Screen education
from film appreciation to media studies

Foreword

We are very fortunate indeed to have this meticulous chronicle of the Society for Education in Film and Television and its prickly and stimulating relationship with the British Film Institute. Tracing a history that goes back to the 1930s, the book you hold in your hands manages to recreate moments almost lost to our present memory, when public institutions and civil society merged in a vibrant, politicized way.[1] Terry Bolas proves to be a skilled and even remorseless researcher and guide to these earlier periods. I found his reconstruction of the turmoil in the Education Department of the BFI thirty-five years ago especially fresh and compelling. Drawing on memory, oral history, archival investigation, and textual analysis, Bolas illustrates those mythic times when people who were largely excluded from academic posts, were not careerists, and were dedicated to political-economic transformation through the moving image and criticism of it, sought to unlock popular creativity by changing how texts are taught.

I am writing here from the vantage point of someone who spent the late 1980s working in cognate areas of Australian universities, and the period since in the USA.[2] In Australia, there was a rarely-voiced but clear consensus that everyone was pro-feminist, pro-multicultural, skeptical of capitalism, and hopeful for and about socialism and democratic politics. The work of SEFT and the BFI was a lodestone for us. Since that time, a much more aesthetic tendency has dominated film studies in Australia, while media studies more generally has become something akin to a handservant of government and money via the popular uptake of 'creative industries,' complete with a utopic faith in media access that denies the power and malevolence of corporate control and valorizes the folksy myths of entrepreneurship.

In the USA, many segments of media scholarship have always been intensely conservative, because they deny their own conditions of existence; exclude issues of labor and the environment from consideration of the media industries; ignore imbalances in cultural exchange; use neoclassical notions of competition in discussing ownership; fail to attach textual analysis to wider social formations; invest in dustbowl empiricism; peddle cybertarianism; draw on theories from *Screen* and *Screen Education* in the 1970s without acknowledging it as a socialist enterprise; and are driven by puerile academic careerism.

It can hardly be a surprise, then, to find Bob McChesney lamenting that contemporary media studies is 'regarded by the pooh-bahs in history, political science, and sociology as having roughly the same intellectual merit as…driver education' (2007: 16). Or that the *Village Voice* dubs TV studies 'the ultimate capitulation to the MTV mind… couchpotatodom writ large…just as Milton doesn't belong in the rave scene, sitcoms don't belong in the canon or the classroom' (Vincent, 2000). Even Stuart Hall recently avowed that 'I really cannot read another cultural studies analysis of Madonna or *The Sopranos*' (MacCabe, 2008).

So is everything hopeless? Has the institutionalization of screen studies simply birthed one more normal science, bereft of social innovation and epistemological excitement? Was film theory a bust? Did all those young thinkers of the 1970s sitting in London pubs debating the latest in semiotics end up stimulating thousands of readers who spent the 1990s setting up scholarly and publishing concerns that had none of the old political drive to make a difference?

I don't think so. In the days when old-style mail still mattered, my old friend Noel King remembers, the excitement in Australian university libraries was palpable when a new issue of *Screen Education* or *Screen* came off the boat. Why *was* that? I think it was due to a non-professional but not exactly amateur – more mad-inventor – attitude to trying out new things. That stands, for me, as the ultimate tribute to the intellectuals who populated SEFT and the BFI from the 1970s to the 1990s. They had a wide variety of projects, problems, and passions, and they modeled a world of engagement and scholarship that still has the power to captivate and inspire. The anticipation experienced by Noel and many others signified something that doesn't erode, something captured here by Terry Bolas. It can animate us still.

Toby Miller
Chair of Media and Cultural Studies
Univeristy of California, Riverside
November 2008

Works cited

MacCabe, Colin (2008) "An Interview with Stuart Hall, December 2007" *Critical Quarterly* 50, Nos 1–2: 12–42

McChesney, Robert W (2007) *Communication Revolution: Critical Junctures and the Future of Media* New York: New Press

Vincent, Norah (2000, February 2–8) "Lear, Seinfeld, and the Dumbing Down of the Academy" *Village Voice*

Notes

1. For what has happened to the BFI and its publishing since, readers may care to read the dossier published in *Cinema Journal* (47, No 4 of 2008) featuring many greatest hits and latest memories of British screen studies.

2. During the 1970s heyday of *Screen* and *Screen Education*, I was at school in Britain and Australia.

Prologue

If film appreciation is to have more success than literary appreciation a due regard for the approach must be demanded. It must be taken at a time of day when the mind has had time to ease off from the concentration required by the academic subjects, yet not when the body is readjusting after violent physical exercise, nor should the stomach have been just filled or too long empty.

J Wood Palmer *University House Broadsheet* (1944), in which supplementary advice is offered to those using the BFI pamphlet *Film Appreciation for Discussion Groups and Schools* (1942)

I remember my surprise and delight as a young teacher in the early 1960s when I discovered that there existed a society for those who felt film was a sufficiently significant part of British culture for it to deserve a proper place within formal education. I joined the Society for Education in Film and Television (SEFT) and soon found myself on its Committee, then became its Honorary Secretary in 1965. Some 25 years later, when I was on a term's sabbatical, I became a Visiting Fellow in the English and Media Department of the University of London Institute of Education. This was autumn 1989 and my personal brief for the term was to take stock of what had been achieved for media education at this point. But the resource that should have been my starting point – SEFT – had gone out of existence earlier that year. My researches continued minus SEFT, though I was both concerned and intrigued that an association which had existed for almost 40 years (during a period when for most of the time media education had been marginal within educational institutions) had disappeared at the point when media education and media studies in particular were better represented than ever before in formal education.

There has been much scholarship invested in broad cultural studies of the United Kingdom from the perspective of the second half of the 20th century, while other scholars have looked in detail at the theories which nurtured the rise of film study and subsequently of media education within the UK. This account will seek to demonstrate how a flexible institutional apparatus while operating within the culture nevertheless for four decades facilitated the study of a marginal discipline. Today it would be highly improbable for a similar intellectual journey to be undertaken by committed and gifted 'amateurs'; nor does a significant aspect of the culture remain unexplored outside the Academy, still awaiting the arrival of such determined theorists as happened upon film in the 1970s. This account will trace how a pioneer movement organised and evolved in a sequence of very particular circumstances.

How did the study of film and television, and subsequently of media, shift its position from the margins of the curriculum in secondary education in the 1950s to become firmly established and widely available in higher education at the end of the 20th century? To position SEFT in the history of the UK film education it is appropriate to investigate the early years of the film appreciation movement from the 1930s, since several pre-war activists would become part of the founding committee of the Society of Film Teachers (SFT) in 1950. SFT then became SEFT in 1959 after a year-long debate about the relevance of studying television. The Society was disbanded in early 1989.

I knew from research I had undertaken for an MA dissertation that the intervention of the journal *Screen* in the 1970s was another key moment.[1] But in that exercise I had focused on the journal itself – as had many other commentators across a very wide range of texts. The bigger task was to step back and ask additional questions. How was the phenomenon of *Screen* possible? How had the second series of *Screen Education* which emerged from the back pages of *Screen*, transformed the dynamics of the screen education movement? The 1950s – during which period the Society's interest was in film – was one of steady growth and achievement as its regular publications, *The Film Teacher*, *Film Teacher* and then the original *Screen Education*, all testify. However the changes over the following two decades were more important because they were to be more influential. Having been personally involved in the movement in the mid-to-late 1960s I was aware of the preliminaries that preceded the arrival of *Screen*. But there was more to SEFT than *Screen* and it was important to ensure that the whole period under investigation had a broader coherence. During a period of approximately two decades – the 1960s and 1970s – there was the greatest momentum for change, albeit the eventual manifestation of that change took place in the 1980s within a range of educational institutions. The British Film Institute Education Department and the Society for Education in Film and Television were the two key organisations throughout this important period and were manifestly very different operations at the start of the 1980s from those they had been at the end of the 1950s.

If this inquiry is asking the basic question, 'How did they do it?', any answer will provoke the further question, 'Why did they bother?' Some 40 plus years ago, I felt able to answer it confidently.

In the beginning there were enthusiasts: teachers who enjoyed the cinema and wanted to communicate their enthusiasm to the next generation. They saw in film an art form which children enjoyed spontaneously. More significantly film did not have the same built-in hierarchy of values that literature had. There was no rift like that between what the children read from choice and what the school, for a whole variety of reasons, selected for them to read. The screen education movement therefore had its origins in the enjoyment of the local cinema programme – something which would never be forgotten.[2]

It is not a statement I would need to contradict today, but I would have to add that, at the time of writing, in most institutions screen education was frequently extra-curricular: the film society and film-making club.

As film and television study began to find niches within the timetables of sympathetic institutions, the mood changed. 'Often it seems tensions develop between film teachers and their colleagues, for it is somehow implied that film is subversive in the school context.'[3] Nobody had felt threatened while film was associated with out-of-school activities. It was even acceptable in the mid-1960s as a 'Newsom' subject.[4] Few objected to what was considered a distraction for the early school leavers.[5] In further education it was similarly tolerated as part of the Liberal Studies programme for block and day release students. But when in schools film and television courses competed with more traditional subjects in option block choices, there developed an interventionist anti-media attitude. Some determined teachers felt they had a duty to advise able students against making a decision with, they implied, adverse long-term career implications.

There was a further intervention with unexpected consequences when, in the 1970s, schools and colleges began to introduce 'educational technology'. These developments were not universally welcomed but where they were welcomed, it was generally in terms of teachers making better use of audio and visual aids. The benefits were seen simply as those of facilitating and reinforcing the transfer of existing patterns of knowledge. I observed at the time how benignly this invasion was viewed and what might be the consequences of taking this limited perspective.

> …it is not seen as a problem in the way that popular culture was. What evidence there is suggests that children are far more adept at mastering the techniques of the visual media than their teachers, understandably so since teachers are essentially experts with words whose tradition is a literary one and who owe their present position to their expertise in written examinations. Unlike the children and students of today their education was based on reference to a very wide range of books as directed by their teachers. They were not regularly exposed to television from an early age where the channels are so few that there is little opportunity for selection and everyone's terms of reference are the same. We have therefore a situation where the experience of children is not only highly specialized but is common to a whole age group.[6]

What were perceived by educators as mechanisms for making the transference of knowledge more efficient, were considered by their students as having a more sophisticated potential.

It is now accepted as unremarkable that children will readily access, explore and find ways of engaging with technological change and as a consequence educators must aim continuously to connect with these developments and become as proficient as their students. In the 1970s, however, it was the Trojan horse of educational technology that encouraged a cohort of dissident insiders to move on to the attack. There were by this stage certain teachers and lecturers who readily recognised the contradiction demonstrated by their colleagues who welcomed change but only as long as it made easier the communication of the familiar. These dissidents were of the generation that had in the 1960s expressed dissatisfaction at university where both the organizational structures they encountered and the courses they attempted had served to alienate rather than educate them. They still had personal educational agendas with unfinished business. This fuelled their engagement with screen education, with media and with cultural studies. What better arena for dissident energy than the territory disowned and discredited by most of their predecessors and some of their contemporaries?

An important resource for my investigation was the recollections of those who had played major roles in the years of film appreciation and screen education. Many of those whom I interviewed recalled how frequently – whether in schools or higher education – they had encountered and fought against institutional opposition to screen/media education. This opposition was, some thought, fuelled in part by an anti-media stance of the Press. Usually it seems the very existence of this opposition served to validate the importance they wanted to give to those aspects of media education they intended to introduce. Even now it is still possible to find spectacular evidence of a situation bedevilled by contradiction. Christine Geraghty has put the following on record.

> Nearer home, Professor Graham Sellick, Vice-Chancellor of the University of London was reported as having told the Headmasters' Conference that "so-called academic courses in media and cultural studies" were valueless', a rather dispiriting comment for those of us who have the temerity to teach such subjects in his august institution.[7]

As someone who was an active 'screen educationist' in the 1960s, I have become familiar with the 'histories' which form the introductory sections of accounts of the evolution of media education. I was concerned at the emphases that were routinely given only to developments post-1970.[8] In the 1960s I had encountered and worked not only with the emergency trained cohort of teachers from the late 1940s but also with some of their predecessors, the activists who had been developing aspects of film appreciation since the 1930s. It was from these two groups that SEFT's founding body the Society of Film Teachers had emerged in 1950. This book will attempt in part to do justice to the pioneers of the period from the 1930s to the late 1950s. The explosion of interest in the last twenty years belies the long haul during the previous fifty.

This was a movement from the grassroots up, and not a higher education project which had been modified as it reached down into the schools. This process should be contrasted with the situation in the USA where, as Dana Polan has revealed, the study of movies was well established in both schools and colleges during the 1930s.[9] All the more intriguing therefore that SEFT survived the lean years and passed in a time of plenty when film and media were finally being accepted in the Academy. Having played a part in this movement I had nevertheless to acknowledge that I was largely ignorant of its origins and did not understand its ending. I had therefore to include in my investigations how SEFT had started and then trace the history through to its demise. Why had it ceased precisely when the potential for it to recruit new members appeared to have increased so significantly?

In the 1950s both SFT and BFI were comfortable with the proposition that a more discriminating audience would, by its very existence, ensure that films of a better quality would be produced.[10] It was never explained how this might work in practice, nor was the process of discrimination investigated. Such terminology tended to be deployed rather than scrutinized. The most obvious instance of this practice was in the use of the term 'film appreciation'. The process of appreciating a film was never adequately defined, but it implied that, with time, it was possible to achieve a state of passive connoisseurship. In the 1930s pioneering teachers had shared a consensus that they were developing 'film appreciation', probably drawing on the United States model where there was already the practice of 'movie appreciation' in both schools and higher education.[11] By the 1980s, film had lost its dominance and the descriptive terminology had broadened out to 'media studies' and 'media education'. There was, it seems, an evolutionary process at work: between the film appreciation decades (1930s – 1950s) and the media education decades of the 1980s (and later) there were the 1960s and 1970s. These were the transitional years of 'screen education'.

The term 'screen education' was coined in 1959 by the Society of Film Teachers with its move to extend the Society's remit to include television and the consequent need to change the Society's name appropriately.[12] The BFI Education Department was never able to accommodate the term for institutional reasons and used 'film and television teaching/study' instead. But 'Screen Education' gained authority from its use in the titles of three SEFT journals. The first *Screen Education* was published from 1959 to 1968. Then *Screen Education Notes* emerged from the back of *Screen* in 1971 and continued until 1974 when it became *Screen Education* again. It finally ceased publication in early 1982.

A particular feature of the 1960s and 1970s was that these decades provided a period of technological stability which facilitated both the wider establishment and more intensive development of film teaching/screen education in the UK. Viewers had a choice between just three television channels. The big technological change during the period was the introduction of colour television, but compared with other broadcasting innovations this made least change to the practice of television study. Access to film viewing was still controlled and communal. Films were to be seen projected on 35mm in cinemas or in 16mm in institutions like schools, colleges, universities or film societies. Films became available for hire on 16mm well before they might subsequently be broadcast on television. In the present century where cinema exhibition of film has become little more than the trailer for subsequent DVD sales, it is important to recognise just how different were those 'screen education years' for filmgoers. An influential role was therefore inevitably assumed by those who chose films for screening in an educational environment. Perhaps even more significant were the interventions of those working in BFI Education who selected the material which teachers were to use in the classroom during those two decades. Their choice of material for film extracts would have a determining effect on the shape of screen education.[13] The BFI Lecture Service which provided speakers throughout England and Wales on behalf of the Institute and the British Film Academy drew only on a tiny number of regular contributors, thus reinforcing the apparent unity of the message.[14] The introduction of Channel 4 in 1982 and then the spread of home video recording and viewing would produce a very different environment in the 1980s, which would transform not only television study but also approaches to cinema.

But if the background elements of these two decades remained stable, it was also the case during this period that developments in this embryonic subject area were mainly transmitted by the two bodies already identified: SEFT and the BFI Education Department. Teachers would dispatch separately to each organization identical letters requesting help, since to the outsider there was no obvious way of distinguishing between them and the priorities each had for supporting practitioners.[15] Indeed such was the mutually shared role of the two organisations that each felt obliged to publicise the existence of the other. But in practice the two bodies were very different in their operation. Under its Head, Paddy Whannel, the BFI Education Department became in the 1960s, as I intend to demonstrate, a 'film academy-in-waiting' where Departmental members were encouraged to develop research interests and where the establishment of film study at university level was considered to be an essential bridgehead. SEFT was very energetic in the early 1960s and produced a series of no-nonsense publications which were designed to be sent to those teachers who had questions about getting started as screen educationists. These two organizations, having developed distinct differences in the 1960s, would swap roles in the 1970s. This exchange of activities was not the result of consultation and assessment. It was *force majeure* in the shape of intervention by a small group of BFI Governors in 1971. Under the Chairmanship of Asa Briggs they produced their Report on the BFI Education Department.[16]

This was the report which resulted in the resignations of Whannel and five of his colleagues[17] but which, as a consequence, enabled SEFT to have total operational independence from the BFI. The concentration of resources on its new journal *Screen* was part of a move to explore more theoretical territory which in turn attracted an intellectual élite to the Society while the Report imposed blight on the Education

Department which would persist for almost a decade. The Governors insisted the Department, now re-named as Educational Advisory Service, should play only a supportive and not a developmental role in film and television education. The consequences are explored in the chapters that follow. But it is remarkable that no one, not even those who resigned in protest, has retained a copy of the report. The BFI's own archive of Governors' papers has no copy. Of course it may be that what the report said was actually less significant than the construction the BFI establishment of the time was able to put upon it.

During the 1980s, after *Screen Education* had ceased publication, once again there was a swapping of roles between the Society and the Institute's Education Department. The BFI became extra vigilant about the use made of money it paid to the Society by way of grant and consequently pressured SEFT to adopt an ever wider caseload of activism in relation to external developments in the media, while the Education Department took on a more pedagogic approach to the field of media education. SEFT moved further and further from its original aim of addressing the interests of teachers till eventually it was left with no effective constituency from which it might draw support.

There is one aspect included within this enquiry with which readers are likely to be familiar: the SEFT journal *Screen*, which has for the last three decades attracted regular scrutiny and detailed commentary in numerous books. Such has been the influence of this journal, and specifically of its intervention in the 1970s, that the authors of almost all new works of film theory have felt bound to acknowledge *Screen*'s contribution. It rapidly attracted serious academic attention, particularly from scholars in the United States. The first PhD to be completed as a study of *Screen* was submitted by Philip Rosen to the University of Iowa in 1978.[18] Perhaps the first home-grown attempt to address the importance of *Screen*'s intervention came with Anthony Easthope's contribution in *The Politics of Theory* in 1983.[19] In 1985 *The Cinema Book* makes multiple references to *Screen* as the source of controversy in various debates, though without featuring the journal as a phenomenon in itself.[20] This was followed in 1988 by David Rodowick's *The Crisis of Political Modernism* and Robert Lapsley and Michael Westlake's *Film Theory: An Introduction*.[21] By the 1990s the authors of film theory compendiums in the English-speaking world might wish to dissociate themselves from 'Screen theory' but could only do this if they first addressed the specifics of what *Screen* had promulgated. This may be detected in *Post Theory* (1996),[22] *The Oxford Guide to Film Studies* (1998)[23] and *Reinventing Film Studies* (2000).[24] *Screen* continues in regular publication as an academic journal and is the most obvious legacy from SEFT. However it is only a part of the story and as the most well-known part will for that reason receive less attention in this account.

While its theoretical positions have generated extensive and learned responses, curiously there has been little interest in how the journal came about and how, in a decade when film/cinema journals were created, blossomed intermittently, faltered and disappeared, somehow *Screen*, then regarded as the most impenetrable of them all, was in regular quarterly publication. Indeed, some of those who were closely connected with

Screen in the 1970s lacked curiosity as to its provenance as comments by Heath, MacCabe and Wollen have in subsequent years revealed.[25] On the other hand, *Screen Education* in its 1970s manifestation has received scant attention, but as I intend to demonstrate, this journal made the more lasting contribution to the evolution of media education. For these wider areas of inquiry that I wished to pursue, there was relatively little by way of commentary. My priority has therefore been the search for the original documentation, or the part of it that has survived. Neither SEFT nor BFI were proficient at archiving materials and though regimes of meticulous minute-taking were routinely adopted through the decades, the sequences of surviving documents are incomplete and anyone attempting to draw conclusions from such intermittent records faces the risk of over-interpreting the evidence.

Since so much of the Society's record has proved to be incomplete, its journals have acquired increased importance. The emphasis with which they document developments helps to provide evidence of what may be taken as the priorities of the time. Alongside the SEFT journals were the publications from the BFI. During the 1940s, before it had any department which would directly address educational issues, the Institute produced several pamphlets for teachers, but these demonstrate barely any relationship to each other. The 1950s was the decade when SFT's journal *Film Teacher* was published regularly. In the 1960s, both BFI Education and SEFT produced occasional publications, addressing specific sectors of the growing movement. In the 1970s when SEFT's resources went into *Screen* and *Screen Education*, the BFI's publications became more substantial with a new emphasis on television while duplicated documentation supported the sequences of revision characterized by the ILEA Sixth Form Film Study Course.[26]

Faced with an incomplete documentary record, a key resource has been the recollections of those who were participants at the various stages of this history. There was however a frustrating – if revealing – problem in contacting potential interviewees. Whereas it proved easy to reach those activists from earlier decades who had remained within the advisory or university teaching worlds, those who had continued in schools and moved on or retired proved impossible to trace. This was not perhaps unexpected in that a career structure in film/television education had not been available before the 1980s. In those earlier years career advancement came from reverting to more conventional routes. Having taken such a route myself, I was not surprised at my failure to track down those with whom I worked on the SEFT Executive Committee in the 1960s. What was both surprising and gratifying was to discover the large number of activists and contributors from the SEFT of the 1970s and 1980s who now occupy key positions in the film and media education world of the twenty first century. This diaspora represents the real legacy of SEFT.

Notes

1. Terry Bolas *'Projecting Screen'* Unpublished MA thesis Middlesex University 2003
2. Terry Bolas 'Film and the School' *Screen Education Yearbook 1967* London: SEFT November 1966 p 25
3. Terry Bolas 'Afraid of the Dark' *Screen Education* No 42 January/February 1968 p 6
4. See below Chapter 5 for discussion of the Newsom Report *Half Our Future* London: HMSO 1963.
5. Early school leavers were a group that had to be catered for until the school leaving age was raised to 16 in 1973.
6. Terry Bolas 'Developments in Film Education' *Screen* Vol 11 No 3 [May/June 1970] p 101.
7. Christine Geraghty '"Doing media studies": reflections on an unruly discipline' *Art, Design and Communication in Higher Education* Vol 1 No 1 p 26
8. See for example Jim Cook and Jim Hillier *The Growth of Film and Television Studies 1960–1975* London: BFI Education 1976 and David Buckingham *Media Education* London: Polity 2003.
9. Dana Polan *Scenes of Instruction – The Beginnings of the U.S. Study of Film* Berkeley: University of California Press 2007
10. See for example Stanley Reed *A Guide to Good Viewing* London: Educational Supply Association 1961 which was aimed at a child readership.
11. See Helen Rand and Richard Lewis *Film and School* New York: D Appleton – Century Company 1937. Here the authors want to replace the familiar term 'moving-picture appreciation' with 'evaluating motion-pictures'.
12. For a concise account of the first ten years of SFT/SEFT see R C Vannoey 'Ten Years On' in *Screen Education Year Book 1960–61* London: SEFT October 1960.
13. The endorsement of American cinema established at this time is now being identified by some academics as having distorted the development of the serious study of film. See below Chapter 6.
14. *The British Film Institute Quarterly Gazette* gives detailed lists of lectures and who gave them on the Institute's behalf between 1952 and 1965.
15. The author became aware of this frequent duplication when working simultaneously for both organisations in 1969.
16. The two other members of the Committee were Helen Forman and Paul Adorian. It was planned that Karel Reisz should also be a member of the group, but he resigned from the Governors before the Committee met.
17. The others who resigned were Eileen Brock, Alan Lovell, Gail Naughton, Jennifer Norman, Jim Pines.
18. Philip Rosen *The Concept of Ideology and Contemporary Film Criticism: A Study of the Journal Screen in the Context of the Marxist Theoretical Tradition* Unpublished PhD thesis University of Iowa 1978
19. Anthony Easthope 'The Trajectory of *Screen* 1971 – 1979' in Francis Barker *et al* (Eds) *The Politics of Theory* Colchester: University of Essex 1983

20. Pam Cook (Ed) *The Cinema Book* London: BFI 1985
21. Robert Lapsley and Michael Westlake *Film Theory An Introduction* Manchester: Manchester University Press 1988; David Rodowick *The Crisis of Political Modernism* was first published by the University of Illinois in 1988 and reprinted by the University of California Press, Berkeley 1994.
22. David Bordwell and Noel Carroll (Eds) *Post-Theory Reconstructing Film Studies* Madison: University of Wisconsin Press 1996
23. John Hill and Pamela Church Gibson (Eds) *The Oxford Guide to Film Studies* Oxford: Oxford University Press 1998
24. Christine Gledhill and Linda Williams *Reinventing Film Studies* London: Arnold 2000
25. See Bolas (2003) op cit
26. The BFI publishing arrangements were altered following the Briggs Report. Previously the Education Department had been a publishing unit distinct from that part of the BFI which published *Sight and Sound* plus other books. In the 1970s the latter section became dominant.

1

Cinema under Scrutiny

It is a paradox to realize the great power of the commercial cinema and then to introduce the cinema into the schools bereft of its essential characteristics.

E Francis Mills, Demonstrator, London School of Economics 1936

During the 1930s mass entertainment for the working class provided in the cinemas is widely perceived as having the potential to do harm. Children in particular are identified as vulnerable and civil society is roused on their behalf. The concerned voices are not those of the teachers in the state elementary schools who are generally silent, while others in more socially prestigious employment make the running. Teachers in the private sector however start to investigate the educational potential of what films have to offer. The British Film Institute through Sight and Sound *provides space for the writing-up of their experiments and then offers some holiday time teacher training.*

The aim of this investigation is, put simply, to trace the part played by a small-scale teachers' organisation in the evolution of media education in Britain, where, given the separate national identities it embraces, 'Britain' has to be a flexible concept. The Society of Film Teachers was founded in October 1950, but this particular date is not the appropriate starting point for this account. The momentum for such an organisation was developing in the 1930s and, had a war not intervened, SFT might have started sooner. Subsequently pre-war pioneers were able to continue their work, albeit at more influential levels, in the post-war period. They were then joined by ex-service personnel whose wartime introduction to the power of film had been very immediate. However recognition of the potential for education in media or, more accurately for the period, the case for film appreciation had been established with the coming of the talking pictures and of the dream palaces which showed them.

The Film in National Life

Although the term 'film appreciation' acquired only passing importance in the history of film and media studies, its gradual introduction during the 1930s and 1940s was an important feature of the coming to terms with film that preoccupied influential elements in British society and some educationists. During the 1930s children, education, film, the institution of cinema and their interrelationships were repeatedly described and interpreted. When the decade began, 'film appreciation' was absent from the work of those who wrote about the cinema. That there was an interest in the cinema and its programmes and in the wider use of film is indicated by a number of events and publications, the most significant and influential of which was the Commission on Educational and Cultural Films and its 1933 report *The Film in National Life* which led to the formation of the British Film Institute and the attendant quarterly *Sight and Sound*.[1] The Commission, funded by the Carnegie Institute, was an unofficial grouping of educationists from the British Institute of Adult Education and its creation was part of their campaign

> ...to encourage the use of film as a visual aid in formal education as well as to raise the general standard of film appreciation among the public.[2]

In fact the specific term 'film appreciation' is absent from the text of the Report. When not directly considering the visual aid use of film, the Commission is concerned about the 'public appreciation of film' and the shaping of 'taste'. It seems possible that the spread of sound cinema in the late 1920s and early 1930s became the catalyst for increased interest in the cinema as a social phenomenon. However, there persisted a lasting and unhelpful legacy of attitudes that persisted from the era of 'silent' films.

The terms of the relationship between the cinema and society in the United Kingdom had been set out in stark detail in *The Cinema: Its present position and future possibilities* published in 1917 by the National Council of Public Morals, described in the Introduction by its own Director and Secretary, James Marchant as 'one of those unofficial organisations which are the pride of English endeavour'.[3] Essentially setting out to investigate the cinema as an institution, the Commission also delved into the world of education and the role that the film might play there. On the basis that 'the lure of the pictures is universal', the Commission considered nothing to be off-limits so that its report could state in the opening paragraph that

> ...we leave our labours with a deep conviction that no social problem of the day demands more earnest attention. The cinema, under wise guidance, may be made a powerful influence for good; if neglected, if its abuse is unchecked, its potentialities for evil are manifold.[4]

The cinema's potential for doing harm was to persist as a notion that successive generations would have to address. Fear of this potential would be manifested in a variety of ways. The cinema as a venue would be seen as presenting problems by its very nature: it would be perceived as harbouring disease, providing the cover of darkness for illicit activity and as keeping children from their beds while harming their eyesight. The films shown in the cinemas would be denounced as requiring censorship, lest they entice the young into delinquency or inflict psychological damage on them by terrorising them with horrific sights. Furthermore, films, and in particular sound films, in the classroom might usurp the role of the teacher by undermining control. Probably the most lasting legacy of the Commission was that it became a model for the many separate inquiries that would be set in train by public bodies, which would each individually seek to investigate certain aspects of cinema. Perhaps for politicians, involvement in such an inquiry would provide a convincing demonstration of their integrity in the face of these presumed threats to society. Undoubtedly these extra-curricular activities presented early film educationists with the additional problem – beyond that of identifying their object of study – of also having to try to retrieve film from its many dubious associations.

From the 1930s to the 1960s film educationists were few while others who wished to promulgate their views on the cinema were plentiful. Not only were members of the clergy, politicians and journalists eager to comment but their vigilance was endorsed by numerous voluntary societies that existed to represent specific interest groups and attitudes, particularly among the middle classes. Such bodies were to continue over the next two decades, persistent in their involvement, striking attitudes and taking positions about popular culture and the media. Nowhere would the survival of such groups be better demonstrated than by the organisations represented in the attendance list of the 1960 National Union of Teachers' Conference on 'Popular Culture and Personal Responsibility'.[5] At that conference, as in so many of the debates before then, the voice of the teacher would barely be heard.[6]

For a screen educationist in the 1930s, not only was there a need to be heard among the clamour of voices that wanted to pronounce on the cinema but there was also a need to distinguish clearly the ways in which film and education interrelated. The debates in the 1930s began to be considered separately. There was the relationship between children and the cinema; there was the use of film in classrooms and then there was the study of film for itself. The first of these was the one which was most conspicuous to everyone: huge numbers of children were going frequently to the cinema, as was adult society. Consequently, even in depression hit Britain, cinemas were a growth area.

Children and the Cinema

The mid-1930s in the United Kingdom saw a great expansion of cinemas. During the decade the number of cinema-goers attending on a regular basis increased as more accommodation became available in new cinemas. A significant proportion of this expanded audience was young. Oscar Deutsch went from owning one cinema in 1933 to having 220 under the Odeon brand in 1937 with a further 35 under construction.[7] As a consequence, by 1939, Deutsch was one of the first exhibitors to offer a cinema club for children: the Odeon's Mickey Mouse Club.

Most children were educated in elementary schools, which they left at age 14 and potentially then were wage earners. In the literature of the time those still at elementary school were usually referred to as children, those at work and under 21 as adolescents. The two categories were distinguished in the minds of the cinema operators so that the groups attending children's matinées or Saturday morning pictures were essentially those that would now be regarded as of primary school age. Though references were regularly made to the relationship between adolescents and the cinema, in practice in the 1930s when conferences met or groups convened to investigate 'children and the cinema', it was generally to the issues around the attendance of the younger group that they addressed themselves. In post-war Britain, with the raising of the school leaving age and consequent enlargement of the school population, the perceived issue of adolescents and the cinema would be addressed more directly.

In November 1936 the British Film Institute, held a two-day conference on 'Films for Children'.[8] To judge from the Foreword to the Conference Report, published in January 1937, the event had been organised to counter an earlier conference in summer 1936, organised by the Cinema Christian Council and the Public Morality Council.[9] The BFI's event was 'to summon a further and fuller conference representative of all shades of opinion',[10] with the clear implication that the nature of the organizers of the previous event had perhaps guaranteed a predictable, if unhelpful, outcome. The shades of opinion deemed by the BFI as appropriate to speak formally were: the Home Office, a film renter, a child psychiatrist, two exhibitors, the Mothers' Union, a Director of Education and a member of the National Union of Teachers' Executive.

The positions taken were generally unsurprising, though the Home Office speaker (S W Harris, later to become Chairman of the British Board of Film Censors) introduced proceedings and advanced the idea that the young should be introduced to the 'art of film appreciation' since the films of the future 'would largely depend on the tastes of the children of today'.[11] The film trade representatives drew attention to the limited potential of children's matinées as generators of income; the child psychiatrist was reassuring as to the child's imperviousness to suggestibility by films and the educational input was to argue for more local control of what was shown. A separate case was made for the BFI to take an initiative in editing down longer adult films so that they might be shown to children in the condensed version.

The final, rather bland, motion urging co-operation with the BFI reveals that 95 organisations were represented at the conference. Thus given the predictable composition of the audience some familiar themes emerge in the comments reported from the discussions that followed each speaker:

- presumed links between juvenile delinquency and films
- the adolescent as a problem
- cinemas were warm and dark with all that implied
- fresh air was preferable
- films were degrading the English language and replacing it with American.

Whether teachers were in the audience is unclear. However one 'ex-teacher' is reported as stating that the cinema trade had a better understanding of children than teachers had. The most direct outcome was the publication and extensive distribution by the BFI of its first list of eighty entertainment films recommended for children's programmes. Additionally short films were listed in categories devised by the Children's Film Society based at the Everyman Cinema in Hampstead.[12]

In 1938, the League of Nations Advisory Committee on Social Questions produced a report *The Recreational Cinema and the Young*, based on information collected from the governments of some 46 countries.[13] That it should have had a strong Anglo-American focus, rather than an international perspective, is probably the result of the presence of A C Cameron and Oliver Bell both representing the British Film Institute, together with Edgar Dale, representing the United States Payne Fund investigations. However, perhaps most significantly, the report was prepared by S W Harris, who had represented the Home Office at the 1936 conference. Whilst dismissing some of the more extravagant claims as to the harm done by cinema attendance, the familiar health hazards of eye strain and sleep deprivation from late-night viewing are repeated.

There is, however, a section headed 'Teaching of Film Appreciation' which shifts away from giving children special films to view toward preparing them for visits to the commercial cinema – which they were attending in any case.

> The answer to this question would appear to be found in some method of encouraging the young to discriminate between what is good and what is bad.[14]

Harris had of course hinted at this in his introduction to the 1936 conference. Here he is more specific in identifying the task as one of shaping 'taste' to influence commercial film-making:

> The young people of today are the future patrons of the cinema, and if their taste can be formed so as to encourage the production of films of good quality, there could be no better way of bringing about a general raising of the standard.[15]

He continued to demonstrate where a start had been made. In the United Kingdom, the *Monthly Film Bulletin*, recently introduced by the BFI, added to the censors' categories four of its own in order better to define which films were suitable for what audiences. The refined categories were:

A: adults only
B: adults and adolescents (over 16 only)
C: family audiences
D: films for children

Such refinement, however, was only a first step. It was the use which was subsequently made of the films that mattered:

> ...in several countries, efforts are being made in the schools to cultivate an intelligent appreciation of films amongst the children and to teach them to discriminate between the good and the bad.[16]

Seven of the states of the USA had by this stage included the teaching of film discrimination in the school curriculum. The BFI is credited with having kick started a similar activity in the United Kingdom, though no specific instances are mentioned. The opening sentence of the Conclusions section of this League of Nations publication is revealing. 'The present inquiry would have been justified if it only serves to draw attention to a problem, which is common to the whole world.'[17] Quite how far the classroom teacher would have been complicit in this conclusion is questionable. For many, having concerns about the influence of the cinema would have seemed to be an issue of lesser importance than attempting to understand the opportunities/threats that the introduction of educational films into schools would bring.

Connecting Film and Education

In the 1930s significant attempts were made in both the United Kingdom and the United States of America to establish the nature of the relationship which might exist between film and education. In both countries, a variety of books was produced examining the implications of the relationship. The clarity of the two most distinct links between films and education emerged only slowly: film was a visual aid, contributing to the better understanding of a wide range of areas of knowledge, and then there were the beginnings of the acceptance of film itself as the object of study. Curiously, the name that might be given to the second of these became established long before there was any consensus as to what the study itself might involve. This area of inquiry became known as *motion picture appreciation* in the USA and *film appreciation* in the United Kingdom. As a term in general use in the UK, film appreciation persisted into the 1960s. If there was a significant moment for its discontinuation, it may have been in 1958/9, when the BFI's Film Appreciation Department was re-designated as the Education Department.

The term 'film appreciation' (as distinct from references to 'the appreciation of the film' first appears in *Sight and Sound* in 1934 when an article about 'The School Film Society' by A Maxwell Lewis identifies one of the aims of such a society as 'a means of training the child in film appreciation'.[18] Coincidentally, in the same issue, Paul Rotha reviews *How to Appreciate Motion Pictures*, which had been published in the USA in 1933 as 'a manual of motion picture criticism for high school students'.[19] Since the term 'motion picture appreciation' seems to have had earlier currency in the United States, it may be that – with suitable trans-Atlantic modification – it became 'film appreciation' in the United Kingdom. Both Lewis in his article and Rotha in his review make it clear that film appreciation is in effect a shorthand way of making reference to the training of film taste, and that by such training – as *The Film in National Life* had proposed – a better informed audience 'with higher standards of taste' would be for the good of cinema in the longer term.[20]

However, in 1933 *The Film in National Life* does make specific reference to the relationship between the school, the child and the cinema.

> The taste of the next generation is largely formed at school; therefore the school cannot afford to neglect so important a factor as the film in the education of a generation which goes regularly and naturally to the cinema.[21]

The report when dealing with the entertainment of the public returns to this theme. The paying cinema audience is seen as composed of three tiers. At the base are the general public, some ninety per cent of cinemagoers. (The remaining ten per cent is divided between educated opinion holders and film society members.) For this ninety per cent the commission identifies the need for 'an education in taste' which 'can best begin with the children'.[22] Interestingly, the report is reluctant to differentiate between the entertainment and the teaching film on the matter of training taste. Given that the teaching film will be the one viewed most frequently by teacher and pupils, that film will have a 'cultural influence in the school'.[23]

This point is acknowledged by J A Lauwerys, a lecturer at the London University Institute of Education, when editing *The Film and the School* in 1935, though the remit of this work is in the audiovisual area. He writes of the training of 'film-taste' but feels it is best accomplished through film-making.[24] Also in 1935, W H George, a schoolteacher, states in his introductory chapter to *The Cinema in School* that 'the cultural aspect of the cinema thus concerns the teacher more than does the film as a teaching device…'.[25] His experiments out of school hours involved showing a range of silent films, including narrative, cartoon and general interest films, as a result of which he noted 'a gradual improvement in the art of seeing a film'.[26] His conclusion was that:

> In secondary schools and schools where pupils remain to ages of 16 and over, there is a wide field for the teaching of the appreciation of films.[27]

A third book to be published in 1935 was *The Cinema in Education* by Charles D Ottley, apparently a cine enthusiast with limited professional involvement in education. The style is ponderous and grandiloquent and he makes no reference to film appreciation. Despite its subtitle as *A Handbook for Teachers* the 'Introduction' states bluntly: 'No attempt will be made at an exhaustive analysis of the art of teaching nor yet of the art of the film'.[28]

Paul Rotha in his Foreword to his book *Documentary Film* in 1936 states that he had intended 'dealing with the importance of the cinema as a factor in modern education' but then decided that the 'educational film should be considered separately from the documentary movement'.[29] He then endorses George's *The Cinema in the School* [sic] as the best of the various books recently published. Also included in those books was almost certainly also, *The Grammar of the Film* by Raymond Spottiswoode that Rotha had reviewed for *Sight and Sound* and to which reference will be made later.

In trying to separate the documentary, from the educational, film Rotha was responding, as did a number of his contemporaries, by attempting a classification of non-entertainment films. He gives priority to the 'general illustration film' rather than to the 'direct teaching, or instructional film'.[30] Lauwerys makes a rather different binary distinction between 'foreground' and 'background' films, the former is an 'intrinsic part of the lesson'; the latter helps 'to broaden the outlook of the pupils'. He continues:

> Possibly, therefore, we ought to sub classify background films themselves into
>
> (a) those that are mainly informative
> (b) those used mainly for training taste.[31]

Category (b) would seem to be approaching film appreciation. Indeed, Lauwerys then quotes *The Film in National Life* in support of his assertion that 'films to be shown to children should be aesthetically valuable'. He refers to the earlier report's claim that 'the taste of the next generation is largely formed at school'.[32]

Early Film Theorists

Not all influential works that attempted to offer ways into understanding the cinema and film were conceived in a specifically educational context. *Scrutiny of Cinema* (1932) was written by William Hunter, a former student of F R Leavis and a contributor on the cinema to the journal *Scrutiny*. The book is about the silent cinema, with only a postscript on sound cinema, which was perhaps indicative of the slow acceptance of the sound film as a lasting phenomenon. Hunter poses the question as to whether the sound film has increased the possibilities of the cinema as a means of personal expression or was it an exhibit of 'valueless virtuosity'.[33] Hunter's stance here, and in an article written for the first issue of *Scrutiny* in the same year, was to doubt whether film was comparable to other arts. 'It must always remain to some extent popular and democratic, and on a lower level than its contemporary art forms.'[34] He favours the output of the Soviet Union and is dismissive of American films, where he sees the director as more an engineer than an artist. Those who write about film are attacked for their lack of discrimination. Where Hunter differs significantly from the popularly held view is in his belief that the 'second-hand' experience offered by the cinema, was more dangerous to adults than to children.

Two authors whose work proved to be more durable and outlasted the 1930s were Rudolph Arnheim and Raymond Spottiswoode. What was to become ultimately the most influential English language book of this period had its origins as *Film als Kunst* by Arnheim, first published in Germany before Hitler came to power. An English translation was published in London in 1933 with the title *Film*.[35] While current books on film theory will recognise the importance of Arnheim among early theorists, there is little evidence that his views gained much currency in the educational world at the time in the United Kingdom. In fact, his stance would have been readily accommodated by many of the activist groups of the time since he perceived film art as under threat. While he was unequivocal in his claims for film as a distinct art form, he felt it was in danger of being compromised by the poorly educated audience that went to the cinemas and by the financial imperatives that lay behind its mass production. The relevance of Arnheim's stance was not lost on the reviewer in *Sight and Sound* who saw the book as making the case for training the young in 'critical appreciation'.

> It would be a splendid thing if headmasters and headmistresses and teachers generally could be persuaded to study this book and so be equipped to give positive advice instead of the usual negative moral objections.[36]

When *Film as Art* was published in 1957 it was a reprint – with modifications – of *Film*.[37] Arnheim wrote a foreword that indicated not only had there been a rigorous analysis of what he had previously written – albeit much was preserved – but that he now felt more optimistic both about those who made films and those who watched them. As an established academic in the USA, Arnheim had fulfilled the promise that the *Sight and Sound* reviewer had foreseen in 1933: that in Arnheim's book 'a case has been made out for including the art of the cinema in the curriculum of universities'.[38]

In 1935, a recent graduate from Oxford University, Spottiswoode produced *A Grammar of the Film*, subtitled *An Analysis of Film Technique*.[39] In attempting to establish parallels between a written language and that of the film, Spottiswoode – who on his own admission had no experience of film-making when he wrote the book – took a highly academic approach, which was ultimately condensed into an elaborate fold-out genealogical grammar table at the end of the book. Whether many readers could follow the density of the book's arguments is perhaps doubtful. In his review of the book, Grierson complained about this attempt to anatomise film into laws of grammar while it was still in its infancy as an art form. 'The atmosphere of the mortuary is not absent from Mr Spottiswoode's book.'[40] Crucially, it seemed like a dead end for those who were looking for a better way of interpreting the cinema. As Grierson complained 'I cannot catch the accent of appreciation (or *valuation*), and I feel we ought to, if the laws are to be real laws'.[41] What is clear is that the concept of 'film grammar' as an accessible approach gained a hold in the world of film appreciation and much simplified versions of Spottiswoode's idea were to persist into the 1960s. *A Grammar of the Film* went into a second edition twenty years later. There was clearly perceived to be a demand for such a book, and possibly the claims implicit in its title stimulated this demand. However, unlike the re-issue of Arnheim's work in 1957, here the only difference from the 1935 edition was a statement inserted at the front of the 1955 edition to say that it was an unchanged reprint of the 1935 edition.[42]

The British Film Institute Finds a Voice

In the *British Film Year Book* of 1947/48 the editor comments that the six years from 1933 to 1939 'were indeed a period of experiment for classroom teaching'.[43] He was referring specifically to what would subsequently be seen as the use of film as an audiovisual aid. By 1939 Gaumont British (through two subsidiary companies) had produced sufficient 16mm educational films and 16mm projectors for this 'sub standard' gauge to have been established as the standard for educational use. But it was not simply the technical aspects of the equipment that had been evolving during the 1930s. The relationship between the cinema and the school was being tested. After World War II it was generally the view of all but a small number of film teachers that the cinema was the appropriate location for entertainment films and the school for the film as visual aid. Yet in the 1930s there was regular use of cinemas for showing instructional/ educational films to mass audiences of school children. On occasions these would be organized by education authorities; at other times a prototype children's matinée organized by the cinema would show the same kind of programme to a paying child audience.

Uncertainty as to how film might function in both education and the wider society lay behind the expectations of what a National Film Institute might be able to do. A C Cameron had been a prime mover in the Commission on Educational and Cultural Films, the body that produced *The Film in National Life*. He put the position clearly when he wrote in the first issue of *Sight and Sound* (at that time published by the British Institute of Adult Education).

> The entertainment film and the teaching film are two separate things. Any attempt to make the one improving or the other amusing is fatal. A National Film Institute would be concerned with both, but I hope it would never confuse them. If it were concerned to improve the public taste in entertainment films, it would inculcate discrimination, not priggishness.[44]

The British Film Institute, was subsequently set up with the task of attending both to the development of the educational film and to the appreciation of the entertainment film. Gradually during the 1930s, the practical implications of separating the two in educational establishments became clearer. In the first issue of *Sight and Sound* to be published under the aegis of the BFI in Winter 1933/34, the responsibility for raising the 'cultural and educational status of the cinema audience' is said to lie with the directors and producers of documentary films.[45] The argument that follows goes like this: the resultant audience will be selective in its visits to the cinema and, through its acts of discrimination in favour of certain films, will influence what films the commercial cinema is prepared to produce.

But other options were subsequently offered. After the establishment of the BFI as a national institution in London, where the film trade and the educationists came together, numerous other local Institute Societies were to follow where there would be a similar meeting of the two interests. Thus, the *Sight and Sound* editorial 'The Film and the Public' in Spring 1934 states:

> Through the membership of the provincial Film Institute Societies a stream of new patrons is being brought back to the cinemas, more discriminating, perhaps, in their tastes than others who have fallen away, but equally insistent to see the pictures they want.[46]

Later in the same issue R S Lambert, Editor of *The Listener* puts the responsibility more widely:

> The film is making us more eye-conscious as a nation; so that it lies in *your* hands to raise the whole standard of film production and exhibition in the future.[47]

By the Summer of 1934 and the next issue of *Sight and Sound*, there is a new section 'Films and the School'. In it A C Cameron writes:

> The chief interest of the film for children as for adults is in the public cinema. But a great source of entertainment may become a great power in education; and, within a generation, I personally believe that it will be accepted as a duty of the school to educate the taste of a child in its film-going as much as in its reading, or in its musical appreciation. The teacher, if he is to do his part, must know the cinema and treat it as a friend and not as an enemy.[48]

It was of course to be a much longer process before film and media began to get general acceptance in education. Later in the 'Films and the School' section there is an article by Ernest Dyer, billed as Chairman of the Tyneside Film Society, but revealed in his article as a teacher of English. He argues strongly that the development of taste 'is a task to be addressed in the classroom and not in the film society or film making group'.[49] In subsequent generations it was of course the English lesson that would provide the curriculum base for film and television study in the secondary school. Nevertheless, the film society and/or the film making group remained staples of screen education territory for many years, frequently the preserve of teachers who were film enthusiasts, but whose subject was not English.

Classroom Pioneers

This spread of enthusiasm for film teaching is demonstrated by some of the early contributors to *Sight and Sound's* educational pages. A Maxwell Lewis was assistant physics teacher at Hemel Hempsted Grammar School, E Francis Mills (whose later role in the Society of Film Teachers was considerable) was a Demonstrator in Geography at the London School of Economics, G Buckland Smith was Visual Education Organiser at Brentwood School and William Hunter was Film Officer at Dartington Hall. Each in a different way sought to demonstrate, by using experimental techniques, how influential/instrumental the use of film might be.

In 1936 A Maxwell Lewis was the first to lecture on Film Appreciation at a BFI Summer School, having first used the term 'film appreciation' when writing for *Sight and Sound* in summer 1934 where he had begun with a quotation from *The Film in National Life*.

> The training of the school-child's taste in cinematography by teaching, interest and entertainment films is the basis of the intelligent audience of the future.[50]

His account sets what is to become a familiar pattern for accounts of film appreciation during the decade. He works in a private independent school, where money is available, as is student time outside school hours. So for Lewis the school film society has two sections. There is the Production Group which makes films and models its organisation on an industry based hierarchy of demarcated roles; it concentrates on filming school activities. Then there are also film screenings and visits to the cinema which form the basis of lectures and discussions. Whereas the film-making process is accounted for in great detail, the information provided on how film appreciation is organised is detail free:

> Lectures should be arranged on points of film art and the technique of production in order that the children will understand films, and will be able to appreciate the good and deprecate the bad in the films which they will see outside the society. They should not be given the impression that the school film society is to replace visits to the public cinema, in their private life, but that is to make their enjoyment of these visits more complete. In this way the ideal of 'the intelligent audience of the future' will be realised.[51]

In the next issue of *Sight and Sound* Lewis is taken to task by Dyer, the state secondary school teacher in Newcastle, who points out that 98 per cent of children are not in well funded private schools. He also challenges the assumption that film-making by children is an effective way into film appreciation.

> Film taste is not trained by assisting in the production or watching the subsequent exhibition of a film of fifth rate quality.[52]

Dyer also regrets that Lewis provided no details about the technique he adopted in film appreciation. Dyer's own position is that 'the proper place for the training of film taste is in the classroom' and that it is appropriate there to draw on children's existing familiarity with film and its forms. 'I have been especially surprised to find the degree to which boys think in filmic terms.' Given the difficulty of adding a new area to the curriculum, Dyer argues for English as the obvious home for film study. Here, he too is surprisingly short on detail.

> The main aim is to substitute a critical and intellectual approach for the normal (uncritical and emotional) approach, and to base such criticism on an understanding of the nature of cinema as an art in its own right.[53]

His principal technique was to get students to devise what amounted to literary story boards – no drawn images, just written language description. Using film as a stimulus to writing, Dyer found that some of the best results came from the 'non-literary' members of the form.

In 1935 Lewis wrote a further article 'Training Young Critics', and this time decided to test the effectiveness of what he was doing. Although he perceived this 'experimental research' to be about film appreciation, it was primarily not about viewing entertainment films, but was to

> ...test the effect of training in film observation and appreciation upon the ability of a child to learn from an instructional film or from a film made specially for teaching purposes.[54]

Children were divided into an experimental group and a control group. Both groups viewed the films at special matinées in a local cinema, but only the experimental group had a further lesson on 'the technique of film observation in film appreciation' where students learned about 'an alphabet of the essential properties of the medium'.[55] Unfortunately no detail of the method is provided beyond the fact that the study started with monochrome moving pictures and ended with the introduction of sound and colour.

The experimental group also got to make a film as a demonstration of what they had learned, but the main experiment was to be evaluated on the basis of questionnaires completed by the students at various intervals after the screenings – so Lewis had 110,000 answers to scrutinise at the conclusion of the experiment. He had not completed the task when the article was published! Consequently, the reader had to be content with Lewis's qualitative results where, unsurprisingly, all the children proved to be keen and interested, whether in the experimental or control group. Nothing is said about how the students evaluated the classroom lectures. Ever the enthusiast, Lewis is sufficiently buoyed up by the experience to advocate such courses of film appreciation in other schools.

Of particular interest during this period is E Francis Mills, who was to become a key figure in the post-war period when, as a lecturer in an emergency teacher training college, he enthused his students in the role that film could have in teaching. Subsequently he was an important contributor of evidence to the Wheare Committee on Children and the Cinema and a founder member of the Society of Film Teachers. In 1936 when he wrote for *Sight and Sound*, he was billed as a Demonstrator in Geography at the London School of Economics. Quite apart from his particular contribution to the history of the Society of Film Teachers, the trajectory of his involvement with film education would provide the model for many other early SFT activists. These were people whose initial area of study might be quite distant from the timetabled subject of English, which came to be perceived as the natural home for embryonic film educators. The way into film education for geographers, historians, scientists, teachers of physical education or religious studies was to be through a fascination with film.

Writing in *Sight and Sound* in Spring 1936 Mills reports on an experiment 'designed to give practical guidance to the teacher who uses films in the classroom and to the film producer'.[56] The experiment was focused on the lesson type rather than on the film shown to illustrate it. There were four types of lesson: B, R, Q and L. Group B students never saw the film and theirs was designated the control group. Group R saw the film (on the regional geography of the British Isles) and was then asked questions about it. The Q lesson started with the teacher posing a question that could be answered from careful observation of the subsequently shown film. Those who had the L type of lesson had to experience the film's screening being extended throughout the lesson. It would be broken up into sections and the film stopped for questions to be asked 'step by step'. The conclusion of the experiment was in favour of type Q usage with 'material improvements of the order of 30 – 40 per cent'. More revealingly Mills concludes his report, by claiming that his experiment was

> …a demonstration that the film can be used as a real educative medium, not merely by 'bringing reality into the classroom' but by encouraging constructive thought on the part of his pupils and creating a more active cooperation in his subsequent teaching.[57]

Perhaps here were the first stirrings of film appreciation, though the term does not appear in either parts of the article. What is implied is that viewing and considering the film represents a shared experience between teacher and class and through that sharing a different relationship of 'active cooperation' is achieved.

By autumn 1936, when he concludes the second part of the article on his experiment, it is in two distinct sections. The first deals with geography films, where the familiar distinction is made between teaching and background films, with the need for more of the former to be produced. The second section entitled 'Teachers must be film-minded' is of much greater importance to this inquiry. Still arguing his case from the vantage point of the geography teacher, Mills begins to reveal his increasing enthusiasm and awareness as to what might be possible with the combination of film and education. His involvement with film was soon to range beyond its geography teacher origins. These are the two key paragraphs in his second article.

The greatest success is not to be attained along any of these narrow lines, for unless teachers understand something of the nature and idiom of filmic expression, the peculiar genius of the cinema will remain untried in the classroom, and very great benefits to education may be missed. How many teachers have studied the cinema for its own sake, have tried to understand its nature, and then seriously thought of the possibilities that this new medium might have in store for education? How many have considered the best ways of introducing – rather than adapting – the cinema into the classroom, to help teach a generation of film minded children?

How many teachers have thought of the possibilities of using the emotional power of the film as a means of leading the strong feeling and quick sympathies of the adolescent into educational channels, as scouting has directed the boy's physical energies? Psychology teaches us that feeling is the fount of all curiosity and effort.[58]

Essentially, Mills's position is stated at the end of the section.

It is a paradox to realise the great power of the commercial cinema and then to introduce the cinema into the schools bereft of its essential characteristics.[59]

Clearly Mills's intellectual position had yet to be developed. He is beginning not only to ask questions about what using film might involve but he is also asking questions not being asked elsewhere. Whereas many of the authors of similar surveys chose to conclude with watertight results, Mills is suggesting that far from slotting film screenings into the existing classroom regime, the very nature of the classroom experience is to be questioned.

The second person to lecture on film appreciation at the British Film Institute Summer School was G Buckland Smith, Visual Education Organiser at Brentwood School, an independent public school. Writing in early 1937 and already billed to speak at that year's summer school, Smith's account of his work demonstrates a familiar pattern. His emphasis is on encouraging the use of films in established curriculum areas and the costs of investing in the equipment were justified on this basis. Film appreciation had no place in the 'ordinary school curriculum' but 'the institution of a School Film Society was the best alternative'.[60] While acknowledging the limitations of this volunteer approach to film appreciation, Smith nevertheless felt the need to vindicate his enthusiasm for the subject by testing film society members at the end of the course against the control group of non-members. His claim that this provided evidence that the standard of film appreciation had been raised seems a spurious validation. The members then went on to film the school sports day. Smith claims that this exercise benefited from the expertise students had acquired through their film society's screenings and lectures.

Writing in *Sight and Sound* two years later, Smith produces a more reflective account. The influence of *The Film in National Life* is still there.

> If a standard of films is to be set which will truly represent our national culture it is essential that a higher standard of public demand should be achieved, and this can only be done for tomorrow by the education in film taste of the younger generation of today.[61]

Smith argues for a greater recognition of film in schools and that there should be curriculum time for appreciation on its own or as part of English or Drama. He then states that there are a few schools in the United Kingdom (which he does not identify) where film appreciation is taught in this way, but he acknowledges that in many more it is in the film society '...where training in film taste is provided in out-of-school hours'.[62] Once again, the term film appreciation is deployed but there is felt to be no necessity for providing an explanation as to what it might involve. He concludes by making the case for the training of teachers, not specifically in film appreciation, but in promoting all aspects of successful film use in schools.

William Hunter had not given up on film. By the end of the 1930s he was heading the Dartington Hall film unit, a school unit that was busily engaged in making silent educational films, about which Hunter wrote in *Sight and Sound*. Hunter's career development is perhaps indicative of the 1930s. It was the decade when everyone was learning to cope with film and modifying their responses to it over time.

The Exhibitor's Viewpoint

In 1939 Richard Ford's book, *Children in the Cinema*, was published.[63] The author worked for Oscar Deutsch and was responsible for children's film matinées in the Odeon cinemas. It was a significant publication in that it attempted to connect the various strands which had persisted in the 1930s between the commercial cinema, educational institutions, films, psychology and the cinema audience. Also it sought to depict the national situation. What is notable about this work is its authorship. Such was the distance between the academic world and that of the cinema, it was left to a member of the trade to survey the territory and to attempt to gather together the evidence from a wide range of sources and witnesses. A large part of the book is taken up with presenting evidence of the case for and against the cinema as an influence on children. That the author draws on a wide range of quotations on both sides of the argument is indicative of the importance the issue had in society at the time. It is equally clear everyone had a view and that while teachers had remained largely silent, others had rushed to judgment. Particularly evident in making the case for the defence are the contributions Ford cites from psychologists and psychiatrists.

Ford's concluding chapter is 'Teaching through Entertainment' and its final section is 'Film Appreciation as a Classroom Subject'. In it he makes a clear attempt to offer a balanced critique of the status of film appreciation in the United Kingdom and contrasts the status of its development with that of motion picture appreciation in the USA. He draws on the experience of some of the established British writers on the subject, particularly Dyer and Buckland Smith. His is the first attempt to provide a bibliography on the subject of film appreciation, albeit one dominated by the US experience. Writing from his perspective as a cinema exhibitor, there are two key elements to his position. Firstly, film appreciation is not a neutral exercise. It is a mechanism for addressing the perceived problem of children's viewing of films lacking in quality, a lament he identifies as being articulated in 'every conference, in every speech or paragraph devoted to Children in the Cinema'.[64] Secondly, he regards teachers as deficient in addressing this problem, because they do not attend the cinema regularly. Moreover he argues teachers generally regard the use of film as a visual aid in school as an adequate way of satisfying the child's interest in the cinema. Essentially for Ford, the objective of film appreciation is 'to persuade the child itself to want to see the films that are wholesome'.[65]

A large part of this concluding chapter (before the final section on film appreciation) is devoted to the value of films for demonstrating to children appropriate attitudes to road safety, dental care, and the proper treatment of animals. Film appreciation is fitted awkwardly into this model since the health and safety propaganda films have the intention of benefiting the child, but film appreciation here is presented as a quasi moral movement, which enlists the child in a campaign to influence the films that are to be produced for commercial exhibition. The wholesome films would presumably appeal to a family audience and thereby attract bigger queues outside the local Odeon.

Beyond the Teachers

Sight and Sound published a wide range of material about aspects of film during the 1930s (including some technical articles for those wary of the mechanics of introducing the necessary equipment). But it is difficult to estimate how representative a picture may be built up from this evidence. Other documentation survives but frequently lacks a context. At the end of the decade the British Film Institute did attempt to build up a better national picture, for example by organizing a survey of the number of projectors on educational premises.[66]

Probably as a part of this attempt to get a national picture, a typescript document *The Cinema and Education* was prepared for the BFI in June 1937 by A A Denholme in which the author surveyed the investigations and enquiries that had been undertaken by various local education authorities in relation to film. What is immediately clear is that such initiatives were in practice very local. While numerous authorities were experimenting with the use of film as a supplement to existing classroom practice and as a way of illustrating the established curriculum, there appeared to be a wide-spread reluctance to draw upon the conclusions of reports produced elsewhere; only home-grown experimentation would be trusted.

One of the limitations on the process was the very restricted availability of projectors and films. The report estimates that there were 1,000 projectors in schools, though no supporting evidence is offered for this, and other sources suggest fewer. The BFI's own survey in Summer 1937 had shown a total of 812 projectors in England, Scotland and Wales combined, though a number of schools had yet to reply. But not all projectors in the report would have been equal. While silent projectors were in the majority, some of these were hand-cranked by the teacher/projectionist. The film gauges in use included 9.5mm, 16mm and 35mm with several schools having 35mm sound equipment. Film availability depended on a variety of national rather than local film libraries, and on advance bookings, the timing of which would impinge on syllabus planning and delivery.

Nevertheless, it is clear from the survey that, where enthusiasm existed, films were being used and some structured approach to its potential for children's learning was being tested. Results where children showed more interest and better retention of knowledge hardly seem surprising today, but clearly were providing significant evidence then in the face of sustained opposition to film from some quarters. The report is entitled *The Cinema and Education* and so it would appear that the institution of the cinema might be appropriately included in the survey. Yet the report does not deal with cinema-going by children or the role of entertainment films. Cinemas are however mentioned in some examples as where the London County Council used local cinemas to show interest and instructional films to some 14,000 children in a large-scale experiment.

The most revealing part of the report is when 'backward' children are discussed. Their interest in, and responses to, films were shown to be much closer to those of children who were not designated as backward. Consequently films were then judged to have a particular importance for this 'backward' group. This was an attitude that was to persist post-war. What unfortunately did not follow from this experimental revelation was any scrutiny of the teaching methods that had defined a group of children as backward when an alternative teaching approach had demolished this categorisation. Instead, one can note the beginning of what became a long association in both secondary schools and further education colleges of film with the education of less-able students.

Only at the end of the report when quoting the Erith Education committee of October 1931 does film appreciation get an implicit reference when the committee is quoted in support of Denholme's assertion that 'films should be used to develop taste and judgment'.

> The cinema is, for better or worse, becoming rapidly the literature of the people. The schools, through the use of films of sound artistic and literary merit, can do much to raise the standards of public taste in films as they are undoubtedly doing in printed literature. This can only be done by meeting the cinema problem on its own ground, rather than by ignoring it. We must raise a generation critical of the films shown them by exhibitors. This is surely a task which can only be successfully undertaken by the schools.[67]

Perhaps it is indicative of the perceived limited effectiveness of the BFI at the time that this report, prepared for the BFI, concludes rather lamely: 'Without overstating for the cinema, there seems adequate proof that suitable films, related to the work of the school, are worthwhile.'[68]

While individual teachers and some local education authorities were experimenting with the potential of film as a visual aid as the Denholme survey shows, other local politicians had been 'investigating' the effects of the commercial cinema on children throughout the 1930s. The timing of the onset of their attempted interventions would suggest it was the establishment of the sound film that became the catalyst for this upsurge of concern. In 1930 Birmingham set up a Cinema Enquiry Committee and was followed in 1931 by the Birkenhead Vigilance Committee's report on *The Cinema and the Child*.[69] Both reports included the responses of children to a range of questions. However, in each investigation, the presentation of the responses is unsystematic and is, predictably, revealed as supporting each council's very specific target. Birmingham was in the process of petitioning the Home Secretary in favour of greater censorship; Birkenhead was mounting a campaign (albeit unsuccessfully) to get local magistrates to tighten cinema regulations affecting children.

In 1930 the London County Council had approached the issue more professionally by obtaining a report from its Chief Inspector of Schools on the effect of the attendance at cinema performances on the minds of children. This was a more cautious enterprise and was conducted systematically so that the reactions of children had been collected in such a way as to prevent them from giving answers which were shaped to fit the prejudices of their interviewers. Accordingly much of the evidence was gathered from the children's writing, and here again it was noted that the 'dull' child was transformed when responding to film. The report is not free from anxieties about eye-strain or the possible permanent damage to be done to some children by the 'one distinct evil' of the cinema – where they are frightened by films. Nevertheless, the report is clearly constructed to head off the more extreme anti-cinema allegations:

> ...in spite of the strong opinions of some able and devoted headteachers to the contrary, the preponderance of evidence is that the actual effect of the pictures on the children is not substantially harmful.[70]

The alternative offered is that there should be more open-air opportunities.

> It is a great misfortune that thousands of children should spend Saturday afternoon in cinema houses, not because it does them moral injury, but because it is clearly inappropriate expenditure of time. Time spent playing in the streets is better spent.[71]

The report concludes by recommending expenditure on alternative facilities for children. Such a conclusion may have been judged by the officers presenting the report to be an effective way of silencing the potential critics among politicians: it offered an alternative which would have required considerable public expenditure. The reporting officers clearly wanted to limit the involvement of their political masters. The report begins by stating plainly that producing a psychological report would have been a lengthy enterprise and was therefore not to be attempted. The report's comments on children's 'taste' are brief, since what is described are children's preferences for particular types of film, which tend to shift with increasing maturity. There is no suggestion that the schools have any role to play in shaping taste or approaching commercial films from what would then have been considered a film appreciation perspective.

By the late 1930s there is evidence of a greater accommodation of the cinema by British society. An intriguing umbrella organisation was formed at the initiative of the well established Tyneside Film Society. This was the Northern Counties Children's Cinema Council. In support of its offshoot organization, the Film Society was still quoting the Commission on Cultural and Educational Films:

> If the standard of public taste in films is to be raised, we must begin with the children. It is important to train their taste in films, as in music; from the social point of view, more important.[72]

The Cinema Council's aims and objects were threefold:

1. To foster interest in and to promote the use of the film and other visual aids in education.
2. To encourage the training of film taste and discrimination in children.
3. To act generally as a clearing house of experience in film matters amongst Educational Administrators, Teachers, Parents and Social Workers.

The council had two sub-committees, one for film appreciation and the other for 'teachers and others who wish to experiment with films'.[73] With this remit it hoped to encourage the participation of northern local education authorities and other child-centred organisations. By way of encouragement, it provided evidence of organised activity in other parts of the United Kingdom.

In 1939 the Council produced a pamphlet *Film Appreciation in the School*, which was distributed by the British Film Institute. It begins almost apologetically, by stating that it is not a plea for formal courses in film appreciation in schools. Instead, it outlines what were subsequently to be the strategies of post-war film teachers: find any potential opportunity for children to demonstrate their responsiveness to the commercial film. As was to be the case a decade later, English lessons are seen as presenting the most opportunities.[74] Nevertheless, it was considered important that the teacher should be a regular local cinema patron, and consequently address students on an equal footing. As was also to be the case with later advocates, the school film society was to provide significant opportunities

...to encourage children to notice and discuss such points as the rhythm and cutting of a film, parallel action, the emotional effects of background music, the social values implied. A child's power of discrimination can often be aroused by an intelligent question; but the questioner should never have a preconceived idea as to what the answer will be or ought to be.[75]

Elsewhere in the pamphlet an extended quotation from the *Handbook of the Scottish Educational Film Association* demonstrates an ingenious conjunction of the study of Shakespeare with the study of feature films so the comparison might be made between the respective uses of dramatic irony, comic relief or soliloquy. The teacher is however advised not to try this approach unless they are as well-versed in film appreciation as in the works of Shakespeare. Of particular interest to the would-be film teacher is the two-page booklist that concludes the pamphlet.[76] Divided into six sub-sections, books are listed under

History Criticism and Appreciation	eight books
Technique and Aesthetics	seven books
Film-making, Film-writing and Scenarios	three books
Music	one book
Cinema as a Social Force	three books
For Younger Children	three books

To have eight books in the first section is impressive. In fact half of them – those that might be seen as coming under the film appreciation heading – are of United States origin. The remaining four (of which three are by Paul Rotha) are essentially about film history. That the US should dominate the appreciation section is indicative of the substantial funding and much greater spread of the work in the United States.

Discovering the BFI's Role

The 1930s was not a period when in-service training of teachers was provided. Consequently, a deterrent to the general acceptance of film in educational institutions was the lack of familiarity of teachers with both the equipment and the materials available to them. Help was provided by the British Film Institute in organising short intensive courses during the school summer holiday period. When the first such school took place in August 1935, its emphasis was on practical film-making. Known as the Scarborough Film School it was organised in conjunction with the Educational Handwork Association. The BFI claimed it was 'the first summer school for teachers in this country'.[77]

At the 1936 Summer School there was to be a slight change of emphasis in that while some 72 students were mostly gaining experience of making films, among the evening lectures was the one on Film Appreciation by A Maxwell Lewis, the physics teacher whose article in *Sight and Sound* had been the first to use the term 'film appreciation'.[78] At the third summer school in 1937 there was a further lecture on film appreciation, on this occasion by G Buckland Smith, the Brentwood schoolteacher who had in fact been present as a student at the 1936 school, having won a scholarship to attend.[79] The beginnings of a pattern may be detected. Buckland Smith was the first of many who, over the decades, would graduate from being student to lecturer at the summer school. The schools were to become so well established that by the 1970s and early 1980s the British Film Institute's annual summer event was almost obligatory for those who wanted to engage seriously in the rapidly evolving area of theory around film and media study.

By 1938, the British Film Institute was again collaborating with the Educational Handwork Association. There was the usual emphasis on practical film-making but no reference to film appreciation this time. In 1939, the BFI's partner was to be the government in the shape of the Board of Education and the course content was 'optical aids in school'.[80] The Board's collaboration in this rather functional summer school suggests only a limited commitment to film in education. In fact the Board had been lobbied by the BFI on a range of issues and was becoming more receptive about approaches to film. In its 1937 *Handbook of Suggestions* for teachers, the Board recommended that in schools where there was no projector 'sympathetic discussion' of films shown in local cinemas would do a 'great deal' for children.[81]

Although the Institute's Summer Schools seem to have temporarily eliminated film appreciation from their agenda, elsewhere in the Institute there were signs of interest as *Sight and Sound* reveals in its Winter 1940 edition. Brian Smith, an established 16mm educational film-maker, in an article called 'The Next Step', identified 'an urgent need for an authoritative Manual of Film Appreciation'.[82] The article was written in part as a response to one by Ernest Lindgren in the previous issue of *Sight and Sound*. Lindgren had linked film appreciation to the potential aspirations of the post-war world where the cinema would have its 'proper function in the development of post war society'.[83] Nevertheless, whilst calling both for the establishment of 'the tenets of a sound theory of film criticism' and for the training of film teachers, Lindgren still sees film appreciation as being complicit in the moulding of 'the taste of the audiences of tomorrow'. But Lindgren, as Research Officer of the National Film Library, was promoting a very particular approach to film appreciation: that of film history – which was the approach that his film library was best able to accommodate.

Smith's article does take as its model the historical framework proposed by Lindgren, but then he details how such a study 'for sixth forms or WEA groups' might be organised into stages. His proposed stages are very interesting because, although they are linked to the 'historic' resources the National Library might provide, there are to be sections on the film as industry, the marketing of stars, the complexities of film finance and its social implications, together with 'the problem of reality on the screen'. Then, provided they were available on 16mm, contemporary American and British feature films would be studied through 'representative examples' where ideally the teacher would have access to 'an anthology of one reel or two reel extracts from film classics'.[84]

This short wartime piece anticipates not only much of what would form the basis of syllabuses for film study courses in the 1970s (such as the Associated Examining Board's O/A level in Film Study or the ILEA Sixth Form course) but also the means of their delivery by film extracts. Indeed Smith would probably have found himself in agreement with the founding editors of *Movie* twenty years later when he writes of the exciting but exacting task of the film teacher.

> He would warn his pupils against mistaking good intentions for film craftsmanship; films about great scientists played by sincere and capable actors, as well as documentaries informed with social purpose, might sometimes be observed to remain stuffy, wordy and cinematically dead.[85]

By the time these articles were published, wartime austerity had greatly reduced the number of pages in *Sight and Sound*. Consequently when Smith responded to Lindgren, the journal's typeface had been made smaller in order to accommodate his article in newly narrowed columns. However, it is clear from what he writes that there had been an evolution of thinking in the 1930s, and that not only was it possible film appreciation might gain some conceptual identity as an area for investigation, but certain of the ways in which that investigation might proceed had been identified. Whilst the war would temporarily interrupt the further development of these ideas, it would, also through the strategic use of film deployed as part of the war effort, shape the attitudes of the next generation of film teachers.

Notes

1. Commission on Educational and Cultural Films *The Film in National Life* London: George Allen & Unwin 1932
2. Christophe Dupin 'The postwar transformation of the British Film Institute and its impact on the development of a national film culture in Britain' *Screen* 47.4 Winter 2006 p 443
3. The Council had apparently gained credibility from an earlier report that it had produced on the causes and effects of the declining birth rate. It was dominated by representatives of organized religion.
4. National Council of Public Morals *The Cinema: Its present position and future possibilities* London: Williams and Northgate 1917 p xxi
5. NUT *Popular Culture and Personal Responsibility Verbatim Report of Conference* List of Attendees London: National Union of Teachers 1960
6. This did, however, work to the benefit of the Society for Education in Film and Television as will be demonstrated in Chapter 4. Two of its members (who were the only teachers formally to address the three-day event) were able to use to their advantage the audience's lack of familiarity with the notion of taking film and television seriously in the classroom. They were able to demonstrate the work that the Society for Education in Film and Television (SEFT) was promoting to an audience that 'wanted something to be done about the media'.

7. There has been much interesting research into the cinema and society in the 1930s: Jeffrey Richards *The Age of the Dream Palace Cinema and Society in Britain 1930–1939* London: Routledge 1989; Anthony Aldgate and Jeffrey Richards *Cinema and Society from 1930 to the Present* London: I B Tauris 2002; Jeffrey Richards (Ed.) *The Unknown 1930s An Alternative History of the British Cinema 1929–1939* London: I B Tauris 1998; Nicholas Pronay and D W Spring *Propaganda, Politics and Film* London: Macmillan 1982; Stephen G Jones *The British Labour Movement and Film* London: Routledge & Kegan Paul 1987.

8. BFI *Report of the Conference on Films for Children* 20–21 November 1936 London: British Film Institute 1936

9. This organization is not to be confused with the National Council for Public Morals which had, subsequent to its report on the cinema in 1917, become the National Council for Race Renewal.

10. Ibid p 3

11. Ibid p 8

12. 'Films for Children' *Sight and Sound* Vol 6 No 23 Autumn 1937 p 117

13. *The Recreational Cinema and the Young* Geneva: League of Nations 1938

14. Ibid p 27

15. Ibid p 27

16. Ibid p 29

17. Ibid p 30

18. A Maxwell Lewis 'The School Film Society' *Sight and Sound* Vol 3 No 10 Summer 1934 p 75

19. Paul Rotha Review 'How to Appreciate Motion Pictures' *Sight and Sound* Vol 3 No 10 Summer 1934 p 81

20. *The Film in National Life* p 66

21. Ibid p 58

22. Ibid p 83

23. Ibid p 66

24. J A Lauwerys *The Film and the School* London: Christophers 1935 p 29

25. W H George *The Cinema in School* London: Sir Isaac Pitman & Sons 1935 p 17

26. Ibid p 26

27. Ibid p 34

28. Charles D. Otley *The Cinema in Education* London: George Routledge & Sons 1935 p xi

29. Paul Rotha *Documentary Film* Boston: American Photographic Publishing Co 1936 p 18

30. Ibid p 18

31. Lauwerys op cit p 19

32. Ibid p 20

33. William Hunter *Scrutiny of Cinema* London: Wishart & Co 1932 p 51

34. William Hunter 'The Art-Form of Democracy' *Scrutiny* Vol 1 No 1 May 1932 p 62

35. Rudolf Arnheim *Film* London: Faber and Faber 1933

36. Review *Sight and Sound* Vol 2 No 6 Summer 1933 p 61

37. Rudolf Arnheim *Film as Art* London: Faber and Faber 1957
38. Review *Sight and Sound* Vol 2 No 6 Summer 1933 p 61
39. Raymond Spottiswoode *A Grammar of the Film* London: Faber and Faber 1935
40. John Grierson Review *Sight and Sound* Vol 4 No 16 Winter 1935–36 p 157
41. Ibid p 57
42. Spottiswoode (1955) op cit
43. Peter Noble (Ed) *British Film Year Book* London: Skelton Robinson 1947 p 197
44. A C Cameron 'The Case for a National Film Institute' *Sight and Sound* Vol 1 No 1 p 9
45. David Schrire 'The Psychology of Film Audiences' *Sight and Sound* Vol 2 No 8 Winter 1934 p 123
46. Editorial *Sight and Sound* Vol 3 No 9 Spring 1934 p 2
47. R S Lambert 'How to Get the Films You Want' *Sight and Sound* Vol 3 No 9 Spring 1934 p 7
48. A C Cameron *Sight and Sound* Vol 3 No 11 Autumn 1934 p 125
49. Ernest Dyer 'Training Film Taste' *Sight and Sound* Vol 3 No 11 Autumn 1934 p 135
50. Lewis op cit p 75
51. Ibid p 136
52. Ibid p 77
53. Dyer op cit p 134
54. A Maxwell Lewis 'Training Young Critics' *Sight and Sound* Vol 4 No 14 Summer 1935 p 81
55. Ibid p 82
56. E Francis Mills 'The Film Lesson' *Sight and Sound* Vol 5 No 17 Spring 1936 p 33
57. Ibid p 35
58. E Francis Mills 'The Classroom Film' *Sight and Sound* Vol 5 No 18 Summer 1936 p 41
59. Ibid p 41
60. 'Brentwood School Shows the Way' *Sight and Sound* Vol 6 No 21 Spring 1937 p 39
61. G Buckland Smith 'Wanted – A Sympathetic Understanding' *Sight and Sound* Vol 8 No 30 Summer 1939 p 85
62. Ibid p 85
63. Richard Ford *Children in the Cinema* London: George Allen and Unwin 1939
64. Ibid p 208
65. Ibid p 208
66. *Sight and Sound* Vol 6 No 22 Summer 1937 p 94; Vol 6 No 23 Autumn 1937 p 152; Vol 7 No 25 Spring 1938 p 38; Vol 7 No 28 Winter 1938–39 p 175
67. A A Denholme *The Cinema in Education* London: British Film Institute 1937 p 15
68. Ibid p 15
69. Birmingham Cinema Enquiry Committee *Report of investigations April 1930–May 1931* Birmingham Council 1931; Birkenhead Vigilance Committee *The Cinema and the Child A Report of investigations* June-October 1931 Birkenhead 1931
70. London County Council *School Children and the Cinema* London: LCC 1932 p 5
71. Ibid p 6

72. 'Northern Counties Children's Cinema Council' Newcastle: NCCCC 1938 p 4
73. Ibid p 5
74. Ernest Dyer who had previously advocated this connection with English lessons in *Sight and Sound* was now Chairman of the Executive Committee of the Children's Cinema Council.
75. NCCCC *Film Appreciation in the School* London: BFI 1939 p 4
76. Ibid pp 7–8
77. 'BFI Summer School' *Sight and Sound* Vol 3 No 12 Winter 1934–35 p 185
78. 'London Film School' *Sight and Sound* Vol 5 No 17 Spring 1936 p 9
79. 'Film School for Teachers' *Sight and Sound* Vol 6 No 21 Spring 1937 p 16
80. 'Optical Aids in Schools' *Sight and Sound* Vol 6 No 29 Spring 1939 p 39
81. Board of Education *Handbook of Suggestions* London: HMSO 1937 p 52
82. Brian Smith 'The Next Sep' *Sight and Sound* Vol 9 No 36 Winter 1940–41 p 69
83. Ernest Lindgren 'Nostalgia' *Sight and Sound* Vol 9 No 35 Autumn 1940 p 49
84. Ibid p 69
85. Ibid p 69

2

Film Appreciation

It is probably vain at this stage to press for the inclusion of film study within the curriculum. The critical standards which have been evolved for the older arts cannot be applied wholesale to this new one: teaching methods, and most importantly teaching tools, are still at best experimental, indeed the last are virtually non-existent. And there is the further difficulty that when it comes to knowledge of the subject, in many cases the class can give the teacher a long start.

J Denis Forman, recently appointed Director
of the British Film Institute, January 1950

As civil society is reconstructed, the phenomenon of Saturday morning pictures disturbs the middle classes and a government committee is set up and then sits in on these junior picture shows. But it is the evidence taken from those promoting the teaching of film appreciation that starts to move the process on. Meanwhile the die-hards fear the creation of a new generation of children addicted to films which they will be condemned to view through permanently strained eyes. The 1944 Education Act creates an environment where not only will opportunities be found to teach about films, but equipment will be provided to project them. There will now be teachers who can legitimately be recruited to the Society of Film Teachers.

The Second World War had important consequences for film appreciation. Most fundamentally the use of film – and specifically 16mm sound film – in the training of troops, in the dissemination of public information and in the provision of entertainment in non-urban locations had, by 1945, become established on a national scale. The importance of film and the portability of its performances were embedded in the consciousness of the population.[1] While generally the study of film *per se* within education had to wait for the ending of hostilities, there had been numerous attempts during the war to signal how things might change with the coming of peace. This chapter will describe how the notion of Film Appreciation (frequently spelt with the capital letters F and A) first identified in the 1930s, persisted throughout the 1940s and 1950s. A range of activities became established in education under the recognition of acceptability which the term was perceived as affording. There were, however, also those whose response to film and particularly to the institution of cinema was hostility.

Defining Film Appreciation

The impetus that war-time was to provide for film appreciation may be demonstrated by contrasting a memo written in 1938 by BFI Director Oliver Bell with the situation two years later.[2] Bell regards 'film appreciation' as a new term, though it had been used in *Sight and Sound* and at BFI summer schools from the mid-1930s. He then details four ways in which the Institute is promoting film education work: through the publication of the *Monthly Film Bulletin* and *Sight and Sound*, through education (particularly teachers' groups) and through the work of the National Film Library. What he does not provide is any description of what film appreciation might actually involve. By 1940 and the onset of war-time conditions, the British Film Institute had engaged with film in education directly and seconded four teachers as Teacher Organisers who covered different parts of the country to promote the use of the cinema for educational and other purposes. The Organisers reported that they had found film appreciation in 'surprsingly few schools'.[3] In 1941 the process was repeated over a longer period of almost a year. This time the report records that in a few locations successful attempts are being made to develop film appreciation.[4] As a consequence the BFI was persuaded of the need to establish a Travelling Representative to contact educational authorities and institutions on a permanent basis.

Throughout the 1940s the BFI felt the need to maintain a level of interest in film appreciation in a succession of pamphlets.[5] In November 1942 there appeared the first edition of Lindgren's *Film Appreciation for Discussion Groups and Schools*. Then, Dorothy Grayson, appointed as the BFI's first non-seconded Travelling (Educational) Representative, produced *Films and Youth Organisations* in June 1944. This was followed in November 1944 by *The Elements of Film Criticism* described as 'a simple introduction to film appreciation'. In January 1946, the more wide ranging pamphlet *Visual Education* had a section on 'Film Appreciation as a School Topic'. Later in October 1946 with a substantial 40 pages came *A First Course in Film Appreciation*, to be followed in November by a revised edition of *Film Appreciation for Discussion Groups and Schools*. Subsequently, in April 1948, came a revision of Grayson's pamphlet. There was a strong BFI connection with two further 1944 pamphlets *The Cinema* by Ernest Lindgren and *The Cinema and the Public* by Roger Manvell.[6]

In addition, film appreciation featured in other BFI events. The pamphlet recording the proceedings of the 1943 conference 'The Film in National Life' and the publications following the 1944 and 1945 summer schools in Bangor contain references to film appreciation.[7] The 1943 conference was, according to Sir William Brass, BFI's Chairman of Governors, an attempt by the BFI to address issues that were being raised with it about 'the international and sociological aspects of the film'.[8] These words were to be decoded by Dr John Murray, the Principal of the University College of the South West in Exeter where the conference was held, in his welcoming remarks. His interpretation of the international aspect may be inferred from his remarks about the American cinema, where he objects 'to having the cinema that some other nation deserves'.[9] The sociological aspect, he sees in a very specific context:

> The nation has suddenly become adolescent conscious, and that I consider a most unprofitable and a most unfortunate mood, and one with which those who are infected with it are always trying to infect other people.[10]

The record of Brass's own subsequent introductory comments is revealing:

> We are convinced, he said, that we are dealing with a new art form and one which is worthy of respect and intelligent study. It is for this reason that the Governors have encouraged the Film Society movement and why they are now fostering what we call Film Appreciation.[11]

In practice film appreciation was not the subject of any lecture at the conference. It was however, the topic for one of the discussion groups. The report back was given by G P Meredith, newly appointed to the recently created/part BFI funded post of Lecturer in Visual Education in University College, Exeter. His task was not an easy one. In three paragraphs are contained a range of contradictory stances. There appeared however to be some consensus around four criteria by which to judge films: craftsmanship, psychological insight, social awareness and integrity.[12]

Perhaps the problem of finding common ground for a definition of film appreciation made planners of the summer schools in 1944 and 1945 more cautious. Both featured sections on film appreciation in the programme, but its applicability was a given and not to be contested. Under the umbrella that film appreciation provided, a series of lectures was organised on what were seen as relevant topics. The authority of the lecturers would guarantee the applicability of the content and each speaker would stay within the limits of a demarcated role. Thus if you wanted to know about film direction, you heard Thorold Dickinson. If you wanted to understand audience reaction, then you listened to the views of the Past President of the Cinema Exhibitors' Association. There was still some discussion of the use of film in youth clubs and the role of the BFI's Education Panel. These however, were to be found in another part of the summer school programme: Visual Education.[13]

In all this, the wartime context must be considered. Undoubtedly film had played a huge part in the war effort and thus in the long-term created conditions in which the study of film might be encouraged and developed. In the short term the war made contact between those who wanted to teach film almost impossible. The BFI pamphlets represented an important link to a larger body of teachers than those who were able to attend the summer schools. However no means exist for gauging how widely distributed or read that they were. There appears to have been little controlling editorship with each pamphlet in the BFI 'Film Appreciation' series being a one-off publication with minimal cross-referencing.

In making 'The Case for Film Appreciation' in 1942 Lindgren takes the view that since there will be little chance of film study gaining a place in the school curriculum, the emphasis for its development must fall on out-of-school activities and adult education. In practice this model was to be characteristic of film education until the 1960s. The pamphlet followed a predictable pattern, where three main aspects are distinguished: how a film is made in the studio, the internal structure of the film and the history of the cinema. Very rarely do particular films get mentioned by way of illustration and the emphasis is on whatever films were to be seen currently at local cinemas. Yet underlying the process is the persistent belief that once you have a more discriminating audience 'a positive demand for better films will naturally and inevitably spring'.[14]

Given the frequency with which this notion was to be advanced during the 1940s and afterwards, one is bound to wonder quite how the model of a discriminating audience seeking to effect improvements on the quality of films might work in practice. Since the audience has to put money upfront in order to see the film, dissatisfied customers have few options. Do they demand money back from the exhibitor? Do they picket a producer's subsequent output? The only practicable way of being in a position to avoid supporting a film that might fail to match up to the discriminating filmgoer's standards would be for the filmgoer to endorse the views of published film critics and only attend films that have achieved some kind of quality hallmark from the reviewers.[15] Underlying this expression of a need for a discriminating audience was an attitude that, not only were many films not good enough, but also that the audience was incapable of detecting this lack of quality. If the films lacked quality yet found an audience, that audience must lack taste. Only at the end of the 1950s would 'taste' itself come to be questioned in the film education movement.

Grayson's pamphlet bears the marks of her travels and offers useful organisational tips. It is also ready to acknowledge that the young audience will have acquired the basis of what might now be called cine literacy but which she refers to as 'tecnics'. But although conceding their expertise, Grayson sees the youthful audience as deficient in 'judging the fundamental moral merits' of the film. Here the remedy is to be found in Film Appreciation – 'or in other words, the inculcation of the elements of film criticism'.[16] Perhaps her use of the term 'film criticism' was a deliberate trail for *The Elements of Film Criticism* to appear a few months later. Produced by C H Clarke, Youth Organiser for Wembley, half of this 28 page pamphlet is a reprint of articles from *Sight and Sound* under the title 'The Critics Speak'. Five film reviewers from the national press had been invited to write about their work. Each had followed a personal pattern and the pamphlet provides no contexting of what they write or any connection with Clarke's contribution in the first half. The Governors' 'Foreword' is convinced 'they are making a valuable contribution to the general welfare of the community in publishing this short guide to film criticism'.[17] Under two principal headings of 'The Story' and 'Production' the reader is provided with a range of questions that might be asked in a group discussion and examples are drawn from films that s/he might have seen in local cinemas. Clarke himself makes no great claims for what may be achieved other than that the viewer may have enriched 'enjoyment of good work'.[18]

Visual Education, described as 'Some notes by W Waters', a Hounslow teacher, provides a very basic guide to visual aids but also includes sections on 'Film Appreciation as a School Topic' and 'Film-making as a School Subject'.[19] Whilst limited space would necessarily preclude Waters from being prescriptive, his stance is one that encourages teachers to seize opportunities for older children in secondary schools and think in terms of film appreciation as 'a subject worthwhile in itself' and therefore appropriately to be accommodated within the school timetable.[20]

No context is provided for *A First Course in Film Appreciation* and no introduction is offered for its authors, Ceinwen Jones and F E Pardoe. Subsequent articles will reveal that the former is a secondary school teacher and the latter, Chairman of the Manchester Film Institute Society. These authors claim the moral high ground from the outset:

> This is the real basis of a course on film appreciation – the intelligently directed seeing of carefully selected films in order to acquire a knowledge of good films made by sincere and conscientious artists.[21]

Whilst initially accepting that studying basic techniques of film-making is straightforward and that film history will turn off beginners, thus apparently clearing the syllabus for more relevant approaches, the detailed 'Lectures on Film Appreciation' provided by the authors seem to ignore this precept. Instead, almost all of the 12 lectures are preoccupied with either technique or history. The attitudes displayed in the section on 'Reasons for Film Appreciation' are revealing. We are told that it is the fictional film which presents the real problem. The authors deplore the spread of American idioms (as did many other contemporary writers in Britain). They then list those alarming tendencies, the exposure of which film appreciation must have as its ultimate aim: 'a false idea of life, an over-emphasis on hedonism, a refusal to treat any serious topic in other than a puerile way, a disregard for good taste or the truth'.[22] The course will conclude with the making explicit of this moral stance by the analysis of a short film.[23]

Jones applied to the BFI Governors in 1947 and was awarded £30[24] to support an experiment in film appreciation which was reported subsequently in *Sight and Sound*.[25] The work had been based in a girls' secondary modern school in Oldbury. It was perhaps the first film appreciation class to make use of what the authors refer to as a 'text book': *Good Films and How to Appreciate Them*, published by the *Daily Mail*.[26] Despite its title the book does not deliver on its promise. Its emphasis is on the making of British films and it too ends on an anti-American note.

Possibly, a level of desperation at the BFI had allowed the publication of the *First Course* document. The Annual Report, earlier in the year, had revealed that the BFI was under pressure to educate the public about film appreciation.

> Were it not that Dr Roger Manvell is on the Institute's staff and can devote almost his whole time to lecturing on the matter, it would be frankly impossible to accede to many of the heavier requests. During the year, he has given nearly 200 lectures.[27]

Those requesting lectures would have received a menu of the seven 'Public Lectures and Talks for Discussion Meetings' that Manvell offered, most of which could be delivered without 'the use of films and other illustrative material'.[28]

Marketing Film Appreciation

Indeed, two members of the Institute staff were important in shaping film appreciation: Lindgren and Manvell, though not in the Institute's own publications. Manvell became very prolific in the post-war period. As Director of the newly created British Film Academy from 1947, he maintained close links with the BFI, where he had previously been Research Officer.[29] Lindgren spent almost all his working life time heading the National Film Archive at the BFI, until his death in 1973.[30] As the war ended, each produced a potentially influential pamphlet.

Both were addressing non-specialist audiences, covering a wide range of people. In *The Cinema* Lindgren wrote for the Association for Education in Citizenship, which sought to stimulate discussion about the post-war world. He writes reassuringly that going twice a week to the cinema is 'a normal part of social behaviour'.[31] He recognises that 'the cinema audience is a young audience and (because the prices are cheap) is predominantly a working-class audience'.[32] Nevertheless, he is dissatisfied with how things are and there is the predictable argument that films will only get better if the audience has higher standards of taste, and therefore there is a need to 'recognise some kind of film appreciation work as a necessary part of education'.[33]

Manvell wrote *The Cinema and the Public* for the Army Bureau of Current Affairs, a tabloid mixture of the insightful and the populist. Reassuring in that it implies that any of his readers can become an effective film critic, nevertheless once the status of film critic is achieved the reader's skill will be

> ...to sift the bogus entertainment from the genuine, and to be able to recognise those moments of greatness and distinction in the films of exceptional quality which come along the way.[34]

While dismissing the claims of the American Payne Fund studies that delinquency was aggravated by watching films,[35] he questions whether 'two of the great democracies in the world' are well served by the 'Hollywood tradition that the majority of films should make a display of luxury and financial success'.[36] He then claims that the greatest instrument of adult education will be the (British) documentary film.[37] Manvell's output of books on film published in the UK was so extensive at this time that Lindsay Anderson was moved to take him to task in *Sequence* for his 'painstaking appreciation of good films'.[38]

Post-War Education

These BFI wartime precedents, most of which promoted an involvement with film as an appropriate activity for the less privileged participants in state education, set a pattern for at least the next two decades in Britain. Subsequent events were to reinforce this. As a consequence of the 1944 Education Act the school leaving age was raised to 15 in 1947, which would in turn require more teachers to enter an educational environment where many older teachers, who had had to carry on working during war-time, would be retiring. The solution was the emergency training college. Here student teachers recruited from returning ex-service personnel would be trained in a single year. Two factors would combine here. The schools needed to find useful ways of providing education for the 'non-academic' 14 year olds they had previously lost and the mature students training to teach them were more likely to think independently about what the new curriculum areas might be.

With the raising of the school leaving age some lecturers in the training colleges identified a new potential textbook market. In the post-war world and its spirit of reconstruction, civil society was reviving. Consequently, citizenship became recognised as a teachable notion and the English lesson was identified as one of its potential bases. Given that the remit of English was to be thus extended, films and the cinema might now be included in its scope. In 1946, Margaret Laurence, an English lecturer at Bingley Training College, produced *Citizenship through English*.[39] She made a fundamental assumption that the Modern School Child was different from the Grammar School Child, the former having a relationship with the outside world at age 14 which the latter would only attain at age 17. Taking as a starting point the report of the BFI's 1943 Conference, her view is that the teacher should tap into the film experience children had already acquired in the cinema and attempt to use this to enable children 'to evaluate films as works of art, as well as entertainment'.[40] These ideas, however, are only briefly developed and there is a clear expectation by the author that in classroom discussion students may well mention 'a film, which raises some moral issue or standard, which it may be interesting to question or affirm'.[41]

Towards the end of the decade a more substantial attempt to involve film came with the publication of *English for Citizens* (Evernden and Holloway).[42] This was a four book series, with each book being aimed at a specific cohort of the Modern School population. In 1950 Book IV entitled *Our Own Language* appeared, designed for the fourth (and final) school leaving year. Although the term is not used, about half the book is given over to what might be considered film appreciation. The priority given to film and the detail in which it is covered are probably explained by the fact that its authors acknowledge the help received from Stanley Reed and his West Ham Secondary School colleagues who operated in a Local Education Authority where film appreciation and school film-making had been established from the 1930s. A different note is struck from the outset.

> If we can make ourselves intelligent cinema-goers, we shall become better citizens.[43]

A distinct change of educational philosophy is to be noted. Previously, the newly trained intelligent cinema-goers would have been identified as potential foot soldiers in the long march to demand better films. Here the benefits will be felt by the children themselves.

Given that citizenship is the underlying issue, the approach to films is distinctive: 'When we say a film is good we usually mean that it is true to life'.[44] For the young citizen this is to be the crucial test of a film's quality. This concept leads the authors into strange pedagogic territory at one point. They outline speculative fantasy narratives for films and invite the students to say how things might alternatively have been in real life. The book introduces both a thematic and genre approach to film study. In a section called 'Wedding Bells', romance on screen is contrasted with the prospect of life for the young marrieds in austerity Britain. Genres, particularly Western and Gangster films, are examined both as having distinctive generic elements but, given the writers' goal of 'citizenship education', these films inevitably also have to face the reality test. In a section on 'Heroes, Heroines and Villains', a start is made in the consideration of representation and stereotyping in the cinema.

What was probably the most novel and enlightening section for the teacher is the one called 'Examining the Workmanship of a Film: *Night Mail'*.[45] A detailed commentary is provided covering the first half of the film, which is not merely descriptive but also interpretative and offers detailed analyses of, for example, how the movement of the train is conveyed in eight different ways. For the second half of the film it is over to the students who are expected to respond to detailed questions which explore the construction of the film, how elements of the soundtrack are used to provide meaning and how narrative elements are deployed.[46] Given Reed's own background as a film-maker and his enthusiasm for film-making, it is no surprise the book concludes with a section on film-making in school supported by the familiar justification.

> By learning to make films, we shall learn to watch them with understanding and full appreciation of the art with which they were created.[47]

From today's perspective, it is perhaps important to see the publication of this book as something of a landmark. Much of what preceded it had been opinionated and often made pronouncements about film appreciation that were devoid of context. Here are some of the approaches to film study which would become established in the 1960s.

There was a very practical circumstance which also influenced how film appreciation might reach the schools post-war. This was the introduction of visual aid equipment. Whilst it inevitably took time to equip schools with 16mm projectors, the experiences of wartime meant there was an expectation that such deliveries would take place and schools looked forward to their arrival. Thus with the greater availability of projectors, film study became a possibility. Rationing was to play its part with different authorities choosing to be restrictive in their provision, with some schools sharing projectors. The legacy of pre-war attitudes where some favoured silent films for educational purposes was used to legitimise the provision of only (cheaper) silent projectors. A variation of this discrimination persisted for many years in the London County Council, where secondary schools were each allocated a sound projector, but primary schools had to make do with silent equipment.

A large constituency in post-war provision was that of the Youth Service. War-time reports sought to anticipate matters by planning for peace. Included in these reports were proposals for the use of films in the clubs not simply as a distraction but as the basis for structured discussion. In 1943 the Board of Education was categorical: going to the cinema four or five times a week was 'a dangerous addiction'.[48] Consequently it urged that more attention be given to discussion 'in school hours and in clubs'. The follow-up publication by the re-designated Ministry of Education is less strident and wanted the informal discussions to explore technique, taste and truth. Youth club members were to develop a critical attitude to 'commercial amusements'.[49]

Children and the Cinema – The Wheare Committee
There was a further element in the background to the teaching of film. Children's Saturday matinées and Cinema Clubs had existed in the 1930s. They had continued during wartime, to the extent that the Rank Organisation had made special films for them from 1943.[50] Post-war they attracted attention as a social phenomenon which was without precedent. Huge numbers of children, mostly between seven and twelve years old, attended cinemas unaccompanied by parents and then were supervised by a tiny number of adults – cinema staff untrained in dealing with children *en masse*.

Such were the reverberations in society about these events that the government in 1947 established a committee to investigate the situation. The membership of the Committee did not include representatives of the BFI, despite protests from the Governors.[51] The existence of the Departmental Committee on Children and the Cinema (often referred to as the Wheare Committee, after its Chairman, a Professor of Government at Oxford) was seized upon by many groups that had views about the cinema. Along with those who tended to view negatively the relationship between children and the cinema were also included those who were both experimenting with, and advocating, film appreciation. It is clear that Wheare himself became sympathetic to this new movement. In an early note on the Committee's work in April 1948 he wrote:

The need to develop film appreciation for children and for teachers has been mentioned by several witnesses, and I think it would be helpful if we could have further information on what has already been done in this field and also suggestions as to how this work can best be carried out.[52]

The Committee's brief had not mentioned film appreciation. E G Barnard, Chief Education Officer of Portsmouth and a member of the Committee, writing an account of its work following publication of the Report in early 1950 sketches the background.[53] The committee had been set up, firstly as a result of a Parliamentary debate in November 1946 on children's cinema clubs and secondly in response to a deputation in 1947, representing local authorities and teachers organisations. The committee had two elements to its brief:

(a) to consider and report on a the effects of attendance at the cinema on children under the age of 16, with special reference to attendance at children's cinema clubs;

(b) whether, in the light of these efforts, any modification is desirable in the existing system of film classification, the existing position with regard to the admission of children to cinemas, or in the organisation, conduct and management of children's cinema clubs.

The advocates of film appreciation were not, however, in a position to present a united front and it was indeed the existence of the Wheare Committee itself which served to provide a focus for a range of individuals and institutions that had been operating independently. Those who were variously involved in the advocacy of film appreciation saw that submitting evidence to the Committee or appearing as witnesses would be the best possible opportunity for promoting their work. It is also clear from material in the National Archives that there was a more informal channel of contact, maintained by Mrs Marcousé, the Joint Secretary to the Committee from the Ministry of Education, who presumably played an important role in shaping the form of the Committee's final report.[54]

Correspondence in the National Archive reveals the readiness of Mrs Marcousé to meet and learn from E Francis Mills, albeit not until mid 1949 when the draft of the report was already being compiled. Mills, who was at this stage lecturing at Gaddesdon Emergency Training College, had submitted a detailed statement of work being done in film appreciation and had hoped to make available a 'final report'.[55] However, time constraints prevented this. It seems very likely that this report was to become the basis of the document *School Film Appreciation* that would be circulated in early 1950 with the blessing of the BFI.[56] It is also clear that the committee received a copy of Maurice Woodhouse's paper summarising the work that he was currently then undertaking on film appreciation at Leeds City Training College.[57]

In practice, the published report explored other areas, responding to the wide range of evidence it had received. [58] Section VII is called 'Raising Standards: Two Aspects' and the two aspects are 'Educating Children's Taste in Films' and 'Raising the Standard of Films for Children'. The consideration of the first aspect concentrates specifically on film appreciation, which the report acknowledges has only a subsidiary connection with the enquiry itself. Members had

> ...heard of the benefits which children and young people might derive from the teaching of film appreciation, but few concrete suggestions were made as to how this could best be done.[59]

The problem for those who wished to advocate film appreciation was not necessarily opposition from members of the Committee but the limited supporting evidence with which it was presented. The Committee was, however, ready to acknowledge the evidence that children enjoyed the cinema and that it was overwhelmingly the art form to which they responded. The Committee was also confronted by those who demanded this was a phenomenon about which something should be done. The Report could make certain recommendations which might help to satisfy these complainants, such as introducing a higher age limit of seven for the admission of unaccompanied children to the cinemas, but there were very real limits on the practicability of what they might propose. It had judiciously avoided tackling the claims being made as to the damage done to children's physical and psychological health by the device of referring to these as issues for subsequent substantial and properly funded research. Children were clearly going to carry on going to the cinemas, so the only feasible options were to suggest possible ways of improving both the children and the films.

Thus, the committee had to come up with ways of 'Educating Children's Taste in Films' and given the limited amount of work available for them to consider, they had to 'doubt whether film appreciation ever could, or should, become a school subject in itself'.[60] In fact, despite this statement (which may have been included to satisfy the more sceptical members of the committee) there are three pages devoted to film appreciation and a proper deployment of what evidence they had. The work of the Northern Counties Children's Cinemas Council, which had been set up in the 1930s, was described in detail. The Liverpool Youth Organisations' Committee had developed a guide in the form of a wall chart to draw attention to the current film releases and this also was described and commended.

Witnesses who appeared before them or submitted evidence included Stanley Reed and Maurice Woodhouse.[61] Only two instances of the implementation of the appreciation in schools are quoted in detail. The descriptions of this work in the Report would suggest sufficient correspondence with work described elsewhere for it to be assumed that the accounts are of Reed's work in West Ham and Woodhouse's in Leeds. Other witnesses included Frank Farley and B Gillett, teachers who had each had substantial periods of secondment with the BFI during and just after the war.[62]

Although apparently recognising that film appreciation would not get into the school curriculum, nevertheless the Report picks up on the need for there to be an acknowledgement of the place of film in teacher training.

> The first need, therefore, is more opportunity for teachers to equip themselves with a better knowledge of the cinema, as so many have already done with drama and music. We believe that many would like to do so, if the opportunities existed.[63]

The Report then targets a range of educational and other institutions that should collaborate in order 'to provide the training, which is so greatly required'.[64] The underlying assumption in this promotion of appreciation is that the child will benefit in a very specific way.

> We agree with the view of one of the schools mentioned above, that the most important function of film appreciation for children and young people is to develop film discrimination.[65]

This is reinforced by a long quotation from evidence submitted by the BFI, which in the Committee's view best sums up their own views. The BFI had, in effect, provided the committee with the means both to justify and yet diminish the role of film appreciation because it presents film appreciation as a starting point from which a proper appreciation of other arts may be achieved.

> In this way they can be brought to consider forms of art which normally they would regard as quite outside their experience and which, if approached more directly, they might feel to be dead and academic.[66]

Perhaps the BFI felt it had to submit this rather defensive approach, since its remit in relation to film appreciation was unclear following the setting up in 1946 by Local Education Authorities of the National Committee for Audio Visual Aids in Education (NCAVAE).[67] This latter organisation was in no doubt as to how things stood. Approached for its views on film appreciation following Professor Wheare's initial decision to investigate that area, the NCAVAE Secretary responded

> …that it had been specifically agreed when an inquiry into Children and the Cinema was instituted that the question of film appreciation in schools was a matter for which the National Committee would ultimately be responsible.[68]

That said, the NCAVAE had nothing much to offer other than that

The promotion of standards of good taste with regard to film appreciation is, of course, one of the functions of the National Committee, and the Committee is at present considering the means by which this can best be achieved.[69]

Film appreciation had, it appears, now reached sufficient significance for it to be a disputed area of influence which was to be fought over between national organisations.

When it was finally published in early 1950 the Wheare Report was not the damning document some might have wished for. In particular, it called for more research on the contentious areas, whilst giving a nod of official approval to the teaching of film appreciation. There were, however, passages which implicated the cinema in the encouragement of false values, and these in particular gained publicity. Nevertheless, the supportive paragraphs were to be quoted as evidence of official recognition for some fifteen years until the publication of *Half Our Future* in 1963 gave a stronger push for the acceptance of film study. Once again it seemed appropriate to advocate the uses of film in school in anticipation of a further raising of the school leaving age, now set to become 16, albeit this was not to be achieved for a further decade.

Appreciation and Discrimination in the School

As has been shown, the BFI had made several contributions to the study of film in pamphlet form in the 1940s. The provenance of these publications is unclear and they do not form a detectable sequence, each apparently being a one-off. What was more influential were the regular summer schools scheduled to attract teachers in the long school summer holidays. These courses had restarted in 1944 at a time when the BFI was under attack from the Dartington Hall Trust which carried out a wartime survey (the Arts Enquiry)

> …which severely criticised the BFI's limited achievements and lack of influence, in particular in the field of formal education, which had been its main activity.[70]

The Enquiry, circulated in confidential draft form in 1944,[71] had felt it necessary in order to make its case against the BFI to offer the following definition of what the Institute should have been doing.

> The purpose of film appreciation is to show people how to recognise what is good and bad in the form, the content and the technique of the film. It is therefore an extension of the work of film criticism, in that it aims at providing information and at inculcating standards of judgment.[72]

Quite how widely accepted this definition might have been, one cannot judge. By the time that the final version of the Arts Enquiry was published in 1947 no such all embracing definition was attempted.[73] Instead it declared, in the Summary chapter under 'Film Criticism and Appreciation', in a less prescriptive manner:

> Much remains to be done to increase the public's appreciation of the film and to raise its standards of judgment.[74]

Indeed, the BFI's own report of June 1946 had made the following pronouncement:

> Film appreciation is a loose term and no exact definition of it has been formulated. At the moment it ranges from training children's taste to advanced study of the structure of a particular film.[75]

According to Christophe Dupin, the Arts Enquiry formed a crucial part of the debate in Labour government circles around the future of the BFI.[76] The outcome for the Institute was the setting up of the Radcliffe Committee and the publication of its Report in 1948,[77] which, quite apart from its proposals for reviving the organization and purpose of the Institute, gave it a clearer brief in relation to the newly formed National Committee for Audio Visual Aids in Education (NCAVAE) over the delivery of film appreciation.

> But we should be concerned to learn that education authorities were indifferent to the importance of developing a right appreciation of films among children or that they thought that such appreciation could be imparted by a teacher without having the opportunity of expert training or advice. The evidence that we received gave us some reassurance on this point and we recommend therefore that the Institute should aim to assist education authorities on these lines, while recognizing that the direct responsibility in the school must lie with them.[78]

Several inter-related events then took place. Denis Forman (former chief production officer at the Central Office of Information) was appointed BFI Director in 1949. At the summer school that year a number of students declared an interest in film appreciation and as a result letters appeared in various educational journals, urging others with a similar interest to get in touch.[79] Some 60 teachers responded. In the following February a duplicated document *School Film Appreciation* with a supportive foreword by Forman went out to the teachers who had responded.[80] In his introduction Forman reported that Stanley Reed would start work in April 1950 as the Institute's first Film Appreciation Officer.[81] The signatories to *School Film Appreciation* were E Francis Mills, the pre-war pioneer of film appreciation while at the London School of Economics (LSE), Tony Hodgkinson, Jack Smith and John Huntley. The first three had signed the letter that urged teachers to respond. Huntley – a sound engineer at Denham Studios and a part time BFI lecturer – joined them subsequently. Mills had established a very active film group in his training college. Hodgkinson, by now a Secondary Modern School teacher, had been one of Mills's former students. Smith taught in a Grammar school.

With the support of both Forman and Reed the momentum was maintained and plans were made for the formation of what would become the Society of Film Teachers. Following on from a conference on Film Appreciation in October 1950 organised by the English New Education Fellowship, the inaugural meeting of SFT took place.[82] At its formation, the aim of the Society of Film Teachers was to focus on film appreciation. The statement of SFT's aims, regularly repeated in its publications in the early 1950s was:

> THE SOCIETY OF FILM TEACHERS exists to promote the teaching of film appreciation in colleges, schools and the Youth Service. Membership is open to all who are actively engaged in education and wish to teach film appreciation as a curriculum subject, or organize junior film societies, discussion groups or similar activities.[83]

The connotations of the term had to be taken on trust by the Society's members since, as has been shown, though it was increasingly widely used, there had been either a reluctance to define it or a readiness to assume it meant whatever you wanted it to mean.

Perhaps it was the catch-all nature of its applicability that enabled so many different enthusiasts to gather together in a Society where each would independently do her/his own thing outside the Society. One notable early instance which demonstrates the breadth of interest of the SFT membership occurred in 1953, when A W Hodgkinson, styling his byline as a Founder Member of SFT, wrote in the January issue of *Visual Education*, describing his classroom use of two films.[84] In the March issue, he was taken to task by Jack Smith, another founder member.[85] The debate between them illustrates the tentative nature of what film appreciation might be considered to embrace at this stage. Hodgkinson, teaching in a Modern School, had sought to demonstrate how well his students, aged between 11 and 15 years, had responded to extracts from *Nanook of the North* and *Kameradschaft*. The children had been shown the silent igloo-building sequence from *Nanook* and *How to Build an Igloo*, an instructional sound film in colour. Invited to give each film marks for 'beauty, humour, truth, entertainment value and instructional value', the children preferred the earlier silent film. When responding to Kameradschaft, the children were encouraged 'to write imaginative, eye witness accounts of the disaster'. Hodgkinson's conclusion was that 'good films were better teaching aids than uninspired "text book" films'. He attributed this to a characteristic of Modern School children for whom 'knowledge and understanding are acquired more through the senses and sensibilities than through the use of the intellect'.

Smith argues that 'in attempting to make the widest possible use of his films, [Hodgkinson] has wandered away from the true field of the film appreciation lesson'. He tackles Hodgkinson firstly for not drawing the students' attention to the role of the film-maker in constructing the film. Then, perhaps writing from the stance of a grammar school teacher, Smith resists the use of *Kameradschaft* as the inspiration for creative writing.

> It is every child's right to be shown how to read and how to get the most out of books; study of the film should be used, whenever possible, to stimulate literary as well as film appreciation – and particularly in the Modern School where literature as a "subject" must appear so unprofitable and be so difficult to teach.

In the early fifties teachers were experimenting both with the kinds of films that might be shown in the classroom and with the subsequent educational practices that followed screenings. It would be a lengthy process before any consensus would develop around the nature of film teaching. Smith, however, wrote from his private address and did not reveal to *Visual Education* readers that there was any SFT connection. The next chapter will explore the early years of SFT's quest to define the shape of film teaching/screen education as it is documented in the Society's publications.

What film appreciation might involve is explored in some detail in 1952 by Maurice Woodhouse in his PhD thesis, albeit his theoretical references are literary ones.[86] When he needs to demonstrate practice, he is obliged to compare two current newspaper criticisms of the Orson Welles' *Macbeth*, one from *The Observer* and the other from *The Times Educational Supplement*. In the absence of any academics writing constructively about the cinema, the newspaper critics were his only source of documentation. This had also been the case for the BFI publication *Elements of Film Criticism*, where a range of critical stances was documented with each critic proposing her/his own position with no editorial attempt to context individual contributions. Woodhouse claims that the term 'film study' would be a more appropriate term for the work he was attempting in schools. Curiously, he proposes this not because it would involve the use of a neutral and descriptive term but because it implied a lower level of scholarship than the term 'film appreciation' and in that way 'the kind of training which can be given to the majority of school-children might be described, perhaps, more simply and more accurately'.[87] His premise is that appreciation is 'a complicated process, which demands an emotional sensitivity, coupled with a degree of intellectual maturity'.[88]

Training the audience to appreciate the film was perhaps a legacy of the culture of war-time, when so many had to tackle the unfamiliar and training was a necessity and sometimes meant the difference between life and death. Stonier, in the collection of essays *Made for Millions* (1947), describes the options as follows:

> Audiences can either be left to sink below their natural level (which, in general, is the policy of the 100,000,000 circulation film-maker) or trained to develop taste and intelligence.[89]

This collection of essays was intended to investigate 'the situation in which artist and audience find themselves today as a result of the inventions which have revolutionised the means of publishing information and works of art'.[90] In practice half of its contributors were the reviewers employed to consider the arts in the national press. Their common position was that the arts could no longer be the preserve of an élite in an age of the reproducibility of art.

> The machines have come to stay and in our view it is now a question of mass culture or no culture.[91]

The Editor's 'Epilogue' takes the line of hinting rather than stating that the producers of mass art will only improve the product if the audience demands a better one. Only by training a more discriminating audience will things improve.[92] This remained a widely held view in the post-war years, and certainly found echoes in the film appreciation movement.

Young Cinema-Goers Receive a Caution

While the debates around children and the cinema continued, children intrigued by the phenomenon of cinema wanted to read for themselves about their new found interest. However certain books about the cinema which were intended specifically to be read by children were written from the perspective of religion rather than from any independent concept of film appreciation. Andrew Buchanan (a producer of educational and religious films who had lectured at BFI summer schools in 1936 and 1938) addressed his *Going to the Cinema* (1947) to the 'Adult Cinema-goer of Tomorrow'.[93] These prospective spectators were alerted from the outset that commercial films were not art, though there might be rare exceptions. After reading the book, Buchanan hopes his readers will 'be so much more critical that you will hesitate to spend your time and money on shows that are not up to standard…'.[94] His position becomes more explicit when he states

> On the whole, British films contain more good sense and good taste than most American films, but sometimes they appear to us to move rather slowly.[95]

He then opposes 'British quality and American quantity' and indeed anti-Americanism is a theme of the book, perhaps picking up on a populist mood of the time.[96] His ideal film would blend the methods of the documentary with those of the feature film. Some of the notions around quality that Buchanan advances here were part of a wider debate among film critics of the time – a debate that would be reinvestigated decades later by John Ellis.[97]

In 1951, Buchanan published two books. *The Film in Education* is a substantial work intended for an adult educational readership. Its significance here is that the attitudes to which it gave currency were in direct opposition to what both SFT and the BFI Film

Appreciation Department were setting out to achieve in relation to films that were readily accessible locally. Buchanan regards the Secondary Modern schoolchild (about 80 per cent of the state school population) as 'backward'.[98] He is disgruntled that the Wheare Committee (to which he had given evidence) was out of step with his views.

> I also hold the opinion that children are harmed morally by constantly seeing adult films, and that even in cases where no moral harm is done, the practice of cinema-going (to adult programmes) by children plants seeds in their minds during a most critical period, gives emphasis to superficial and unimportant aspects of life, directs attention from fundamentals and creates preciousness and restlessness.[99]

His second book was *Focus Film Course*, published by the Catholic Film Institute and intended as a briefing pamphlet for those attempting to teach film appreciation.[100] As a working definition of film appreciation he adopts that of the Arts Enquiry in 1944 and in order to fire up the missionary zeal of the teachers they are told that

> There is also no doubt that the spiritual and mental development of the individual is not advanced by film going.[101]

That Buchanan was widely accepted as an authority on children's cinema is evidenced by the contributions he made to *Contemporary Cinema*, the short lived Church of England monthly film journal. In articles introducing film appreciation Buchanan informed his readers that merely wishing to be entertained was an insufficient reason for going to the cinema.[102]

Another author promoting a Christian approach to film was Vernon Sproxton (1948) who set a context for his attitude to cinema as a fall from grace.

> It is not insignificant that the picture house really established its hold on our national life during the sad and squalid early nineteen-thirties…The cinema's popularity is not so much a cause as a consequence of the breakdown of virile home life.[103]

Thus prepared the reader finds listed 'The Canons of Film Appreciation'.[104] These turn out to be a list of elements of film eg photography, characterisation, editing etc, and under these headings questions are asked. Some are bewilderingly abrupt: *Was the editing good?* Others encourage respondents to be judgmental: *Had the characters sufficient motive for what they did? Was the story too paltry for film, or* vice versa? Sproxton still feels able to include the section on his Canons by reassuring readers that 'we are concerned with the form and not the content'.[105] All things are relative and by the end of the final chapter on the Christian Approach to the Cinema, the questions provoke unashamedly judgmental answers:

Were the conclusions of the film moral and the scenes depicted decent? What was the understanding of man? Was he shown as 'captain of his soul' or as a somewhat tragic figure in need of redemption?[106]

The prevalence of these anti-cinema attitudes (presented with the explicit endorsement of religion and often targeted specifically at child readers) provided an important part of the potentially hostile context in which both SFT and the BFI Film Appreciation Department had to operate when they were seeking to become established.

BFI/SFT Collaborations

There is no doubt that the 1950s was the decade in which close collaboration persisted between SFT and BFI, with a number of joint ventures. In part this was a result of the limited number of staff in what became the Education Department of the BFI and of the readiness of the SFT committee to participate in what was at this stage seen as a joint-venture to promote film appreciation and (as an offshoot of that) children's film-making as proper components of the curriculum in schools. Schools contained the most students and were therefore the likeliest target area. However, a series of deaths among SFT activists who had an extra-school connection may have reinforced this tendency. SFT's first chairman R R Jones, Deputy Director of Education in West Ham (where film activity in schools was well established) died as a result of a car accident in December 1950.[107] A year later, G T Hankin who had recently been an HMI and contributed to SFT meetings, died.[108] The following December, 1952, Dr Maurice Woodhouse, the first person to receive a research qualification in the area of film appreciation, died.[109] In 1954 Janet Hills, the film correspondent of *The Times Educational Supplement*, who had championed the work of both BFI and SFT (where she had been on the committee) died suddenly at the age of 36.[110]

Stanley Reed at the BFI did much to promote film appreciation. His energies went in several directions. His articles appeared in assorted journals and he lectured widely.[111] Under his former secretary, Lectures Officer Molly Lloyd, the lecture service and the summer schools became very well established. There were also two deliberately promotional activities Reed established, one for the members of the BFI and the other for the schools and youth clubs. BFI members received, as part of the National Film Theatre booklet, a smaller insert called *Critics' Choice*.[112] Each month film critics from leading newspapers met over lunch to decide by vote which was the 'film of the month'. This information and reviews were then circulated. The schools received what might perhaps be regarded as a junior version of this: *Film Guide*. Produced over a decade from 1950 to 1961 by the Film Appreciation Department, the *Guide* was a wall chart for display in the classroom, which focused on recent film releases and drew the attention of students to them.[113] Eventually re-designated *Screen Guide* this chart was produced by both the BFI and SEFT as SFT had become known. In 1959 the Society of Film Teachers had become the Society for Education in Film and Television. The names of both the Society and the *Guide* had been changed to accommodate the greater interest being given to television by the late 1950s.

The model for *Film Guide* had been a wall chart produced in Liverpool for display in youth clubs and which had been given as evidence to the Wheare Committee.[114] That earlier version had concentrated on films in Liverpool cinemas. *Film Guide*'s long-term problem was that it had to accommodate the scheduling of both London openings and provincial release dates. Alongside the film reviews, other information was provided about films and film-makers. Most importantly, the re-designed later version from January 1954 had a tear-off slip intended for the teacher or youth leader. The conscientious recipient of the *Film Guide*, as it was published each month, would have compiled an early guide to teaching film appreciation by assiduously filing all these slips. The significance of these wall charts was that they were directed at children in schools and at members in the youth clubs. These charts represented the first material specifically for students which the BFI was to produce.

The Film Appreciation Department had been enlarged by the addition of John Huntley and then, following Reed's promotion to become the BFI's Secretary, by the appointment of Tony Hodgkinson, the SFT activist. Reed's earlier promotional activities bore fruit in that international contacts were established, where the joint presence of BFI and SFT gave the UK some pre-eminence in the developing European world of film appreciation. The records of international conferences provide opportunity not only to discover a British position on film study in relation to that of other nations but also to detect the 'official' evolution of that British strain of film appreciation.

Indeed, the nature of the conferences around issues of children and film had changed since the 1940s when they had had a specifically British dimension. Then the organisational impetus had not necessarily come from those directly involved in film teaching work – since there were hardly any in that position – but from other concerned bodies. The note of concern had been reflected in the styling of the conferences. In the early conferences the child had been considered in relation to the institution of cinema; later s/he was to be positioned in confrontation with the changing nature of the moving image. In 1946 the National Council of Women had collaborated with the BFI on 'Children in the Cinema', triggered by 'the ever growing importance of this problem today'.[115] In 1949 the English New Education Fellowship and the University of London, Institute of Education staged 'The Impact of the Cinema on the Child'.[116] By 1950 the event which preceded the creation of SFT was significantly a conference on Film Appreciation.[117] By the time of the international gathering of film teachers in Amsterdam in 1957 the styling was 'Film Education and Youth'[118] with a follow-up event in London in 1958 entitled 'Film, Television and the Child'.[119]

In the 1950s the work of both SFT and BFI was strong on organisation and on propagandising but weak on establishing a theoretical basis for what was so enthusiastically being propounded. Little changed following the conference which had provided the backdrop to the formation of SFT and had included a lecture from Stanley Reed on 'Film Appreciation in the School', drawing on Reed's years of teaching and advising in

West Ham. In it he established some of the tenets that were to apply in the early years. Most important was his emphasis (which became a SFT one also) that the films which mattered were those screened at local cinemas and which consequently were routinely accessed by the children. Secondly he promoted discussion as the process by which children were to engage with an understanding of film. Thirdly he saw children's film-making as an important part of their achieving this understanding.

It is however relevant to note that Reed recorded several reservations about how the work should be developed, but subsequently others tended to ignore his cautionary remarks.[120] He favoured using extracts from feature films and not documentary films (which were often to be used simply because they were available on free loan). He did not favour the translation of 'the mechanics of studio practice' into school as the basis for making films. Nor did he feel that the teaching of film history should have any degree of priority for children. Although he promoted film-making, this was as a means and not as an end in itself. The quality of the finished film was irrelevant: the learning process was in the translation of an idea into visual terms, where the group construction of the ideas in the shooting script mattered more than the film which might eventually get made. Yet in subsequent years SFT/SEFT would encourage the use of sponsored free loan films, include a film history section in its *Handbook for Screen Education*[121] and promote children's film-making competitions.[122]

By the time Reed was addressing the Amsterdam conference in 1957 he was now Secretary of the BFI and perhaps less prepared to offer suggestions as to what should happen in the classroom. Instead he stands back, though it is clear he is certainly aware of the differences between the British approach and that which was being advocated by J M L Peters of the Netherlands Film Institute who had identified three elements as the domain of film education:

> Without a certain knowledge of film language one cannot be able to appreciate the film aesthetically, neither evaluate a film critically.[123]

By gaining access to film language, the student may be enabled 'to see actively'. From this state it is, Peters claimed, a natural extension for the child to co-operate with the film artist and engage in 'creative seeing'. The third stage is that of 'seeing critically'. Here judgments are involved. The child is expected to evaluate 'the (social, moral) contents of the film as positive or negative, as acceptable or objectionable, as useful or harmful, as 'good' or 'bad'.[124] It asks for 'discrimination and independent judgment'. In the resolutions passed at this conference Dr Peters's threefold approach was accepted as the model for 'training in discrimination'.[125]

Faced with this certainty, Reed had felt it necessary to defend the British position:

> I would like to dispel any idea that may exist in respect of film teaching in Britain that because we are doing good deal of practical work we are not interested in theory.[126]

He then in effect states that the British cannot hang around waiting for theory when there is clearly a job to be done now. He advocates following two principles: taking 'the positive approach' and aiming to educate the ordinary cinema-goer. From Reed's very particular insistence that he is concerned to provide a non élite education, we may take it that he is committed to the education of the Secondary Modern schoolchild. It was therefore unsurprising that when the follow-up conference was staged in London in 1958, organised by BFI and SFT, there was a strong emphasis on practice rather than theory.[127] On the first full day delegates visited schools to see teaching in progress and then discussed television programmes with members of the Society. The second full day saw the delegates in the audience at the NFT for one of the regular presentations by the BFI for children from London County Council (LCC) schools. The programme was called 'Are They Real?' The third day being Saturday found the delegates at the Ritz in Richmond for a Saturday morning cinema club programme, followed by a demonstration of teaching methods by SFT.

Education Through Art

Attitudes however were changing. In 1957 Paddy Whannel had replaced Tony Hodgkinson as Film Appreciation Officer, and it was specifically through his influence that both the BFI and SFT became involved in a loose federation of educational groups, known as the Joint Council for Education through Art. The Council had a distinctive strategy. It brought together the educationalists and the creative artists at a number of significant events where the BFI and SFT collaborated with the Council. The most influential of these was a series of lectures/screenings and discussions with the title 'Visual Persuaders' on eight consecutive nights at the newly opened National Film Theatre building in 1959. By extending the range of contacts and the expertise of the personnel involved, an engagement began to be made with issues around what was beginning to be identified as popular culture.

Before this more formal linkage under the Council, the BFI had collaborated with one of Council's key organizations, the Society for Education through Art. In 1956 SEA published an issue of its Journal, *Athene*, produced with the co-operation of the British Film Institute.[128] Here the beginnings of a new form of association may be detected. The alliance of the two institutions had begun with the joint organisation of an Easter Film Course in 1955 on 'Art, Films and Film Art'.[129] In his introduction to the joint issue of *Athene* Herbert Read, President of SEA, makes clear what he sees as the priority.

> It is the use of film for the teaching of art that we have uppermost in mind on the present occasion.[130]

Much of the joint issue does reflect Read's attitude, with only one article attempting to address the notion of film being an art form. This is 'Teaching the Art of Film' by Hodgkinson, then the BFI's Film Appreciation Officer.[131] A revealing picture of where things stood in the mid-50s is contained in Hodgkinson's article. Having acknowledged that film teaching draws its adherents from those trained in both visual and literary cultures, he attempts to outline what all can actually agree upon. Firstly, the teacher must respect the popular cinema and his children's taste for it. Secondly, all film teaching should be closely related to current films available to children. Then he distinguishes three broad approaches: sympathetic, guided discussion of current films; the showing of worthwhile and entertaining films to enlarge and deepen the child's film background; and finally, the teaching, by suitable means, of the elements of film art.

What is significant here is the rather bland nature of what is being offered by the BFI's Film Appreciation Officer. Given the emphasis this SEA/BFI publication was demonstrating, perhaps Hodgkinson was treading cautiously in unfamiliar territory. The sub-headings matching his three approaches generally precede sections which encourage readers to take things further by contacting either the BFI or SFT. Where he does become prescriptive is in relation to children's film-making.

> The production of a film by children must never be regarded by the teacher as an end in itself, and it is for this reason that the Institute and the Society of Film Teachers have forborne to publicise widely this aspect of film appreciation work.[132]

Despite this caution he then argues that the films children make do demonstrate their 'sure grasp of cinematic convention' and using 'this unconscious taste for what is fundamentally good in cinema' perhaps 'we shall have gone some way towards creating that more discriminating public, which the report of the Departmental Committee on Children and the Cinema, published in 1950, rightly postulated as the only way in which the art of the cinema could be improved'.[133] It seems that the official approval, implicit in the Wheare Report, for raising standards by improving the audience's power of discrimination was still being exhibited. Indeed, Herbert Read's brief introduction already quoted had contained the following endorsement:

> If the critical taste of the public is ever to be raised from its present indifference or docility, it will be through the formation of a critical attitude at school.[134]

The SEA subsequently held an ambitious conference at the Royal Festival Hall in April 1957 on 'Education through the Arts'. The conference and the report of the event were under the auspices of the new umbrella body: the Joint Council for Education through Art, which became very active in promoting educational events in the late 1950s. Among these conferences was 'Art, Science and Education' in 1958. Two of the contributing societies were the British Film Institute and the Society of Film Teachers. These two became much more influential in the Joint Council so that by May 1959 they organised the week-long event 'The Visual Persuaders'. No record exists of 'The Visual Persuaders' beyond the programme details. However, there is a record of the earlier 1957 conference,[135] and also a booklet published in 1958 *Artist, Critic and Teacher*.[136] In these a definite change of educational direction may be detected. Brian Groombridge is among those who begin to question the process of educating taste, and he specifically raises issues of class.

> One must take great care not to confuse education with the imposition of middle class or aristocratic standards on people who are not themselves middle or upper-class.[137]

Groombridge rejects the attitudes of teachers whose commitment to teaching is limited so they deliberately avoid any engagement with the interests of their students. He also rejects those who seek to indulge the children's preferences today in order to wean them to something better tomorrow. He wants teachers to share the pleasures of the mass media with their students.[138] His views are complementary to those of Whannel, who at the 1957 conference had attacked the patronising teacher whose attitudes Groombridge subsequently challenged:

> …the teacher, obsessed with a raising standards of taste. This assumes that there is a sound and established body of taste, and that it is the aim of education to pass this on in diluted doses to the masses.[139]

Whannel makes a specific plea that the teacher should be concerned to distinguish what is good and bad in popular culture. In so doing a context was set for the developments that were to follow in the 1960s.[140]

The Academy Keeps its Distance

Much of the early activity around teaching film was focused on the 'grass roots' – schools – and received very little attention in higher education from the 1930s to the 1960s. Events might have turned out differently: immediately post-war, Alexander Korda funded a research trip by Oxford academics to the USA to investigate the use of film in higher education.[141] Given the constraints imposed on transatlantic travel by the exigencies of the immediate post-war period, their expedition had to be curtailed. Crucially, the academics never got beyond the east coast. Their proposed visit to Hollywood never happened. Significantly, what also failed to take place as a consequence of their remaining on the east coast was a visit to the University of Southern California, scheduled to have happened while they were in Los Angeles. Had the Oxford dons seen how developed and substantial the academic standing of film study had become at USC since it offered the first undergraduate major in 1933,[142] perhaps the long wait that the study of film had to undergo before gaining any academic acceptance in the United Kingdom might have been reduced.

The cinema and the serious study of film met opposition from within the academy. While C M Fleming (1944), a social psychologist, had refused to denounce the cinema as a bad influence,[143] J P Mayer in *Sociology of Film* (1946) was certainly alarmist, claiming that children at the cinema were 'victims of emotional possession'.[144] Predictably, he promotes film appreciation as a mechanism that will confront (and presumably exorcise) this possession. Mayer chooses to draw heavily on the work of the 1930s Payne Fund Enquiry in the United States, ignoring the later publications in America which had discredited much of the findings. The context of his own work had been an enquiry on behalf of the Rank Organisation into Children's Cinema Clubs. The reviewer of Mayer's book in *Documentary Newsletter*, points out that the questionnaires completed by the children and the essays submitted by them 'are not sufficiently representative of the various classes, occupations, age groups etc for any findings to be at all valid as a sample survey'.[145] Nevertheless, Meyer's book was reprinted three times – until 1970.

Elsewhere in the academy, film had attracted little attention. Herbert Read in *Education through Art* (1943) makes no mention of film, though he does discuss the concept of appreciation in relation to art.[146] Earlier he had paid attention to the cinema when in 1932 he considered what might be meant by a film aesthetic. His purpose then had been to provide endorsement for the notion that film was an art form and to raise the status of the film artist who would have 'the visual sensibility of the painter, the vision of the poet, and the time-sense of the musician'.[147] In his involvement with the Society for Education through Art mentioned above, Read had continued to promote the primacy of the 'art film'.

Stanley Reed always maintained that only when film was established as a proper area for investigation at university level would it have sufficient purchase within the educational system to give status to the study of film at other educational levels.[148] Indeed according to Leslie Heywood, a founder member of SFT, Reed's attitude was decisive in determining the choice of an author for the BFI's first book on the subject of film appreciation, *Teaching Film*.[149] She was Grace Greiner, a lecturer at Goldsmiths College, University of London. Alone of the SFT pioneers she was based in a university, the other higher education representatives were all in teacher training colleges. Although film as an object of university study was a long way off in the 1940s, in certain departments of education interest in the phenomenon of children and the cinema was receiving attention. At Birmingham University in the late 1940s, Wall and his researchers produced several papers from a psychological perspective.[150] In Leeds, Maurice Woodhouse was carrying out classroom research, which eventually led to his 1952 PhD thesis *Film Appreciation in the School*.[151]

As to consideration of whether the universities might themselves engage with film – other than as a visual aid – Bristol University Drama Department took the initiative, both in introducing a highly innovative course and with the organisation of a conference on 'The Relation between Universities and Films, Radio and Television' in 1954.[152] An earlier undergraduate attempt to encourage academics to consider the cinema had occurred in 1947 when the film journal *Sequence* approached several leading Oxford dons asking them to nominate the best film each had ever seen – with mixed results.[153] There was a formally constituted body that might have been the basis for injecting film study into the Academy: this was the British Universities Film Council which had been founded in 1948. However, the priority of BUFC was to influence universities to accept film as a visual aid, rather than as an object of study in itself. As late as 1968 Stuart Hall, writing in the BUFC's *Journal* notes how little developed film study was at university level then, compared with its status in further education where there had been developments during the 1960s.[154]

Film study did however find a home on the fringes of the Academy – in extra-mural provision. The most enduring instance of this was that provided under the auspices of London University and which, until the 1980s, was organised and controlled by the BFI. It started in 1953, taught almost entirely by John Huntley on a peripatetic basis. Once established in the BFI's own premises by 1955, the course subsequently achieved University Certificate status with progression over two, then three years. Later a fourth year was added for students who wished to proceed to a Diploma. For many years its lecturers continued to be drawn from the BFI's own staff.[155]

Highly influential in the pattern of the dissemination of film appreciation was the BFI's Lecture Service, firmly established by 1952. An early agreement was reached with the British Film Academy that the BFI would be the agency for handling lecture requests received by both organizations.[156] As part of the arrangement, some Academy members would make themselves available to the BFI as lecturers. This latter group was called upon particularly in the staffing of summer schools in the 1950s.[157] From the records in the BFI's *Quarterly Gazette* it is clear that most of the demands made on the Lecture Service throughout the 1950s were met from within the BFI's own staff. In the period 1954 – 1957 three members of staff – Reed, Huntley and Hodgkinson – delivered about 60 per cent of the lectures, almost all in the context of adult education. In 1958–1959 the pattern was maintained when Whannel replaced Hodgkinson. There was to an extent a geographically determined metropolitan focus, but lectures were given at venues throughout England and Wales. When adult educators wanted to develop film appreciation in the regions, it was to the BFI that they looked as when Roy Shaw started to develop the study of film at Keele.[158]By the end of the 1950s a tight structure had developed around the dissemination of film appreciation in Britain. The BFI with its close control, by a small group of employees, of the Extra-Mural course, the summer schools and lectures to adult education groups, was complemented by SFT/SEFT, an entirely voluntary organisation, attempting to establish a wider support provision for teachers and schools.

Notes

1. A source of useful wartime background wartime information is Dilys Powell *Films Since 1939* London: Longmans Green 1947.
2. Oliver Bell *Memorandum on the promotion of film appreciation in Great Britain* London: BFI 1938
3. *Report of an Educational Film Campaign* London: BFI March–July 1940.
4. *Report of an Educational Campaign organised by the British Film Institute* May 1941–April 1942 London: BFI July 1942

5. The pamphlets were: Ernest Lindgren *Film Appreciation for Discussion Groups and Schools* London: BFI 1942; Dorothy Grayson *Films and Youth Organisations* London: BFI 1944; C H Clarke *The Elements of Film Criticism* London: BFI 1944; W Waters *Visual Education* London: BFI 1946; Ceinwen Jones and F E Pardoe *A First Course in Film Appreciation* London: BFI 1946.

6. Ernest Lindgren *The Cinema* London: English Universities Press 1944; and Roger Manvell *The Cinema and the Public* London: Army Bureau of Current Affairs 1944

7. *The Film in National Life* Conference Report London: BFI 1943; George Pearson *The Film as a Visual Art* London: BFI 1945

8. *The Film in National Life* (1943) p 2

9. Ibid p 4

10. Ibid p 3

11. Ibid p 5

12. Ibid p 37

13. *Film Appreciation and Visual Education* London: BFI 1944 pp 79–89

14. Lindgren 1942 op cit p 3

15. Possibly the closest this model came to finding an operational reality was with the publication by the BFI Film Appreciation Department of *Critics Choice* and *Film Guide* which are described later in this chapter.

16. Grayson op cit p 3

17. Clarke op cit p 2

18. Ibid p 11

19. Waters op cit p 2

20. Ibid p 10

21. Jones and Pardoe op cit p 9

22. Ibid p 4

23. Ibid p 12

24. British Film Institute Governors' Minutes 28 October 1947

25. Ceinwen Jones and F E Pardoe 'Film Study' *Sight and Sound* Vol 18 No 70 Summer 1949 pp 91–93

26. Jympson Harman *Good Films and How to Appreciate Them* London: *Daily Mail* School Aid Department ?1947

27. British Film Institute 13th Annual Report 30 June 1946 p 7

28. BFI Special Collections Box 91 0/91/4 British Film Institute *The Film* Lectures offered by Roger Manvell BFI London c 1946

29. *British Film Academy Quarterly* 6 July 1949 p 2

30. Ivan Butler *To Encourage the Art of the Film* London: Robert Hale 1971 has useful information on Lindgren's various roles at the BFI.

31. Lindgren (1944) op cit p 7

32. Ibid p 11

33. Ibid p 17

34. Manvell op cit p 12

35. Ibid p 13
36. Ibid p 14
37. Ibid p 15
38. Lindsay Anderson 'The Manvell Approach' *Sequence* No 2 Winter 1947 p 34
39. Margaret Laurence *Citizenship Through English* Edinburgh: Oliver and Boyd 1946
40. Op cit p 19
41. Ibid p 21
42. S C Evernden and R.G. Holloway *English for Citizens* Book IV *Our Own Language* Leeds: E J Arnold & Sons 1950
43. Op cit p 11
44. Ibid p 134
45. Ibid p 171
46. Ibid p 176
47. Ibid p 190
48. Board of Education *The Youth Service After the War* London: HMSO 1943 p 13
49. Ministry of Education *The Purpose and Content of the Youth Service* London: HMSO 1945
50. Mary Field 'The Child Audience' *British Film Academy Journal* Summer 1955 p 3
51. Information on the backgrounds of the Committee Members is to be found in the *British Film Academy Quarterly* April 1949 p 13. The Chairman was Professor of Government and Public Administration at Oxford. Ten of the twenty members were employed in jobs directly related to education.
52. National Archives File No ED121/579 'Note on the Committee's work by the Chairman' 28 April 1948 p 2
53. E G Bernard 'Children and the Cinema' *Visual Education* Vol 1 No 6 June 1950
54. National Archives File No ED121/580 Letter from Marcousé to A Wall 16 August 1949
55. National Archives File No ED121/580 Letter from Mills to Marcousé 31 July 1949.
56. See later in this chapter.
57. M T Woodhouse 'Children's Film Judgments' *Researches and Studies* No 1 December 1949 pp 33–45
58. *Report of the Departmental Committee on Children and the Cinema* London: HMSO 1950
59. Op cit p 74
60. Ibid pp 94 and 96
61. See agenda item 'Examination of Witnesses' for the meeting of the Committee on 18 March 1949. National Archive file ED121/579.
62. Wheare op cit p 75
63. Ibid p 75
64. Ibid p 74
65. Ibid p 75
66. Ibid p 75
67. NCAVAE had been set up in 1946 to service Local Education Authorities though its commercial arm the Educational Foundation for Visual Aids. When the Radcliffe Report proposed changes within the organization of the BFI in 1948 it had to take account of the sensitivities created by the existence of NCAVAE.

68. Letter from R J Thom to Marcousé 6 August 1948 National Archive file ED121/580
69. Ibid
70. Christophe Dupin 'The postwar transformation of the British Film Institute and its impact on the development of a national film culture in Britain' *Screen* Vol 47 No 4 Winter 2006 p 445
71. *Interim Draft of the Factual Film in Great Britain* London: The Arts Enquiry 1944
72. Op cit p 181
73. *The Factual Film* The Arts Enquiry Oxford: Oxford University Press 1947
74. Op cit p 30
75. BFI Annual Report June 1946 London BFI 1946 p 7
76. Dupin op cit p 447
77. Cyril J Radcliffe *Report of the Committee on the British Film Institute* London: HMSO 1948
78. Ibid pp 8–9
79. See for example correspondence in *Film User* Vol 3 No 37 November 1949
80. A.W. Hodgkinson, John Huntley, E Francis Mills, Jack Smith *School Film Appreciation* London: BFI 1950
81. Op cit p 1
82. The inaugural conference which preceded the formation of SFT included a presentation by Stanley Reed on 'Film Appreciation in the School' Society of Film Teachers *Bulletin* Vol 1 No 1 December 1950 pp 3–6
83. See *The Film Teacher* Summer 1952 p 2 and *The Film Teacher* Spring 1953 inside back cover
84. A W Hodgkinson 'Two Film Lessons' *Visual Education* Vol 4 No 1 January 1953 pp 2–3
85. Jack Smith 'Film Appreciation' Correspondence *Visual Education* Vol 4 No 3 March 1953 p 8
86. Maurice T Woodhouse *Film appreciation in the School* Unpublished PhD thesis Department of Education University of Leeds January 1952 pp 24–35
87. Op cit p 24
88. Ibid p 24
89. Frederick Laws (Ed) *Made for Millions* London: Contact Publications 1947 p 12
90. Ibid p 95
91. Ibid p 98
92. Ibid pp 95–98
93. Andrew Buchanan *Going to the Cinema* London: Phoenix House 1947
94. Op cit p 13
95. Ibid p 131
96. Ibid p 150
97. John Ellis 'The Quality Film Adventure: British Critics and the Cinema 1942–48' in *Dissolving Views* Andrew Higson (Ed) London: Cassell 1996 pp 66–93 and 'Art, Culture and Quality – Terms for a cinema in the Forties and Seventies' *Screen* Vol 19 No 3 Autumn 1978 pp 9–49

98. Andrew Buchanan *The Film in Education* London: Phoenix House 1951 p 197

99. Op cit p 225

100. Andrew Buchanan *Focus Film Course* London: The Catholic Film Institute 1951

101. Op cit p 15

102. 'Film Appreciation 1 – The Right Approach to the Screen' in *Contemporary Cinema* Vol 2 No 3 March 1948 pp 106–110

103. Vernon Sproxton *Watching Films* London: SCM Press 1948 pp 15–16

104. Op cit p 33

105. Ibid p 35

106. Ibid p 50

107. *Society of Film Teachers Bulletin* Vol 1 No 3 July 1951 p 2

108. *The Film Teacher* Winter 1952 p 12 has a 'stop press' announcement of Hankin's death. He had been a founder member of SFT

109. *The Film Teacher* Spring 1954 p 9 has an obituary of Woodhouse whose death occurred only a few months after he had joined the SFT Executive Committee

110. *Fragments Janet Hills 1919–1956* was published posthumously and privately by her family in 1956. It contains a first chapter of *Birds Eye View*, a proposed book in which she intended to look critically at a range of approaches to film appreciation

111. For examples of Reed's promotional writing see 'Appreciating the Film' in *The Photographic Journal* August 1950 pp 285–291 and 'Film and Child' *Visual Education* Vol 1 Nos 9–12 (September – December) 1950.

112. *Critics Choice* edited first by Stanley Reed, then by David Robinson, ran from No 1 April 1952 to the final issue in February 1956.

113. The *Film Guide* wall chart was published monthly from January 1951 to September 1959.

114. See *Look and Listen* Vol 4 No 9 September 1950 for an account by Frank Tyrer on the development of *Film Guide* in Liverpool.

115. *Children and the Cinema* April 9 1946 Conference Report London: BFI June 1946

116. BFI/National Council of Women *The Impact of the Cinema on the Child* March 1949 Conference Report, English New Education Fellowship *Bulletin* No 55 April 1949

117. Editorial *Society of Film Teachers Bulletin* Vol 1 No 1 December 1950 p 2

118. *Film Education of Youth* 22–24 November 1957 International Conference Report Amsterdam Instituut Film en Jeugd 1957

119. *Film, Television and the Child* October 1958 Conference Report London: BFI/SEFT 1958

120. Stanley Reed 'Film Appreciation in the School' *Society of Film Teachers Bulletin* Vol 1 No 1 pp 3–6.

121. Alex Richardson, R C Vannoey, Don Waters *A Handbook for Screen Education* London: SEFT 1963

122. SEFT along with BFI was involved with the Young Film Makers Competition when the original *News Chronicle* Competition was taken over by the National Union of Teachers in 1960. Subsequently from 1966 SEFT also sponsored the London Co-operative Society competition for children's film making.

123. Instituut Film en Jeugd op cit p 3

124. Ibid p 4

125. The resolutions were incorporated into the Report of the follow-up Conference 'Film, Television and the Child' held at the NFT in October 1958 and published by the BFI. See p 52.

126. Ibid p 6

127. Tony Hodgkinson 'The London Conference' *Film Teacher* No 15 December 1958 pp 3–7

128. *Athene* Vol 7 No 4 June 1956

129. Op cit p 7

130. Ibid p 7

131. Ibid p 12

132. Ibid p 13

133. Ibid p 13

134. Ibid p 7

135. *A Consideration of Humanity, Technology and Education in Our Time* 22–27 April 1957 Conference Report London: Joint Council for Education through Art 1958

136. Paddy Whannel and Alex Jacobs (Eds) *Artist , Critic and Teacher* London: Joint Council for Education through Art 1958

137. Op cit p 24

138. Ibid p 28

139. *Art, Science and Education* Whitsun 1958 Conference Report Joint Council for Education through Art London: 1958 p 113

140. Op cit p 114

141. A H Smith, Maurice Platnauer, T C Keeley, Nevill H Coghill *Report of the Oxford Drama Commission* May 1945

142. See Dana Polan *Scenes of Instruction The Beginnings of the US Study of Film* Berkeley: University of California Press 2007 p 176

143. C M Fleming *The Social Psychology of Education* London: Routledge and Kegan Paul 1944

144. J P Mayer *Sociology of Film Studies* London: Faber and Faber 1946

145. *Documentary News Letter* Vol 6 No 56 April/May 1947

146. Herbert Read *Education Through Art* London: Faber and Faber 1943 pp 90–94

147. 'Towards a Film Aesthetic' Herbert Read in *Cinema Quarterly* Vol 1 No 1 Autumn 1932 p 11

148. See Stanley Reed *The Film: United Kingdom* London: BFI 1955 p 15 and 'Film Education in Schools' Report of the International Conference *Film, Television and the Child* Amsterdam: Instituut Film en Jeugd 1957 p 11.

149. Grace Greiner *Teaching Film* London: BFI 1953. Heywood's observations were made in a telephone interview with the author on 30 May 2004.

150. W D Wall 'The Adolescent and the Cinema' *Educational Review* Vol 1 1948–1949 pp 34–46 and 119–130; W D Wall and W A Simson 'The Effects of Cinema Attendance on the Behaviour of Adolescents as seen by their Contemporaries' *British Journal of Educational*

Psychology Vol XIX Part I February 1949 pp 53–61; W D Wall and E M Smith 'Film Choices of Adolescents' *British Journal of Educational Psychology* Vol XIX Part II June 1949 pp 121–136.

151. See end note No 86

152. Glynne Wickham (Ed) *The Relation between Universities and Films, Radio and Television* London: Butterworth 1956 is a collection of most of the papers delivered at the Bristol Conference in March 1954.

153. *Sequence* 2 Winter 1947 p 26

154. Stuart Hall 'Impact of Film on the University' *University Vision* No 2 October 1968 pp 28–31

155. See *BFI Quarterly Gazette*.

156. *British Film Academy Quarterly* April 1949 p 5

157. *British Film Academy Quarterly* April 1950 p 2

158. Sir Roy Shaw in interview with the author 29 September 2004

3

Searching for Room at the Top

Until provision is made, at a university or elsewhere, for the academic study of film, and for the study of teaching methods at training colleges, full advantage cannot be taken of the growing disposition towards this work now existing in formal education.

Stanley Reed, Secretary of the British Film Institute 1955

As the number of television sets increases, concerns about the influence of the cinema diminish. But for some teachers the question is: should the study of television be considered on a par with film? Eventually SFT is persuaded and becomes SEFT in recognition of the impingement of the new medium on the perceptions of children and young people. Consequently film appreciation is replaced by screen education. But who is to teach it? The single year of training offered as emergency provision after the war was followed by a standard two year course. This is now to be replaced by training that will last for three years. The optimists plan that the additional time now available in the colleges will provide the opportunity for a breakthrough in training teachers of screen education.

The previous chapter strayed beyond the early 1950s in recounting how SFT had collaborated with the BFI Film Appreciation Department in presenting itself in the public arena during that decade. From its inception it also addressed its members in a succession of regularly produced publications commencing with *Bulletin* Number 1 in December 1950 just a few weeks after the Society was established. The sequence of regular publications was maintained, if occasionally a little erratically, until the last *Screen* to be published by SEFT appeared in 1989. The aim of this chapter is to consider how the regular publications of the Society reflected the first decade of film and television teaching and how the influence of the Society may be detected in other key publications of the period.

Metropolitan Origins

Given the Society's beginnings in a Britain still suffering from a legacy of wartime austerity and given that its initial membership was small, its first publication, the quarto size duplicated *Bulletin*, was of necessity a modest product with articles that were brief. Nevertheless, number 3 published as a Special Festival Issue in July 1951 contained 40 pages. What the *Bulletins* reveal however, is that SFT was experimenting with various means of addressing its potential audience. It would seem from the locations of the early committee members that SFT had a very metropolitan focus and London appears to have been the accepted venue for advertised events to which non-members were invited. *Bulletin* number 1 announces that SFT would also make short films on film craft and that the first, to be called *The Camera Moves*, is already in production.[1]

The Society was efficient in getting its activities mentioned in other appropriate publications, particularly the national monthly visual aids journals, *Look and Listen* and *Visual Education*. Its biggest early promotional event was an SFT exhibition 'The Teacher in School and Out', part of the College of Preceptors' Exhibition staged to coincide with the Festival of Britain. This was the event where *The Camera Moves* was premiered.[2] Lectures were given on film appreciation and recruitment at the event took the total membership beyond 150.[3]

But the limitations of the duplicated *Bulletin* as a vehicle for promoting a society concerned with the visual were becoming apparent. In Summer 1952 there appeared the first issue of *The Film Teacher*, now printed and on sale for two shillings, edited by Derek J Davies. According to the editorial its publication was an act of faith in response both to the Society's steadily increasing membership (which by then approached nearly 300) and to a grant in aid of £50 from the BFI.[4]

> In fact, we regard the appearance of *The Film Teacher* as marking a turning point. The day when film appreciation was either unknown or regarded as the province of cranks is fast receding.[5]

With its 32 pages of small print text, *The Film Teacher* had space for longer and more considered articles. The issues it explored are indicative both of the concerns about films, the cinema and children that were around in the early 1950s and of the Society's readiness to engage with those issues. The Wheare Report had recommended the creation of local Cinema Councils to oversee the quality of children's film entertainment. An editorial deplores the negligible legislative response to Wheare's 31 recommendations.[6] Clearly SFT wanted to promote these councils, yet the article is constantly drawing attention to the considerable opposition being expressed to children's cinema clubs – particularly from teachers. The Society's consequent fear was that the Councils might become platforms for its opponents to occupy.

Also drawing inspiration from the Wheare proposals is an article by Sidney Harris, President of the British Board of Film Censors. The BBFC had found itself, as a result of a Wheare recommendation to be part of a permanent Consultative Committee, alongside representatives from both local authorities and the film industry. This Committee had in turn set up an Advisory Sub-committee where educational representatives might make their contributions. Both SFT and BFI were on this Sub-committee and accordingly Harris had been invited to write for *The Film Teacher*. In his article Harris advocates 'isolation' and 'immunisation' as effective child protection measures.[7] Isolation is achieved by clear censorship categories, the most significant of which, following Wheare's recommendation, had been the introduction of the 'X' Certificate.

Immunisation – 'the training of children to protect themselves' – is presented as a better long-term solution. What has to be found is 'some method of encouraging the young to discriminate between what is good and what is bad'.[8] Harris continues by endorsing the 'energy and enthusiasm' of SFT in carrying out this 'essential task'. There is no editorial qualification as to the appropriateness of this role for the Society. Subsequent writers, looking back from the 1960s and 1970s, were wont either to see this immunisation approach as being the prevalent one in the 1950s or one where the basic impulse of the film teaching movement had been 'to protect young people from the possibly corrupting influences of the cinema and then of television.[9] Such notions were regularly repeated, but to identify them as embracing the attitudes of the whole film teaching movement is misleading. *The Film Teacher* on the opening Editorial page of its first issue states simply that the SFT journal is 'for those who want to help young people to enjoy their film-going'.[10]

In another editorial article, 'Teaching the Teacher', there is an account of the Society's attempt to promote film appreciation at the Annual Conference of the London Schools' Film Society.[11] An effort was made at the conference to get the Film Society's members to support a resolution 'calling for the inclusion in the London County Council's (LCC) film library of material for use in teaching film appreciation and for the provision of teacher training courses in film and film teaching'.[12] The motion was eventually carried but the preceding discussion had concentrated on a 'singularly unreconstructive complaint…and questions revealed suspicion and ignorance of film appreciation teaching'. Since this took place at a meeting of the London Schools' Film Society, the extent of the opposition is significant. Those present were already involved in showing films to children as an extra-curricular activity and yet were not readily prepared to support a more structured approach to film in the classroom. Hodgkinson, moving the motion as Secretary of the London Schools' Film Society, was clearly promoting the agenda of SFT. However, his statement to the meeting that 'no teacher need hesitate to start film appreciation, because he lacked specialist knowledge of film aesthetic or film history'[13] could have been interpreted by sceptics present as undermining the case for taking film appreciation seriously. Earlier in the same meeting, Stanley Reed had offered hesitant teachers the more reassuring option of drawing on BFI and SFT experience 'of the wide scope of work already done in film appreciation'.

In the short-term, the meeting bore fruit in that, although film appreciation extracts were not then added to the LCC film library catalogue, by the start of 1953 district inspectors in London were able to nominate up to three individual schools per district to receive additional capitation funding specifically for hiring films and film extracts for film appreciation purposes.[14] The LCC and its successor body, the Inner London Education Authority (ILEA), were in subsequent years to develop close links with both SEFT and BFI in a variety of film teaching experiments. These will be referred to later. Given that both BFI and SFT/SEFT had an inbuilt metropolitan focus anyway, endorsement by London's education authority was not wholly beneficial for the Society's expansion in the regions, as the gap was seen to widen between what was readily facilitated in the capital and that which frequently faced opposition and ignorance elsewhere.

A Positive Approach

Perhaps in a deliberate attempt both to move the debate beyond London, and to draw lessons from the experience of the London Schools Film Society meeting, the SFT Secretary Jack Smith wrote an article for the national audio visual journal *Look and Listen* a few months later. [15] The relevance of the Wheare Report is accepted but a new tone emerges.

> For the Wheare Report, valuable as it was in its balance and lucidity, seems to have had the effect of focusing public attention on the magnitude of the problem, which the cinema presents, instead of upon the positive steps that can so usefully be taken.[16]

This call for a 'positive approach' harks back to a BFI publication of 1951, *Films and Children: The Positive Approach* by Janet Hills. With its publication following the appointment of Reed as Film Appreciation Officer and the formation of SFT, Hills offers a comprehensive account of the evolution of film appreciation in Britain since the 1917 inquiry.[17] The 'Introduction' by BFI Director, Denis Forman, is largely at one with the prevailing view that children need training in discrimination in order to appreciate films. But he argues strongly that

> ...the object of teaching film appreciation is not so much to discourage children from going to bad films as to encourage them to select the better ones and to derive a deeper enjoyment from their film-going.[18]

The creation of SFT is noted by Forman as particularly significant in this respect, the tone being indicative of the close relationship between his Film Appreciation Department and the Society. The Society of Film Teachers is given a whole appendix to itself in the body of the text.[19]

There are extensive listings in the various appendices to assist potential teachers and these offer a snapshot of the state of film appreciation in 1951. However, it is the concluding section that is most revealing from today's perspective. The BFI identifies the range of materials it intends to produce – films, film strips, display material, books – but immediately a caveat is introduced, reflecting the Institute's pragmatic approach.

> Materials are very important and so are activities such as film-making, but it is essential not to mistake a method for an aim.[20]

Despite the very early recognition of this issue, one of the consequences of the kinds of materials produced by the BFI over succeeding decades was that its carefully selected materials, particularly film extracts, were to influence significantly how media teaching developed. Nowhere is this legacy more explicitly demonstrated than in the evolution of the BFI extract catalogue into the first two editions of *The Cinema Book*, the structures of which reflect its ancestry.

The beginnings of another long-standing dispute within the BFI may be detected here in *Films and Children* where it is the declared intention of the Film Appreciation Department to issue a series of publications on methods of film study. The back cover of the booklet however already advertises BFI film study publications, particularly a new series of monographs 'on the work of important film directors'. These were not however published by the Film Appreciation Department, but originated from the *Sight and Sound* stable under the General Editorship of Gavin Lambert, that journal's Editor. There was to be tension in succeeding years between these two BFI departments. Film Appreciation and Publications Departments did however combine in the production of *The Film Guide* to which reference has already been made. The viewing panel that watched films for possible inclusion in the guide was 'composed of the critics from the *Monthly Film Bulletin*, together with a group of experienced youth leaders and educationists'.[21] SFT too had formed a viewing panel by November 1951.[22] Viewing panels were to become a regular feature of SFT and SEFT during the 1950s and 1960s producing reports on individual films. Unfortunately, no record seems to exist of the process by which the panels constructed their reports, though Viewing Panel Reports were frequently republished in several of the Society's regular publications.

If the issues raised by the Wheare Report provided the focus for the first edition of *The Film Teacher*, external developments continued to impinge on subsequent issues, indicating perhaps not only that the new society felt it needed to have a presence wherever matters connecting film and children were to be found, but also that SFT was uncertain as to what its constituency might properly include. Thus the second issue of *The Film Teacher* led with an article about the recently formed Children's Film Foundation, an organisation of British film producers whose joint enterprise was to facilitate the making of films for showing at children's matinées.[23] The CFF had an agenda which to an extent overlapped with that supported by SFT.

> …the products of the new organisation will aim at first class production which will give young audiences the right material on which to develop into discriminating adolescent film-goers.[24]

External Pressures

By the third issue of *The Film Teacher* in Spring 1953, another external issue dominated: 'the question of violence'. Not only was there a three page editorial comment on 'Violence in Films' but the topic was also raised in an extended interview by the Society with Alexander Mackendrick at Ealing Studios.[25] The inside front cover contains an advertisement for a BFI pamphlet, *Are They Safe at the Cinema?*[26] whose author, Janet Hills, is recorded in the same issue as having recently resigned from the SFT Committee, as her 'many other activities now made it impossible for her to attend our meetings'.[27] Concern over violence and its possible links to the cinema had a very specific contemporary origin: the murder of a policeman in London by Christopher Craig, during whose trial links were made under cross-examination between his actions and his regular film-going. Both Hills in her pamphlet and *The Film Teacher* are specific as to what occasioned their interest in films and violence,[28] for as *The Film Teacher* editorial put it 'so unprecedented a case has almost certainly raised public feeling against the cinema to an unusually high level.'[29] Film teachers were beginning to feel the onslaught and both BFI and SFT had to respond because

> ...critics ranging from colleagues in the common room who avoid both the cinema and new ideas, to local authorities preoccupied with economies, can dismiss film teaching as so much unnecessary encouragement of the young to go to the devil more quickly.[30]

Stanley Reed had publicly adopted the stance of the Wheare Committee which was that, until properly funded substantial research was undertaken, uninformed opinion would make the running. This was demonstrated early in 1953, when at a tea discussion meeting organised by SFT with a range of speakers, views from the floor demonstrated that 'at the moment, we seem to be a long way from even reasonably acceptable generalisations'.[31] The Society was in danger of being manoeuvred into a compromise position. Some argued that it might achieve a face-saving role by marketing its teaching of discrimination on an anti-juvenile crime ticket. This was resisted and the Society allowed itself to favour only certain of the blander solutions put forward at the meeting: 'Saturday morning shows, Cinema Councils, film appreciation'.[32]

More thoughtful readers of that issue of *The Film Teacher* would have found Mackendrick's views on the topic more to the point. When asked to comment on what false values he found more objectionable, his response was to attack how 'in a certain type of film...the way in which vicious behaviour is disguised, presented in a form in which audiences can enjoy it with a clear conscience'.[33] Elsewhere in the interview Mackendrick raised a more fundamental point, which his SFT interviewers did not challenge, yet his views questioned certain SFT assumptions about the ring-fencing of matters about children and film.

I've been talking as if I don't distinguish between adult, adolescent and child audiences. Intentionally so. Youngsters are obviously more imitative and impressionable. But this makes the problems different only in degree, not in kind. The principles are surely the same.[34]

If these were the views of SFT, rather than Mackendrick's own, it would run counter to that of Hills. In both her books for the BFI, she is pessimistic about what may be achieved by the film teacher.

If children who will never reach more than elementary discrimination are pushed into aesthetic deeps, then they will drown, discrimination and all.[35]

Film teachers have, for instance, while keeping their own standards unshaken, to decide exactly what compromises to make in their work with children, many of whom will never reach full discrimination...[36]

It is perhaps important to read these comments in the light of Hills's earlier statement: 'Film appreciation work in Britain began in the field, and so is not over-encumbered by theories'.[37] She takes the same position that Reed would later present at the Amsterdam Conference in 1957 and detailed in the previous chapter. The absence of theory and more importantly the absence of any recognition that this might be a problem had consequences for SFT and SEFT. Its journals for almost two decades were ready to publish accounts of a wide range of teaching experiences and practices. Provided an author could argue that her/his approach had been successfully accomplished, the account of that experience would be published. As a result SFT/SEFT found itself implicitly endorsing what was published in its name, even if some form of disclaimer were printed saying that the views expressed were not necessarily those of the Society. The existence of all this activity encouraged Hills in this instance (though others did so too elsewhere) to offer readers reassurance. Having SFT and the BFI Film Appreciation Department operating across a wide range of activities connecting film and children was regularly presented as the beginnings of a solution. Being presented so positively would hardly induce introspection in either organisation.

The aftermath of the Wheare Committee was still in evidence in the Autumn 1953 edition of *The Film Teacher* which contained an account of the recently formed Cinema Consultative Committee by John Trevelyan. But two other external developments preoccupied the journal and were of a different order. The lead article is entitled '3D and TV', which topic had dominated SFT's fourth Annual General Meeting Conference. By contrast, the centre spread of the issue is headed 'Film Morality and Film Taste' consisting of some 'points' made by Father John Burke of the Catholic Film Institute, printed without comment, other than those implicit in two accompanying stills.[38] Trevelyan's article is in effect an account of the work of the Consultative Committee's Advisory Sub-committee which had a sizeable educational input, in addition to the representatives from BFI and SFT. Trevelyan, a former Director of Education, was then a British Board of Film Censors (BBFC) Examiner. Subsequently as Secretary of the BBFC, he remained on the Advisory Sub-committee and was crucial in getting formal backing in 1958 for the BBFC pamphlet *The Teaching of Film* which was heavily influenced by SFT and BFI.[39] Here Trevelyan's article is concerned with the limited recommendations made by the Sub-committee about children's cinema clubs.

The '3-D and TV' article was a report of speakers at the 1953 SFT Conference where the Society was both acknowledging the cinema's technical innovations in response to competition from television and anticipating the proposed introduction of commercial television planned for 1955. Raymond Spottiswoode had spoken about 3-D from an industry perspective; Freda Lingstom, as Head of BBC Children's Television, had described work in her department. But it was *The Film Teacher* Editor Derek Davies who had raised the more fundamental issue: how far 3-D and TV were legitimate fields of SFT activity. 3-D was seen by him as central to the SFT brief, but with a huge attendant practical difficulties. About TV, Davies had his doubts: it 'was much less clearly a film teacher's responsibility'.[40] In parentheses it is then recorded that within the SFT Committee '…there were sharp divisions of opinion on the standing of TV as an art-form, and whether that mattered when it was so clearly a major social influence'.[41] Whether the Society should address the issues presented by television was a debate which continued throughout the decade, coming to a head at the Annual General Meetings in 1958 and 1959. The initial response, following the 1953 conference, was the creation of a TV Sub-committee.[42]

The 'morality' debate across the centre pages is an unexplained curiosity. There is no background information as to why *ex cathedra* statements from a Catholic priest should be privileged in this manner. The only commentary is that provided by the accompanying stills and a final statement that 'we should [ie not 'would'] welcome members' views on any of these moral issues'.[43] Perhaps readers were to draw their conclusions from the stills. One is of Marilyn Monroe in *Niagara*. The other still is from *Red Planet Mars* and shows a newspaper seller in front of a billboard proclaiming 'GOD SPEAKS FROM MARS'.[44]

The final issue of *The Film Teacher* in its printed format appeared in Spring 1954. As with the preceding four issues, it ran to 32 pages, had a card cover and sold for two shillings. The cover illustration remained unchanged throughout – a sketch of children heading for a queue outside the cinema, overseen by a uniformed commissionaire – providing further evidence of the pervasive influence of the Wheare Report on the Society in the 1950s.[45] What does change across the five issues is the proportion of content devoted to providing readers with information and reviews. What had taken up five pages in the first issue, occupied fifteen in the final one. When the decision was taken to cease printed publication and return to a duplicated version of *The Film Teacher*, the problem of providing up-to-date information to members, particularly on new books and 16mm film availability no doubt served to support the decision to produce the first *Film Teacher's Handbook* in 1956.

Film Teacher and Teaching Film

It was only with this final issue that *The Film Teacher* appeared free of the need to respond to external circumstances. Its lead article was on 'Diploma Course Work' in the University College, Leicester.[46] The philosophy of that Education Department was to provide background courses which would contrast with the postgraduate diploma students' teaching specialisms. Film Study was offered in this context and chosen by ten to fifteen students per year. It was timetabled for half a day per week: a contrast with other teacher training institutions, where film was only available to students as an extra-curricular option. The article offers little information about course content, but does identify three clear aims which are themselves indicative of the course organiser's desire to separate out and address issues that were tending to be amalgamated and confused in the promotion of film teaching at the time.

(i)   To develop the study of film, among the students themselves.
(ii) To discuss with them, what can be done by way of film study in schools and review some possible methods of approach.
(iii) To examine some of the sociological implications of cinema-going, especially in relation to children.[47]

Further articles focus on work in a Secondary Modern School and in a Grammar School. The former article is important because it records an already well established two year Film Appreciation Course with 14–16 year olds in a Nottingham School, which is available to all the students 'in the A, B and C streams'.[48] The author adds

> One should not assume that low reading ability necessarily implies a correspondingly low response to visual impressions. There appears to be little or no correlation here.[49]

The author provides plentiful illustrations, as to the material he uses and it is clear that he makes regular but selective use of the BFI's expanding library of film extracts, and also of its *Critics' Choice* publication. By contrast, the article on the Grammar school is a report of another SFT Tea Discussion meeting at which Jack Smith, then SFT Chairman, spoke of his work in organising film as an extra curricular activity in the face of prejudice, which actively opposed development of the work.[50]

> The prejudice is especially marked in grammar schools, whose arts teachers must so often resent the threat which mass-entertainment media offer to traditional cultural values.[51]

While this does provide further evidence of the antagonism toward film teaching, it is revealing in illustrating how the battle lines around attitudes to popular culture were being formed – at school level. Intriguingly, presumably because Smith was addressing a sympathetic audience, the discussion that followed was pre-occupied with the question of who should teach film. As so often in the 1950s, these grass roots enthusiasts for film saw the only solution to their search for acceptability in the provision of courses at university level.[52]

The first substantial publication to come from BFI's Film Appreciation Department in 1954 was *Teaching Film* by Grace Greiner, a lecturer at Goldsmiths College in the University of London.[53] This was an attempt to provide a comprehensive guide to classroom methods for use in Infant, Junior and Secondary Schools. Its author had been a founder member of SFT and the book's Foreword was provided by the Chairman of the BFI, its publisher. Like so much published in the 1950s its acknowledged antecedent was the Wheare Report and among those who are publicly credited as having assisted the author were members of SFT and the BFI Film Appreciation Department.

Undoubtedly, the author's position was in line with the SFT/BFI project of encouraging and enabling established teachers to make a start in teaching film, while identifying the inherent problem of there being almost no provision in initial teacher training for anyone to take up an appointment with some form of accredited recognition as a film teacher. Greiner's approach is to offer teachers as many options as possible (appropriate to children's ages) as to ways of focusing on film, whether in the classroom or outside it. For Infant and Junior schools (with which, to judge from the children's quotes, the author was more familiar) film is generally presented as a stimulus to a range of other educational activities.

At secondary level there is to be a more direct engagement with film, usually within structured discussions, overseen by the teacher. Five approaches are identified: moral, sociological, critical, technical and historical.[54] The author appears to be uncomfortable with the first of these suggesting the moral approach be used in denominational schools, Sunday Schools and Church Youth Groups.[55] The moral approach 'involves the consideration of the behaviour of the characters, and of the standards and values implied in the story of the film'. Greiner's commitment to inclusiveness has led her into the kind of compromise which afforded acceptability to any teacher who used film. The sociological approach, as advocated, invites students to judge the representation of the world in the films they see against their own experience of living in society. Here Greiner is approaching an embryonic thematic approach to film study. By contrast, the critical approach does focus on the film by dissecting it, identifying the story, content and theme and only then considering form and technique. The author warns against over concentration on either form or content. A model for detailed analysis of films is provided and its provenance is acknowledged: it is the same as that which SFT had produced for *The Film Teacher*, in effect a checklist against which the attributes of any film might be ticked off.[56]

It is clear that despite the various approaches Greiner advocates, the student response is always channelled into some form of discussion. Indeed, the author seems more adept at offering a range of strategies for the structuring of discussion than in addressing what might be specific to film teaching. How far these constraints were a consequence of wanting to recruit all potential film teachers, rather than discourage them, is impossible to determine. What is clear is that many of her contemporaries were consulted about the text and are implicated in its presentation.[57] Indeed Alexander subsequently claimed this book was a direct outcome of 'notes and other material relating to work being carried out in Primary and Secondary schools' SFT had accumulated.[58] But if the development of theory or indeed how to think about teaching film seems rudimentary, the concluding chapter on 'The Film Teacher' does illustrate some of the problems which had to be faced by would-be film teachers. The most committed of students in the most progressive of locations might take a two-year basic course in film and training in teaching method, provided this was taken as an additional subject super-imposed on a full timetable and on the understanding that the student would receive no credit for having done it on her/his Teacher's Certificate.[59] Given the positive message her book sought to promote, Greiner clearly underplayed the extent of the problems the new subject would face in getting established, though she identified both the marginalisation of film in colleges and its total absence from the Academy.

Following the disappearance of *The Film Teacher* in its first incarnation, the *Newsletter* was introduced with the intention of it being published both more frequently and regularly than its predecessor. It also represented a considerable financial saving, being duplicated rather than printed. It appeared only three times: before the October 1954 AGM, then in the following December and February. The December issue reported the Committee's decision to produce 'the first of an annual series of *printed handbooks*'.[60] These *Film Teacher's Handbooks* would represent a big commitment for the voluntary organization.

No record exists of issue 1 of the *Newsletter*, which appears to have been combined with notice of the October 1954 SFT Annual General Meeting. Between issues 2 and 3 of the *Newsletter*, the Society passed through a transitional period. Number 2 contained a report of the Society's 1954 October Conference on 'The Responsibilities of the Film-maker'. Familiar territory was explored here: how the British Board of Film Censors went about constructing its 'C' list of films and what were the special problems facing a director of children's films.[61] These were still the preoccupations dating from the Wheare years. The next *Newsletter* printed an article on 'The Challenge of Television' by SFT's Chairman Jack Smith. This had originally been given as an address to the Conference of Educational Associations. Smith's lecture had been sponsored by the Society as a result of its decision 'to extend its activities to include television'[62] and it constituted 'the first public statement for the Society on the question of television'.[63]

The address was in anticipation of the start of commercial television later that year. Smith focused particularly on the supervisory role of the Independent Television Authority (ITA) and was arguing that SFT should have a place on the Children's Programmes Advisory Committee, which was to be set up under the 1954 Television Act. Indeed the meeting passed a resolution supporting this claim.[64] Smith made the case for children becoming discriminating viewers of television as a consequence of teacher encouragement. Subsequent discussion revealed that teaching television appreciation was regarded by his audience as different from film appreciation in some rather fundamental ways in that television study material would not exist and even owning a television set was not necessarily a priority for teachers. While it is clear SFT felt the need to position itself in relation to television, thinking was at an early stage. Smith could still, at this stage, refer to television as 'our latest eye – looking outwards onto the bright world and into the darker corners too'.[65] The meeting closed with a screening of 'two American commercial television shorts which had been put on film, and which left the audience hoping we would not be subjected to the same high-pressure sales assault'.[66] The mood of expectation from these teachers was of their being on the receiving end of what was about to happen. Whereas film appreciation had begun to consider notions of institution and of audience in its approach, the carry over to television was certainly incomplete.

On its re-appearance in April 1955, at the start of the new financial year, the New Series of the Society's Journal was called simply *Film Teacher* and was edited by Jan B Hoare.[67] It consisted of twenty pages (including the covers) of duplicated typescript, each page being half of a foolscap sheet, the standard larger paper size of the period. It contained only one major article, again from A J Baker, the Nottingham teacher whose Film Appreciation course (taught for 60 hours a year over two years) had by now been running for some five years. This article complements his earlier one by giving a sequential account of the course. While the author tries to link with screenings in local cinemas, the course structure is heavily influenced by the nature of BFI extract material available. In the second year of the course Baker adopts the device of showing features in serial fashion across two weeks' lessons, while welcoming recent additions to the BFI extract library.[68]

By issue 2, *Film Teacher* is apparently finding it hard to find contributors, with nine of its sixteen pages consisting of two articles re-printed from elsewhere.[69] It is the back page that shows evidence of developments. There is a job advertisement for a teacher to join the school where E Francis Mills, the long-time champion of film teaching, was headteacher, and where presumably the successful candidate would teach some film. The second development is the announcement that the Society's Viewing Panel is to be split into three separate panels with R C Vannoey co-opted to the Committee as organiser.[70]

In *Film Teacher* 3 the only substantial article is about group film-making in a girls' Secondary Modern school.[71] The author's account is one of trial and error. The values she detects in the projects are unusual. Firstly, children's notions of film as a glamorous activity are replaced by concepts of planning and hard work. Secondly, the sustained debate and discussion which accompanies the process serve to improve students' command of English. Thirdly, film-making instils values of teamwork. Later generations of film teachers would also come to value process over outcomes. In the same *Film Teacher*, Hodgkinson, by now Film Appreciation Officer at the BFI, reports on the 'Films and Children Conference', held in Luxembourg in spring 1955.[72] Here Hodgkinson, records his satisfaction at the 'unanimous international acceptance of the 'positive attitude' adopted by British film teachers'.[73] He is convinced Britain leads the way, though it has nothing to match France's 'enviable number of enthusiastic 'filmologists', many of whom are working in the field of education'. But by failing to write up the work being developed…

> It is in this respect, that we Britons, with our scorn of theory and pragmatical, 'practical' approach, are most likely to fall down.[74]

Film Teacher 4, scheduled to appear in October 1955, became a matter of dispute between SFT and the company that did the duplication. The copies were judged to be of too poor a quality to be distributed and the issue's content was circulated as part of a Special Bulletin in February 1956. When *Film Teacher* 4 did eventually appear in July 1956 it was the last to be edited by Jan Hoare who opened his final editorial with news that members would already have received the first *Film Teacher's Handbook* (which he had been largely responsible for editing) and Information Sheet No 1.[72] Issue 4 has two features of particular interest. There is an account of film teaching in Norway which reveals a course very heavily dependent on approaches originating in Britain.[76] Then there is a request for SFT to hear from 'members who have used instructional films (such as on geographical or scientific subjects) to teach film appreciation'.[77] There was undoubtedly among SFT members a determination to look as widely (and cheaply) as possible for material which might be salvaged for film appreciation purposes.

Film Teacher 5 in September 1956 was edited by H R (Ray) Wills, who continued as the sole honorary editor of the Society's journal until the last issue of (the first series of) *Screen Education* in September/October 1968, a total of 59 separate issues produced mostly on a bi-monthly basis. Wills had had a primary school teaching background before becoming a lecturer in a teacher training college. *Film Teacher* continued as a duplicated publication until May 1959 and for the purposes of this chapter it is this journal that will be considered. *Film Teacher* was a publication of the Society of Film Teachers; the renamed Society for Education in Film and Television (SEFT) published its successor journal *Screen Education*. Under Wills's editorship *Film Teacher* became more substantial although still a duplicated publication, usually averaging between 24 and 28 pages. It appeared regularly every alternate month with a three-month gap in the summer when *The Film Teacher's Handbook* was published. Certain features of the Wills style became apparent. He was always ready to address and exhort his readers on behalf of the Society. His editorials were best read as personal statements rather than as the views of the Society's Committee, which on occasions meant he promoted issues of his own.[78]

Although Wills did receive assistance from other committee members, it was inevitably in ways that would not impinge on his editorial control. There were, over the decade during which he edited *Film Teacher* and *Screen Education*, several SFT/SEFT members who volunteered to work on getting advertising or on increasing circulation or on designing the layout and who were to operate effectively in these prescribed roles. Producing a bi-monthly magazine on time over a ten year period was a notable achievement for Wills who devoted much of his spare time to the task, but his dedication was not without problems for the Society. The journal frequently reprinted articles from elsewhere which Wills felt merited reproduction and, as he always had to operate without a budget to pay authors, this was the only means by which 'names' would be found writing for the Society. Since its journal was the most obvious return members received for their subscriptions and since Wills always delivered on time, it meant that other committee members were probably reluctant to interfere, since to do so might have precipitated a crisis. Indeed, Wills remained in charge until 1968 when others not only challenged the Society's publications' regime but were prepared to take over responsibility for it.

Wills's first editorial reports on the growing interest in film appreciation in Europe and the USA and he comments that it has 'become an international movement'.[79] He then speculates that 'Perhaps in the not too distant future it will be possible to organise some form of conference for the interchange of ideas and experiences'. Yet in *Film Teacher* 3 there had been a report of just such a conference in the previous year.[80] Other subsequent instances of Wills's disconnected attitude will become evident. *Film Teacher* 6 contained an eight page central insert on gold coloured paper where the new editor addressed the readership directly. In part he sought information from those readers who ran school film societies or made films with children about their practice. But his main purpose was to motivate readers in their role as SFT members in a section 'Jobs for the Willing'. Here they were encouraged to join viewing panels, suggest possible film extracts, report on television work, but most importantly, form regional groups as a means of countering 'our London centredness'.[81] The 'Cuttings' sections of Wills's *Film Teacher* were to become a regular feature in which he reported in brief on a range of events and publications he considered to be of interest. Fifty years on, these 'cuttings' contain both minutiae valuable for cross referencing and also intriguing accounts of work in progress. Issue 6 reports on a weekend course 'The Film in Youth Work', which had been organised by both SFT and the Berkshire Education Committee and attended by ten members of the Executive. The innovation explored on this occasion was the tape recorder, which was increasingly becoming available in schools. The course set out to 'explore the possibilities of making tape recordings, which would provoke discussion about set film extracts'. The Editor having attended remained doubtful about the value of the exercise, though he added 'it is good to see various methods of approach being subjected to practical test and experiment'.[82]

The next two issues were 'special numbers'. Number 7 was a 'Special University and Training College number' and number 8 a 'Special International Number'.[83] Issue seven starts with a 'Training College View', which is interesting in demonstrating just how restrictive the promotion of film teaching was. In this particular college the only contact that students had with film teaching was when they were 'confronted with the problem of Children and the Cinema'.[84] The article that offered most was 'Film Appreciation at the University Level – A General Survey'.[85] However, this account of the work of the British University's Film Council (BUFC) demonstrates how limited was its engagement with film appreciation. It does confirm the existence of a joint, BUFC/BFI/SFT committee, which was looking into the establishment of a University lectureship in Film, though no subsequent reference to this committee is to be found. The main area of the BUFC interest at that time was apparently in filmology, then a current area of interest in France.[86]

More revealing were the remaining two accounts in the issue: an update of the work in University College, Leicester, previously reported in *The Film Teacher*[87] and a report from SEFT Committee Member Leslie Heywood of Borough Road Training College on 'Film in the School Curriculum'.[88] The structure of the Leicester course had remained much the same as in the earlier account, but what had become apparent were the limitations of the students who arrived at university with almost no background experience in watching movies. The author hints that this results from attitudes to film in grammar schools and points to other more successful developments in film study in the extra-mural programme with older students. Reference has been made earlier to the hostility to film to be found in 1950s' grammar schools. Nowhere is this better demonstrated than in *The Journal of Education* in February 1958 where a Senior English Master, T R Barnes, describes the art of the cinema as both 'ephemeral' and 'parasitic'.[89] In an introductory editorial comment supportive of Barnes, Stanley Reed is taken to task for wanting to look forward to a time when all generally trained teachers might be able to teach about the popular arts. 'Mr. Reed may not realize how many grammar school masters regard this as part of their province.'[90]

Heywood's article is important because it confronts two realities. At this time headteachers had complete power to determine what was to be taught in their schools. If a head wanted to have film study in her/his school, there was nothing to prevent it. Where a committed film teacher wanted to teach film, and where the head was sympathetic, things could always happen. However, Heyward, concentrating on the practicalities, goes on to argue that although no specific obstacle prevented the establishment of film courses, English lessons offered the best potential entry point for the introduction of film into schools. The English specialist had to be trusted to teach film and not in effect use film as a form of visual aid to back up English teaching. Heyward correctly anticipates what would happen in the 1960s, when film did become established in numerous English lessons.

When an issue is billed on its cover as a 'Special International Number', knowing the provenance of the articles it contains would be useful, but it is never clear how far articles in the journals that Wills edited were commissioned, and how far he published those sent to him speculatively.[91] Wills introduced this issue by stating that if its predecessor, *Film Teacher 7* had been concerned with the 'quality of film teaching', *Film Teacher 8* was about the 'quantity of film teaching', an introduction that would disconcert rather than enlighten readers.[92] This was however, the first SFT publication to print an article from the USA: 'How to Evaluate the Mass Media' which was significant also as the first to indicate a move from an interest specifically in film and television to recognition of the wider relevance of the mass media.[93] The article is not presented as a reprint from elsewhere, but there are number of factors that suggest it was. The references and mode of address throughout suggest it was written for an American audience. The author Edgar Dale had been an established – if controversial – figure in the USA since the publication of his book *How to Appreciate Motion Pictures*, published as part of the Payne Fund Studies into children and the cinema.[94] It seems extremely unlikely he would have submitted this article to the *Film Teacher*, or indeed have been invited to write for it.

The article does have certain elements that would have recommended it to SFT, in particular statements such as 'the increased teaching of discrimination of the radio, movies, TV, and press in high schools, helping youngsters choose their fare more wisely is a hopeful sign'.[95] But Dale's argument is essentially that evaluating the media involves having a set of values against which the behaviour of characters in the media may be judged. It seems his concept of the media focuses on its presentation of fictional characters. But his principal pre-occupation here is with screen violence, which is carefully tabulated in such a way that he can declare that in the US cinemas there are 7.8 acts of violence per film, while in New Zealand it is half that at 3.9 per film. This then leads into a debate on how to judge violence in the mass media, which in turn becomes a sermon about the mass media being used to develop 'the free individual in the free society'.[96] Dale concludes 'the effort we are trying to produce is a man who is free to grow toward perfection'.[97] The inclusion of such a piece – as evidence of the quantity of work happening under the umbrella of film teaching and printed without further comment – does suggest that Wills had a rather cavalier attitude to content.

Others however did submit material and one US author, Jack Ellis, became a regular contributor first to *Film Teacher* and then to *Screen Education*. What Wills had achieved under the SFT brand was a publication in a developing area of expertise where there was nothing else to match its regular appearance or increasing circulation. As the SFT membership grew and the journal became better known, so some familiar contributors were featured in successive issues. Ellis, a SFT member from North Western University in Chicago, wrote first about film teaching in the US in general and subsequently about North Western's courses in detail.[98] Dai Vaughan, who would later be one of the editors of the short-lived film journal *Definition*, placed several pieces in *Film Teacher*, covering a range of topics which extended well beyond the scope of the journal's usual preoccupations.[99]

Among the authors in the final issue of *Film Teacher* was the BFI's Film Appreciation Officer, Paddy Whannel, whose post had been recently renamed as Education Officer.[100] He contributed an annotated booklist in which he reveals that he had indeed been asked to contribute.[101] He provides the context for the request to which he was responding as concerns around the 'new social and cultural problems that have emerged with the development of the mass media and the growth of the welfare state'.[102] In fact the list is substantially annotated so that it is clear where Whannel positions himself in relation to the recent books from Hoggart and Williams among other authors. But nowhere is his personal stance better demonstrated than in his concluding comment: 'What the cinema needs is a Leavis'.[103] It is clear from the opportunities Whannel was finding to develop and promote his ideas (as already demonstrated in the previous chapter) that he would welcome the chance of addressing the SFT membership. Indeed, Whannel was to work closely with the newly created SEFT during the next few years. As Education Officer, Whannel represented the BFI on the SEFT Committee. In particular, a strong alliance built up between Whannel, who had joined the BFI in spring 1957, and Tony (A P) Higgins, who had become chairman of SEFT in the previous year.

Preface to Film

One of the books to which Whannel makes specific reference is *Preface to Film* by Michael Orrom and Raymond Williams.[104] It was published by Film Drama Limited and was planned to be the first of a series of publications from this organisation, which had been 'brought into being to associate creative workers in a number of artistic fields in the production of films of a new and distinctive kind'.[105] Thus, while SFT and BFI saw a discriminating audience as the means by which films would be improved – albeit in ways that were never defined – Film Drama set itself a comparable task within film production, and one it acknowledged would only be achievable with access to public money. The book does provide a revealing context against which the work of SFT may be set. Williams is insistent from the outset that he is not attempting to provide a theory of film[106] and in that respect his stance reflects that of the pragmatic SFT approach. In Orrom's piece with its emphasis on detailed technical explanations, it becomes clear just how unfamiliar even the university educated person of the 1950s was with the mechanics of film production. As a consequence of this lack of familiarity, the notion arose that if the technical aspects were properly understood, more original and inventive forms of film would be created. The book demonstrates that, while the general population went to the cinema, at this time there were few to think through the nature of what this audience was actually experiencing. The field was consequently left clear for the opposition to make the running with their anti-cinema pronouncements, and it was against this backdrop that SFT members were having to make their claims for the emerging importance of the mass media in the nation's consciousness.

Preface to Film is in effect two separate essays. Williams writes on 'Film and the Dramatic Tradition', Orram on 'Film and its Dramatic Techniques'. Williams's contribution is dominated by his much greater familiarity with drama than with film. He discusses concepts like naturalism and realism with ready reference to the theatre and the work of specific playwrights. His references to actual films are few and fleeting.[107] Perhaps the greatest importance of this essay is that it provides a demonstration of how little the qualities of popular cinema had by this time impinged even on an academic as potentially sympathetic as Williams. What he intends to do is to set up parameters of expectation for Orrom's subsequent essay. Williams establishes that film may be regarded as a form of drama by virtue of its display of performance and imitation which he regards as the defining qualities of drama. Film has the particular advantage, since it becomes a finished product, of allowing total expression, by which Williams means its unity of speech, movement and design. However, he argues that with the coming of sound, films became over dependent on dialogue and therefore this delayed the integrated film form which had yet to be achieved: 'the principle of integrated expression and performance, in which each of the elements being used – speech, music, movement, design – bears a controlled, necessary and direct relation, at the moment of expression, to any other that is being then used'.[108]

Having argued thus far, Williams ends by leading into Orrom's essay with the expectation that only by understanding the techniques of cinema will the search for new conventions of cinema be found. These conventions will be different from those of the theatre and allow cinema as an art form to come closer to expressing 'the structure of feeling' which 'lies deeply embedded in our lives' but which devices of naturalism in the theatre have failed to articulate.[109] Orrom's account marshals evidence from a range of films and is interesting in drawing examples from both classics of European silent cinema and Hollywood films of the early 1950s, though almost all are found lacking in relation to the guiding principles the author defines in order to escape from the 'rigidities of naturalism' seen as the convention which was restricting the development of cinema.[110] These principles are all forms of technical constraint: montage is to be replaced by the use of cutting only for its particular virtues (of providing alternative objective observations of a scene), while the fluidity of the moving camera becomes the fundamental technique of preference. Screen acting will become more like the movements of ballet; speech and music will be in balance on the soundtrack, while décor and lighting will be deployed to true psychological significance.[111] Given the certainty with which these prescriptions are made, it is interesting to note that the home-grown film movement which did emerge later in the 1950s – the Free Cinema movement – was to demonstrate the total antithesis of this approach.

SFT becomes SEFT

As the final issue of *Film Teacher* reached members in May 1959, its companion publication *The Film Teacher's Handbook 1959/60* was about to go to the printers. This was the fourth such publication and the third to be edited by C Cain and R C Vannoey, both of whom had previously been involved with SFT Viewing Panels. This Handbook had 120 pages, 16 of which were taken up by paid advertising, double the number of pages sold in the first (1956/57) handbook. By the time that the 1957/58 handbook was distributed to members and sold to others all of the thousand copies printed had gone. Consequently for the 1958/59 version, the print run was increased to 1500 copies.[112]

The handbook's success lay in the careful targeting of its contents at a time when there were almost no reference books available to those teachers who could not easily gain access to the specialist BFI Library.[113] By the 1959/60 edition, the staples of the successful format had been established. For those teachers who were already operating confidently there were items such as up-to-date lists of teaching materials and constantly revised listings of the ever shifting hierarchy of 16mm film libraries. For those who wanted to show films but were uncertain how to handle the subsequent discussions, there were 'Films to Use' sections, with expanded versions of Viewing Panel Reports.

For those who wanted to extend their own knowledge of the cinema, there were the bibliographies produced by Cain and the Directory of Directors introduced by Vannoey. Each issue also contained a limited number of articles, some of which became the basis of occasional SEFT publications, as did 'Film Making in Schools' in the very first handbook.[114] From today's perspective particular value may be found in the full listing of members at the end of each handbook. The list is arranged by county for individual members in England where the greatest concentration of the membership was located, otherwise members are located by country. New categories of membership had been added to the individual one: Corporate in 1958 and Group in 1959. During this period the membership rose steadily year on year starting at 274 in 1956 and increasing to 385 in 1957, 457 in 1958 and reaching 565 in 1959. This last figure is an underestimate in that it includes 65 group members, organisations in each of which there would have been more than one member

By the end of the 1950s the Society of Film Teachers was part of the changing media education environment where the primacy of film as the object of its attention was being challenged. Other bodies were wanting to engage with what was becoming an area of controversy. The event which not only embodied the concerns of the late 1950s but also looked forward to the very different environment of the 1960s was the National Union of Teachers' Conference 'Popular Culture and Personal Responsibility' in October 1960. However the influence of that conference was enhanced by its timing – after other bodies, notably the British Board Film Censors and the Association of Teachers in Colleges and Departments of Education, had demonstrated, through publications, their readiness to become involved in the evolution of media education. The appearance of these publications coincided with the variety of meetings being organised by the Joint Council for Education through Art and described in the previous chapter. In all these activities the joint influence of BFI/SFT may be detected. Specifically it was the energy of Paddy Whannel, supported by Stanley Reed, which seems to have been the strongest factor linking all these activities. Whannel in turn, having at that point no other professional staff in his department, made very effective use of his connections with leading members of the SFT Committee.

This evolutionary process was to be manifested within the Society of Film Teachers itself. At its Annual General Meeting in May 1958, a proposal to change the Society's name to the Society of Film and Television Teachers was, according to the Editorial in the June 1958 issue of *The Film Teacher*, 'decisively rejected after a lively discussion'.[115] The distinction which had apparently convinced the meeting to vote against the proposal was that while 'film is an art form worthy of serious study' television 'is a means of communication, which can admirably capture immediacy'. It had consequently been accepted that 'this very liveness denies it an aesthetic'. The Editorial was written by Wills who seems to have been personally opposed to the change.

However simultaneously with the reporting of this decision, the Society's *Film Teacher's Handbook* for 1958/59 was ready for the printers with two "challenging" articles both promoting the study of television.[116] Significantly, the *Handbook* also contained a lengthy Policy Statement.[117] In the television section of this statement, an alternative view from that of *Film Teacher* was being propounded.

> Thus television is a powerful part of our modern environment and, as film was many years ago, a potential art.[118]

Clearly not all SFT members had accepted the decisive rejection of television from the Society's name. By the time the next *Handbook* (for 1959/60) was about to be sent to the printers in June 1959 it had become the 'Annual Journal of the Society for Education in Film and Television' with an editorial recording that at the April 1959 Annual General Meeting 'Almost unanimous approval was given to the change of name to the Society'.[119] As a consequence it was reported that 'our bi-monthly *Film Teacher* will now become *Screen Education*, and this *Handbook* will, in future, appear as *Screen Education Yearbook*'.

The pattern of bi-monthly issues of *Screen Education* together with an annual *Screen Education Yearbook* persisted until 1968 when the final issue of *Screen Education* appeared in September and the *1969 Yearbook* followed in December 1968.[120] Had the Society had to bear the costs of distributing its publications, the size of the Journal and Yearbook might have had to be more modest in order to reduce mailing costs. However, as the 1958/59 *Handbook* reveals about its relationship with the British Film Institute at this stage:

> The Institute also affords the Society some clerical and similar practical assistance under the authority of the Report of the Committee on the British Film Institute.[121]

The relevant section of that report, which was being interpreted to the Society's benefit (probably by Stanley Reed, who was by then BFI Secretary), was listed as the third of the objects that the Institute should have '...to encourage, support and serve other bodies working in the same field'.[122] The costs of mailing the Society's regular publications were therefore met by the BFI while volunteer effort by committee members filled the envelopes. The stability of the processes of production and distribution for its publications in the 1960s had come about after a more chaotic publishing history in the 1950s.

Wheare's last legacy
While the debate had continued around the importance for the Society of appropriately recognizing television, the Wheare Report continued to have an effect some nine years after its publication. The Cinema Consultative Committee, set up under the auspices of the British Board of Film Censors, published a report, *The Teaching of Film*.[123] This report was the work of the Cinema Advisory Sub-committee whose provenance was to be found among the Wheare recommendations which 'included one emphasising the need for encouraging film appreciation teaching in schools'.[124]

This Sub-committee was unique among the groups which considered film appreciation in the 1950s in that included in its composition were representatives of both the film trade and relevant Scottish organisations. As a result, *The Teaching of Film* includes sections on 'The Position in Scotland' and 'The Film Trade's Contribution'. Both the recognition of national sensitivities and the avoidance of a potential demarcation dispute may be deduced from the statement that '…in Scotland it was felt that there was no need for the establishment of an organisation akin to the Society of Film Teachers.' The equivalent functions to those carried out by SFT are to be found shared between the Scottish Film Council, the Scottish Educational Film Association and the Federation of Scottish Film Societies.[125] Trade sensitivities are addressed by reassurances that the film teacher 'must seek to understand the trade's special problems and difficulties in providing entertainment for a mass-audience if his work in school is to be fully effective'.[126] Unsurprisingly, since both SFT and BFI were represented on the Sub-committee, the familiar reference to the 'positive approach' is repeated. The assistance of the Trade to the 'general development of film teaching in schools' requires 'the trade to keep in mind, always the positive nature of the teacher's approach' and in order to 'carry out their job effectively' the teachers need the trade to provide 'many more extracts'.[127]

It is apparent that the report is driven by SFT and BFI, not only from the allusions to those organisations, but also from references to activities with which both organisations were significantly involved, such as the 1957 Amsterdam Conference and the 1958 follow-up in London. These activists saw *The Teaching of Film* as an opportunity to be much more specific in what they wanted to promote. As the first of the Report's Conclusions states, 'The experimental stage in film teaching is now passed and the time has come for a planned extension.'[128] This extension would involve more courses in teacher training colleges (possibly taught by seconded teachers with experience), and in the establishment of 'a university course in film, leading to a recognised qualification'.[129] But there is perhaps a rather more innovative approach being signalled.

> Though a popular art, cinema has need for an *élite*, and if children of higher attainment and fuller education are brought up to consider the newer arts as worthy of a place alongside the established media, this will be to the advantage of the cinema.[130]

Here the traditional territory of film appreciation is being extended in two ways. Cinema is being recognised as one of several popular media arts and worthy of equivalent study. Whereas film teaching had received recognition only among the less academic students in a divided education system, claims were now being made for it to reach the grammar schools, which was where 'children of higher attainment and fuller education were to be found'.

Filling the Gap Year in Teacher Training

The Teaching of Film was to be followed by a more substantial report, which it anticipates in the following statement.

> It is encouraging that a recent meeting organised by the British Film Institute in collaboration with the Association of Teachers in Colleges and Departments of Education was attended by representatives of 71 teacher training establishments, and a resolution was passed setting up a joint committee 'to consider the introduction of the teaching of film appreciation into Training College courses'.[131]

In an over-optimistic front-page comment early in January 1960, the *Times Educational Supplement* (TES) stated

> In five years from now we can expect considerable numbers of young teachers to emerge, after completing the study of the film as a main course, with a fund of knowledge and a body of critical principles which should be of great value to the children they will teach.[132]

This comment was a response to the publication of *Film and Television in Education for Teaching* launched earlier that week at a conference held at the National Film Theatre.[133] A report of the launch conference under the heading 'The Good with the Bad – Positive Effects of Mass Media' is to be found in the same issue.[134] Whilst summarising the report's conclusions, the TES article leads with the address given by Whannel who had used this occasion to advance the argument he was already making elsewhere against the notion that there was an orthodoxy of taste which teachers should be concerned to transmit to their students. He was advocating that judgments still needed to be made, but 'for many children these media represented their only major aesthetic experience, and they must be encouraged to use them to make judgments on this experience'.[135]

The publication he was launching was rather less committed, but its agenda was similar. The committee that produced it had included both a heavy BFI representation at senior staff level and SEFT representatives, some of whom were also in the Association of Teachers in Colleges and Departments of Education (ATCDE). Its Chairman was David Johnston, who ran the Teachers' Centre at the University of London Institute of Education. He was both a member of ATCDE and a Governor of the BFI. From the autumn 1960 intake onwards, students entering training colleges would be on three-year courses, not two years as had been the norm once the post-war emergency training scheme ended. This fifty per cent increase in student attendance time was seen as presenting a unique opportunity for film and television study to be included in such courses. This report was to make the case for their inclusion. The 'official' case for the training colleges to recognise the relevance of film study had been made in the McNair Report of 1944 when referring to broadcasting and the cinema.

We should expect such studies to be part of an enlightened course in education or social studies, and to result in the schools doing something to influence children's taste.[136]

But the training colleges were institutions with problems. A damning survey had appeared in *Scrutiny* in 1932. Although based on rather impressionistic but substantial evidence, the article had been damaging. The colleges were seen as symptomatic of the 'general state of English culture' and of standards lowered by such agencies as the cinema.[137] In response to these perceived external influences, the colleges were seen to do nothing to 'encourage an adult sense of responsibility'.[138]

There were more than echoes of this observation in *Film and Television in Education for Teaching*. The document clearly addresses the issue of how to get film and television study into training college courses, but it also reflects at some length on the shortcomings of training college students in a chapter called 'The Training College Situation.' *Scrutiny* saw the institutions as failing the students; here it is the inadequacies of the students themselves which are highlighted. They are neither as intellectually able as those of their contemporaries who have gained university places, nor as emotionally developed as those who left school at fifteen.[139] The case is then made that a film and television study course would be very appropriate for such students 'since by their lack of experience they are themselves sitting victims for the false values of the popular television show and by the demands of their profession are greatly in need of a sharpened discrimination'.[140] They will need this 'sharpened discrimination' because, the argument goes, once the school leaving age is raised to 16, these newly trained teachers will be faced with students, who will be 'more independent, more vocal, more sophisticated, more imbued with the common patterns of television values'.[141]

An uneasy parallel was implicitly being drawn: film and television study had become acceptable in the secondary modern school for those who had not made it to the grammar school; here it was being deemed appropriate also for the training college students who had failed to get into university. It seems the Working Party felt that attacking on this particular front might be productive. If the educational case for including film and television in courses might not be sufficiently powerful, perhaps the social case might prove overwhelming. In the 'Summary and Conclusions' chapter, the case is put starkly.

> In view of the particular needs and resources of Training College students, the Working Party consider that a course on film and television can serve to bring under review and unify many of the problems of the personal and social development of the students in a way that is not possible in separate courses.[142]

The document is very much of its time, drawing on both the Wheare Report and the more recent *Television and the Child* in a chapter on 'The Growth of Public Concern'.[143] Both these previous reports called for the audience to be educated about the particular medium on which they were reporting. The working party, still felt it had to nod in the direction of the 'immunisation' mode of thinking. 'In the last resort the defence of the individual rests within himself.'[144] Nevertheless, it concludes the chapter saying 'that positive education of viewers, particularly child viewers, as distinct from attempts at negative control, is desirable as a part of the general educational process'.[145]

A substantial part of the pamphlet is taken up with strategic issues around the nature of training college courses and what options might be possible within Main Courses on the one hand and Curriculum Courses on the other. The principal practical difference was that the curriculum course, being both shorter and internally assessed, might offer an easier route along which film and television study might make inroads. For the non-specialist reader the four principal conclusions provide a clearer focus as to why the general case was being made, albeit one senses that the authors were trying to cover as many options as possible.[146]

> Firstly, the working party regard film and television as important for the influence they can exert on the outlook and values of ordinary people.
>
> Secondly, the Committee regard film and television as a substantial body of art.
>
> In the third-place, film and television constitute an excellent medium for the serious study of contemporary life and culture.
>
> Fourthly, film and television provide an excellent medium for the study of human relationships and values.

The third and fourth conclusions together became part of the thinking behind the thematic approach to film, which was developed in the 1960s. Similarly, during that decade, the second conclusion began to be realised, as more scholarly publications on film appeared. It is the first conclusion which reflects a residual culture. The reference to 'ordinary people' as a particularly vulnerable category is revealing, as is the extension of that conclusion to suggest those most at risk have 'immature or unsettled personalities'.[147]

Given that *Film and Television in Education for Teaching* was written by a committee, it was perhaps unavoidable for it not to be a totally coherent document. Perhaps the most anomalous ingredient of all is to be found in Appendix VI. This contains a reprint from *Universities and Left Review* of the film review by Paddy Whannel of *Room at the Top*.[148] Its inclusion is to support the arguments being advanced for film and television study as a Main Course. The assertion is that the review demonstrates 'the profundity of issues raised by the discussion of film' and in Whannel's review 'the reader will find the examination of character and personality provocative and the contrast between the novel and the film a contribution to an understanding of the role of the film as a vehicle for the presentation of human qualities'.[149]

Whannel's review takes a predictably Leavisite approach with both some detailed textual analysis and a clear moral stance.[150]

In its frankness before physical love, its willingness to explore social experiences representative of the post-war period, and its refusal to smooth away all ambiguities of motive and character shaped by social forces – this film is far ahead of anything produced by the British cinema, certainly since the war.[151]

The choice of this review of this particular film may be explained firstly by Whannel's readiness as a member of the Committee to offer his own work as a test case and secondly by the controversy which had surrounded the release of *Room at the Top* in 1958, when the Report was being written. Given an X certificate, Rank cinemas had refused to screen the film, which had consequently been released only in smaller independent cinemas. By praising the film in this manner in a journal of the Left, Whannel was purposefully courting controversy. By reprinting it in the Report as a model of good practice the Committee nudged forward the rather conservative territory of film appreciation. As film study developed in the 1960s, it would be the Leavisite model that would be initially influential.

Notes

1. *SFT Bulletin* Vol 1 No 1 December 1950 p 12
2. *The Mini Camera* Vol 5 No 11 1951 p 31 There is no evidence that any subsequent films in the proposed series were ever produced. A W Hodgkinson in 'Amsterdam and the Virtual World' *Film Teacher* 12 March 1958 refers to his 'enthusiastic efforts' to make *The Camera Moves* in 1951. His view had changed by 1958 and he saw no need for such films. In the 1960s copies of a film made by long time SEFT activist S G P Alexander called *Telling a Story in Pictures* were regularly advertised for sale in *Screen Education*.
3. *Look and Listen* Vol 5 No 8 August 1951 p 170
4. *The Film Teacher* Summer 1952 p 27
5. Ibid p 1
6. Ibid p 3
7. Ibid p 7
8. Ibid p 10
9. See Jim Cook and Jim Hillier *The Growth of Film and Television Studies 1960–1975* London: BFI April 1971 p 11. They refer to 'the protective or inoculative approach'. Peter Harcourt in 'Towards Higher Education' in *Screen Education* No 26 September/October 1964 advances the protection from corruption hypothesis.
10. *The Film Teacher* op cit p 1
11. Ibid pp 20–22
12. Ibid p 21
13. Ibid p 21
14. *Look and Listen* Vol 7 No 1 January 1953 p 9

15. Ibid pp 21–22
16. Ibid p 21
17. *The Cinema: Its present position and future possibilities* London: Williams and Northgate 1917
18. Janet Hills *Films and Children: The Positive Approach* London: BFI 1951 p 4. As related in the previous chapter, Reed was particularly associated with this term and presented it almost as a form of rebuttal when challenged on the lack of British film theory in Amsterdam in 1957.
19. Ibid p 47
20. Ibid p 33
21. Ibid p 30
22. *Look and Listen* Vol 5 No 11 November 1951 p 239
23. Mary Field 'The Children's Film Foundation' *The Film Teacher* Winter 1952 pp 1–5
24. Ibid p 5
25. *The Film Teacher* Spring 1953 'Violence in Films' pp 2–4; Interview 'As I See It' with Alexander Mackendrick pp 8–12
26. Janet Hills *Are They Safe at the Cinema?* London: BFI 1953
27. *The Film Teacher* op cit p 31
28. Hills op cit p 3; *The Film Teacher* op cit p 2
29. Ibid p 2
30. Ibid p 3
31. Ibid p 4
32. This compromise seems to have forced the Editor to append the following footnote to the 'Violence in Films' editorial. 'The still which heads this article is from *Sound of Fury*. But note that in this film – a study of lynch-law – the violence is artistically essential. Without it the film would be, in fact, less moral.' (Ibid p 4).
33. Ibid p 11
34. Ibid p 11
35. Hills 1951 op cit p 34
36. Hills 1953 op cit p 23
37. Op cit p 21
38. *The Film Teacher* Autumn 1953 '3D and TV' pp 2–6, 'The Consultative Committee' pp 8–11, 'Film Morality and Film Taste' pp 16–17
39. British Board of Film Censors Cinema Consultative Committee *The Teaching of Film: A Report and Some Recommendations* London: July 1958.
40. Ibid p 2
41. Ibid p 2
42. *The Film Teacher* Spring 1954 p 25
43. *The Film Teacher* Autumn 1953 p 17
44. Ibid p 17
45. The cover design was an original one for *The Film Teacher* Summer 1952 by Geraldine Spence. See p 32 of that issue.

46. I E Roberts 'Diploma Course Work' *The Film Teacher* Spring 1954 pp 2–4

47. Ibid pp 2–3

48. Allan J Baker 'Opening Shots' *The Film Teacher* Spring 1954 pp 6–9

49. Ibid p 7

50. *The Film Teacher* op cit pp 10–11

51. Ibid p 10

52. Ibid p 11

53. Grace Greiner *Teaching Film* London: BFI 1954

54. Ibid p 22

55. Ibid p 22

56. Ibid p 23

57. Ibid p ii

58. S G P Alexander 'We've Come a Long Way' *Screen Education* 31 September/October 1965 p 54

59. Greiner op cit p 28

60. *Newsletter* No 2 December 1954 p 2. This issue also recorded that Derek J Davies, who had edited *The Film Teacher* throughout, had left the Committee having moved from London. It is impossible to determine how far his departure influenced SFT's publication decisions. He was publicly thanked at the AGM for bringing 'such prestige' to the Society (p 5).

61. Report of Don Chaffey, speaking at the annual SFT conference, *Newsletter* No 2 December 1954 p 6

62. Editorial in *Newsletter* No 3 February 1955 p 2

63. 'The Challenge of Television' *Newsletter* No 3 p 3

64. Ibid p 5. There appears to be no record of the Society ever having held such a position.

65. Ibid p 5

66. Ibid p 5

67. There had been an increase in the BFI grant to SFT for 1954/55 as the Treasurer reported at the October 1954 AGM. This allocation was presumably carried over as the new annual amount in 1955/56. *Newsletter* No 2 December 1954 p 5

68. 'One Approach to Film Appreciation in the Secondary Modern' *Film Teacher* No 1 April 1955 pp 4–6

69. The two articles are 'Story into Screenplay' by Victor Thompson, an account of an activity based approach used in youth clubs and 'Don't be so ashamed of your school reports now' by Frank Hazell, reprinted from the trade press. Hazell was a senior executive of a film exhibition chain who had published a pro SFT article saying that it was in the interests of cinema managers to get on good terms with local film teachers.

70. R C Vannoey was to become a very energetic and productive member of the SFT/SEFT committees from 1955 to 1969.

71. E M Pointon 'Beginners All' *Film Teacher* No 3 August 1955 pp 6–10

72. The author has been unable to find any further report of this conference.

73. A W Hodgkinson 'The Continental Scene' *Film Teacher* op cit p 12

74. Op cit p 12.

75. According to S G P Alexander in 'We've Come a Long Way' *Screen Education* No 31 September/October 1965 p 57 five Information sheets were produced in all, edited by Alan Whittaker during the period April 1956 to March 1958.
76. Leiken Vogt 'Film Teaching in Norway' *Film Teacher* No 4 July 1956 pp 8–14
77. *Film Teacher* op cit p 7
78. See *Film Teacher* 12 March 1958 pp 2–3 where the Editorial 'Hi Kwai or Die' is subtitled 'Some thoughts on the Future of British Cinema'.
79. *Film Teacher* 5 September 1956 p 2
80. A W Hodgkinson 'The Continental Scene' *Film Teacher* 6 November 1956 p 13
81. *Film Teacher* 6 November 1956 p 13
82. Ibid p 20 The event was given a particular interest by the participation of Celia Johnson in the group that recorded a discussion about the extract from *Brief Encounter*.
83. *Film Teacher* 7 was published in January 1957 and *Film Teacher* 8 in March 1957.
84. C E Fitchett 'Film Teaching – A Training College View' *Film Teacher* 7 January 1957 p 5
85. E W M Heddle 'Film Appreciation at the University Level – A General Survey' Ibid pp 11–14
86. Ibid p 13
87. I E Roberts 'Diploma Course Work' *The Film Teacher* Spring 1954 pp 2–4
88. L Heywood 'Film in the School Curriculum' *Film Teacher* op cit pp 17–20
89. T R Barnes 'Art and Ketchup' *The Journal of Education* Vol 90 February 1958 p 61
90. 'A Negative Light' *The Journal of Education* Vol 90 February 1958 p 43
91. In *Film Teacher* 14 September 1958 p 28 Wills, having completed two years as Editor, observed: 'My thanks go first to those few who have sent me unsolicited articles; secondly, to those who having been solicited supplied their copy before the deadline'.
92. *Film Teacher* 8 March 1957 p 2
93. Edgar Dale 'How to Evaluate the Mass Media' *Film Teacher* 8 March 1957 pp 14–18
94. Edgar Dale *How to Appreciate Motion Pictures* New York: The Macmillan Co 1933
95. *Film Teacher* op cit p 18
96. Ibid p 16
97. Ibid p 18
98. Jack Ellis 'Film Societies and Film Education in the USA' *Film Teacher* 13 pp 15–19 and 'Film at North Western University' *Film Teacher* 15 December 1958 pp 19–25
99. Dai Vaughan 'The Poem as Film' *Film Teacher* 12 March 1956 pp 4–8; 'What is Free Cinema?' *Film Teacher* 14 September 1958 pp 11–17; 'A Seat for the Tenth Muse' *Film Teacher* 15 December 1958 pp 16–19; 'Films of Innocence' Film Teacher 17 May 1959 pp 25–27
100. The author has not been able to track down a copy of *Film Teacher* 16.
101. Paddy Whannel 'Towards a Positive Criticism of the Mass Media' *Film Teacher* 17 May 1959 pp 28–30
102. Ibid p 28
103. Ibid p 30

104. Michael Orrom and Raymond Williams *Preface to Film* London: Film Drama Limited 1954

105. Op cit Promotional comment on rear dust jacket

106. Ibid p vii

107. Ibid pp 26 and 39

108. Ibid p 54

109. Ibid p 54

110. Ibid p 116

111. Ibid p 116

112. *Film Teacher* 12 March 1958 p 21

113. For example *Halliwell's FilmGoer's Companion* was first published in 1965 – and then only in hardback.

114. Sidney Rees and Don Waters 'Film Making in Schools' *The Film Teacher's Handbook 1956/7* London: SEFT 1956 pp 11–19. This was subsequently published as *Film Making in Schools* London: SEFT 1960 and then revised and published as *Young Film Makers* London: SEFT 1963.

115. *Film Teacher* 13 June 1958 p 2

116. C L Heywood 'The Challenge of Television' pp 23–26 and A P Higgins 'Television: Meeting the Challenge' pp 27–29 *The Film Teacher's Handbook 1958/59* London: SEFT 1958. According to Alexander, Heywood had seconded Hodgkinson's motion to rename the Society at the previous month's AGM. See S G P Alexander 'from SFT to SEFT' *Screen Education 29* May/June 1965 p 67

117. Ibid pp 61–67

118. Ibid p 63

119. *The Film Teacher's Handbook 1959/60* London: SEFT 1959 p 3

120. Whereas *The Film Teacher's Handbook* had been timed for summer production and distributed in advance of each new academic year, the *Screen Education Yearbook* was produced in the autumn and distributed to reach members before the start of the new calendar year to which it applied. The Society seems to have judged it an acceptable economy that, after the November/December 1961 issue of *Screen Education*, members would no longer have an issue of the journal distributed at the same time as the new yearbook. Thus subsequently there were to be only five issues a year of the bi-monthly *Screen Education* from 1962 – 1968 inclusive. The title *Screen Education* was of course revived by the Society in the 1970s when it was published from Spring/Summer 1974 until Winter/Spring 1982. However the first issue of that journal in 1974 was published as number 10 since it was in effect a continuation of *Screen Education Notes* established in Winter 1971. The confusion of numbering of early issues of *Screen Education Notes* is dealt with in a later chapter.

121. *The Film Teacher's Handbook 1958/59* p 61

122. *Report of the Committee on the British Film Institute* Cmd 7361 London: HMSO April 1948 p 5

123. *The Teaching of Film A Report and Some Recommendations* London: The Cinema Consultative Committee 1958

124. Ibid p 5
125. Ibid p 11 The Association for Media Education in Scotland (AMES) was started in 1983.
126. Ibid p 12
127. Ibid p 13
128. Ibid p 14
129. Ibid p 14
130. Ibid p 8
131. Ibid p 8
132. *Times Educational Supplement* 8 January 1960 p 25
133. Association of Teachers in Colleges and Departments of Education/ British Film Institute *Film and Television in Education For Teaching* A Report of the Joint Working Party of the Association of Teachers in Colleges and Departments of Education and the British Film Institute London: BFI 1960
134. Ibid p 40
135. Ibid p 40
136. Board of Education *Report of the Committee to Consider the Supply, Recruitment and Training of Teachers and Youth Leaders* [McNair Report] London: HMSO 1944 p 137
137. L C Knights 'Will Training Colleges Bear Scrutiny?' *Scrutiny* Vol 1 No 3 December 1932 p 259
138. Ibid p 259
139. *Film and Television in Education for Teaching* p 18
140. Ibid p 19
141. Ibid p 20
142. Ibid p 42
143. Hilde Himmelweit *Television and the Child* Oxford: Oxford University Press 1958
144. ATCDE/BFI op cit p 15
145. Ibid p 17
146. Ibid p 41
147. Ibid p 41
148. *Universities and Left Review* – soon to become *New Left Review* – was edited by Stuart Hall. Whannel was on the Editorial Board.
149. Ibid p 25
150. Ibid pp 63–66
151. Ibid p 63

4

Discrimination and Popular Culture

The fields of media studies and image analysis are developing fast. We urgently need development of checkable research strategies…When we are developing those techniques, we must not kid ourselves that we can avoid involvement in the controversies in the political field about these issues. But in any particular case, the implication is that we cannot know in advance exactly where we will be standing. We know only one group that we oppose: those who refuse to analyse, choosing again exactly the same moralistic censorious role that I have described in the 1950s. Their 'refusal to theorise' must be our first target.

> Martin Barker, commenting in 1984, on how the 1950s
> campaign against horror comics must not become the
> model for shaping responses to media education

In October 1960 the NUT Conference puts popular culture permanently on the educational agenda. During the 1960s the Conference's legacy is still to be found in a range of books aimed at different parts of the educational market. Almost simultaneously the respectful critical position for worthy films still preserved within the BFI comes under attack from Oxford Opinion. *These new critics, whose preference is for detailed textual analysis, also produce a legacy in* Movie, *a potential rallying point for a younger generation of film teachers. While key SEFT officers engage with the popular culture debate, its journal* Screen Education *is in danger of missing the big picture.*

Certain key events at the start of the 1960s were to have long term consequences for the development of media education and that would impinge on SEFT and its activities. The momentum for change started with two books published in the late 1950s which had focused on cultural issues and provoked debates: *The Uses of Literacy* and *Culture and Society*.[1] But if the territory that these works explored had excited the intellectuals, the coming of commercial television and its popular appeal had stirred the population at large. Controversy increased as to whether the BBC or commercial television would be granted the third television channel with the result that the Pilkington Committee was set up in 1960 to decide the matter.[2]

Teenagers Rock: Graduates Write

SEFT's new journal *Screen Education* soon found itself in a crowded film publications environment. Journals appeared which challenged *Sight and Sound*: *Definition* (1960), *Motion* (1961) and *Movie* (1962). *Movie* had developed from *Oxford Opinion*, which had set out directly to confront *Sight and Sound*. *New Left Review*'s new film critic Lee Russell was in reality Peter Wollen, who had replaced Paddy Whannel on that journal in 1962. UNESCO publications focused more directly on film and television in education, with the appearance in 1961 of *Teaching about the Film* where the Dutch author J M L Peters drew heavily on BFI and SEFT experiences.[3] Later in 1964 *Screen Education* was published in UNESCO's Reports and Papers on Mass Communication series where the writings of leading SEFT members, Hodgkinson and Higgins, predominated.[4]

Although not directly involving SEFT, there was a development which both SEFT and the BFI had promoted for a long time. A university presence for film was finally found at the Slade School of Art, under the aegis of University College, London, with the appointment of Thorold Dickinson as Lecturer in Film at the commencement of the 1960/61 academic year. A committee would subsequently be set up in 1965 to investigate the possibility of a national film school – an item which had appeared repeatedly on the agenda of the Governors of the British Film Institute since 1958.[5]

The election of a Labour Government in 1964 would lead to the appointment of a Minister for the Arts who would then respond positively to the pressure which had been coming from the BFI about a change in its funding mechanism. Whereas previously the Ministry of Education had been cautious in responding to requests from both BFI and SEFT, the re-named Department of Education and Science would agree to fund the BFI whose Education and Regional Departments, in particular, benefited as a consequence. SEFT would benefit too from the establishment of a BFI funded BFI/SEFT joint appointment in 1967. Detailed consideration of these developments will form the basis of the next chapter.

A new identity was emerging in the population – the 'teenager' – a term which quickly replaced the 'adolescent' as a descriptor. In the 1940s the adolescent, making the transition from school child to worker at age 14, had been seen as potentially vulnerable in a world of austerity. The next cohort in the 1950s, leaving school at 15 and entering better paid employment, were potential consumers entering a society of increasing affluence and who were increasingly perceived as not vulnerable but menacing. By 1960 this phenomenon, repeatedly featured in the popular press was coming under academic scrutiny. It was with the conjunction of these and other cultural events that an anxiety was articulated at the National Union of Teachers' Annual Conference at Easter 1960 and only a few months later, a conference 'Popular Culture and Personal Responsibility' was organised. SEFT featured prominently in one of its sessions and in the follow-up publication.

'Popular Culture and Personal Responsibility' in October 1960 is recognised as a 'landmark' event in the evolution of what came to be identified as Cultural Studies.[6] Two emerging areas of intellectual investigation coincided at the Conference: cultural studies and what would become media studies. It is important to note a certain similarity in their origins: each had developed at the margins of formal education. Cultural studies had, in Steele's view, evolved in the extra-mural classes of universities,[7] while film and television study had begun among the non-examinable students in the secondary modern schools. In the period from 1945 to 1960, it is reasonable to infer that both adult and school students in these very different institutions were largely drawn from the working class. Such students would have fewer preconceptions of how their teachers should select and present objects for study. It was the distance from the élite core teaching bases of the university campus and the grammar school which gave the extra-mural tutors and modern school teachers the freedom to experiment. Subsequently, by the mid-1960s, both cultural studies and media education were to have separate embryonic academic institutional bases – in the Birmingham Centre for Contemporary Cultural Studies and in the Education Department of the British Film Institute.

Undoubtedly, the conference was in part a response by a particular professional group to the writings about popular culture of Raymond Williams and Richard Hoggart though Stuart Laing is clear in citing the 'rapid expansion of the television audience (particularly for ITV)' as the trigger for the concern.[8] But both Fred Jarvis and Brian Groombridge, key figures in the organisation of the conference, whilst not disregarding the intellectual stimulus provided by Williams and Hoggart, each separately emphasised another key influence: *Blackboard Jungle*.[9] Screenings of this film in 1956 had led to 'audience participation' where young audiences had responded in some venues (perhaps less to the depiction of a school out of control than to the rock 'n' roll soundtrack accompanying the credits) by vandalizing those cinemas. Press coverage – and outrage – had been considerable. Predictably its depiction of United States inner urban secondary school chaos would have registered with teachers in the United Kingdom as a portent of the future for British education. The vandalizing of cinemas persisted. The level of concern was such that *Screen Education* published an account of the manager of a small cinema in a Welsh mining village who described the problems he had with his teenage patrons. He pinned his hopes of producing a more responsible generation through the popularity of the 'Boys and Girls Own Cinema', as his cinema's own Saturday matinée was described.[10]

In the early 1950s, during the trial of Christopher Craig and Derek Bentley for the murder of a policeman, Craig's defence sought to implicate his frequent cinema-going as a contributory cause of his delinquency. This had fed concern about the negative effects of cinema.[11] Now there was a parallel discourse to which *Blackboard Jungle* contributed. Furthermore it was an American film, and one American cultural product had recently been dealt with – by the law. Horror comics, in effect American imports, were outlawed in 1955 as a result of the Children and Young Person's (Harmful Publications) Act. As Martin Barker's research has shown, the essential impulse behind those who campaigned for this legislation was the anti-Americanism of the British Communist Party.[12] The extent of this covert influence had been somewhat disguised by the presence of an organization which at that time enjoyed public esteem: the National Union of Teachers, which had joined the campaign, albeit belatedly. Undoubtedly, some NUT members had perceived their union's intervention as an appropriate response to an alien form of culture, to judge by the references to it at the October conference.[13]

A further strand in the influential elements, and one emphasised by Groombridge, was *The Teenage Consumer* published in July 1959.[14] Its author, Mark Abrams, defined the teenage consumer as a young person who had disposable income, who was predominantly working-class, who was very influenced by the trends set in the United States, and who was distinctive by her/his patronage of the mass media. Teachers might only encounter the younger versions of such teenagers, prior to their becoming wage earners, but they would have had plentiful hearsay evidence to support Abrams's thesis. There had been official recognition in 1959 of how the media, teenagers and education coincided in the school room (and where responsibility was assumed therefore to lie) when the Crowther Report had pronounced:

> Because they [the mass media] are so powerful they need to be treated with the discrimination that only education can give…There is also…a duty on those who are charged with the responsibility for education to see that teenagers, who are at the most insecure and suggestible stage of their lives, are not suddenly exposed to the full force of the mass media, without some counterbalancing assistance.[15]

The National Union of Teachers' Conference 1960

At the union's Annual Conference at Easter 1960, a motion was put forward and carried unanimously. Although the wording suggests the motion might have arrived at conference fully formed – and with supporters – Jarvis's recollection is that its content evolved during the conference.

> Conference, whilst recognizing the vital part played by teachers in developing the moral and cultural standards of the nation and its children, considers that this is a task in which others must co-operate.
>
> Although today more young people than ever are actively engaged in intellectual pursuits and appreciate or participate in the creation of art, literature, music or drama, Conference believes that a determined effort must be made to counteract the debasement of standards which results from the misuse of press,

radio, cinema and television; the deliberate exploitation of violence and sex; and the calculated appeal to self-interest.

It calls especially upon those who use and control the media of mass communication, and upon parents, to support the efforts of teachers in an attempt to prevent the conflict which too often arises between the values inculcated in the classroom and those encountered by young people in the world outside.[16]

Several features of the conference organisation would have been simply impossible by today's standards. All the speakers who were invited during May and June accepted for the following October. No one declined. No one expected or received any payment. Speakers who were not London based were put up in the homes of the organisers. Indeed, for a union to organise such a conference on a non-industrial topic was very unusual. The NUT had recently become the first union to establish a public relations and publicity department and it was this department's first big project under its new lead officer, Fred Jarvis.[17] Admission was by free ticket, the funding for the conference coming from an unspent fund which had been accumulated in readiness for industrial action which had not taken place. The NUT Executive felt that using the money in this way would be acceptable to members. Although no speakers were paid, the Union did pay for a verbatim record of the whole conference, which included all contributions from the floor. Undoubtedly, the comprehensive nature of this permanent conference record contributed to the enduring status of the event.

The list of conference members does demonstrate both a potential attendance of some five hundred people from three hundred organisations and an absence of teachers.[18] Such was the pressure from organisations wanting to be there that the members who voted to have the conference were largely excluded. To address this issue, the NUT produced a *Study Outline* to the conference, edited by Groombridge, which was made available to NUT branches and members in 1961.[19] The guide is a careful exercise in drawing out from the various speakers' contributions, threads of the main themes of the conference.

The task the original Easter Conference motion specifically wished to be addressed was that of 'developing the moral and cultural standards of the nation'. The phrase was echoed in the NUT President's introduction to the October event.

This is not the first time that, in the interest of the child, teachers have had to express their concern for moral and cultural standards. A few years ago, we conducted a vigorous and successful campaign against 'horror comics'.[20]

The frontispiece of the *Verbatim Report* defines the event as:

...a Conference of those engaged in education, together with parents, those directly or indirectly concerned with the welfare of children and young people, and people involved in the mass media themselves to examine the impact of the media of mass communications on present-day moral and cultural standards.[21]

NUT General Secretary Ronald Gould's introduction to the *Verbatim Report* concludes optimistically with the expectation that reading the report will make 'those in the mass media' 'ensure that these media are used to raise moral and cultural standards'.[22]

The wide range of extra-educational organisations in attendance at the conference is probably accounted for by this ostensible aim of engaging with moral and cultural standards. In practice most of the platform speakers had been invited because they would have something to say that was relevant to the scrutiny of popular culture, not of morals. Indeed, the styling of the conference had clearly separated what was being addressed – popular culture – from the issue of responsibility. Quite why the conference juxtaposed popular culture with personal rather than social responsibility is never explained. Given the conference's scheduling in autumn 1960, when it coincided with the formation of the anti-nuclear weapon Committee of 100, it was perhaps a time when it seemed appropriate for individuals to identify their personal commitment as had the hundred named individuals who were protesting against the establishment of nuclear submarine bases in Scotland.

The conference was opened by R A Butler, the Home Secretary, whose credibility with an educational audience derived from his period as Secretary of the Board of Education when he had successfully steered the 1944 Education Act through Parliament. In what he presumably intended as a supportive gesture, Butler, remembering how a change in the law had appeared to offer a resolution to the horror comics campaign, made it clear that if any of the issues to come before the conference were susceptible to being solved by legislation, then he would be ready to listen.[23] Butler was not the only speaker to refer to the Children and Young Persons (Harmful Publications) Act. It had been cited in the NUT President's introduction[24] and later from the floor, Horace King (an NUT sponsored MP) proposed 'the successful horror comics campaign' as a model for action.[25]

Whannel and Reed were influential in the design of the conference, and in advising on speakers.[26] Reed was an NUT member and had assisted the union in setting up the making of its publicity films: *I Want to go to School* and *Our School*. Whannel brought in the format and contacts from the Joint Council for Education through Art, where the creative artists and the educationists were placed in direct dialogue. Here, rather than the creative artists, it was the producers of the media who were lined up: Gerald Beadle, Director of Television Broadcasting at the BBC, Norman Collins, Deputy Chairman of Associated Television, Mary Grieve, Editor of *Woman* and Cecil King, Chairman of *Daily Mirror* Newspapers. All appeared in the session 'the responsibilities of the provider'. The creative artists were Huw Weldon, Colin Morris, Karel Reisz and Francis Williams who addressed 'the restrictions of working in the media'.[27]

These sessions were scheduled for the final day when, as it were, the case for the prosecution had been made. But in their addresses to conference, King and Collins moved on to the attack. King predictably gained press headlines with his comment

In point of fact it is only the people who conduct newspapers and similar organisations who have any idea quite how indifferent, quite how stupid, quite how uninterested in education of any kind the great bulk of the British public are.[28]

Collins decided to turn the accusation towards the teaching profession: 'the overwhelming mass of the letters we get are illiterate, they are ungrammatical, they are deplorably written'. But it was not the illiteracy alone that he condemned but also the content of the letters requesting fan material and the screening of 'music hall type' programmes, 'I hold the teachers very largely responsible, if that is the attitude of the people in their teens and early twenties'.[29] If the organisers had hoped to achieve a consensus, there was to be none.

Tony Higgins and Don Waters from SEFT were the only teachers to address the conference, making their contribution on the previous afternoon. Their tape recordings of children discussing films and the screening of a school made film would have been novelties for many in the audience. Their cinema session was deliberately separated from the debate about television, which was included with radio. Unlike the other media under scrutiny, films were not represented on the platform by any one engaged in film production. Only later when speaking at the television event did G H Elvin (speaking on behalf of the Trade Union Group, the Television and Radio Safeguards Committee) draw attention to how he felt the SEFT contribution had served only to distract the audience.

This afternoon, I was very disappointed at the way the session at the National Film Theatre went; teaching teachers how to teach children film appreciation is all very well, but that session did not face up to the purpose of this conference.[30]

Yet the terms of the Higgins/Waters presentation had been set by Whannel at the outset.

It is because we in this particular session want to make a stand upon the question of values and our own personal commitments, because we want the matter to be stated in positive terms, that we have given over most of our session, not to talking about what we can do about it but demonstrating what two teachers are doing about it in their schools every day.[31]

As Higgins later put it 'we should not regard the film as a problem at all but as an opportunity to open a vast world of rich experience to young people'.[32] Although

Whannel defined his task as giving 'an extended introduction to Don Waters and Tony Higgins', he had chosen to insert at short notice an extract from the film *Nice Time* at the start of the session.[33] He explained this last-minute addition of the film as his reaction to the morning's proceedings at which

> I was really disturbed about the general view that things are as they are, they will continue to be like that and all we have to do is some more research, and in the meantime not do anything rash, perhaps have a few conferences.[34]

Nice Time, with its direct social comment, perhaps demonstrated Whannel's exasperation. It was his hasty attempt to challenge the inertia and hand-wringing which the conference appeared to be inviting. He, on the other hand, clearly saw the conference as an important opportunity to promote the kind of work with which he was already heavily involved.

> We need within education to develop the whole movement which already exists for extending that part of education which deals, not with the giving of knowledge but with the evaluating of experience, extending that into the area where people really are experiencing all these things, such as popular music, films, television and so on. We have to extend that and embrace that area within education and critical judgment terms.[35]

It is then additionally clear that by having as speakers two experienced practitioners in Higgins and Waters, Whannel was determined not only to change the terms of the debate from what should happen to what was already happening but also to highlight the potential quality of debate about popular culture.

Higgins outlined his approach which was to discuss with children what films and television programmes they had seen, and to attempt to ask general questions of them about what might now be considered issues of narrative, stereotyping and representation. But he had a further strategy. Having established the kind of films or programmes which children enjoy, the teacher then attempts to steer them towards preferred examples: '... the answer to bad television is good television'.[36] The school film society, he argued, can develop and widen children's taste through judicious screenings. This was open to interpretation. There were some for whom widening taste meant moving children away from popular culture while others saw the importance of exploration within popular culture.

Waters took up the case for the screen education lesson and demonstrated how the availability of the short film extract had made teaching film within the constraints of the school day possible. But his greatest enthusiasm was for film-making. When children were making a film, Waters argued that for him the priority was the end product (the finished film that demonstrated accomplishment) not the means (the lessons that might be learned from the film-making experience). Having the opportunity to be creative in a form that was such a central part of their popular culture was, for Waters, a process the value of which was 'difficult to overestimate'.[37]

It seems likely the conference audience would have been sympathetic to what was being demonstrated and few would have challenged Higgins's closing statement that 'the purpose of education in film and television…is to help children to enjoy to the full all that is best in film and television'.[38] Higgins reported directly to SEFT members about the Conference which he chose to describe as 'the NUT mass media conference'.[39] His session with Waters had occasioned a positive response. What concerned him was that most of his audience had had no idea such work was taking place in schools. This would perhaps have been a matter of greater concern for SEFT if most members of the audience had been teachers but, given the wide representation from civil society which dominated the audience numerically, this display of ignorance was perhaps unsurprising.

Cultural Texts

Since so few teachers had been able to attend the very conference which NUT members had voted into existence, clearly there was a need, both practically and politically, to find a way of engaging as many members as possible in the subsequent debate. The task of trying to attempt to edit down the 348 foolscap pages of the *Verbatim Report* fell to Groombridge, who had to find a structure which would contain the conflicting emphases of different speakers and of the responses that they had drawn from the floor. This became *Popular Culture and Personal Responsibility: A Study Outline*.[40] Whereas concern over moral and cultural values had been emphasised in previous pronouncements, Groombridge begins by offering two rather different reasons for the conference being called and ones which probably more accurately reflected the aim of Jarvis and others engaged in the planning of the conference:

(1) to discover to what extent other organisations concerned with education and social welfare shared both its anxiety over some features of the contemporary cinema, television, journalism and pop songs, and its desire to improve their quality;

(2) to enable representatives of these organisations to discuss the problems and opportunities created by the mass media with some controllers of the media and with some of the writers and artists attempting to work creatively within them.[41]

Groombridge was an active member of the BFI's lecture panel and he and Whannel had collaborated previously. Their shared views are best summarised in an article for the *Times Educational Supplement* in early 1960 which anticipates certain of the reasons for the conference outlined above.

> It is important for the educationists to know the difficulties they face, rather than denounce the media as such; conversely, it is important for the producers to meet those who are responsible for their audience's taste.[42]

They see a danger in there being two kinds of outsider: both the children and their teachers.

> Both sets of outsider are agreed that there are two cultures, popular and traditional, vulgar and respectable which are mutually exclusive and enemies.[43]

The children associated the traditional and respectable culture as not being for them while their teachers 'look on appalled at the candy floss world which their charges revel in'. With this as a model for what teachers face, the authors detect three distinct responses. There is the teacher who resolutely defends his or her own standards by refusing to acknowledge any value whatever in popular culture. There is a less confrontational teacher who seeks gradually to wean his pupils away from the popular arts and recruit them to the highbrow arts – but this concerns the authors who ask: 'Does the small group of recruits for the highbrow arts justify leaving the rest to attend to their own critical defences?'[44]

The authors then opt for a third possibility.

> It suggests that [the popular arts] have already produced works of art in their own kinds, and that by the proper enjoyment and study of these, standards and criteria appropriate to these new forms can be worked out.[45]

As illustration of good practice in this respect, SEFT and its approach to the cinema is offered as a successful model, where children 'can be led to understand the role of discrimination in heightening enjoyment in other arts at the same time as they learn to take films seriously'. The authors, perhaps recognising the readiness of the SEFT journal *Screen Education* to accommodate all comers, provide their resumé of good practice.

> 'Film appreciation' should be more than a narrow understanding of the techniques of film-making. It involves awareness that technique expresses a style, and that through style a director conveys his personal vision and scale of values about the purposes of life and society. Equally, the teacher should beware of pushing film study in the direction of an academic historical survey of the cinema.[46]

Unsurprisingly, Groombridge allows his extracts from the SEFT speakers at the conference to have a sizeable section of space in his chapter in the *Study Outline* on 'The educational response and the practitioner's voice'. It was strategically important – both at the conference and in the *Study Outline* – that a solution should be there to be found already in operation, and in the hands of an established teachers' organisation with a ten year track record of 'considered experience'.[47]

Almost within days of the NUT Conference, the Council for Children's Welfare published *Family Viewing – a study of early evening television*.[48] Prominent among its authors once again was Tony Higgins, Chairman of SEFT, and there was the predictable plug for the Society, which 'has already advanced far in this field and has devised various methods to help children get the best out of television'.[49] The SEFT methods are declared to be: classroom discussion, encouraging children to 'watch the better programmes' and 'the formal study of television as a classroom subject along the same lines as the study of the older arts and means of communication'. The advance being claimed seems to have been the transfer of the approach of viewing and discussing film to the inspection of individual television programmes.

The basis for the study had been the monitoring of programmes shown between 6 pm and 8 pm from November 1959 to April 1960, where 'ten monitors in two groups watched every ninth programme'.[50] This report had been set up in the wake of the dismissal by both BBC and ITA of the recommendations contained in *Children and Television Programmes*, the report of the BBC/ITA Joint Committee.[51] In its title, *Family Viewing* embodies both the dilemma and the solution. Since parents and children were assumed to watch these potentially inappropriate programmes together, the report is clear as to where responsibility lies: with both Television Authorities and with parents. It is 'a dual responsibility, with parents taking an increased share as the evening advances'.[52] When it comes to encouraging children to discriminate, then it is a shared responsibility between parents and teachers.[53]

Clearly, there was a view that popular culture was getting out of hand, and there was the need in society for some group to be prepared to take responsibility to head off the threat. Perhaps in the context of the Cold War, the engagement with popular culture was perceived as the battle of the home front. The home front battle had at least one specific focus: the Pilkington Committee set up to advise on where control of the third television channel should be allocated. SEFT submitted evidence to the committee as detailed in *Screen Education* 8. SEFT used the opportunity to attack the ITA which had 'not carried out its responsibility under the 1954 Television Act' to ensure the ITV companies produced programmes of a high general standard of quality.[54] It also used the opportunity not only to promote the work of SEFT, but to make a plea in general for money.

> We recommend therefore that the importance of providing children with education in television should be acknowledged and that to encourage the provision of this education and help more fully those already engaged in it, SEFT should receive regular sufficient financial assistance.[55]

A rather more considered response, also involving Higgins in its construction, was published in *New Left Review* as a 'Television Supplement'. This was the joint work of

Higgins, Whannel and Raymond Williams. Although delivering recommendations to the Pilkington Committee, the Supplement has a major section on 'Tasks for Education' with separate recommendations as to what the education service should be targeting.[56] Given that BFI/SEFT representatives were involved in producing the supplement, the recommendations are unsurprising, but defined here in rather broader terms. *NLR* calls for 'courses in critical appreciation of the mass media' so that film and television are no longer distinctively identified. Teachers should have the opportunity to be trained 'in the field of popular communications'.[57] Whereas the SEFT evidence to Pilkington wanted to see a Television Institute established as an offshoot of the BFI, *New Left Review* wants an independent 'institute of communications research' to help 'those teachers and lecturers in popular communications subjects'. The Supplement concludes with the repetition of a familiar argument about the role of education in relation to the media.

> In the end, the quality of the service provided will depend upon the critical awareness of the audience, the sense of responsibility on the part of those who serve that public, the conditions in which the service is received, and the cultural life of the society as a whole.[58]

There were several publications other than Groombridge's *Study Outline*, which appeared after the NUT conference and which declared a specific connection to it: *Britain in the Sixties: Communications* (1962), *The Popular Arts* (1964), *Discrimination and Popular Culture* (1965) and *Understanding the Mass Media* (1966).[59] *Britain in the Sixties: Communications* contains a reference to the conference in the Acknowledgements where Williams describes it as 'the most remarkable event of its kind ever held in this country'. The book draws heavily on the verbatim record of the conference. The early chapter on the history of communication is a development of the paper Williams gave on the opening day. The fourth chapter, 'Controversy', quotes extensively from subsequent conference speakers. The concluding chapter, 'Proposals', seeks to move forward from the conference's expressions of concern by allocating tasks to both education and to media institutions. But it is clear, as Steele has noted, that Williams at this stage 'still deplored the contemporary incarnations of mass media'.[60] Consequently he has radical proposals for keeping commercial interests away from the channels of communication and for extensive public ownership, repeating the call for state involvement which had characterised *Preface to Film*. Williams does not attempt to theorise what he is observing; he perhaps hoped to use the momentum of the conference to press for change.

The structure of *The Popular Arts* is designed to be inclusive. The chapter on 'Topics for Study' extends across different media, but nevertheless specific topics tend to be located within particular media. 'The Avenging Angels' deals with crime writers, specifically Spillane and Chandler, where the authors then opt for Chandler as embodying good popular art. 'The Young Audience' is about popular music, but it is clear where the authors' preferences lie.

Throughout this chapter, we have constantly made comparisons between pop music and jazz. This is because, though there are many individual pop songs worth listening to, in general jazz seems an infinitely richer kind of music, both aesthetically and emotionally.[61]

Here the Leavisite approach is transferred to the popular arts, where the worthy and the unworthy are contrasted. Stuart Hall has maintained that the authors were mindful of the strong influence of Leavis among English teachers and felt that taking a Leavisite approach would make the ideas of the book more marketable amongst a cohort of committed teachers and more likely to be put into practice as a consequence.[62] Since both Hall and Whannel were essentially Leavisite in their approach at this stage, perhaps this was an inevitable marketing strategy. The negotiation with the publishers was conducted by Whannel, who promoted the book on the basis of its substantial reference section and its suggested 'Projects for Teaching'. Unfortunately, this would prove to be a problem for a book of nearly 500 pages. By the time it was published some of the suggested material was likely to have been superseded or replaced, given the very nature of the media with which the book was dealing. The authors' dilemma is embodied at the end of the chapter on 'The Young Audience' where there is an extended end note (added just before going to press) on The Beatles. The authors struggle appropriately to acknowledge this emerging phenomenon and yet also to place it in the context of their existing thinking.[63]

Discrimination and Popular Culture claims the greatest direct connection with the conference and yet had none.[64] It does reflect certain aspects of the conference in that media are separated and written about in isolation and by different authors. It also has an unsympathetic introduction, perhaps rather closer to the thinking of the original sponsors of the NUT annual conference motion, which sought to apportion blame to the providers of popular culture. Published as a paperback original, it became sufficiently successful to achieve a substantially revised hardback second edition ten years later. Much of *Discrimination and Popular Culture* was unequivocal in its opposition to popular culture. In the Editor's 'Introduction' Thompson states:

The hypothesis of this book is that the shortcomings of popular culture are with us, because the mass media just listed have become the expression and mouthpiece of a particular type of civilisation.[65]

He quotes extensively from the speakers at the Conference and implicitly draws authority from an assumed association with the Conference, at which he states:

The most predictable thread running through the proceedings was the express hostility of teachers towards the way in which the mass media are used at present.[66]

This might have been an accurate reflection of the feelings that produced the original Easter Conference motion, but it can hardly be true of the October Conference itself, since there were hardly any teachers able to be present, other than those representing professional associations.[67] On the issue of responsibility, Thompson is clear that 'those who control the mass media, must be made fully responsible to the society in which they live'.[68]

An important part of Thompson's thinking is in accord with what SEFT and BFI were saying about the importance for all schools to address the various forms of popular culture with the strategy of teaching children to discriminate between good and bad.[69] He also stresses the importance of there being a supply of trained teachers from the training colleges.[70] Seizing on the freedom available in the curriculum in the 1960s for schools to innovate, Thompson promotes an élitist notion of experts in the sphere of cultural health, who would keep alive 'our distinctive national culture', a phrase which is not adequately explored.[71] The model offered for the practice of the cultural health team is curious, if not quaint: it is that of the peasant in the Middle Ages who, by attending Mass, 'learnt unconsciously something of the standards of art and music and oratory, which were the pride of Europe'.[72] He concludes by re-instating the familiar case that the pioneers of film appreciation had promoted.

> No great improvement can be expected till more and better education makes its impact and the media are met by a consciously discriminating public.[73]

Discrimination and Popular Culture rather upstaged the original conference, on the existence of which the book had justified its own publication. Indeed, Robert Hewison subsequently believed the book was a collection of the 'almost despairing papers' given at the Conference.[74]

The last of the books inspired by the conference is subtitled 'a practical approach for teaching' and acknowledges a debt not only to the conference but also to Hoggart, Williams, Thompson, Leavis, SEFT and *The Use of English*. The author, Nicholas Tucker, had also seen *The Popular Arts* in manuscript. Thus *Understanding the Mass Media* represents a summation of the contemporary attitudes and became the first book to promote in detail ways of teaching the range of the mass media. Its structure is a legacy of the conference in that each medium is isolated and described separately, following the structure in which individual speakers at the conference had made their presentations. The author does not attempt to offer approaches that look across the media to see what attributes they might have in common. The book is directed to the innovative teacher and provides such teachers with practical classroom strategies for approaching the various media.

Screen Education

Screen Education[75] published by UNESCO in 1964 also derived from a conference, the International Meeting on Film and Television Teaching held in Norway in 1962. Most of the book is written by Hodgkinson, who was about to leave for a teaching post in the USA.[76] He uses the occasion both to establish a wider use for the term 'screen education' to cover teaching film and television and also to attempt an analysis of what that term might involve from a more theoretical perspective, drawing on a range of sources. His argument begins with an examination of what screen language might be, though he does not follow the model of screen grammar that Spottiswoode had introduced. Instead he deals with the issues of production, reproduction and interpretation, where the combination of the various means of communication and reception possible through film and television serve to emphasise the power of screen language.[77] What then has to be addressed is how the educator should respond to the omnipresence of the screen language.

Here Hodgkinson draws on the work of Hoggart and Williams. From the latter, he concludes that 'the intermediaries – the controllers of the media – have become or are becoming the most important parties to communication'.[78] From Hoggart he infers that a means of communication so publicly processed must result in a 'bland culture'.[79] Hoggart had been influential in the Pilkington Report and accordingly Hodgkinson quotes from that report's findings: 'What the public wants and what it has the right to get is the freedom to choose from the widest possible range of programme matter. Anything less than that is deprivation'.[80] Concerns of the period about mass media were particularly focused on the effects on children. Hodgkinson diverts from his general case to quote from the Wheare and Nuffield reports and reverts to the Wheare Committee's solution of the necessity of producing through the schools a more discriminating public.[81]

If the means for achieving this is to be found, Hodgkinson argues there is a prior need to gain recognition for film and television as forms of art as a first step to their inclusion in the school curriculum. Starting from an organisational position, he draws on the work of Herbert Read, who had argued that what a child could cope with educationally was closely related to its development with age. Read believed that only at 14 were children capable of logical thought, 'and any attempt to force an early development of concepts is unnatural, and may be injurious'.[82] Hodgkinson modifies this to the extent of lowering the age of logical thinking to 11 or 12, but does not challenge Read's assumption. The new lower age designated for the onset of logical thinking, however, would conveniently allow screen education into the secondary school curriculum from the entry year.[83]

Having argued that children are ready for screen education, the need is to define it in such a way that both film and television qualify for inclusion in the curriculum. Williams's work assists here, since he demonstrates that new art forms are regularly resisted by those who see themselves as the custodians of the existing arts, so that Elizabethan drama and 18th-century novels were similarly discounted by the élite minority of their contemporaries. The ephemeral nature of television proves particularly challenging to its acceptability as an art form. But what it does enable is for children to become familiar with 'the basic conventions of the language' long before they attend school.[84] Hodgkinson is therefore in the curious position of acknowledging that children may read this visual language, which is 'unconsciously assimilated', but following Herbert Read he would then argue that only at secondary school age may the teacher intervene to educate them in the '*formal* qualities of screen art'.

Once the children are in a state of preparedness, what then are the aims of screen education? Here again Read is invoked and specifically his argument that 'the work of art, however concrete and objective, is not constant or inevitable in its effect: '*it demands the co-operation of the spectator.*'[85] Hodgkinson, takes this engagement of the child spectator with the screen's images as a starting point for screen education. What the child then proceeds to do with the empathy experienced is to contribute personally – 'which renders discussion of films and television such a rewarding and vital part of screen education'.[86] This then leads into an extensive quotation from a published account of discussions following screenings in a further education college. The experience of the teacher had been that his students were less concerned with the stance taken by filmmakers and more concerned with their own emotional responses to circumstances portrayed in the films.[87] Acceptance of this emotional unburdening by individuals, as an aim of screen education underpinned certain thematic approaches, which culminated in the use by the Humanities Curriculum Project of extracts from film and television fictional narratives as neutral evidence in discussions on topics such as war and youth.[88]

Having identified this over-riding aim of personal revelation through discussion, Hodgkinson needs to find a methodology. Once again he draws on Read and the latter's prescription for the three activities involved in art teaching: self-expression, observation and appreciation.[89] Self-expression had traditionally been manifested in the film-making area of screen education, where SFT had promoted the idea of the group-made film. Whatever educational justification had been advanced for this procedure, it did make a virtue of necessity. Classes were large; film-making equipment was expensive; film stock and processing were costly. Hodgkinson feels the need to accommodate the views of those like Don Waters, who argued not only for the value of the group film-making experience but also for the simulation of professionalism it encouraged.[90] However, Hodgkinson also anticipates the kind of work that would be developed a few years later at Hornsey College of Art when he foresees the use of 8mm cameras and portable tape recorders, allowing 'untutored forms of self-expression in a truly individual fashion'.[91]

Observation as a method would seem to accommodate many of the more traditional activities expected of children in relation to their viewing of films. Here Hodgkinson abandons Read and draws on Williams who proposes 'teaching the institutions'.[92] Much of the first decade of SFT had been focused on the scrutiny of the finished product, rather than on any process of mediation by which that product had been developed and presented. By introducing the concept of institutions in *Screen Education* the author was initiating the process of establishing a significant area of investigation for media education in the future.

The third method – of 'appreciation' – might have been presented as screen education coming full circle back to its film appreciation origins. But whereas film appreciation had started at a time when audiences were unfamiliar with television, now teachers were faced with media saturated children, so that their first task was to arouse enthusiasm for what might be an over familiar experience. Here both Read and Williams are invoked: the former to advocate the teaching of enjoyment, the latter to demolish the received and often repeated wisdom that by learning to appreciate the good, recognition of the bad would follow automatically.[93] Hodgkinson, having got to this point, withdraws from the challenge of where it might lead and concludes by asserting that it is the enthusiast who must lead the unspecified way.

What Hodgkinson then does in a separate chapter which takes the form of the appendix is to promote a specimen screen education syllabus he had developed and used over the first three years of a mixed secondary school. It is a curious mixture, which is probably the result of a process where the curriculum content was being revised in phases. The first year is distinctly old-fashioned in its concentration on the mechanics of film and photography, the history of the cinema and the introduction of notions of film grammar. By contrast, the second year is mostly about institutions and about other media. The final year combines both the thematic and genre approach and ends – albeit only 'for suitable classes' – with film-making.[94]

It becomes difficult to disentangle ends and means at this point:

> ...*the factual knowledge which the children acquire in this subject is of no value whatsoever except in so far as it enables them to approach these deeper and more valuable aspects of their education with confidence, understanding and a degree of objectivity.*[95] [Hodgkinson's italics]

The value of the course is that

> ...when the children have thoroughly acquired the habit of close analytical looking and listening, we enjoy each other's confidence, share a common language and enthusiasm, and are able to discuss freely the many questions of human behaviour, social *mores*, moral attitudes etc, which the best films and television programmes illumine.[96]

While one might readily accept that the knowledge of optics and of cinema history might be of limited value to the non-specialist, the author's argument is compromised. To spend a year looking at institutions and other media and then state that knowing this information is valueless, is an extraordinary claim when he is advocating discussion of human behaviour, which must inevitably be proscribed by those very institutions and agencies he has taught about. But then issues of representation did not find their way into his syllabus.

Inoculation

UNESCO produced a number of publications about film and media in the early 1960s (and continued to do so regularly in subsequent decades). One of the most substantial to be published before *Screen Education* arrived in 1964 was *Teaching about the Film* by J M L Peters, Director of the Netherlands Film Institute.[97] Drawing heavily on examples from British and American films (copiously illustrated with stills) and on the work of SEFT and BFI, the book seemingly aimed to be definitive on the subject. Its assertions were so emphatic that later screen educationists would have been able to quote from it as being sufficiently authoritative as to illustrate the limitations and idiosyncrasies of film teaching being undertaken at the time.

Such was the author's desire for precision there is a detailed appendix, identifying the skills and capacities of children in relation to film at any given age between 7 and 18. The four elements by which their progress may be determined are: understanding film language, aesthetic appreciation of films, critical assimilation of film content, and methods and practical possibilities. These in turn are tabulated against three aspects of the students' general mental development: perception and thinking, aesthetic receptiveness and creativity, and interest and criticism. So extreme were the claims being made that the book seems to have had negligible effect on film teaching developments in Britain. One of Peters's statements is notable, not for its insight but for its persistent legacy.

> Film-teaching (or film education) means helping young people to develop a critical defence towards those films which rely for their primary attraction on the display of technical novelties, on expensive-looking stars and on other superficial factors properly belonging more to the sphere of advertising, rather than on the true and inherent qualities of the cinema. Young people should, as far as possible, be helped to immunize themselves against the spell-casting power of films which use such means.[98]

The medical metaphor of immunization that Peters uses here was probably still thought appropriate at this stage of the post-war period, when children were becoming used to receiving a series of injections to ward off the diseases that had previously been life-threatening. Indeed, as already noted, S W Harris, President of the British Board of Film Censors, had used the term 'immunisation' in *The Film Teacher* in 1952, as a way of dealing with the 'spread of infection'.[99] But it is clear that in Peters's view this 'self immunization' process was not to be regarded as the whole of film education. During the 1960s, the phrase was not used and Peters's book had little influence beyond being listed in bibliographies, having been superseded in UNESCO's publications by *Screen Education*. As has been shown, there had always been a current of concern about the influence of the media on children, and this had been regularly addressed by those who wished to promote media education.[100] But it was only when later media educationists wanted to describe a history for their area that the related term 'inoculatory' was introduced. The re-emergence and persistence of this shorthand and dismissive term of reference is relevant to this investigation.

Roy Knight writing a lengthy editorial introduction to the BFI produced *Film in English Teaching* in 1972 traces the history of film in English teaching. At no point does he make mention of the 'inoculatory' approach.[101] Yet four years later Jim Cook and Jim Hillier emphasise the 'protective or inoculatory' approach in their paper introducing the BFI/SEFT 1976 Film and Television Studies Conference.[102] Len Masterman makes reference to 'the old inoculation theories' in 1980.[103] Ten years later James Halloran and Marsha Jones refer to the 'inoculatory or moral approach' and it is their paper that is subsequently quoted by the BFI in 1992.[104] None of these sources is able to direct readers to articles where media teachers make the case for the inoculatory approach, because none exist. The common authorities quoted are Leavis and Thompson,[105] the Spens Report,[106] the Crowther Report[107] and the Newsom Report.[108] None of these sources use the term 'inoculatory'.

The authority for the prevalence of the 'inoculatory approach' derives from Graham Murdock and Guy Phelps of the Leicester Centre for Mass Communication Research researching on behalf of the Schools Council in 1973.[109] The Council had initially thought that the conclusions of the research would enable them to make suggestions about 'relatively simple curriculum reform, perhaps with regard to media-appreciation classes or media-based teaching generally'.[110] But Murdock and Phelps were not subsequently instructed to discover what media teachers were doing. The focus of their research on behalf of the Schools Council evolved from that initial brief to become:

(a) the ways in which mass media impinged on the school situation, and
(b) the relationship between children's use of, and attitudes towards, the media on the one hand – and teachers' attitudes towards the media on the other.[111]

Subsequently after further modification

...it became the main aim of the study to determine the extent to which the differences in patterns of social relationships and systems of communication between schools on the one hand and leisure environments on the other are complementary or contradictory.[112]

Halloran, Director of the Leicester Centre, later revealed that the researchers' ultimate conclusion was 'about the quality of the relationship between teachers and pupils and the assumptions on which these relationships rest and, beyond that, about the kind of society we want'.[113]

It is essential therefore to understand in the light of these statements that Murdock and Phelps were not reporting on the teaching strategies of those who were designated as teachers of media or of those who had timetabled film or media lessons; they were looking at teachers' attitudes more generally. Part of their research was to compare the attitudes of those who taught science and those who taught English. The latter group included those who were expected in some schools to introduce their pupils to aspects of media. Whereas science teachers generally were required to teach only science, the researchers found that the English specialists were often to be found also teaching subjects other than English, and to feel as a consequence all the more strongly that their fundamental role was essentially the 'transmission of literary values'.[114] Therefore some teachers of English were on the defensive when completing the research questionnaires about their attitudes to the media, whereas science teachers did 'not need to be on the defensive, since not only is their basic subject matter relatively unambiguous, but they also spend the majority of their time teaching it'.[115]

Murdock and Phelps found among a sample of English teachers that there were four distinct approaches to media:

Approach 1 Media material seldom if ever introduced into lessons.
Approach 2 Media material not introduced and any attempt by pupils to introduce it is resisted.
Approach 3 Teachers actively combat the countervailing influence of mass media by exposing examples to criticism (the 'inoculation' approach).
Approach 4 The positive approach.[116]

The most frequently quoted part of the research is where the authors, carefully putting quotation marks around the word 'inoculation', state that this third approach 'commanded considerable support from both the comprehensive (32 per cent) and secondary modern schools (36 per cent) in our sample'.[117] But what does not get quoted is the description that follows which reveals in detail that the approach they are describing stems from an attitude to the media similar to the attitude to certain films of the 1950s, as identified by Peters.

> Underlying this approach is a particular view of the process of media influence.
> According to this view, the mass media can be seen as a series of machines controlled by self-seeking, and occasionally evil, men. These machines send out sounds and images which enter the uncritical minds of the passive audience and then turn them into compliant zombies who will willingly accept the implanted ideas, and may even act them out and behave in an anti-social manner.[118]

The language the researchers use to describe the attitude of these teachers is surely designed to signal to the reader that the inoculatory approach is a designation to be applied only to those instinctively hostile to the teaching of media, not a description of an authentic teaching strategy.

In more recent times, it is clear that the term 'inoculating' has come to be used as a portmanteau reference into which a wide range of past approaches may be bundled. Buckingham, citing Halloran and Jones and Masterman, states

> This process of training students in 'discrimination' and 'critical awareness' has been described by subsequent critics as a form of 'inoculation' – in other words a protection against disease.[119]

Over time the various references to 'inoculation' have been taken out of context and used indiscriminately to include and discredit a wide range of earlier approaches to media education

Movie Stirs

If the NUT Conference inaugurated a period when it became legitimate to explore a wider cultural landscape from the educational perspective SEFT had promoted, there were contemporaneous developments in which the traditional approaches to film criticism in the wider society were being revalued. These more analytic approaches were associated with a new generation of university educated film critics. Almost all had no formal film education and indeed their subject specialisms covered a wide range of both the arts and the sciences. What they had in common was years of frequent and regular visits to local cinemas to watch and enjoy mainstream films. That they were able to draw so productively on this ordinary experience was a practical vindication of what SEFT had long maintained: simply by going to the cinema and enjoying the experience, it was possible to acquire the necessary skills to become a discerning viewer.

50 Famous Films 1915–1945 was published by the BFI at the point when Huntley had replaced Reed as Controller of the National Film Theatre.[120] Described in the Foreword by Director James Quinn as 'one of several innovations', the book was designed for NFT regulars, who would have a permanent collection of the programme notes of what were the NFT's most predictable archive screenings. Authors of the notes on individual films are not credited and their comments follow no set pattern or length. It was, in effect, a collection of miscellaneous programme notes of rather more than 50 films, chosen without any coherent structure but masquerading as a serious BFI publication. The film reviewers of *Oxford Opinion* (specifically Ian Cameron and Victor Perkins) pounced, seeing it as 'worth examining for the light it throws on the standards and prejudices of this country's cinematic establishment'.[121] Previously, according to Cameron, they had planned that in that issue they would 'devote our space to a dissection of that distressing journal [*Sight and Sound*]'. But instead *50 Famous Films* provided a better target for attacking film criticism in Britain, as it demonstrated 'the pallid philanthropy that has always provided its criteria for evaluation'.[122]

Cameron was then approached by the Federation of Film Societies to write a piece for their journal *Film*, where the argument was presented in a more condensed form. Cameron saw traditional criticism as judging a film, 'on the acceptability of its social and political attitudes', where a significant proportion of the review might be the plot synopsis.[123] At the core of his criticism was the accusation that *Sight and Sound* and the *Monthly Film Bulletin* demonstrated intellectual laziness. What they did not do was talk about style.

> To judge a film on anything other than its style is to set up the critic's own views on matters outside the cinema against those of its maker.[124]

Responses came both from Penelope Houston, Editor of *Sight and Sound* and Peter John Dyer, Editor of *Monthly Film Bulletin*. Houston devoted six pages of the autumn 1960 edition of *Sight and Sound* to her reply to the original *Oxford Opinion* article.[125] Her tone is patronising and she seeks to present *Oxford Opinion* as parroting the ideas of others: 'A lot of this comes from *Cahiers du Cinéma*, along with the list of admired directors.' Choosing to interpret *Oxford Opinion*'s engagement with film style as 'reviewing a film in terms of half a dozen striking shots', her punch line was that 'cinema is about the human situation, not about spatial relationships'.[126] Dyer maintained the patronising distance in *Film* when he responded to Cameron's article in an earlier issue of that publication.

> I wouldn't employ them, because of their judgment, or rather their lack of it; and because it follows that they will enjoy neither influence nor staying power.[127]
>
> Their much vaunted obsession with style is backed up by nothing in their own criticism to encourage one to believe that they know the first thing about style.[128]

The NUT Conference had had an agenda about ways of approaching popular culture and of raising the expectations of its audience. At the same time the debate triggered by *Oxford Opinion* was confronting some of the issues which were around in the Popular Culture debate. A group of Oxford graduates was championing the most popular of popular art forms and challenging the assumptions of those whom they perceived as defending those 'quality' films from which the cinema was supposed to draw its credibility as high art. The 1950s had seen such intergenerational differences being the source material for controversy in various art forms. If there was a detectable difference in attitude among those attending the NUT conference, where some were hostile and others accepting, it had perhaps been anticipated by art critic Lawrence Alloway, writing in 1957. He described what he saw as an essentially fundamental, generational split. Born in 1926, he distinguishes the characteristics of his generation in two ways.

(1) We grew up with the mass media. Unlike our parents and teachers we did not experience the impact of the movies, the radio, the illustrated magazines. The mass media were established as a natural environment by the time we could see them.

(2) We were born too late to be adopted into the system of taste that gave aesthetic certainty to our parents and teachers.[129]

The implication of this argument is that the older conference members were likely to be separated from the younger because each cohort had a fundamentally different concept of cultural normality.

Alloway wrote on a range of topics connected to the visual and popular arts in the 1950s. He also lectured on film, but did not publish any writing on the subject at the time, although he did subsequently.[130] However, as a successful and influential art critic in the late 1950s, Alloway made radio broadcasts of some film reviews. Towards the end of this broadcasting period, in December 1960, he devoted a broadcast not only to praising the 'impressive film criticism' to be found in *Oxford Opinion* but additionally to dismissing the writings of its opponents at the BFI as 'stale and boring'.[131]

Now it seems to me that the Oxford critics have this sense of the movie as something complex and extensive, whereas the BFI writers and the weekly ladies have lost both their wonder and their curiosity.[132]

He also detects a similar spirit of rebellion in the Cambridge journal, *Granta*, which was following Oxford's lead. Charles Barr, then reviewing films for *Granta*, acknowledges the shift toward the Oxford journal's 'purposeful and committed line on cinema', which accelerated when Barr became Associate Editor of *Granta*.[133] Alloway does have one major criticism of both *Oxford Opinion* and *Sight and Sound*. 'Both groups are equally neglectful of the iconography of the movies'.[134] By the time that the *Oxford Opinion* writers had become editors of *Movie*, they were more persuaded by Alloway's arguments and it was in *Movie* that Alloway's writings about cinema were finally published.[135]

To have such controversy around British Film Criticism encouraged the London Region of the Federation of Film Societies to set up a debate in the following January where Penelope Houston, Peter John Dyer and John Gillett would appear for *Sight and Sound*.[136] Consequently, when Cameron, Perkins and Shivas turned up to put the *Oxford Opinion* case, they expected to be opposed by *Sight and Sound/Monthly Film Bulletin*. Instead however the BFI was represented by Paddy Whannel and Alan Lovell who had apparently volunteered to stand in for Houston and Dyer.[137] Unsurprisingly, the account of proceedings as reported in *Film* was not quite the antagonistic heavyweight encounter that its readers might have expected. Indeed, whilst listing the *Oxford Opinion* three as present, the *Film* account diplomatically avoids identifying who was actually opposing them.

The critical debate staged by the London Regional Group at the end of January did not lead, as was hoped, to an advance into more fruitful fields of argument.[138]

Although Cameron had a piece in a subsequent issue of *Film*,[139] it seems that he reserved his major response for *Screen Education*.[140] He writes mostly about the evolutionary process the *Oxford Opinion* writers had gone through as they reviewed films for that journal and in the process discussed their shared responses as a group. He begins however, by rounding on the institutional critics and in particular on Houston's attempt to discredit *Oxford Opinion* when she accused them of being attracted to 'jazz and the excitements surrounding it'. What excitements Cameron asks: 'alcoholism? drug addiction? prostitution?'[141] Though, as he acknowledged elsewhere, Houston's original response had been very effective in making a much wider readership aware of *Oxford Opinion* than that journal would ever have achieved on its own.[142]

A decade earlier, involvement in the Oxford based journal *Sequence* had provided a route for its editorial team of Gavin Lambert, Lindsay Anderson and Penelope Houston to various roles within and for the BFI, as Houston acknowledged.[143] If they had a banner to fight under it would have been Anderson's 'Stand Up, Stand Up'. The *Oxford Opinion* writers were different. They appeared to eschew a political stance.

> In view of our stated ideas about form and content, it is ridiculous to say that we 'prefer form to content', or that we 'refused to talk about meaning'. What we refuse to talk about is whether we agree with the attitude expressed in the film, and to judge it on that basis. This does not prevent us from going as far as we are capable in working out its meaning.[144]

When these same authors persevered and produced the first issue of *Movie* in Summer 1962, it started to become clear that what they were committed to was detailed textual analysis. When he wrote for *Screen Education*, Cameron was still at the point of needing to refute Houston's claim that 'cinema is about the human situation, not about spatial relationships'. Cameron dismissed this misinterpretation of the *Oxford Opinion* position by likening it to informing a reader that the novel was not about punctuation.[145] As Cameron's byline in *Screen Education* explained he was 'Late of *Oxford Opinion*, now teaching in London'. The first issue of *Movie* was a year away, and the piece in the SEFT journal was enabling Cameron to disengage from what was clearly an unproductive debate. As he concluded:

> In the end, the only way in which one can support one's critical theories is by writing criticism, rather than arguing about it. I'm fed up with writing about criticism. I'd rather write about films.[146]

Screen Education fails to hold the ring
It seemed briefly that *Screen Education* would be the vehicle for the continuation of this debate when Dai Vaughan, Co-editor of *Definition*, replied to Cameron.[147] *Definition* was a new film journal which first appeared in February 1960. Its principal editors were Alan Lovell, Boleslaw Sulik and Dai Vaughan, the latter having been a regular contributor

to SEFT journals. Vaughan attacks Cameron's assumption that it is possible to discuss a film and be neutral about the attitudes expressed in it. He asks 'How can we agree or disagree with the "attitude" that we ourselves have conferred upon a work in our act of response?' If *Oxford Opinion* and subsequently *Movie* were to be noted for avoiding the taking of a political stance, *Definition* was very much a journal of the Left. Like *Oxford Opinion* it had attacked *Sight and Sound*. Lovell had detected that 'the vitality of *Sequence* is changed into the complacency of the established magazine'.[148] He saw it as reluctant to offer any substantial critique of the British film industry largely because of the BFI's delicate relationship with the film industry. Consequently, the BFI funded journal that had both security of publication and distribution was perceived as merely reflecting 'what is happening without enthusiasm or insight'.[149] Vaughan in his challenge to Cameron was trying to shift him into the ranks of committed critics.

But *Definition* 3 rather than *Screen Education* saw three-way battle lines being drawn. Houston had responded to Lovell, and as with her response to *Oxford Opinion* she was essentially patronising, claiming that *Definition* was 'a trifle rocky on its feet'.[150] In the same issue Robin Wood – soon to become one of *Movie*'s regular writers – joined the *Oxford Opinion* position whilst making his own Leavisite leanings very clear.

> We urgently need a sharpening of critical instruments, some means of analysing what Dr F R Leavis would call 'local life', some method of practical criticism of *mise-en-scène*.[151]

Wood too could not resist patronising Lovell: 'One must be able, Mr Lovell, to analyse and understand these things before one has the right to dismiss Hitchcock as a "second rate director"'.[152] This was the first skirmish in what would later become a major critical debate between Wood and Lovell, under SEFT auspices in *Screen*.[153]

Probably the most significant of the contributions to the debate in this issue of *Definition* was that of Whannel, whose position, according to the Editorial, coincided with that of *Definition*. In fact, Whannel's article attempts to adopt a viewpoint which offers a panorama across the contemporary critical scene. Having by this stage already identified himself as both a critic from the New Left and a Leavisite, Whannel is least sympathetic to the 'general run of critics who claim a vague liberal position', by which he must mean his BFI colleagues on *Sight and Sound*. They are 'consistently taken in by the big subject, ever ready to judge a film by its plot outline and discuss it or approve it for its subject matter and overt moral position'.[154] However, he appears to align himself with Houston on the matter of *Oxford Opinion*'s French influenced position. He summarises her attack on *Oxford Opinion*.

> Not a difficult task, certainly in the English form, where the specific judgements seemed to have been taken over but the theoretical basis left in Paris.[155]

Whannel then offers a compromise position.

If we see our problem as teasing out the values embedded in the style of the film I think this undercuts most of the confusions that have cropped up in the argument.[156]

But, as a Leavisite, he has to offer a further mechanism for judging the film.

A film is an act of collaboration with the viewer. All the time, we are being asked to respond to hints and suggestions and create a world. In the good film these clues are many, the life portrayed is closely textured. In the bad film the clues are slight, the life portrayed is schematic.[157]

If in the matter of criticism it fell to Whannel to try to map out the territory, so after the success of the cinema session at the NUT Conference it was again Whannel, who wrote in *Screen Education* 'Where do we go from here?' 'Here' he defined as having two main obstacles – the absence of a clearly defined place for film within academic education, and the lack of a serious critical tradition. To take the second point first, Whannel makes no mention of the debates around the various journals with which he was then involved: 'The cinema has produced no great critics' was his view but his concern is however more specific. It is less that there is no 'literature of quality' about film, it is that critics are not seeing a relationship between popular education and serious critical writing.[158]

The bulk of his article derives from his concern with the place of film in the Academy. It soon becomes clear that for Whannel establishing film in the Academy is simply a starting point. Thus he describes in only the briefest reference the appointment in the previous October of Thorold Dickinson at the Slade School of Art as the first lecturer in film at a British university.[159] What exercises Whannel now is how a place in the Academy would alter the status not just of film, but also of popular culture, in the school. Whannel's emphasis on the importance of film's acceptance in the university as the means by which film would get proper recognition in schools was always a fundamental part of his thinking.[160] He is forced to look back thirty years for a model – to *Culture and Environment* and *Education and the University*.[161] These are not ideal models as he has to concede, since they embody the notion that high culture must be defended against popular culture.[162] He identifies the cinema as particularly important – sufficiently established and recognized as a popular art form to provide a model for approaching other popular art forms.

That both Cameron and Whannel should chose *Screen Education* 7 as the appropriate publication to publish the concluding pieces for their respective involvements in the *Oxford Opinion* debate and the NUT Conference would appear to demonstrate SEFT's position at the centre of events. It would be incorrect to draw this inference. At the time it was the only regular journal in publication which had significant numbers of readers with an interest in both debates. Cameron's 'Purely for Kicks' is printed as the second of a sequence of two articles headed confusingly 'University Report'. It follows a descriptive account of a university student film society. There is no context provided to link 'Purely for Kicks' to the previous series of articles published elsewhere that made up this important debate.

The Editorial to *Screen Education* 7 fails to respond to any of the issues that Cameron or Whannel raises. Instead, in the double page spread headed 'Concern for Children', Wills takes a view similar to that which had apparently triggered the original NUT conference motion.

> The child has seen crook and cop, outlaw and marshall, wife and mistress, all employing the same means to achieve their ends. He has been deluged by the devices of an acquisitive society which appear to offer him extravagant luxury on 'extended and easy terms'. Superficial, trivial and shallow conformity has been put on a pedestal for him to admire.[163]

He is in effect refusing to engage with how Whannel is defining the post-conference position. It would be several years before the Society would address the issue of its journal's idiosyncratic and increasingly marginal role.

Notes

1. Richard Hoggart *The Uses of Literacy* London: Chatto and Windus 1957; Raymond Williams *Culture and Society* London: Chatto and Windus 1958
2. *Report of the Committee on Broadcasting* (Pilkington Report) London: HMSO 1962
3. J M L Peters *Teaching about the Film* Paris: UNESCO 1961.
4. A W Hodgkinson *Screen Education – Teaching a critical approach to cinema and television* Paris: UNESCO 1964
5. *The National Film School – Report of a Committee to consider the need for a national film school* London: HMSO 1967
6. The term 'landmark' was first used by Marghanita Laski in proposing the vote of thanks at the end of the Conference. *The Schoolmaster* November 4 1960 p 948.
7. Tom Steele *The Emergence of Cultural Studies 1945–65* London: Lawrence & Wishart 1997 Chapter 1 pp 9–32
8. Stuart Laing *Representation of Working Class Life 1957–1964* London: Macmillan 1986 p 193
9. Brian Groombridge in interview with the author 3 August 2004 and Fred Jarvis in interview on 15 July 2004.
10. J Morgan Roberts 'Cinema Behaviour Problems' *Screen Education* 9 July/August 1961 pp 42–43
11. In *The Film Teacher* of Spring 1953 much of the issue was devoted to consideration of 'the question of violence'. Simultaneously the BFI published *Are They Safe at the Cinema?* by Janet Hills.
12. Martin Barker *A Haunt of Fears* London: Pluto Press 1984
13. See below for the references made by Butler, Exworthy and King

14. Mark Abrams *The Teenage Consumer* London: Press Exchange Ltd July 1959
15. 15–18 (Crowther Report) London HMSO 1959 pp 222–223
16. Stuart Hall and Paddy Whannel *The Popular Arts* London: Hutchinson Educational 1964
17. Interview with Jarvis op cit
18. National Union of Teachers *Popular Culture and Personal Responsibility* Verbatim Report London: NUT 1961 pp 341–347
19. Brian Groombridge *Popular Culture and Personal Responsibility A Study Outline* London: National Union of Teachers May 1961
20. *Verbatim Report* p 1
21. Ibid Frontispiece
22. Ibid p iii
23. *The Schoolmaster* November 4 1960 p 941
24. Ibid p 941 The President was SW Exworthy
25. Ibid p 942
26. Interview with Jarvis op cit
27. Popular Culture and Personal Responsibility Conference Programme October 1960
28. *Verbatim Report* p 253
29. Ibid p 251
30. Ibid p 178
31. Ibid p 96
32. Ibid p 98
33. *Nice Time*, a product of the BFI Experimental Film Fund directed by Claude Goretta and Alain Tanner was a short film about a typical Saturday night in London's Piccadilly Circus.
34. Ibid p 94
35. Ibid p 95
36. Ibid p 98
37. Ibid p 104
38. Ibid p 104
39. *Screen Education* 6 January 1961 p 31
40. Brian Groombridge op cit
41. Ibid p 5
42. Brian Groombridge and Paddy Whannel 'Pop, Posh and Pedagogue' in *Times Educational Supplement* 5 January 1950 p 217
43. Ibid p 216
44. Ibid p 217
45. Ibid p 217
46. Ibid p 217
47. Ibid p 217
48. Mildred Masheder, Anthea Holme and Anthony Higgins *Family Viewing – a study of early evening television* London: Council for Children's Welfare November 1960
49. Ibid p 39

50. Ibid p 1 The authors acknowledge assistance in devising their research methods from Hilde Himmelweit and Joseph Treneman.

51. Ibid p II

52. Ibid p 40

53. A similar exercise was repeated (but with considerably greater publicity) in 1983 by the Department of Education and Science under Sir Keith Joseph. See the references to *Popular TV and Schoolchildren* in Chapter 10.

54. 'The Pilkington Committee A summary of evidence submitted by the Society to the Committee on Broadcasting' *Screen Education 8* May-June 1961 pp 4–5

55. Ibid p 5

56. 'Television Supplement' *New Left Review 7* January- February 1961 pp 30–48

57. Ibid p 45

58. Ibid p 48

59. Raymond Williams *Britain in the Sixties: Communications* Harmondsworth: Penguin Books 1962; Stuart Hall and Paddy Whannel *The Popular Arts* London: Hutchinson Educational 1964; Denys Thompson (Ed) *Discrimination and Popular Culture* Harmondsworth: Penguin 1965; Nicholas Tucker *Understanding the Mass Media* Cambridge: Cambridge University Press 1966

60. Steele op cit p 184

61. Hall and Whannel op cit p 311

62. Stuart Hall in interview with the author 17 March 2004.

63. Ibid p 312

64. Fred Jarvis in interview with the author 15 July 2004 recalled a phone call asking for his approval when the book was ready for printing.

65. Denys Thompson (Ed) *Discrimination and Popular Culture* Harmondsworth: Penguin 1964 p 9

66. Ibid p 15

67. The teacher quoted by Thompson by way of illustration is Stuart Hall whose attendance at the Conference in a personal capacity was probably more appropriately ascribed to his then role as Editor of *New Left Review*. There is no evidence from the List of Participants that Thompson attended the Conference.

68. Thompson op cit p 19

69. Ibid p 17

70. Ibid p 19

71. Ibid p 18

72. Ibid p 18

73. Ibid p 22

74. Robert Hewison *Culture and Consensus: England, Art and Politics since 1940* London: Methuen 1995 p 105

75. A W Hodgkinson *Screen Education* Paris: UNESCO 1964.

76. Ibid Preface [p 3]

77. Ibid p 9

78. Ibid p 10 The quotes from Raymond Williams are from *Communications* Harmondsworth: Penguin 1962.

79. Richard Hoggart is quoted from his 1960 paper to the Congress for Cultural Freedom Conference in Berlin 'The Quality of Cultural Life in Mass Society'.

80. Ibid p 11 The quote is from *Report of the Committee on Broadcasting* London: HMSO 1962 Cmdr 1753

81. Ibid p 11 The quote is from *Report of the Committee on Children and the Cinema* London: HMS0 1950 Cmdr 7945. The Nuffield Foundation funded H T Himmelweit, A N Oppenheim, P Vince *Television and the Child* Oxford: Oxford University Press 1958.

82. Ibid p 14 Herbert Read is quoted from *Education Through Art* London: Faber and Faber 1943.

83. Ibid p 140

84. Ibid p 16

85. Ibid p 18

86. Ibid p 18

87. The article quoted is by Norman Fruchter 'Two Hours a Week' *Sight and Sound* Vol 31 No 4 Autumn 1962 pp 198–200

88. See below Chapter 5

89. Ibid p 21

90. Ibid p 23

91. Ibid p 23

92. Ibid p 24

93. Ibid p 24

94. Ibid p 27

95. Ibid p 27

96. Ibid p 27

97. JML Peters *Teaching about the Film* Paris UNESCO: 1961 Almost simultaneously there appeared *The Influence of the Cinema on Children and Adolescents* Paris: UNESCO 1961, an annotated international bibliography. In 1964 *Screen Education* (Hodgkinson op cit) was published.

98. Peters op cit p 20

99. Sir Sidney Harris 'The Child and the Cinema' *The Film Teacher* Summer 1952 pp 6–10

100. Particularly the Centre for Mass Communication Research at Leicester University, the London School of Economics and the University of Leeds.

101. Roy Knight (Ed) *Film in English Teaching* London: Hutchinson 1972

102. Jim Cook and Jim Hillier 'The Growth of Film & Television Studies 1960–1975' London BFI Education April 1976.

103. Len Masterman *Teaching About Television* London: Macmillan Press 1980 p 19

104. James D. Halloran and Marsha Jones *Learning About the Media: Communication and Society* Paris: UNESCO 1986 pp 55–60 reproduced in Manuel Alvarado and Oliver Boyd-Barrett (Eds) *Media Education: An Introduction* London: BFI/Open University 1992 pp 10–13

105. F R Leavis and Denys Thompson *Culture and Environment* London: Chatto and Windus 1934

106. Board of Education *Secondary Education with Special Reference to Grammar Schools and Technical High Schools* London: HMSO 1938
107. Central Advisory Council for Education (England) London: HMSO 1959
108. Central Advisory Council for Education *Half Our Future* London: HMSO 1963
109. Graham Murdock and Guy Phelps *Mass Media and the Secondary School* London: Macmillan 1973
110. James D Halloran *Mass Media and Society* Leicester: Leicester University Press 1974 p 14
111. Murdock and Phelps op cit p vi
112. Ibid p vi
113. Halloran op cit p 14
114. Murdock and Phelps op cit p 14
115. Ibid p 14
116. Ibid p 33
117. Ibid p 38
118. Ibid p 37
119. David Buckingham *Media Education* London: Polity Press 2003 p 7
120. National Film Theatre *Fifty Famous Films 1915–1945* London: BFI 1960
121. Victor Perkins 'Fifty Famous Films 1915–1945' *Oxford Opinion* No 38 April 30 1960 p 36
122. Ian Cameron 'Films' *Oxford Opinion* op cit
123. Ian Cameron 'All Together Now' *Film* 25 September/October 1960 p 12
124. Ibid p 13
125. Penelope Houston 'The Critical Question' *Sight and Sound* Autumn 1960 Vol 29 No 4 pp 160–165
126. Ibid p 163
127. Peter John Dyer 'Counter Attack' *Film* 26 November/December 1960 p 8
128. Ibid p 9
129. Lawrence Alloway 'Personal Statement' *Ark 19* Spring 1957 reprinted in *The Independent Group: Postwar Britain and the Aesthetics of Plenty* David Robins (Ed) Cambridge Massachusetts: The MIT Press 1990 p 165
130. Lawrence Alloway *Violent America: The Movies 1946–1954* New York: Museum of Modern Art 1971. p 7
131. Lawrence Alloway Transcript of Extract from the programme 'Comment' transmitted 15 December 1960 on the BBC Third Programme p 1
132. Ibid p 1 The 'weekly ladies' is presumably a reference to Dilys Powell of *The Sunday Times* and Caroline Lejeune of *The Observer*.
133. Charles Barr in interview with the author 7 June 2005.
134. Alloway transcript op cit p 2
135. 'Lawrence Alloway on the Iconography of the Movies' *Movie* 7 February and March 1963 pp 4–6
136. 'The Current Picture' *Film* 27 January/February 1961 p 7

137. This is as recalled by Victor Perkins in interview with the author on 19 April 2005. Alan Lovell in interview on 7 June 2005 had only a "vague memory" of the event. It would appear from a report in *Film* 28 March/April 1961 that Gillett was also present.

138. 'The Current Picture' *Film* 28 March/April 1961 p 4

139. Ian Cameron 'What's the Use?' *Film* 28 March/April 1961 pp 10–11

140. Ian Cameron 'Purely for Kicks' *Screen Education* 7 March–April 1961 pp 31–33

141. Ibid p 31

142. Ibid p 31

143. Houston op cit p 162

144. Cameron *Screen Education* 7 op cit p 33

145. Ibid p 33

146. Ibid p 33

147. Dai Vaughan *Screen Education* 9 July–August 1961 p 50

148. Alan Lovell 'The Best we've Got' *Definition* 2 p 3

149. Ibid p 3

150. Penelope Houston 'Enthusiasm for What?' *Definition* 3 p 8

151. Robin Wood 'New Criticism?' *Definition* 3 p 11

152. Ibid p 11

153. Alan Lovell 'Robin Wood – A Dissenting View' *Screen* March/April 1969 Volume 10 No 2 pp 42–55; Robin Wood 'Ghostly Paradigm and HCF: An Answer to Alan Lovell' *Screen* May/June 1969 Vol 10 No 3 pp 35–48

154. Paddy Whannel 'Receiving the Message' *Definition 3* p 14

155. Ibid p 14

156. Ibid p 15

157. Ibid p 15

158. Paddy Whannel 'Where Do We Go From Here?' *Screen Education* 7 March–April 1961 p 7

159. Ibid p 8

160. Alan Lovell in interview with the author 7 June 2005 reinforced this point

161. F R Leavis *Education and the University* London: Chatto and Windus 1948

162. Ibid p 9

163. H R Wills 'Concern for Children' *Screen Education* 7 March–April 1961 pp 4–5

5

Film in Education – The Back of Beyond

The Crowther Report does establish a better balance of blame than the NUT Resolution. But a more fundamental objection can be made to both statements in the way they define the problem itself. Both passages imply a clear distinction between the two cultures – the culture of the mass media and the traditional culture of sophisticated arts. And both see these as standing in opposition to each other.

Stuart Hall and Paddy Whannel, 1964

The Newsom Report provides 'official' support for the introduction of film and television study in schools, specifically in the context of the proposed raising of the school-leaving age. The necessity for providing a liberal studies offer to short-term release students in further education provides another opportunity for screen education at the margins. Publishers become intrigued by the potential this new market offers. But the increased interest from teachers and the number of enquiries consequently received by SEFT puts great pressure on the Society's volunteers. The new Labour Government of 1964 funds the BFI more generously and so its Director and Education Department make SEFT an offer the Society cannot refuse.

During the 1960s the status of film and television study changed considerably and by the end of the decade many more teachers and lecturers were actively involved in a range of developments. BFI and SEFT were both instrumental in these developments and also the beneficiaries of them. There were major events outside the arena of film and television teaching which greatly assisted in the process. The change of government in 1964 was one such defining event. There were others too, affecting in particular the opportunities for screen education in further education colleges and secondary schools. In the former, colleges became obliged to offer students released for specialist training by employers the additional opportunity to participate in liberal or general studies courses. In secondary schools there was the expectation that the long delayed raising of the school leaving age to sixteen was about to happen and that new areas of interest had to be found for these additional students.

The Newsom Report

Consequently the biggest potential area for the expansion of film and television study was to be in secondary schools, where the publication of *Half Our Future* in 1963 had made the clearest call to date for the introduction of film and media teaching into schools, albeit for the 'less able' half of the student population.[1] *Half Our Future* very quickly became known as the 'Newsom Report' after its Chairman, J H Newsom, who had been Chief Education Officer for Hertfordshire in the immediate post-war years. While in post there he had actively encouraged film appreciation and presented reports on a range of related topics to the County Education Committee in 1950.[2] Given Newsom's earlier promotion of film teaching in an educationally progressive county and at a time when his reports would have coincided with the publication of the Wheare Committee's report, it seems that *Half Our Future* had a very sympathetic author when it came to make its observations on film and television in education.

Immediately following the Report's publication, the BFI Education Department seized on the relevance of what it said and produced a duplicated handout detailing the eight paragraphs from the Report that had the greatest relevance for film and television teaching. The Department did not however add any editorial comment.[3] SEFT's response was delayed. This was probably because of the timing of the Newsom Report, which was published in August 1963. Consequently it appeared too late for comment in the September/October issue of *Screen Education* which was ready for distribution at the start of the autumn term, while copy for the *1964 Yearbook* was complete and ready for the printers by early October. In the first *Screen Education* of 1964, there is a brief introduction from Don Waters, then Chairman, but the content of the subsequent article 'Newsom on the Screen Media' was apparently lifted from the BFI's duplicated document, though with the omission of two of the eight paragraphs quoted there.[4] There appears to be no logic as to the exclusion of these two paragraphs, 378 and 479. The former endorses film-making which would certainly have commanded agreement from SEFT committee members at the time. The latter argues for the value of the creative arts in helping young people 'to come to terms with themselves'. Unlike the BFI's publication of its selection of quotations without further comment, Waters's introduction is unequivocal in its endorsement.

> We have had support for screen education in official documents before – the Wheare Committee – the Pilkington Report – but never such powerful advocacy and expressed so much in our own terms as it is in this remarkable document, the report of the Newsom Committee.

But, there never was such ammunition for the teacher and the would-be teacher of screen education. It is the duty of every one of us to use it – on every possible occasion and as effectively as we know how.[5]

There is however a curious postscript to the quoted paragraphs: from Alex Richardson, editor of SEFT's *Film and TV News* which had appeared in the preceding autumn.[6] He was an important presence on the Committee and was later to become SEFT's first paid officer. The postscript is both strident and personal. Richardson taught then at Cornwell School in East Ham, the dilapidated buildings of which had been pictured in the Newsom Report where photographs had been selected to juxtapose images of good and bad facilities in secondary schools. It is on this initial peg that he fixes his response but then contrives to enlist SEFT into his diatribe. His concluding paragraphs are printed below. They demonstrate two important features which affected SEFT's organisation in the 1960s: Ray Wills's apparent reluctance to exert editorial control over *Screen Education* even in instances where SEFT as an organisation was inappropriately invoked; Richardson's readiness to use his position within SEFT to give endorsement to what were his personal views.

I wouldn't mind particularly that Cornwell will not get new buildings for yet another five years (ha! ha!). If I felt that at least Newsom would be backed by money and political enthusiasm. If you could feel that a significant minority really *cared*. But make no mistake about it. I feel badly.

Half Our Future is surely one of the most important Government documents yet prepared – and not just about education. It's about a world which does justice to all its children. They must be taught well. Their real needs must be served first. They must be recognised for what they are: total, vulnerable, powerful human beings. All of them.

When Newsom is finally shelved (by all parties) then it's only the teachers left. In every type of school. We can choose to stay forever with our local children, and teach them, give them everything that can be given with utter honesty and complete concern. Or we can try to become Prime Minister.

You could surrender.

If the quotations printed above from the Report seem like a SEFT manifesto that's how it should be. Teachers *can* effect changes in the greatest conservative system of the twentieth century. SEFT may not win money from people who say screen education is invaluable, but it will still exist when they have built all those universities for the sake of the economy. Because, if nothing else, SEFT represents teachers.

Half Our Future cost the nation only £5,550 to prepare. What's the price of a revolution?[7]

The paragraphs that are quoted by both BFI and SEFT provided powerful support for ideas both organisations had been advocating. Unlike the Wheare Report which made only incidental references to film appreciation within education, the Newsom Report repeatedly stresses the need for teachers to take account of popular culture. The key sentiments of each paragraph are as follows:

87. There is much scope for valuable consumer studies and in examining the influence is extended by newspapers, magazines, comics, advertisement hoardings, films and television. But it would be wrong to leave pupils with the idea that everything they like is bad, or that all criticism is negative. A sound, positive judgement must start with valuing properly the good things they enjoy.[8]

216. We believe that teachers should reckon with these facts, and that their own training should help them to take account of television as a social force, as well as offering them some preparation for the proper handling of school broadcasts in sound and television.[9]

217. Nevertheless, not only through television, but in a very large field of popular culture – music, films, theatre, journalism – pupils can learn, with guidance, to sharpen their perceptions.[10]

474. Here we should wish to add a strong claim for the study of film and television in their own rights, as powerful forces in our culture and significant sources of language and ideas.[11]

475. The culture provided by all the mass media, but particularly by film and television, represents the most significant environmental factor that teachers have to take into account.[12]

476. By presenting examples of films selected for the integrity of their treatment of human values, and the craftsmanship with which they were made, alongside others of mixed or poor quality, we can not only build up a way of evaluating but also lead the pupils to an understanding of film as a unique and potentially valuable art form in its own right as capable of communicating depth of experience as any other art form.

While there is a supply, even if inadequate, of specialist and other teachers with some training in literature, music, art and drama, there are very few teachers equipped to deal with the art forms that most closely touch the boys and girls of this Report. We are glad to note that some training colleges have begun to respond to this challenge by offering courses in film both as major and minor elements in a course.[13]

The production of the Report had been triggered by the prospect of the planned raising of the school leaving age to 16, though this was not in the event to be accomplished for a further decade. Such was the extent not only of the generally positive response given to Newsom, but also of the concerns about the curriculum development that would precede the raising of the school leaving age (ROSLA), that individual film teachers saw an opportunity to offer their subject as an innovative part of the solution. SEFT followed up the comments in *Screen Education* with a Conference in May 1964, 'After Newsom…Making a Start in Screen Education'.[14] An undoubted effect of *Half Our Future* was to raise the profile of film and television teaching and to initiate questions and controversies where, previously in the interests of protecting this embryonic area of study, it had been politic to maintain a consensus. As an initial demonstration of how alliances began to fall apart post Newsom, it is instructive to consider attitudes to the use of the numerous commercially sponsored films available on 16 mm in the 1960s.

Sponsored Films in the Classroom

Many large industrial and commercial organisations had their own production units and film libraries funded as part of their promotional activities. Annual screenings took place at venues such as the National Film Theatre where the latest releases of sponsored films might be viewed. For some years SEFT was formally associated with these Festivals of Free Loan Films organised by the Federation of Film Societies.[15] The particular appeal to teachers was that these films were almost always available on free loan. Such films were valuable as up-to-date and effective visual aids for science or geography teachers, but increasingly some of the films became of interest to film teachers who could, for example, hire *We are the Lambeth Boys* (Karel Reisz 1957) and *Everyday Except Christmas* (Lindsay Anderson 1957) from the Ford Film Library, *Terminus* (John Schlesinger 1961) from British Transport Films and *The Back of Beyond* (John Heyer 1954) from the Petroleum Films Bureau.

To some on the Committee therefore it seemed an appropriate SEFT project would be to produce a booklet on the 'Best of the Sponsored Films', and indeed a sponsored film supplement was published in *Screen Education* where the impending publication of the booklet was repeatedly trailed.[16] Members' views as to what films should be included were sought by questionnaires in the journal. The plans for this forthcoming publication divided the SEFT Committee in 1965. Jim Kitses, by then BFI Teacher Adviser and sitting on the committee as the Institute's representative, led the argument that this was a retrograde step diverting film education away from its more appropriate interest in mainstream cinema.[17]

Undoubtedly there was a benefit to SEFT from the existence of so many free-loan libraries: a significant chunk of its journals' regular advertising income came from the libraries repeated advertisements. This may also have encouraged support for the project among some Committee members. They were however particularly encouraged by learning of the success that a SEFT member, Eric Else, had with an idea that he put to Longmans in 1965.[18] Publishers generally had responded to the huge potential market in secondary schools that the Newsom Report had not only identified but celebrated. Suddenly it seemed appropriate to give textbooks a facelift and perhaps novelty rather than innovation became the driving force. Else's book *The Back of Beyond* is unique. It is essentially a textbook for use in secondary schools, built around the viewing of a single free loan film made in Australia by Shell and distributed in the UK by the Petroleum Films Bureau.[19] The book is now valuable for providing an insight into the confusion of ideas circulating around film teaching which preceded the date of its eventual publication in 1968 and will therefore be considered here in that context.

The book opens with the acknowledgement of two influences: first of the Newsom Report (with the quotation of paragraphs 474 and 476); and of a SEFT interview with John Heyer, the film's director, by Alex Richardson.[20] Else describes the book simply as 'a classroom aid to the study of *The Back of Beyond*'. Its contents include maps, poems, extracts from works of fiction and description, all with linking material by Else. In addition there are thirty pages of very detailed, shot by shot frame analyses of sequences from the film. There is however little indication of the curriculum area that the book is targeting, presumably to enable the publisher to market the book as widely as possible. Only at the end under 'Notes for the Teacher' is there a section 'Appreciation of *The Back of Beyond*'.[21]

The appreciation is a painstakingly detailed chronological account, sequence by sequence, in which Else recalls his responses to the film, with occasional asides to the teacher as to his assessment of the film's effectiveness at particular points. Else's commentary serves to provide any teacher who decides to use the book with a backup of points of cinematic interest, to which s/he might refer in the classroom. In case the teacher might doubt the value of the enterprise, the book concludes with an implicit reference to the British documentary tradition and its revered place in film appreciation.

> *The Back of Beyond* is probably the last of the great romantic documentaries; it is vigorous and life-affirming and has a quality of immediacy that makes it a memorable experience both as a work of film art and as a tribute to the resilience of the human spirit.[22]

Of greater interest now are two very specific aspects of the book. Firstly, Else tries to context an appropriate methodology for looking at the film and attempts specifically to reconcile what he identifies as the approaches of Stuart Hall on the one hand, and Ernest Lindgren on the other. To do so, he draws from *Film Teaching* and *The Art of the Cinema*.[23] The former was the first substantial publication from Whannel's Education Department, the latter a recent revision of Lindgren's 1940s original. Secondly, he provides detailed shot by shot analyses – using frame enlargements – of four sequences from the film. These are accompanied by production stills showing the camera crew at work.

At the time Else was writing, the auteur approach was becoming established as the dominant critical stance and in quoting Hall he is acknowledging the consequent attitude to style which introduces *Film Teaching*. '...not as something imposed upon the subject already given but as the way in which a director conveys to us his inner meanings'.[24] Else's book is a celebration of director Heyer as the film's author. Else chooses to quote from Hall in a way that enables him to link Hall closely to Lindgren.

> One has to start at the other end -- with the whole response; and then, by relating the *content* to the *technique* show how the one has modified the other. The language of the cinema has to be approached by way of the film's *meaning*, and the meaning is what the director wants to say or show (his intention), what he has selected (the content), and how he has translated it into sound and images (his language).[25]

Having established that the 'language of the cinema' is on Hall's agenda, Else is then able to move into the probably more familiar Lindgren territory of film language with an extensive list of the options possible, under such headings as camera setup, camera movement, editing, spoken word, natural sound etc. It is through the constant referencing of these that Else's appreciation is then structured.

The second noteworthy aspect of the book is its display of complete sequences from the film broken down into individual frame enlargements for each shot. Having previously endorsed the authority of film language, inclusion of the author's sequences of frame enlargements is perhaps inevitable, given that he had ready access to a print of the film. But their function in this book seems superfluous. The detail of the breakdown (with information on the content of the various sound tracks accompanying each shot) would be useful for a student tackling an undergraduate film-making course, but understanding the significance of the amount of detailed information which is being revealed here would have been beyond the needs of the 'Newsom' students at whom the book is aimed. Had an enterprising teacher removed these pages and cut the stills into individual shots which the children might then put into order in advance of viewing the film the teacher would have anticipated the photo-play exercises that were to become available in the 1970s.

Changes at SEFT

The controversy in the Committee was such that the pamphlet on sponsored films never reached the printers, though some preliminary work was done on it. The dispute was not in itself the trigger for changes in the Committee, but changes in the composition of its membership certainly would have diminished support for the project, since some of SEFT's longest serving members were to leave the Committee in the mid-1960s, although the final departure of some was protracted by their retaining notional places on the Committee while working abroad. Don Waters left the UK in 1964 to become Head of Educational Television in Zambia. He was followed by Tony Hodgkinson who went to the USA to become Professor of Film in Boston. Tony Higgins gained a secondary school headship in Nottingham and founder member Paul Alexander finally left in 1967 to continue teaching in the primary sector in London. Their respective post-SEFT situations illustrate the dilemma facing film teachers at that time: whether to concentrate one's energy on developing a career within the established UK educational framework or to risk attempting to make a career out of what had begun as a personal enthusiasm. Such significant departures did not go unnoticed. Stanley Reed, Director of the BFI from 1964, confided to the then SEFT Chairman R C Vannoey, who was a survivor from the Committee of the 1950s, that the gaps left by these departures made the Society appear less substantial.[26] Paddy Whannel however chose to view the situation more positively and, anticipating these departures, set out to establish better relations with the Society soon after this author took over as Secretary in 1965.[27]

Whannel, as Head of the BFI Education Department, became the key figure in shaping film education in the 1960s. In *The Popular Arts* both its authors (Whannel and Stuart Hall) propose a 'permanent study laboratory' in which their ideas might develop.[28] In the event Hall was soon deputising for Richard Hoggart and consequently able to set about attracting researchers to the Birmingham Centre for Contemporary Cultural Studies. Whannel in a relatively short period between 1964 and 1970 was to transform his department into the film study equivalent of an 'academy in waiting'. Had they been able to combine the staffing level and facilities that Whannel had achieved for the Education Department with the postgraduate students that Hall was supervising in Birmingham, their ambition for a permanent study laboratory would have become a reality. As Whannel's department strengthened its establishment from the mid 1960s, so SEFT's influence temporarily diminished, although BFI Education continued to promote the existence of SEFT in its literature.

Following its change of name and well publicised presence within the Joint Council for Education through Art and at the NUT Conference, SEFT had started the 1960s with ambitions for growth. There were plans for a range of publishing ventures. Its occasional publications (detailed later in this chapter) proved to be very successful; others proved to be less so and were soon aborted. Among those in this latter category was *Teen Screen*, an attempt to produce an offshoot magazine for teenagers that ran to only two issues in 1962.[29] Probably connected with this publishing project was the proposal SEFT put to BFI that the two organizations should co-operate in the presentation of Saturday morning screenings for teenagers at the National Film Theatre as an opportunity for progression with age from the established children's shows in the commercial cinemas. Reed (then BFI Secretary) declined the proposal because of 'pressure of work on the Education Department'.[30] *Film and TV News* was another short-lived publication which made it only to a first edition in Autumn 1963.[31] Another anticipated but aborted project was to be a filmstrip advertised in *Screen Education* as being ready for purchase in October 1962.[32] To demonstrate the recognition SEFT intended to give to television, the filmstrip was designed to reveal television production methods at the recently opened BBC Television Centre. Issues of copyright ownership intervened after a series of slides had been made around the production of an edition of *The Black and White Minstrel Show* and the project was discreetly abandoned.[33]

Other new projects were however more successful. Teachers of practical film-making were informed in *Screen Education* 19 of the Committee's decision to make available to SEFT members basic film-making equipment.[34] With the assistance of the Rank Organisation, SEFT had acquired three 16mm cameras which together with tripods and light meters were available for hire. These sets of equipment were housed with committee members in different parts of the country and their availability advertised regularly in *Screen Education*. There was also contact with the Rank Film Distribution Library where SEFT was involved in the selection of some extracts from Rank films.[35] In 1962 the first SEFT Summer School was held as a one-week course under the umbrella summer school arrangements of the Educational Development Association (EDA).[36] By 1963 it had become a two-week course in August offering a programme not that dissimilar from the Summer School offered by the BFI, with screenings, lectures, discussion and an important practical film-making element.[37] Based in a training college in Carmarthen this was an appropriate arrangement for SEFT, as the EDA had established publicity machinery and handled all domestic issues. The autonomous BFI school required a much greater level of staffing, though it tended to recruit larger numbers. The SEFT Summer School continued under similar arrangements as an annual event throughout the 1960s, though its location varied.

The Education Department on hold
If SEFT had seemed to be in the ascendant in the early sixties, the Education Department was less confident – at least in public – about its own future. In his 1963 Department Report Whannel identifies the strengths and weaknesses of his situation as he begins to envisage the potential for expansion.[38] His fundamental case is that he is under-staffed, with only Peter Harcourt as Staff Lecturer to assist on the professional side. Harcourt was a recent Cambridge graduate who had been taught by Leavis. In the 1950s the availability of SFT committee members to step in and be available on occasions to strengthen the Department, had perhaps helped to give it a more substantial presence. By the 1960s this arrangement no longer provided the critical and intellectual focus Whannel sought to promote. The inputs SEFT members had made were probably best exemplified by the contributions made at the NUT conference when Higgins and Waters provided evidence of the kinds of film teaching which were possible. By 1963 Whannel clearly wanted to move beyond this stage. He identifies that a point has been reached

> ...in which there is a need for fundamental thinking. The teacher of English Literature can fall back on the work of a long line of distinguished scholars and critics. The teacher of Film has to supply his own scholarship as he goes along, relying on a mere handful of books which in themselves represent an increasingly dated approach to the subject.

This is not a problem isolated from teaching within the school. The work in the classroom will also suffer if it is not supported by original studies.[39]

Typical of Whannel's consistent position is this last sentence. Having been emergency trained as a schoolteacher after the war and having taught in secondary modern schools, he always saw schools as the ultimate beneficiaries of the work he promoted. This was particularly his view when the BFI began to consider financially supporting university lectureships.[40] Here was a fundamental difference with SEFT which had overseen the growth of film teaching from the classroom grass roots upwards and had promoted expertise in that arena. Whannel now wanted to shift the focus of developments and he spells it out that:

> ...we have in the Education Department at the Institute the people who are engaged in film teaching, who regularly in their lectures are forced to feel the need of a thorough and relevant film scholarship to help them in their work, and so care about the kinds of research projects that need to be done. Immediately what is required is some free time for its lecturing staff so that they may work in what might approximate to academic conditions and the freeing of at least one member of staff to concentrate entirely on research and lecturing.[41]

A specific element that he wanted to see introduced was a contribution from teacher training. The Report published by the Association of Teachers in Colleges and Departments of Education had identified the options that might be available with the extension of basic teacher training to three years. Whannel highlights Bede College where for the first time students from 1964 would be able to take Film and Television Study as a main course.[42] But he was also aware of the potential of very promising teachers and lecturers already engaged in teaching film and television whose performance would benefit from further enhancement.

> The problem is further sharpened by the need that the Department feels to establish a more substantial form of training for teachers and lecturers than at present exists. We believe that a number of lecturers would develop the work in film teaching if such training could be provided. We believe that there is a need now to establish, if only for a limited period, a one-year full-time course, and such a proposal has been put to the Ministry of Education.[43]

In the event a one-year course did not prove practicable, but one term courses for seconded teachers and lecturers did follow with BFI involvement both at Bede College and at Hornsey College of Art.[44]

In this 1963 Report Whannel identifies the BFI Education Department publications which will be forthcoming – following the significant gap that had occurred after the appearance of the ATCDE Report in January 1960. The gap

...is because the Institute found it impossible to provide an adequate budget. What little money was available was spent on the bulk purchase of the Society for Education in Film and Television's publications. A reasonable sum of money has now been provided for 1963/64.[45]

During that period of the early 1960s, SEFT's pamphlet publication had peaked, possibly encouraged by the income from BFI's bulk purchasing power. So for a period both BFI and SEFT would have been responding to teacher requests with identical materials. The choice of topics for SEFT's occasional publications in the 1960s was a pragmatic one. Each was designed to provide a ready response to the most frequently received queries from non-members. The material in them was usually reprinted from *Screen Education* or the *Yearbook*. The reprinting was no afterthought: the policy was to set up the material for printing first as articles in one of the Society's two regular publications. This had the double advantage of cost saving and of ensuring that members got access to the information automatically as part of their subscriptions without having to purchase the separate pamphlets.

The first to appear was *Film Making in Schools* in 1960, followed in 1963 by what was to be the most substantial of the series *A Handbook for Screen Education*. Such was the popularity of the former that it was reprinted in 1963 when it appeared under the title of *Young Film Makers*, apparently a deliberate decision to link it to be in the NUT sponsored film-making competition. This was followed in 1964 by *Young Film Makers Symposium*. Also in 1964 came *100 Films for Juniors*. The sequence was completed in 1965 with *A Film Society Handbook* for use in schools and colleges.[46]

The implications of the BFI's dependence on SEFT for publications, the rather conventional contents of which Whannel might have questioned, no doubt served to ensure that the Education Department's subsequent pamphlets and duplicated documents would aim to take a stance which was distinct from the apparent SEFT position on any particular topic. SEFT publications of the 1960s were designed to be encouraging, enabling and inclusive, albeit much of the content tended to be drawn from secondary school experience. Produced in the first half of the decade, they combined a positive approach to popular culture with content determined through access to films or ideas from very particular sources. Thus *A Handbook for Screen Education* has a section on 'Basic Films' that combines historical material from the BFI Distribution Library, extracts chosen by the Education Department and sponsored films. No feature films from commercial distributors are included. Although the SEFT stance from its earliest days had been about stirring children's enthusiasm for films at the local cinema, constraints of cost and time seem to have determined that classroom illustrations could only come from a specialist and limited repertoire. Availability it seems precluded the reality of the courses it was promoting from matching the ambition of the Introduction.

The purpose of the course is not to lead children away from films and television in the hope that they will embrace instead the classical cultures of the theatre and literature. No teacher of screen education despises the media of film and television or the concept of a popular culture. Film is the popular art form of the twentieth century and, while television is a multifarious channel of communication, the development of a new art form within it is inevitable. Children enjoy films and television. By increasing their understanding of the media their enjoyment will be increased and enriched.[47]

A Film Society Handbook, aimed at the after school-hours group, is more catholic in its recommendations, drawn mainly from the commercial 16mm film libraries. Until the widespread use of VHS video tape recorders in the 1980s, school film societies were popular with children, given that there was a lengthy five-year gap between a film's exhibition in the cinema and its subsequent screening on television.[48]

For, in general, the aim of the society will be the same – to enrich young people's experience by showing them, in a congenial atmosphere, examples of the best that the cinema has to offer. Enjoyment should be the keynote of this experience and films should be chosen, initially at least, which have a popular appeal for the audience for which you cater.[49]

SEFT's film-making publications had much in common with the weeklies of the period: *Amateur Cine World* and *Amateur Movie Maker*, being full of tips and encouragement. As *Young Film Makers* states '...it is not the job of this booklet to argue the case for film-making by young people. Its purpose is essentially practical.'[50] The assumption was that anyone writing to SEFT for advice on making films with children was already persuaded of the value of the enterprise. It was simply a question of how.

Approaches to the Ministry of Education
In the section of the 1963 Report headed 'Services' Whannel raises a different issue

The main concern here is, of course, film materials. The Institute, through its Distribution Library, offers a number of extracts of feature films and some special teaching films. This is perhaps the weakest aspect of the provision the Institute makes to the teachers and lecturers. The total number of extracts available is still relatively small and the additions have not kept pace with the growth of work. Further, the collection is unbalanced: a great many Ealing comedies, but nothing from contemporary British films; a good collection of silent classics, but virtually nothing illustrating the Western, the Musical or the modern European cinema.[51]

Whannel, Reed and the then BFI Director James Quinn had a very particular audience in mind when this document was being prepared. They were approaching the Ministry of Education in the hope it might provide an additional source of funding, specifically for the Education Department. In the event the timing of their approach was serendipitous. A significant change was about to take place – one which was to affect both BFI Education and SEFT. This was the switch in the funding of the BFI from the Treasury to the Department of Education and Science which followed the election of a Labour Government in 1964 and the appointment of Jennie Lee as Minister for the Arts. Reed, first as Secretary and then as Director, had been determinedly trying to achieve this switch at least for the Education Department before the change of government, as the internal correspondence of the then Ministry of Education reveals.[52]

SEFT had its own funding concerns. From 1960–1963 it received £150 annually from the BFI as a grant-in-aid body. This was increased to £500 annually from 1964–1967.[53] It was a tiny fraction of the funding of the Education Department and an amount which the Society felt to be inadequate, given the scale of its publications. Indeed, this author recollects that SEFT had been in direct correspondence with Ministry officials at this time about its own funding issues. This request from SEFT received subsequent support from Whannel when making his own case to the Ministry. He asked for it to be 'sympathetically considered'.[54] Unfortunately, none of this SEFT correspondence survives, but its basic argument was to draw attention to the size of its membership in schools and to the frequency and regularity of SEFT's publications and to contrast these with the occasional appearance of BFI printed materials. There is however, archive evidence that the relative reach of each organisation was acknowledged at senior civil servant level.

Material in the National Archives from Summer 1963 provides an enlightening snapshot of the situation current at the time when the BFI was seeking funding from the Ministry of Education specifically for its Education Department.[55] This funding would be supplementary to the annual Treasury grant it already received to cover all BFI activities and from which only eight per cent went to the Education Department. The tone of the civil servants' communications would indicate that the BFI received a relatively sympathetic hearing, probably because its approaches were taking place in the immediate post-Newsom publication environment. Reed had submitted evidence to the Newsom Committee[56] and no doubt he then timed the BFI's approach to the Ministry with the impending publication of the Report in mind.

> We discussed the memorandum with the Inspectorate who thought that the Institute, and its associated body The Society for Education in Film and Television, were providing a worth-while service and that in view of the small resources at their disposal they had so far been very successful.[57]

The BFI wanted more than money. It wanted recognition of the value of its work from the Ministry and felt that this would follow the funding. However while the

Ministry could accept the case for giving BFI money, it dithered over how more formal contact might be set up.

> We have also agreed that we would institute formal contacts with the Institute although we have not yet decided whether an official or an inspector would be most appropriate.[58]

A revealing if ambivalent endorsement of SEFT's work is to be found as the BFI request proceeds up the senior civil servant hierarchy and the case for the desired amount (£7,500) is analysed.

> The Education Department could double its effective strength for £7,000; and the remaining £500 would be passed on to the Society for Education in Film and Television, which assumes the main burden of the work in schools, and, being a largely voluntary body, is also a good bargain.[59]

It would seem from this evidence that SEFT's own attempt at direct contact with the Ministry had backfired. The civil servants had accepted that the Society was important in fostering the work in schools but since it was already operating so effectively on voluntary effort, they saw no reason for SEFT to get more money either from the BFI or directly from the Ministry, this latter option having been somewhat implausibly floated by SEFT.

With the change from Ministry to Department, SEFT tried again with the same arguments and this time succeeded in meeting with officials from the DES in 1965, though with no greater luck. The encounter was reported to members as positively as possible.

> A meeting of the Officers with the Department of Education and Science was especially satisfying. The work of the Society was already well known and the Department was most anxious that the Society's contribution to film work in schools should continue through both membership and publications. Although there can be no direct financing of a professional organisation such as SEFT by the Department the Officers were assured of the Department's desire for the maintenance of a strong Society and of their readiness to give whatever further help they could.[60]

The Committee, aware of the continuing contact of the BFI with the new DES as its key funder, clearly felt that it must continue to signal its own presence and its contribution to the same area of educational development.

The Academy-in-Waiting

In the event the Education Department had obtained the funding from the Ministry to support its 1964/65 budget which included the additional posts of Teacher Adviser and Editor of Materials, to which Jim Kitses and Alan Lovell were appointed.[61] The additional staffing of the Education Department inevitably meant that Whannel's regular involvement of/dependence on SEFT Committee members diminished. In the 1950s, successive Film Appreciation Officers had drawn on the services of SEFT to lecture, to advise and address conferences. The further additional funding achieved by the BFI as the DES replaced the Ministry meant that Whannel was able to continue to strengthen the staffing establishment of his department throughout the 1960s. His strategy was in the spirit of his 1963 Report. He aimed to build up the intellectual strength of the Department by recruiting those who – whatever their paid role might be – would be committed to their own research and writing, as if in a university environment.

A further and significant addition to this 'academy-in-waiting' within the Education Department was Peter Wollen who would have been known to Whannel through their mutual involvement with *New Left Review* where Wollen reviewed films under the pseudonym of Lee Russell and Whannel sat on the Editorial Board. When Peter Harcourt left the BFI Wollen replaced him in having responsibility for publications, while Harcourt's administrative duties as Assistant Education Officer passed to Jim Kitses.[62] Wollen's spell with the BFI was relatively brief but in that period he became involved in the more ambitious publishing project shared with *Sight and Sound* of the Cinema One books which were initially published by Secker & Warburg and then by Thames & Hudson. These books initially concentrated on making available, primarily but not exclusively, approaches to authorship and subsequently to genre studies.[63]

First with Alan Lovell in post as Film Materials Officer and then with his successor Colin McArthur, more money became available. More extracts were selected to fill some of the gaps that Whannel had identified in the 1963 Report. The collection eventually became sufficiently extensive to form the basis of *The Cinema Book*.[64] Access to extracts was hierarchical. Those extracts in the BFI Distribution Library were generally available for hire. Such were the constraints set by distributors over extract availability there were certain extracts not in the Distribution Library but which were available 'for a strictly educational use and can only be borrowed [from the Central Booking Agency] by teachers and lecturers operating a planned course as part of their formal teaching'.[65] The most exclusive use was reserved for the extracts in the Department's Lecture Cupboard 'available only to panel lecturers fulfilling Institute engagements'.[66]

When new extracts became available, they were generally welcomed by teachers. The short 10–15 minute extract was usable within the restricted timescale of the lecture or lesson where the feature film was not. Compared to the hire cost of a feature, the extract was a better bet for film teaching budgets. Only with hindsight have questions arisen as to the long-term influence of this selection process. It could be argued that very individual preferences for a certain type of film and the regular deployment of well established relationships with particular distributors inadvertently shaped what was a very particular approach to the teaching of film, so that an unchallenged dominance of American cinema came to underpin courses on film until the advent of VHS and DVD gave flexibility to the classroom practitioner for the first time who might now use material that had previously been publicly broadcast.[67]

As the Education Department became established with more staff and its own base at 70 Old Compton Street, teachers and lecturers had much easier access to advice. The BFI could now offer a service that neither SEFT nor the old Film Appreciation Department had been able to offer: the opportunity for practitioners to have face-to-face encounters with the advisory staff. From these meetings, a benefit to the Education Department soon became apparent. The number of teachers/lecturers on its list of contacts began to rival SEFT's membership. The department was also in a position to ask those whose classroom practice seemed interesting or relevant to write up their experiences, for which they would then be paid. These accounts were typed up, duplicated and made available free on request.

The scale of this intervention may be assessed by comparing the documents produced in the first and second halves of the 1960s. Of the twenty four 'Syllabuses and Descriptive Accounts' listed as available in 1973, sixteen had first appeared between 1966 and 1969.[68] Only one document dating from before 1966 survived, which was 'Newsom on Film', a selection of relevant paragraphs from the Report, reprinted without comment. There had been earlier documents produced in the first half of the 1960s, but most of these originated from work at Kingsway College by Jim Kitses and Ann Mercer[69] which had already been rewritten as *Talking About the Cinema* (see below).

Education Department Publications

Whannel intended that the publications for teachers to come from his Education Department should be more substantial than previous BFI pamphlets, and that they should also demonstrate greater coherence as a series. A certain caution in relation to what might have been considered as SEFT territory is detectable: consequently the attention to work in schools is limited. The first publication *Film Teaching* (1964) concentrates on courses for adults: in a college of science and technology, a teacher training college, local authority adult education classes and university extra-mural classes.[70] *Talking About the Cinema* (1966) describes work in a further education college.[71] The companion piece *Talking about Television*, which does describe work in schools, is however written by former SEFT Chairman, Tony Higgins.[72]

The Introduction to *Film Teaching* makes it clear that the Editors, Whannel and Harcourt, are expecting an uphill struggle to establish film as an area for serious study.

> Although some progress has been made in film study with young people, it is still rare to meet anyone who, while still at school, has been given any training or guidance, or has even been made to feel that a film could offer a worthwhile experience. In England, even in relatively sophisticated circles, we still make a

sharp distinction between art and entertainment, with the cinema falling decisively in the latter category, where – it is believed – the normal standards of judgment do not apply.[73]

They seek to demonstrate that the process in which they are engaged has been a lengthy one with attempts to enhance the status of the cinema in Britain having originated in the 1920s. But their approach – and the choice of their contributors – is still a cautious one. The notion of authorship is offered as the prevalent method of analysis, though here it is clear there are limits.

It is interesting that the younger writers grouped around *Movie* magazine are preoccupied with similar problems and, despite their attempt to treat art as high culture and to give many minor films a weight of psychological meaning we feel they cannot bear, their contributions…have helped to illuminate some of the issues involved.[74]

Stuart Hall's account of his work within Liberal Studies, and of the three different courses he offers, becomes most interesting in its concluding paragraphs. Here he discusses one course which examines the relationship between the cinema and popular culture, concentrating on the output from Hollywood.

The aim of the course, then, is to break the false connection between quality and taste, and to develop some critical language by means of which the qualities of the cinema as a *popular* art can be discriminated from the great welter of rubbish.[75]

Roy Knight writes of the developments at Bede College, Durham where Film and Television Study had just become available to be taken as a Main Course. This is the most substantial chapter in the book and the one that at the time had the potential to be most influential, since the training colleges were seen (and in some cases such as Eastbourne saw themselves) as the places where screen education developments would most likely take place following the increase in length of the teacher training period.[76] Albert Hunt, an Area Tutor Organiser under Shropshire's unique system for organising adult education had 'the widest possible terms of reference'.[77] He identifies his starting point as answering the question 'What sort of films are likely to arouse interest and start people talking?' His strategy is one of proceeding by stealth in that he would move from *Twelve Angry Men*, which would stimulate discussion much of it peripheral to film study, and seek eventually to screen *Los Olvidados* where that film's imagery would prevent students simply settling for a discussion of social issues. He has to address a wide brief in his work and when speaking to trades unionists deploys the more obvious issues raised by *I'm All Right Jack* and *The Angry Silence*. Although Alan Lovell begins his chapter on Extra-Mural work by making a reference to such extension work in Leeds, Oxford,

Keele and Cambridge, what he describes is the London University Course which had been run since the 1950s by the British Film Institute on its own premises. This access to the BFI facilities, Lovell acknowledges, gives the course great advantages, particularly in facilitating the screening of films under cinema conditions. Of particular historical interest is his inclusion of the detailed syllabuses of the three-year course then current.[78]

Each of these contributors was in his own unique situation. The readers would have found evidence of what was achievable in different sectors, even if there was little scope for adapting wholesale into the readers' situations the courses as described. One observation which is however inescapable is how all courses depend on the relatively small number of extracts available in the period up to 1964 and how therefore the same extract is demonstrated as being used differently in a range of teaching situations.

Talking about Television was seen as following the model set by *Film Teaching* in that it was an account of his work by a practising teacher. Tony Higgins had been a key figure in the Society of Film Teachers in promoting the extension of its remit to include television. Here he seeks to context, within the prevailing attitudes of the time, his approach to television with less able secondary school students. Different types of transmitted programmes form the basis of classroom discussion, albeit with the problem of very limited availability of material for classroom use. Its concluding chapter takes a fundamentally different approach: thematic.

> Parents and children, youth, age, social class, race, politicians, war, policemen, crime, violence, health and disease, housing, fashion, have all entered into lessons held over a period of a few months. Other themes such as work and leisure, falling in love, marriage, animals, scientists, lawyers, teachers etc do not appear in the discussions recorded here, but they are frequently discussed in the television lesson.[79]

This thematic approach was also gaining in importance in film study. The companion publication *Talking about the Cinema* describes work at Kingsway a London further education college. Here teaching is organised thematically.

> It is primarily because of this entertainment bias that we have found the theme to be an important organising principle in our teaching. In taking 'Young People', or 'Personal Relationships', or 'War', and bringing in film materials that treat the subject differently, we have wanted to establish that films do have a connection with reality. We have seen this as a first priority in our courses: at the beginning we have planned our lessons so that students are encouraged to find links between the films they see and the life they experience outside.[80]

Further acknowledgement of the encroachment of the use of themes is to be found in Kitses's supplement *Film and General Studies*, published at the same time. The aims of this course are

(a) to encourage growth, discrimination and expression through the understanding and widening of experience.

(b) to help students to understand their society, its organisations and pressures, and to help them relate themselves to groups and communities within that society.[81]

The authors Kitses and Mercer are opposed to the introduction of examinations into their courses. In this opposition they are echoing the attitude of Harcourt.[82] The debate about the role of examinations was to become central to SEFT's arguments in the 1980s.

The final 1966 pamphlet *Film Making in Schools and Colleges* (which grew out of an Education Department conference in 1965) is organised by education sector to include work in Infant, Junior and Secondary schools, but these reports, written by the supervising teachers, are somewhat overshadowed by the description of work in the Hornsey College of Art Teaching Training Department.

> A word about Hornsey and the place it occupies in this volume. Under the quite exceptional sponsorship of the principal, Mr H H Shelton, film-making plays many roles at Hornsey College of Art, in graphic design, general studies and Teacher Training. We decided it would be a needless falsification of Hornsey's multifarious activities to restrict the length of Douglas Lowndes's contribution in an arbitrary way, and so he has taken a lion's share of the book.[83]

The reality here was that Douglas Lowndes's approach, using simple cameras and a much higher ratio of equipment to children, challenged the group-made film approach which had been promoted both by SEFT and the BFI under Reed. Whannel's colleague, Peter Harcourt, felt it important to publicise this alternative method for organising practical work.[84] Lowndes was also provided with further conference opportunities for promoting his work by the British Film Institute.[85] A degree of tension was created around this with some SEFT committee members, who felt that interesting as Lowndes's work was there were few schools at that stage which would be able to equip their students to Hornsey standards. It was unrealistic for BFI to promote his approach as a generally usable model since this might well discourage some teachers from venturing into practical work.

A SEFT/BFI Rift

Harcourt had already antagonised some in SEFT with his 1964 piece in *Screen Education* 26, a special number devoted to Higher Education.[86] Harcourt set out to review the screen education world at the point when *Film Teaching* was published and in so doing was dismissive of the work being done in schools. Whilst few would quarrel with his opening statement, 'Screen education began in schools and youth clubs', his second sentence, 'it also began defensively' was provocative.[87] When he continues, 'it was generally felt that the greatest need for screen education was amongst the dull', he may have been rather crudely reflecting a reality – in that most of the timetabled work was in the secondary modern school – but the SEFT pioneers bridled at his language. They totally disputed his unqualified claim that 'the basic impulse behind the initial work done in this field sprang from the desire among educationists to protect young people from the possibly corrupting influences of the cinema and then of television'.[88]

Matters were not improved when Harcourt compared the early film teachers unfavourably with those in the Film Society movement. 'Here were no defensive attitudes in relation to the screen: rather there was a real enthusiasm for the cinema', while he sees the film educationists as 'frequently displaying a limited enthusiasm for a great many films, preferring safe and discussable examples like *The Red Badge of Courage* or *High Noon*, often showing little concern or even awareness of how undistinguished, cinematically, such films often are'.[89] The reaction of one SEFT pioneer, Paul Alexander, was to write for *Screen Education* his own version of the history of SEFT which was published in five episodes throughout the 1965 issues of the Journal.[90] Harcourt was using his article to trail what the Education Department saw as its priorities, which he divided into *Fields of Direct Action* and *Services and Materials*. The direct action was to concentrate on the teacher training colleges. In arguing why this approach was the best strategy he takes another swipe at SEFT

> Teachers already in the schools tend to be burdened with their immediate challenges, if not actually set in their ways. Also, we have felt that teachers already in the field who become interested in this work can most profitably be instructed and put in touch with one another through SEFT's information services, publications and summer school, as well as by similar services offered by ourselves. Teaching conditions often impede fresh experiment: whereas in the Training Colleges, when the students are still open to new educational practices, we feel it is easier for them to grapple with the full educational challenge of talking about the screen.[91]

Children's Film-Making

Shifting attitudes to film-making by young people may also be detected in the evolution of the event initially known as the Children's Film Awards. It had begun as a competition organised in the 1950s by the *News Chronicle*. With the demise of that newspaper the sponsorship was taken over by the National Union of Teachers with the detailed organisation being provided first by BFI alone and then by both BFI and SEFT. The first NUT sponsored event was in spring 1961 when it was styled the National Children's Film Awards, with a subheading of 'Film Making – an approach to appreciation'.[92] The competition entry form made strong links between the mood of the major NUT conference of the previous autumn and the particular value of film-making that some had claimed in that connection.

Few challenges are more serious than that of teaching children to withstand the pressure of the media of mass communication, to discriminate between the good, the bad and the indifferent in the mass of material they see, read and listen to in daily life.

By learning to make their own films under the guidance of their teacher, children begin to gain a real insight into the art of the film and their critical faculties are tremendously stimulated.[93]

There was, in the early years, a routine to the arrangements for the competition and the judges usually included representatives from both BFI and SEFT. Frequently a winning entry would come from Cornwell School where SEFT activist Don Waters taught.[94] The changing attitude toward film-making and practical work that had been instituted by Harcourt was sustained by Jim Kitses, his successor as Assistant Education Officer who organised the event in 1967, now styled as the Young Film Makers Competition. Responding to a review in *The Teacher*[95] which had been critical of the judging of the films submitted to the event, Kitses used the opportunity to suggest that some changes in the nature of the event would be appropriate.

The competition in fact began in the days of those polished little story films, traditional group made efforts. But today film-making is penetrating the curriculum in all sorts of ways, ranging from the rough little animated film exercises of an art class, to a Newsom experiment in English, history or geography, to the semi-professional work done in art colleges.[96]

Kitses ends by asking 'Is a competition with its roots in the story film idea an anachronism?'

This shift by the BFI was a significant one. In *Film Study Materials*,[97] a printed pamphlet issued in 1962, the first section (which takes up three of the pamphlet's 16 pages) is headed 'Films Made by Children'. Copies of thirty nine school made films were then available for hire from the BFI. This section, which occupies the same number of pages as the 'Study Extracts: Sound Films' that were also available, is introduced thus:

In recent years, due largely to the efforts of the Society for Education in Film and Television, a number of 16 mm silent short story films have been made by children in school as part of a course in film appreciation. Although in many cases their technique is primitive and content naïve, these films have freshness and charm and have been found particularly valuable both to film teachers and lecturers on film appreciation. By arrangement with the Society, the British Film Institute is making available the films listed below. [98]

By the end of the decade, the Education Department no longer promoted these films as being useful teaching aids. Concerned that the range and quality of entries was falling, it argued successfully that the event should become biennial. Consequently the next event was in 1969 when the name had changed again. It was now 'Young Screen – a Festival and Exhibition of Film Making by Children and Young People'. The following explanation accompanied the entry form:

> Recognising the diversity and educational value of so much that is going on the National Union of Teachers seeks to survey and draw greater attention to this work. We have therefore moved away from the event of a competition with national awards, our past formula which may have placed undue emphasis on the story film, and have embraced the idea of an exhibition. The emphasis is therefore no longer on judging the best film but on selecting and spotlighting representatives of the different approaches and varied uses to which film is lending itself within general education.[99]

Given the changed nature of the event and the need for exhibition space now for three days, 'Young Screen' was held at Hamilton House, the NUT headquarters. The organisation was undertaken by the Teacher Adviser/Secretary of SEFT. Two years later and invitations to 'Young Screen 1971' showed a further distinct shift in the attitude of the three organising bodies

> In our viewing of the submitted material we have found two recurrent polarities: between the functional use of film (eg to record a school activity) and the expressive use (eg an adolescent's projection of his persecution fantasies); and between teacher centred films with their emphasis on formal and social order and the altogether more anarchic child-centred films.[100]

An alternative biennial event had also become available. In 1966 SEFT was approached by the London Co-operative Society who wished to sponsor a film-making event in the metropolitan area.[101] The Co-op ethos ensured that a non-competitive celebration of children's practical work was what the LCS wanted, while the biennial nature of the NUT Festival meant that a ready-made alternative year slot existed to be filled. In the event the 'Co-op Young People's Film and Video Festival' celebrated 25 years of activity in 1991 by which time it had outlasted the NUT event and by continuing into the video era now attracted entries from a very wide range of schools. Significantly too it was no longer a metropolitan fixture, but a national Co-op/BFI event housed in the National Museum of Photography, Film and Television in Bradford.[102]

BFI/SEFT Joint Appointment

In mid 1966 SEFT was approached by Whannel with a proposal for a joint appointment of Teacher Adviser BFI/Secretary SEFT. Such a joint appointment was not unique. The BFI had already established a joint post with the Federation of Film Societies. But it was significant for SEFT, where the voluntary structure had been under great pressure for some time as the demands made on the Society by the expanding numbers of film teachers increased. It seems that the notion for the joint appointment was put forward initially by Whannel, then rapidly received Director Reed's approval. This author (who was Honorary Secretary of SEFT at the time of the negotiations) remembers the detailed agreement with the BFI, no copy of which survives. Perhaps significantly, when the proposal was put to the BFI Governors, the wording of a supporting note from Director Reed indicates that the Governors were encouraged to think that a new Teacher Adviser was to be appointed who would occasionally handle a few routine SEFT matters for a small honorarium.[103] This was certainly not how the joint appointment was viewed by the Society. Nor was it how it operated in practice. By 1968 – after a year's experience of the new post – the BFI was stating in print that SEFT had 'a full-time General Secretary whose office is located within the Education Department of the British Film Institute'.[104]

Such had been the antipathy between some members of the Education Department and some Committee members that Whannel in putting his proposal to the Governors felt he had to acknowledge the rift there had been. As the Minutes record:

> ...while relations between the Institute and the Society had not in recent years been entirely satisfactory, it was felt that nevertheless the Society had been doing excellent work and had produced the very useful journal *Screen Education*, in addition to pamphlets, a Year Book and a list of 16mm film libraries, all of considerable value.[105]

Then to make the case for the benefits the new post would have for SEFT Whannel argued:

> One advantage of this would be that the Society would be relieved of a good deal of the administrative commitments which had so far limited their creativity. Such an arrangement, although it involved the sacrifice by the Institute of a certain amount of the officer's time, would, nevertheless, be of value to them insofar as it served to extend and improve the Society's work, which was of real value to the Institute.[106]

The minutes record, perhaps guardedly, that the 'proposal was generally welcomed'.[107] The reality was that financially this was not a joint appointment. It would be wholly funded by BFI Education, which would house and provide facilities for SEFT. In practice it was a double appointment in that the Teacher Adviser/Secretary would have a full-time secretary working almost exclusively for him. Alex Richardson, who had been on the SEFT Committee since 1960, became the first holder of the joint post on 1 January 1967. With such provision replacing volunteer effort at the core of the Society, there was to be an inevitable shift in the way that SEFT operated. This will be explored in the next chapter.

Also working within the Education Department as a Teacher Adviser by this time was Victor Perkins, one of the Editors of *Movie*. He and Richardson collaborated on aspects of the work. However, the influence of *Movie* on those teaching film at the time was probably a more direct one. In the numerous interviews conducted for this investigation, those who were teaching in the 1960s were very ready to acknowledge the influence that *Movie* had had on them during the period 1962 to 1969 when, although its publication soon became both irregular and infrequent, its reputation guaranteed a loyal and patient readership. But it seems that its influence was less one of inspiring teachers to write articles of *Movie* style textual analysis than to encourage the use of *Movie* methods and preferences in shaping the form and content of their own classroom performance. Not everyone was a *Movie* fan. Roy Knight's view was that

> *Movie* is at pains to demonstrate that good films may be produced in many genres. It argues that the critic's task is to elucidate rather than to evaluate: yet I find in much of *Movie*'s writing not so much elucidation as description.[108]

Knight rejected what he considered to be an uncommitted approach and continued to encourage his students to go further and risk a subjective judgment as to the value of the film. There are occasional articles in *Screen Education* where an individual film is described and analysed in greater detail, perhaps in the spirit of *Movie*, but evidence of its more direct influence was to be found in the London University Extra Mural classes where by 1968 Robin Wood had been recruited to teach 'The Director's Cinema' and in the BFI summer schools where *Movie* writers were guest lecturers for several years.[109]

When SEFT was approached by BBC Schools Television producer Alan Bell for ideas about a Film Study programme for Sixth formers, Richardson passed the inquiry on to Perkins where the most direct *Movie* style intervention of all was consequently to be found in the resultant programme *Cinema*, screened weekly through the Autumn of 1968.[110] This series uniquely linked the programmes transmitted to schools to feature films which were scheduled as imminently to be screened at evenings and weekends on BBC TV. Its advertised ambition was to 'help to put the cinema as an art form on a level with literature as a subject for serious study in schools where it tends to be ignored'.[111]

Shortly after taking up the BFI/SEFT joint appointment, Richardson's book *Screen Education for Schools* was printed by the publishing arm of the National Union of Teachers.[112] The announcement of his new role in the Society is used in the book's promotion. Its style can probably be best described as 'Tips for Teachers' in that the author never hesitates to speak authoritatively and personally from his own classroom experience. This book too is very clearly a product of its time when not only was the 'Director's Cinema' the dominant model but would-be film teachers were compelled to find a variety of ways of introducing film study into their schools. Significantly, therefore, the first chapter deals with the School Film Club, on the grounds that for most children this was the closest experience they would have of film study while at school. Richardson had however previously taught at Cornwell School in East London, which almost uniquely at that time, had a well established screen education programme throughout the school curriculum. Coming from the SEFT tradition, Richardson significantly labeled his practice 'screen education', rather than film teaching and consequently he feels he must offer an explanation as to his preference for using the term: because in studying film and television 'there are no clear aesthetic distinctions to be drawn between the two media'.[113] Also deriving from his SEFT background, Richardson argues for group film-making as an essential part of the screen education experience, and this takes up his third and final chapter. 'I know of nothing else which so swiftly and certainly transforms children's notions of screen art.'[114]

It is this assertion of the value of the individual film as art that underpins Richardson's approach to screen education. In Chapter Two he sees as the two 'crucial advantages' of a timetabled screen education lesson for the teacher:

> He can boldly and single-mindedly present films, which, because they are masterpieces, make children more open to new experiences in art.
> He can ensure that all film and TV study is shot through with opportunities for associated creative work on the part of the children themselves.[115]

This very traditional film appreciation approach is further reinforced by two other approaches, which Richardson identifies but then decides specifically not to endorse. He labels them the *Quasi-sociological* and the *Therapeutic*. The former, which involves an investigation of the organisation of the media industries and of the pressures at work on the construction of various programmes, will he claims 'be disastrous' as a basis for classroom studies.[116] He is more cautious about condemning the therapeutic approach outright, since he has to concede that it is not that different from a thematic approach, which he will subsequently go on to endorse, albeit in a rather restricted mode. But while it is not clear exactly what he is attacking, he cautions that 'Any one teacher (films or no) who chooses to plan a therapeutic course is certainly heading for some big disappointments.'[117]

It is however authorship that dominates his approach.

> It is of the utmost importance that children come to understand, fully and naturally, that films and TV programmes are the work of individual people.[118]

This is an extraordinary statement in its assertion that authorship is a state about which a child will come to have a 'natural' understanding. Presumably this will happen only if the teacher chooses the appropriate films and television programmes for the course. Coupled with Richardson's rejection of any study of institutions, this is a very distinctive teaching method, which is subsequently further reinforced by his approach to thematic studies, where

Different films, sharing a different theme, reveal differences in treatment; they expose the idea of authorship, of a director choosing images, dialogue, music, effects and so on.[119]

So here all approaches, even thematic ones, are made to connect to authorship.

A thematic approach of a different kind became installed in the Education Department in 1967 when Jim Hillier was appointed as Film Research Officer for the Humanities Curriculum Project. This Nuffield funded project set out to produce a range of materials which could be used as evidence for themes such as War and Youth that were to be discussed in the secondary school classroom. Film extracts – from mainly feature films – were to be selected to provide 'evidence' additional to that originating in printed sources.[120]

Screen surfaces

In retrospect it is now clear that if the institution of the joint appointment was the most important development for SEFT in the 1960s, undoubtedly the second was the decision to publish *Screen* in place of both *Screen Education* and the *Yearbook*. The case for ceasing to publish the *Yearbook* was the easier to establish. It had already reached the ceiling in the income it could make from advertising and to maintain publication would require an increase in both the membership fee and the cover price. Whereas when *The Film Teacher's Handbook* first appeared there were few reference sources for film teachers, by 1969 the supply of books of both reference and criticism was much greater. The niche which the *Yearbook* had filled was closing and its Editor Roger Mainds accepted the reality of the situation.[121]

The case for ending *Screen Education* was an altogether more difficult one. Because it occupied a unique position in relation to film study, those wishing to write about their work had only *Screen Education* in which to place their articles. Increasingly US writers, often post-graduate students of Professor Tony Hodgkinson, took up a greater share of the pages. Nevertheless it did accommodate the early writings of authors who would become significant players in the development of film teaching: Charles Barr, Jim Cook, Kevin Gough-Yates, Jim Hillier, Colin McArthur, Robin Wood. Also occasionally featured were writers well-established in other publications: Alan Lovell, Victor Perkins, Paddy Whannel, Peter Wollen.

But it remained essentially separate from SEFT and as the composition of the Committee evolved, questions began to be asked. The fundamental one was about editorship, since whoever controlled *Screen Education* spent the biggest part of the Society's budget and it was by the content of its journal that the Society would inevitably be judged. With new members on the SEFT committee, some recruited by Richardson in his role as Secretary from January 1967, scrutiny of *Screen Education* increased. In 1968 matters came to a head when this author and Kevin Gough-Yates argued the case for a new journal (which would subsequently adopt the name *Screen*). The motion for change was won by a single vote of the Committee.[122]

Notes

1. Ministry of Education *Half Our Future* A Report of the Central Advisory Committee (England) London: HMSO 1963
2. 'A Sensible Attitude to the Cinema – Hertfordshire schools co-operate in evolving a more critical approach' in *Look and Listen* Vol 4 No 4 April 1950 pp 77–76. These reports described: film clubs running in 14 secondary schools; how in another school an intensive study of one film, *Cyprus is an Island*, had been undertaken following the publication of a book detailing its making and its script; and then in a further report a case was made for the making of a film by children, the effect of which would be to 'stimulate a more discriminating approach to the commercial film'. The reports encouraged the committee to purchase a 16 mm camera for the county to be shared between schools to facilitate further film-making.
3. *Newsom on Film* London: BFI Education Department 1963
4. Don Waters 'Newsom' and 'Newsom on the Screen Media' *Screen Education* 22 January/February 1964 pp 7–9
5. Ibid p 7
6. Alex Richardson 'Postscript to the screen education references in the Newsom Report' *Screen Education* 22 pp 9–10. See below endnote 31 for further reference to *Film and TV News*.
7. Ibid
8. *Half Our Future* pp 29–30
9. Ibid pp 73–74
10. Ibid p 74
11. Ibid pp 155–156
12. Ibid p 156
13. Ibid p 156
14. See advertisement in *Screen Education* 23 March/April 1964 p 68
15. See advertisement in *Screen Education* 26 September/October 1964 p 29
16. The first notification of such a booklet is to be found in *Screen Education* 25 July/August 1964 p 36. It is to be called 'Best of the Free Films' and readers are told 'all suggestions welcomed'
17. Author's recollection
18. Eric Else *The Back of Beyond* London: Longmans Green & Co Ltd 1968
19. By the time the book was published there was 'a small handling charge' for this free loan film. See Else op cit p 158
20. Alex Richardson 'Talking to John Heyer' *Film Society News* 9 Summer 1961 pp 3–6 and *Film Society News* 10 Winter 1961 pp 4–6. *Film Society News* began as a supplement to *The Film Teacher* and was edited by Ray Wills for the issues published in 1958/59 (Nos 1–5). The issues 6–12 from June 1960 to Summer 1962 were edited by Alex Richardson and distributed to Group Members of SEFT. This category of membership was abolished with the coming of *Film and TV News*.
21. Else op cit pp 159–173

22. Ibid p 173
23. Stuart Hall 'Liberal Studies' pp 10–27 in Paddy Whannel and Peter Harcourt (Eds) *Film Teaching* London: BFI Education Department 1964; Ernest Lindgren *The Art of the Film* London: Allen & Unwin 1963
24. Whannel and Harcourt op cit p 7
25. Else op cit p 159 quoting from Whannel and Harcourt op cit p 15
26. Author's recollection of a confidential report back by Vannoey in 1966.
27. Author's recollection of private conversations with Whannel in 1965.
28. Stuart Hall and Paddy Whannel *The Popular Arts* London: Hutchinson Educational 1964 p 399
29. Roger Mainds 'The Teenscreen Story' *Screen Education* 18 March/April 1963 pp 53–54
30. British Film Institute Governors' Minutes 2 April 1962 Item 4550 'Education Department'
31. *Film and TV News* was a development of and replacement for *Film Society News* and followed the final (twelfth) issue of the latter in Summer 1962.
32. There is an editorial plug for 'First SEFT Filmstrip' in *Screen Education* 14 May/June 1962 p 38. Members were encouraged to 'Reserve your copies, with cash please'. The cost was £1 to members, 25 shillings to the public.
33. The author remembers glimpsing the slide originals in the safe-keeping of a committee member.
34. 'New Camera Hire Scheme' *Screen Education* 19 May/June 1963 p 47
35. It has proved difficult to obtain details of how this arrangement was originated or maintained. In 'Towards Higher Education' (*Screen Education* 26 September/October 1964 p 26) Peter Harcourt writes 'With the assistance of SEFT, the Rank Organisation have put some twelve new extracts into distribution which should prove useful in the schools…'.
36. SEFT Thirteenth Annual Report 1962/63
37. Advertisement in *Screen Education* 17 January/February 1963 p 45
38. Paddy Whannel *The Work of the Education Department* London: BFI 1963
39. Ibid p 3
40. Alan Lovell in interview with the author.
41. Whannel op cit p 5
42. Ibid p 3
43. Ibid p 4
44. SEFT was involved particularly with the Hornsey Course, having been represented on the Steering Committee and subsequently provided lecturers as reported in the SEFT Fifteenth Annual Report 1965–1966, presented 7 May 1966.
45. Whannel op cit p 5
46. SEFT's publications of the first half of the 1960s were: Sidney Rees and Don Waters *Film Making in School* (1960); Alex Richardson, R.C. Vannoey and Don Waters *A Handbook for Screen Education* (1963); Sidney Rees and Don Waters *Young Film Makers* (1963); S G P Alexander *100 Films for Juniors* (1964); H.R. Wills (Ed). *Young Film Makers Symposium* (1964); R C Vannoey (Ed) *A Film Society Handbook* (1965).

47. Richardson, Vannoey, Waters op cit p 4
48. See Edward Buscombe *Films on TV* London SEFT: *Screen* pamphlet No 1 1971 p 16
49. Vannoey op cit p 1
50. Rees and Waters (1963) op cit p 2
51. Whannel op cit p 6
52. National Archives File ED181/92Memo from D M Basey to P T Sloman CLC7 23 July 1963
53. BFI Interoffice Memorandum 20 January 1992 from Manuel Alvarado to Richard Paterson
54. National Archives File ED181/92 Paddy Whannel 'The Educational Work of the British Film Institute' March 1963 p 10
55. National Archives ED181/92
56. *Half Our Future* p 266
57. National Archives ED181/92
58. Ibid Memo from D M Basey to P T Sloman CLC7 23 July 1963 p 2
59. Ibid Memo from P T Sloman to J F Embling C40/7 20 August 1963
60. SEFT Fifteenth Annual Report 1965–1966
61. National Archives File ED181/92 British Film Institute Education Department proposed budget 1964/65 shows funding for full-time Lecturer/Teacher Adviser and part-time Lecturer/Editor of Materials.
62. Ibid This new budget also had the designated post of Lecturer/Editor of Publications which was initially Harcourt, then Wollen.
63. When the project started individual books were credited either to *Sight and Sound* or to the Education Department. Subsequently the two parts of the BFI shared joint attribution.
64. Pam Cook (Ed) *The Cinema Book* London: BFI 1985 See p (v) for an account of the book's evolution.
65. Whannel (1963) op cit p 7
66. Ibid p 7
67. Ginette Vincendeau in conversation with the author (25 April 2006) expressed the view that the way in which these extracts had been chosen constructed film study as an Anglo-American enterprise with an emphasis on American genre cinema.
68. British Film Institute Educational Advisory Service Documents 1973
69. Ann Mercer would subsequently write as E Ann Kaplan.
70. Whannel and Harcourt (1964) op cit
71. Jim Kitses with Ann Mercer *Talking about the Cinema* London: BFI Education Department 1966
72. A P Higgins *Talking about Television* London: BFI Education Department 1966
73. Whannel and Harcourt op cit p 5
74. Ibid p 7
75. Ibid p 26
76. Ibid pp 28–51
77. Ibid p 23

78. Ibid pp 83–93
79. Higgins op cit p 95
80. Kitses and Mercer op cit p 12
81. Jim Kitses *Film and General Studies* London: BFI Education Department 1966 p 1
82. See below endnote 83
83. Peter Harcourt and Peter Theobald (Eds) *Film Making in Schools and Colleges* London: BFI Education Department 1966 p 4
84. Douglas Lowndes in interview with the author 5 June 2003.
85. ' Film Making at Hornsey College of Art' – all day Film Workshop at the National Film Theatre organized by BFI Education Department January 1966
86. Peter Harcourt 'Towards Higher Education' *Screen Education* 26 September/October 1964 pp 20–30
87. Ibid p 20
88. Ibid p 20
89. Ibid p 21
90. S G P Alexander: 'Not so much a philosophy…' *Screen Education* 27 January/February 1965 pp 6–11; 'Forming the Society of Film Teachers' *Screen Education* 28 March/April 1968 pp 33–40; 'From SFT to SEFT' *Screen Education* 29 May/June 1965 pp 59–67; 'SEFT onwards' *Screen Education* 30 July/August 1965 pp 66–73; 'We've Come a Long Way' *Screen Education* 31 September/October 1965 pp 53–62
91. Harcourt *Screen Education* 26 1964 op cit p 24
92. *Announcing the National Children's Film Awards 1961* London: National Union of Teachers 1961 (From the private collection of Fred Jarvis).
93. Ibid
94. In the report of the 1962 competition (*Screen Education* 15 July/August 1962 p 33) it is stated that 'Cornwell have dominated this section of the competition [Under 16] for so long that the judges were anxiously looking out for challengers.
95. 'Will the judges' choice have a bad effect on future productions?' *The Teacher* June 30 1967 p 7
96. Letters to the Editor 'Young film makers: some words in their defence' *The Teacher* July 21 1967 p 5
97. British Film Institute Education Department *Film Study Materials* London: BFI 1962
98. Ibid p 3
99. *Young Screen 1969* Entry form and information London NUT 1969
100. SEFT Archive Bretton Hall BH/PL/155 *Young Screen 1971* Invitation to the Festival and Exhibition London: NUT 1971
101. Given the existing scheduling of 'Young Film Makers', the first LCS/SEFT 'Let's Make a Film Festival' was incorporated into the 1968 SEFT Annual Conference as reported in the Seventeenth Annual SEFT Report 1967–1968, presented 4 May 1968.
102. Chris Mottershead, Tricia Jenkins *Children Moving Images* London: British Film Institute 1992 p 1 – this booklet accompanies a boxed set of VHS videotapes which demonstrate the range of practical work the event had generated over the years.

103. British Film Institute Governors' Minutes 6 June 1966 Director's note to Item 4859
104. Whannel and Harcourt op cit 1968 reprint p 98
105. British Film Institute Governors' Minutes 6 June 1966 Item 4859 'Society for Education in Film and Television'
106. Ibid
107. Ibid
108. Whannel and Harcourt 1964 op cit p 35
109. Ibid pp 90–91
110. Victor Perkins in interview with the author 19 April 2005.
111. Advertisement in *Screen Education* 46 September/October 1968 p 101
112. Alex Richardson *Screen Education for Schools* London: Schoolmaster Publishing Company Ltd 1967
113. Ibid p 20
114. Ibid p 21
115. Ibid p 20
116. Ibid p 22
117. Ibid p 22
118. Ibid p 25
119. Ibid p 30
120. Jim Hillier and Andrew McTaggart 'Film in the Humanities Curriculum Project' *Screen* Vol 11 No 2 March/April 1970 pp 46–51
121. Roger Mainds (Ed) *Screen Education Yearbook 1969* London: SEFT 1968 Editorial p 5
122. No record now exists of this meeting. It must have taken place in the early Summer of 1968, since the Seventeenth Annual Report of SEFT of 4 May 1968 makes no reference of any change in the Society's publications policy.

6

The University in Old Compton Street

The notion has been put about recently that we (the Society and the Department) have neglected services to the practising teacher…Whatever the source I can tell you nothing has aroused greater anger among my colleagues. If we are to be remembered by anything I think it should be by the quality of the services we provided. Our ideal was never to turn anyone away without giving every assistance possible.

Paddy Whannel, 1971

With increased funding both BFI Education and SEFT accept that they must now find ways of developing the work, not simply do more of the same. For the Education Department this entails finding ways of deputising for the non-existence of university departments of film in the UK. For SEFT it means concentrating the Society's resources on a new journal Screen *which will attempt to be less descriptive and more analytical than its predecessor* Screen Education. *Providing the space for would-be academics to practise does not please BFI Governors. They all but demolish the Education Department and inadvertently offer SEFT the franchise for theorising cinema.*

What had appeared in early 1968 to be the beginnings of a smooth transition to a more professionally organised SEFT with a new journal *Screen*, working collaboratively with a substantial BFI Education Department proved to be mistaken. Within three years a series of events meant that an independent (though part BFI funded) SEFT would be at a distance from a demoralised and reduced department re-branded as the Educational Advisory Service.

SEFT Prepares for the Seventies

When SEFT took the decision to cease publication of *Screen Education* and the *Screen Education Yearbook*, its Secretary Alex Richardson was not at the meeting. He had been absent ill from the spring of 1968 when Terry Bolas had taken on the role of Acting Secretary by the time of the AGM in May.[1] Richardson never returned to work for SEFT and finally was replaced officially on 1 January 1969 by Bolas who then became Teacher Adviser BFI/Secretary SEFT. The long period without a professional officer undoubtedly slowed the momentum of change for SEFT. On a day-to-day basis there was no immediate crisis in that Richardson's secretary, Anna Mathon, continued in post and dealt with routine written enquiries and phone calls. She had two sources of support: the SEFT Committee members and – more immediately to hand – members of the BFI Education Department within whose offices at 70 Old Compton Street the SEFT Office was then located. Separated from the main BFI base at 81 Dean Street, the Education Department was self-contained with projection and viewing table facilities on site. Thus while the Society benefited from the support Whannel and his staff offered at this stage, inevitably the clear distinction between the BFI and SEFT as separate organisations became blurred while the Committee waited in the expectation that Richardson would eventually return to work.

SEFT had started the 1960s proposing a wide range of projects which would support its membership. By 1970, with its commitment to *Screen*, the Society had to concentrate its energies and modify its activities. The Viewing Panels, where a small group of teachers had once produced reports on films for use by others, had been replaced. In both Leeds and London feature film viewing sessions were held regularly which teachers could attend and decide for themselves on the potential usefulness of the films. The summer schools, still under the aegis of the Educational Development Association, had shifted their base to Barry College of Education in Wales which became their regular venue. They were led by SEFT Committee member Kevin Gough-Yates from Hornsey College of Art. A determined effort led by Jim Cook was made to develop SEFT activities in the regions. These would only ever be pump-priming ventures and the Society accepted that its success rate would depend on the energy of individual SEFT members in regional centres.

Conferences became the responsibility of David Lusted.[2] In 1969 two recently appointed Education Department recruits were pitted against each other to demonstrate how the same extract material might be used in their respective educational situations. Jim Hillier demonstrated the use of film to provide 'evidence' of social issues within the Humanities Curriculum Project while Colin McArthur spoke on interpreting the film as a text within the scope of authorship or genre study.[3] In 1970 the conference was entitled 'The Theory of Film Teaching' where individuals outlined the theory behind their individual classroom practice.[4]

One small scale SEFT/ILEA Project in 1970 became the precursor of a much bigger BFI/ILEA Project later in the decade. Bolas negotiated with Leslie Ryder for the ILEA to fund a one term film teaching experiment about genres in one of the Education

Authority's divisions. Students from the seven participating schools came together to view feature films centrally. Follow-up by their teachers in individual schools was supported by material specially prepared for the project. Most students were in their fourth (and at that time final year) of secondary education.[5] The later BFI project would be for Sixth Formers.

The task of editing *Screen* was shared between Kevin Gough-Yates and Terry Bolas, both being volunteers from the SEFT Committee. Plans for the new journal were made during the latter part of 1968. Whannel was supportive of these changes and there was informal agreement between him and the new editors that appropriate contributions from his department would be welcome in *Screen*.[6] It was also the case that Whannel indicated he would like to have a more influential role in that there should be some form of editorial board. The prospective editors resisted this, wanting to establish a distinct SEFT identity. Simultaneously however Whannel was coming under pressure from BFI Governors who were becoming suspicious of the Education Department's emphases.

A University Department

The two BFI departments which had benefited most from the Institute's changed funding arrangements were the Education Department and the arm of the Distribution Department that was setting up Regional Film Theatres. It was the latter which had by far the greater share of new money and that was expanding rapidly but haphazardly.[7] However it was Education that became a target, probably because Whannel had clear plans and priorities and was ready to declare these. It was perhaps inevitable that Governors would challenge the educational proposals because they were detailed and demanded supportive decision-making while there was little at stake in giving a blanket welcome to the general reports that the Regional Film Theatres were spreading the BFI's presence nationally. It is unclear what Reed's stance was at this point, though events were to prove he would become increasingly hostile to the Department he had so assiduously developed over two decades.

Whannel submitted his detailed paper to BFI Governors in November 1968.[8] It is a coherent and well argued paper but there is one statement which, though accurate, now stands out to the reader as a hostage to fortune. He states that 'the department operates like a University Department'.[9] Although this statement is clearly contexted in such a way as to demonstrate its relevance and precision, its apparent ambition might suggest to a governing body dominated by representatives of the film industry that Whannel was taking the BFI into new territory where other agencies might legitimately want to become involved in oversight of the Institute. For Reed whose original Film Appreciation Department had focused so specifically on schools, this must have signalled an impending radical shift in priorities. Perhaps his first organisational response to the paper was in early 1969 to bring the Education Department (plus SEFT) out of its familiar Old Compton Street establishment into the main BFI premises at 81 Dean Street.

Whannel's hand-picked staff of fifteen included Peter Wollen, responsible for publications. Wollen was the staff member most active in seeking to promote an academic atmosphere. Starting in 1967 he organised a regular series of BFI Education Department seminars held originally in Old Compton Street but later in Dean Street. Attendance at these seminars was by invitation only. Most presentations were given by current or former Department staff but among the outsiders invited were Tom Nairn and Sam Rohdie, then a lecturer in Film at the Sheffield Polytechnic, who led two seminars on 'Totems and Movies' and 'Style, Rhetoric and Genre'.[10]

Wollen announced the introduction of these seminars in *Screen Education* where readers were told that the Education Department had 'decided to start an experimental series of film seminars bringing together film critics, film teachers and university teachers and researchers in the established disciplines'.[11] As a taster, the first of these seminars by Alan Lovell on the Western was printed in *Screen Education*.[12] Subsequent seminar papers were however to be 'published in bulletin form by the BFI Education Department'.[13] It is clear that Wollen saw his task as initiating a radically new approach to film study. It is also evident that his focus is specifically film and not any other visual medium. Indicative of his attitude at this point is his assumption that he is entering new territory and may therefore start from scratch. Subsequently members of the 1970s *Screen* Editorial Board were also to consider themselves as prime movers. Wollen begins

> The cinema is a new force, a new mode of communication, a new artform. To think, write or speak about the cinema in some sense necessitates a break with old habits of thought and traditional academic approaches and attitudes.

Later he asserts

> Our general aim was to see what kind of interconnections could be made between the tradition of film criticism, of analysis of individual films and directors, and work being done in mass media sociology, linguistics and semiology etc.[14]

Whether BFI Governors read these comments is doubtful, but the article is indicative of an élitist attitude. Since at that point *Screen Education* was the only journal to be circulated to the great majority of those who potentially might have wished to have sight of the seminar papers, it is extraordinary that no arrangement was sought with SEFT as to the regular publication of at least some of the papers. At a subsequent seminar Alan Lovell delivered a paper 'The Aims of Film Education' which – apart from its centrality to the BFI/SEFT enterprise – acknowledges the existence of *Screen Education* in a positive light, yet his paper was made available only as a duplicated document from the BFI.[15]

For the next two decades, a recurrent feature of the debates around most aspects of media education was to be the split between on the one hand those who saw themselves as the originators of theoretical developments and on the other the classroom practitioners who found they had the task of putting theory to the test. In part it had its origins in the ring-fencing of these and subsequent seminars. But Wollen was pressuring Whannel more specifically on ways in which the Department might engage with research. In a memo headed 'Film Research' in August 1968 he stresses three demands to be made by the Department.

1. Viewing facilities must be made more easily accessible.
2. We should continue to press for Institute research grants.
3. We should try to set up new ways of encouraging a constant two-way traffic between the critic and theorist, working in comparative depth and often in isolation, and the teacher in the school or college.[16]

Wollen follows this up a few days later under the heading 'Research Scholarships' suggesting two possible models:

1. University postgraduates completing a thesis involving the cinema.
2. Teachers seconded to do research.

For the first proposal he envisages a link with the Birmingham Centre for Contemporary Cultural Studies; for the second he is much less clear where the secondment might be located, which could perhaps suggest he had in mind that the Department itself might have been a possibility.[17] When Whannel produced his report to Governors he proposed the BFI fund Research Fellowships 'which could be operated jointly by the Institute and a University Department'.[18]

When Whannel's paper was presented to Governors, it was accompanied by two other papers, one from Martyn Howells, the BFI Regional Education Officer who operated within the Distribution Division, and the other from the British Universities' Film Council, which was another BFI grant-in-aid body. Reed said that 'the papers before the meeting represented the three main aspects of the Institute's educational policy'.[19] SEFT got only the briefest mention in the Whannel paper whereas it might well have merited more substantial recognition. It seems reasonable to infer that since SEFT had been without a professional officer for most of 1968, neither Whannel nor Reed (who only days before had agreed to Bolas replacing Richardson in the post) would have thought it politic to draw attention to the Society at this point

Whannel uses the C Word
Whannel came under attack from Governors Helen Forman and Edgar Anstey. His paper had argued for his Department's central role in developing a film culture and he had used the scale and scope represented by a literary culture as an analogy for what might be achievable. Forman argued that in the longer term it was film's historical importance which would prove more enduring while Anstey wanted to extend the

Department's remit and for it to have a much broader and less aesthetic approach to film. The Governors' minutes provide only the sketchiest account of the debate but it seems clear that although Whannel's arguments were detailed, his opponents refused to engage with the detail. They seem to have registered the carefully argued case as evidence of plotting being already at an advanced stage. Paul Adorian however did challenge the proposals specifically – for wanting engagement at university level. He argued the Department should concentrate on work in schools. Roy Shaw pointed out the Department could only extend its remit at the expense of activities that it was currently undertaking.[20] Discussion of the item concluded ominously when, on the proposition of the Chairman, it was agreed

(i)   that an early opportunity be provided of debating further the policy issues raised by Mr Whannel's paper, as these could not be determined in respect of the Education Department alone;
(ii) that every endeavour should meanwhile be made to build up the educational services of the Institute's own Theatres in the Regions;
(iii) that subject to the further policy discussion proposed in (i) the Institute should continue to interest itself in the wider uses of film as well as in the film as art.[21]

The uninformed reader might have noted with curiosity the fact that when the BFI Governors had held their meeting in November 1968 and mounted opposition to Whannel's pleas for university involvement in film education, there was at the meeting a representative of the British Universities Film Council. The BUFC like SEFT was a grant-in-aid body of the BFI and like SEFT it had an officer post funded by BFI. Nowhere in the minutes is it suggested that Whannel's desire for university links might be encroaching on BUFC territory and that there was already a body in place to do the work he proposed. They did not, simply because the BUFC's priorities were not those of developing film education. Later when celebrating 25 years of existence in 1973 the BUFC in its journal *University Vision* made clear what it considered it had achieved. It had

…sought to draw our attention to the fact that film and other forms of audio-visual materials can play an important and often indispensable role in university level teaching and research, and that the study of film, and latterly of television, is a worthwhile and legitimate pursuit in universities. That this fact is today generally accepted without question is due in very large measure to the diligence and enthusiasm of the many individuals and organisations who have devoted much time, energy and money to the support of the Council.[22]

In the same issue was printed an obituary notice for an Ernest Lindgren, Curator of the National Film Archive, who had been the principal supporter of the BUFC within the BFI. In this it is made clear that Lindgren had promoted a wider university involvement with film than the BUFC had then thought it appropriate to recognise.[23] Essentially BUFC at this stage promoted film as an educational aid; apart from the post held by Thorold Dickenson at the Slade, film as an object of study was not recognised in universities.

In October 1968, the month before the BFI Governors met to consider Whannel's paper, *University Vision* had published an article by Stuart Hall 'The Impact of Film on the University'. He summarises the situation.

> The interest in film in universities seems to be confined – with some notable exceptions – to its technical uses for the purposes of instruction, the reproduction and transmission of information by this new channel.
>
> But anything to match the serious, intense, extended, disciplined study of the cinematic image, of serious film, of the work over years of important directors, of national cinemas styles or of cinematic genres which is the bread and butter of serious intellectual work on the cinema hasn't much of a place.[24]

Subsequently *University Vision* would print an article relevant to film education but which would unintentionally serve to demonstrate the *Vision's* marginal understanding of developments. Liz-Anne Bawden writing from the perspective of the Slade Film Department uses a report in *Screen* as the starting point for her account of 'Film Studies in the University'.[25] The existence of bi-monthly *Screen* then appears to have slipped her memory when she subsequently says there is a 'crying need' for a film studies journal, but she thinks its potential readership is too small for it ever to exist, unless it were to be published in more than one language.[26]

Enter *Screen*

While these internal BFI debates were taking place at the beginning of what was eventually to become a devastating attack by Governors on the Education Department, SEFT was preoccupied with the launch of *Screen*. The Editorial in the first issue divided the journal's intentions into two main areas thus:

> The Editors intend *Screen* to provide a forum in which controversial areas relevant to the study of film and television can be examined and argued. It is by no means clear what the nature of Film Study should be.
>
> At the same time *Screen* will contain articles of considered criticism.[27]

The former intention was distinct from past *Screen Education* practice where accounts of what teachers did in their classrooms had been published usually without comment or context. *Screen* intended to open up debates and within the next two years attempted to do this.[28] There were still to be accounts of classroom practice but these were designed to relate any description to the underlying educational/theoretical position of the teacher.

The editing of the journal had been planned as a joint enterprise between Gough-Yates and Bolas. However by replacing Richardson as the Society's professional officer, Bolas's priorities had to change. Thus Gough-Yates assumed the principal role in commissioning articles and seeking new writers; Bolas while doing some of this took on the organisational and production tasks that were best handled centrally and might sit more easily alongside the SEFT Secretary's many other roles, plus the duties of Teacher Adviser BFI. On a more practical level, the Editors wanted *Screen* to look different from *Screen Education* which had changed layout styles from issue to issue. Its illustrations had frequently been achieved by using printing blocks provided free by distributors wishing to promote their current films. In the new journal illustrations had to relate directly to the articles they accompanied. This point was emphasised from the outset in the article about editing *If* where frames from the film were reproduced within the wide margins that the new design allowed.[29] *Screen* intended that it should look the part of a serious journal about film and how it might be taught.

In its venture into current film criticism, *Screen* was over ambitious. *Screen Education* had never attempted to engage with current film releases. For its readership a practical assumption had been that the journal would only consider writing about a film when it became available on 16 mm. *Screen* abandoned reviewing current films after its third issue. Production difficulties meant that issues four and five had to be combined into a double issue which covered the period from July to October. By the time *Screen* 4/5 would have reached SEFT members any film reviewed would have disappeared from the cinemas long before.

The Editors considered it important to link *Screen* with other SEFT activities. There were obvious ways of doing this: identifying and promoting SEFT events in a more systematic way than had happened previously. Significantly the journal could benefit from work initiated elsewhere in the Society. The articles on Arthur Penn's films printed in the first four issues were written as developments from the previous year's SEFT Summer School where Penn had been studied in the context of the American Cinema.

In an attempt to meet the demands of members for reference information and advisory documentation which had been a feature of the now defunct *Yearbook*, the Society took two different approaches. *Screen* published book listings of a more specialised kind. In doing this it enlisted expert help. The most significant of these contributors was Gillian Hartnoll, the BFI Deputy Head Librarian. She produced a series of lists which – whatever their contemporary usefulness might have been – now have a particular value in providing a snapshot of what was available to the film teacher at the start of the 1970s.[30] Of potentially greatest interest is her select list of available works on film theory which includes only thirteen books. The other approach which was less successful was SEFT's production of duplicated materials. Roy Armes was the Committee member responsible for this area. Reporting to the Society in 1970 he had to acknowledge

SEFT's limitations.[31] A questionnaire to members had revealed a great range of potential demands, some of which could already be met by BFI documents, had members been aware of them. SEFT had clearly to design its provision of materials in the context of what BFI had already available.

The Editors of *Screen* wanted the journal to be the locus of debates about film teaching. The most successful of these ventures was that between Alan Lovell and Robin Wood.[32] When Andrew McTaggart and Roy Armes[33] addressed Peter Wollen's recently published *Signs and Meaning in the Cinema,*[34] a reply from Wollen was sought, promised but never received.[35] Sadly Wollen failed to participate in precisely the kind of two-way dialogue between educationists and researchers that he had advocated so strongly when in post in the Education Department. There was however a response from Richard Collins to Ed Buscombe's article on genre.[36] The important debate for which *Screen* did provide an arena (and that fits into the context of which Whannel was writing) was that between Lovell and Wood. Lovell had held a variety of roles in the Education Department and would subsequently be a significant figure in SEFT and *Screen*. Long associated with, and influential in, the BFI/London University Extra-Mural classes, he was an independent thinker.[37] Wood was firmly committed to a Leavisite position and had become an important critic both through his association with *Movie* and because of his auteur criticism of Hawks and Hitchcock in two groundbreaking books.

In practice the debate commenced with Lovell's seminar paper mentioned above. In it Lovell had identified what he claimed were the three permanent approaches used in film teaching in the late 1960s: 'the Culture and Society position, the Film Language position and the Film and Social Studies position'.[38] He points out the limitations of each. The latter two were identifiable in secondary and further education respectively, though it is unclear as to how extensive each was. He is uneasy at the links made within each approach to what was in practice moral teaching. He argues that as a result of these moral emphases, Film Language teaching comes to favour the social documentary style of film-making while in the Film and Social Studies work, social studies priorities dominate in terms of how the film is presented and discussed. His principal dispute is with the Leavisite approach which had been so widely influential in British education that some film teachers, unfamiliar with alternative methods of teaching film, had – especially within English departments – transferred this Leavisite approach to film. It is clear that Lovell is anticipating the development of the study of mass media: the 'mass media are such an important part of the contemporary environment that the educational system must take some account of the phenomenon'.[39] Leavis's attitude to the mass media had been fundamentally hostile, so Lovell argues there must be a reappraisal of how media teaching should be structured so that the Leavisites were not simply in a position to offer the default approach. He sees the study of cinema as a potential way in to the proper scrutiny of mass media, but acknowledges that it is only one of the options available. In his acceptance of the overarching presence of the media he was in the vanguard of thoughtful opinion of the time.

Given that Lovell saw the Leavisite approach as hostile to the study of mass media, he was an appropriate writer for *Screen* to ask to address the thrust of Robin Wood's criticism which both embodied the Leavisite position and was, by dint of Wood's books, becoming a model of how film study might be undertaken. These books were also widely available and accessible to the uninitiated reader. Lovell's own seminar paper had had a much more limited circulation as a duplicated document. The substance of the Wood/Lovell debate depends on there being a great deal of intricate quoting and cross-quoting from Wood's books. Consequently although the limitations of Wood's stance were to become clearer, the discussion of alternative ways of approaching film and other media is sidelined, as Lovell has to acknowledge.[40] The background to Lovell's thinking was firstly his long-established place within the Education Department and its seminars and secondly his years of teaching on the Extra-Mural Certificate. But Wood's arguments were in the public domain. Consequently although Lovell did expose some of the detailed weaknesses of Wood's position, by so doing he lost the opportunity do more than simply list the broad range of ideas the seminar group were beginning to explore:

> ...ideas derived from structural linguistics and anthropology (structuralism and semiology), from literary criticism and art history (genre and iconography), from sociology (the relationships between art and industry, the nature of movements).[41]

Screen publishes Whannel

Paddy Whannel published very little during his later time as Education Officer. He wrote much, but mainly for internal BFI circulation. With the coming of *Screen* he was able to use its pages to disseminate more widely his thoughts on film education. But by 1971 when he would make his final contribution it was in the extraordinary circumstances that accompanied his resignation. But it is his forecasts in the three earlier reports, that he wrote partly with inclusion in *Screen* in mind, which were to be quoted in the succeeding decades by those who sought to establish their bearings.[42] Whannel's statements have importance not simply because of his accepted status within the film teaching community at that time but also because of their being published in SEFT's journal. The views he expressed were consequently endorsed by SEFT. What Whannel states represented a consensus among the key players at the start of the 1970s. At that point it must have seemed that the movement was well placed to progress. Not only was *Screen* speaking for SEFT as *Screen Education* never had, but there was, it seemed, again a joint enterprise with BFI.

In his three articles for *Screen* during 1969/70 Whannel is consistent in seeking to establish film study in higher education. Even in his first article where he is dealing with the issues of film availability, he mentions the problems faced by those established teachers wishing to have in-service training.[43] Two such one-term courses existed at the end of the 1960s – at Bede College, Durham and Hornsey College of Art Teacher

Training Department. The Bede experiment was short-lived, not because of lack of applicants, but because of the difficulties of their gaining secondment.[44] The Hornsey Course benefited from its proximity to the Inner London Education Authority which, guided by its Aural and Visual Aids Inspector Leslie Ryder, was more sympathetic to such secondments. Significantly the education authority was funded at a level to facilitate secondments to non-mainstream courses. Whannel mentions the attempts by Douglas Lowndes from Hornsey to develop his work into a one-year course at the University of London Institute of Education.[45] Lowndes has revealed how his application failed.[46] The Institute rejected the proposed course because he could not demonstrate that there existed the literature and theory to support it. Yet it was precisely because of this need to develop research in order to produce the back-up documentation for serious study that the MA was being proposed. It was being offered as a necessary stage in the evolution of film study. Several of the students from the one term Hornsey Course: Jim Cook, Jim Hillier, Chris Mottershead were to become significant contributors to SEFT and to the development of film and media education. A decade later the Institute would develop an MA under Bob Ferguson who had been a colleague of Lowndes at Hornsey. Had the Institute responded to Lowndes's proposals, the evolution of film and media study in the 1970s might have had very different emphases.

In a significant shift from the anti-examination stance of his two previous deputies, Harcourt and Kitses, Whannel draws attention to the first joint BFI/SEFT publication for almost two decades: *CSE Examinations in Film*. Researched by Roger Watkins (who would become Chairman of SEFT in 1970), the booklet is cautious in nudging the film education movement towards examinations.

> The purpose of this pamphlet is to acquaint the inquiring teacher with information about examinations in Film and to encourage him to think independently about his own situation.[47]

In his next *Screen* article Whannel tackles fundamental areas. He begins by demonstrating the inadequacy of the terminology that defines what is to be studied. His own emphasis on the priority and specificity of film is clear. He rejects 'Screen Education' because it had been created to include television. As the title of SEFT's re-styled journal it had also been rejected, though for a different reason. Whannel was uneasy that 'Screen' might be too inclusive; SEFT had felt that 'Education' might be a limitation. Subsequently *Screen Education* was successfully reintroduced as the title of a second SEFT journal, once *Screen*'s new identity had been established.

> The fact that there is no agreed term to describe the subject, no equivalent of the term 'literature', for example, is the most obvious indication of the difficulty. All of us shift uneasily between such descriptions as Film Education, with the danger of confusing the subject with audio-visual aids, and the clumsy Screen Education, implying the uncertain and dubious inclusion of television. At times, for the sake

of clarity, we are even driven to return to the old-fashioned term, Film Appreciation, with all its limiting connotations.[48]

Today Film Study has an identity within all levels of education; Media Studies is widely accepted and has a space for film within it. Media education and media literacy are terms that extend the media umbrella even more widely. But in 1970, film as the main object of study was perceived as being under threat. Whannel's previously Leavisite position was being revised as a result; he now felt that it was the economics of the situation that threatened film. The costs of film hire were expensive while other media were available more cheaply.

> The film will not establish itself as a discipline in its own right, with its own body of knowledge and expertise, if its use in education is confined to being a secondary element within some other course. The danger is illustrated by the number of textbooks on Mass Media Studies now available, which offer a sketchy introduction to the cinema over a handful of pages in the context of chapters on such traditional Leavisite concerns as advertising, newspapers and popular magazines and, in some cases, adding the further confusion of sections on topics like the development of printing and telephonic communication.
>
> We have to argue first of all for the *idea* of the study of film as art and entertainment as a distinct discipline having its own particular problems. Secondly, we need to establish centres at all levels in education, but especially within higher education, where such a study can take place.[49]

His argument says that the case for film study must be starkly made – all the supporting secondary arguments may be deployed but it is crucial to state that

> ...the cinema is a significant feature of contemporary culture representing the most developed and distinctive form of art produced by technology with the unique feature that its growth, from its most primitive beginnings, is preserved for study on celluloid.[50]

The late 1960s was a time when the term 'educational technology' was being widely adopted. A range of new equipment useful in the classroom was available and affordable. The once rare 16mm sound projector was well established and had been joined by the 35mm carousel projector and most importantly by the overhead projector. Film study was beginning to be subsumed in this explosion of activity. At Wandsworth Technical College the staff of the Department of Educational Technology included those lecturers responsible for all the Liberal Studies teaching in the college; among them were those who taught film. That department's prime purpose however was to provide training in the use of audio visual aids to all ILEA teachers. Educational technology also then spawned a new kind of educationist: the Media Resources Officer (MRO) whose areas of responsibility were conceived as being wide and flexible. Whannel interpreted the implications of these developments as paralleling the intellectual stance of the then influential Marshall McLuhan. The educational technologist's role emphasised the 'instrumental capacities of media'. The 'imaginative and expressive qualities' were losing out.[51] For much of the post-war period both SEFT and BFI had striven to dissociate their project from that of the audio visual specialist. By 1970 the status of the latter group was clearly in the ascendant.

He also begins to disown the parallel drawn between film and literature, albeit this was the analogy that he had used to BFI Governors. Perhaps here he was shifting his position, knowing how what had seemed an innocuous and appropriate comparison had so antagonised certain governors.

> By and large, the literary culture, with its emphasis on good taste and a refined personal sensibility, *is* narrow. Nothing could be less desirable than to impose such a straitjacket on the cinema which is, after all, not only an art, but also an industry and a form of mass entertainment. The problem is, therefore, to define the content of film study sufficiently rigorously to give it coherence without suffocating it by too narrow a framework.[52]

He then attempts to define the subject, thereby giving a very clear indication of what his thinking was in 1969. He divides the components of the subject into criticism, theory and contextual studies. His brief summary sentences distil very precisely what many involved teachers thought at the time.

Criticism:
There is a need to develop systematic approaches and to find more objective bases for critical analysis than personal taste and sensibility. At present the various ideas clustered around the notions of author and genre would seem to present the most useful starting points.

Theory:
Much must be derived from other fields such as the work in aesthetics and the more specialised studies like semiology and communications theory.[53]

Contextual studies:
[Where he assumes the core of the work will be the study of a particular director.]
Areas to be covered here include the structure of the industry, the production system, the entertainment forms available and the critical climate. Here again the aid of other subject disciplines, such as sociology and economic history, must be sought.[54]

If Whannel felt able to define the fundamental areas of film study for investigation, he was aware that he wrote at a time when for some these issues were irrelevant. Many teachers, some as a result of the Education Department's own promotional publications, were using film thematically. Indeed by housing and supporting the Humanities Curriculum Project's Film Officer, Whannel had encouraged this development, albeit on the strategic basis that it was better to have the project inside rather than outside the BFI. There was a price to be paid for this, both in terms of the increased workload for his advisory staff and in the dilution of what film study might offer

> ...the constant insistence on discussion and on the probing of values, the relative absence of a defined body of knowledge and the lack of a systematic critical procedure, all lead to difficulties of their own which can place some strain on both pupil and teacher. If we add to these difficulties the problem of deciding whether it is the theme or the character of the film which should control and define a discussion, we have a situation which can be rather daunting, especially for the teacher coming fresh to film study.[55]

Manoeuvring in this current – where film was being used in a thematic context – presented a problem and one for which he could offer only two suggestions. The Humanities Curriculum Project was due to be formally reviewed and evaluated. Since the basis of its approach had been thematic, the results of this review might be helpful. A second proposal was that courses might be developed on 'some formal principle drawn from the study of film as art'.[56] It seems clear that the momentum generated by the increasing use of feature film in the classroom was not readily facilitating an investigation of its proper place in education.

The Education Department under Whannel had regularly been confronted with the problem of determining the place and importance of practical work. The members of the department had not been film-makers; they were skilled users of words. On the other hand SEFT had always maintained some film-makers in its key roles, even if their expertise was that of proficient amateurs. The work Douglas Lowndes was demonstrating from his position in teacher training appeared to challenge SEFT's support for the group-made film. The promotion of Lowndes's work by the Education Department was a means by which the department could be recognised as not ignoring the issue of students and practical work. In defending that position Whannel draws a parallel from art education where he maintains there is an accepted and clear distinction between the scholar and the practitioner.

Whannel ends by returning to the project of his department which had so upset the Governors: the development of a film culture. He attempts to put his department's role into context by drawing attention to the other agencies which needed to be involved. These included agencies (as he attempts tactfully to point out) that are within the establishment of the BFI itself, including its publications, the National Film Archive and the National and Regional Film Theatres. What he was not able to say was how separate and indeed hostile to each other these departments then were. To conclude he feels the need to have some proposals as to a way forward. Given that his room for manoeuvre within the BFI was limited, he ends by finding safety in the same project that he had so vigorously championed in the late 1950s with the Joint Council for Education through Art.

> The idea of agency is more dynamic than a concept like museum. The idea of film culture is wider than the notion of film art. The point, therefore, in using the term Agencies of Film Culture is to imply an alliance of artist, critic and teacher in an activist programme.[57]

A decade earlier there had been much broader involvement around this alliance both from within the BFI and beyond it.

A year later Whannel projects a more confident outlook. Indeed much of what he then expected to happen, did. What he did not foresee – or at least did not feel able to commit to paper – was how vulnerable was his own position within that future. In 1969 he had limited his suggestions as to future developments to stating that the coming of videotape would transform the possibilities for studying film.[58] Here he felt able to be more generally positive.

> In the seventies it will move decisively out of its pioneering phase into a period when the outlines of its discipline will emerge more clearly and the study of film, once dependent upon the individual's private enthusiasm, will receive more public and institutional support.
>
> Most of our definitions and formulations are made in the heat of the battle and are therefore provisional.[59]

Where in 1969 he had seemed prepared to acknowledge that the term 'Film Appreciation' still had a value as a point of reference, now he welcomes the extending, if rather indeterminate, scope of film study and identifies as a measure of this achievement the abandonment of the earlier term.

> This was symbolised some years ago by the decision to drop the term 'film appreciation', with all its narrow connotations, from the title of the Department.[60]

The strands making up the identity of the emerging subject have changed somewhat. Theory and criticism remain, but Contextual Studies is replaced by 'the debate about popular culture'. Here also Whannel appears to be shifting away from the moral and Leavisite tone that had been detectable in *The Popular Arts* to allow for a more inclusive and objective approach to popular culture.

It will be broader and more flexible, more dependent on knowledge than on 'good taste' and calling for more diverse lines of attack than the individual critical insight. In this sense once the enormous opportunities for its study have been fully realised it could provide an important challenge and stimulus to the study of art and society in general.[61]

But when he considers the basic territory, he has to repeat the questions of the previous year.

What is the subject Film Study? What are its appropriate teaching methods? How will it become more firmly established as a recognised discipline?[62]

Therefore whilst depicting a greater use of film at all levels of education, he emphasises that the fundamental issues as to the nature and methodology of film teaching remain largely unexplored. He takes some satisfaction from the fact that his Department's seminars are setting out specifically to investigate these. The nature of the debate around practical work has changed too. Jennie Lee had used her visit to open the Young Screen Exhibition in the previous summer to announce the setting up of the National Film School. Its recently appointed principal, Colin Young, had become an occasional visitor to the Education Department.[63] Young's commitment to, and preference for, practice rather than theory would perhaps lead to a redefining of what Whannel might expect from the universities.

Whannel consequently has to acknowledge the specifically British situation around the study of film. Its acceptance in higher education was the final stage of its fitting into the educational hierarchy. Unlike the USA where film study had percolated down into the schools, in Britain it had worked its way up from the schools. He explains this origin by uncharacteristically demonising the process by which the schools had become involved.

Presumably this is because of the paternalistic and moralising approach to the media characteristic of the English (at their best and worst) which sustained the belief that the mass audience needed to be protected from the false values of the movies by being trained in awareness, but that the educated few were saved by having natural good taste.[64]

There were, as has been shown, some vociferous proponents of this view, but it was not the case that this view predominated. For SEFT activists in the two preceding decades, it was their own enthusiasm for film that motivated them.

His article is about servicing the film teacher. Whannel clearly believed that the long term solution was to reverse the 'bottom up' engine that had propelled the study of film during the post-war period. The establishment of film study within higher education was not to be an end in itself. It would be the means by which the many issues and questions that Whannel had identified as impinging on the identity of the subject might be resolved.

> Even given our limited knowledge it seems crucial at this stage to make every effort to establish film study as a distinct discipline at key points within the university. This is important first of all as a strategy. Further advances at other levels are probably conditional on achieving such a status. Secondly, developments in research and scholarship are necessary to sustain the work at the school, further education, adult education and college level. It would seem that a number of problems facing the teacher can only be solved by advances elsewhere.[65]

Where he may be seen as especially prescient – in the light of the developments that took place within SEFT and *Screen* in succeeding years – were in his expectations of the potential that might be detected in the post-1968 generation of young graduates. It is also clear what part he envisages for the BFI in response.

> It is a distinctive feature of this new generation that they are interested in a wide range of film topics, including theoretical questions, but it remains true that formal education provides little opportunity for them to pursue the study of film in a sustained or systematic way.
> ...the Film Institute has an important role to play in this development, especially in the transitional period before fully financed and well-equipped film departments flourish. Already a great many university ventures are sustained by lectures and documentation from the Department and the Institute is now making more money available to support the viewings essential for research purposes.[66]

Clearly aware of the teacher readership of *Screen* he ends his report by reiterating the persistent practical problems that he had identified in previous years. There are certain specifics where he is assertive.

> For some time now we've had requests for definitive film textbooks. These requests have been resisted on the grounds of not wanting to create an orthodoxy and instead we have concentrated on accounts of teaching experiences.[67]

In practice he had begun to provide more substantial film literature through the Department's involvement in the *Cinema One* series. But ever the clear-sighted administrator, Whannel understands that for many teachers it is the costliness of beginning the film teaching enterprise which thwarts them. So he finally concludes by acknowledging how so much of what is or is not possible lies with those who control film distribution.

On the other hand if the needs of film teachers were more clearly understood, if the idea of using a feature for study by a small group were properly distinguished from its showing to the whole school as a holiday treat, and if the idea of creating a population with a film culture was seen in its broad relevance to the changing audience for cinema and the changing exhibition pattern, then we might be able to work towards a more regularised system of discounts related to use.[68]

Enter Sam Rohdie

When Bolas decided to return to school teaching in autumn 1970, the post he had held as Teacher Adviser BFI/Secretary SEFT was redesigned as Secretary SEFT/Editor *Screen*.[69] The redesignation appealed to both BFI and SEFT, but for different reasons. It had become clear that the BFI and SEFT parts of the job did not sit easily together. If the post holder were to be the sole professional officer of the Society s/he had to negotiate on behalf of SEFT with an organisation for which s/he had also the duties of an employee. It was also the case that as Bolas had also been Editor of *Screen*, not a situation envisaged when the original joint appointment was made, the workload of the post had been great. Whannel had been supportive in reducing the BFI advisory element of this workload.[70]

For SEFT therefore it was a much more workable arrangement that the post should be almost wholly concerned with SEFT matters and that the paid professional officer should have editorship of *Screen* which was by far the Society's principal financial commitment.[71] Whannel on the other hand was aware that when the post came to be advertised the Editorship of *Screen* element of the post would attract a much more substantial field of applicants than would the Secretarial role. He saw the opportunity to strengthen the 'academy in waiting' through which Harcourt, Perkins, Kitses and Wollen had already passed. Although this would be a SEFT post, the appointment would remain a joint one by BFI/SEFT.[72] Furthermore, Whannel had got SEFT's agreement that the new Editor would be answerable to a joint editorial board.[73]

Sam Rohdie was appointed Editor of *Screen* and General Secretary SEFT in August 1970 and took up the post in January 1971.[74] During the three years he held the post, the status of SEFT, the project of *Screen* and the scope of BFI Education changed fundamentally. In practice SEFT would be the beneficiary of the BFI Governors' determination to curb Whannel's Education Department. The situation Rohdie inherited at SEFT was one of an organisation in flux. There had been an accelerating process of committee change. Vannoey and Wills, the last of the 1950s' Committee, had left. Watkins, himself a relative newcomer, took over as Chairman for most of 1970 but then, having taken a job in Leeds, he was unable to continue. When Rohdie joined SEFT the replacement Acting Chairman was Jim Cook and the Acting Treasurer was Edward Buscombe, who also took over from a departing long-term committee member Chris Bott.[75] By the time of the 1972 AGM only John Bennett, Buscombe, Cook and David Lusted remained of those committee members who had reported to the 1970 AGM.[76]

A consequence both of his workplace location within 81 Dean Street and of the SEFT substitutions among its voluntary officers, Rohdie probably depended more on the support of staff in the Education Department.[77] It seems however that he was a naturally independent operator who found himself in a situation where he was able to operate independently. His first issue of *Screen* proclaims difference. It has a new and distinctive design by Gerald Cinamon and is now published quarterly.[78] Its Editorial is signed by The Editorial Board and states unequivocally that the 'emphasis in *Screen* on theory is crucial'.[79] As if to place *Screen's* new venture into context the Editorial implies that the journal will not be influenced by what had been written about film in most of the twentieth century. In this Rohdie echoes Wollen's earlier adherence to the novelty of film.

> Above all film must be studied as a new medium, a product of this century and of the machine, and which as a new medium and a new mode of expression challenges traditional notions of art and criticism and the system of education which still in part is tied to these notions.[80]

This statement written in 1971 has clear echoes of what had been written half a century earlier. Subsequently *Screen* did pay great attention to what had been written about the cinema in the early years of the Soviet Union.[81] It must have been interpreted by *Screen's* readers as a rather arrogant anachronism in a journal that already had a twenty year history of promoting the serious study of a medium already seventy five years old.

The trope of the new *Screen* identity may be inferred from its contents. Its principal article is a reprint in translation from *Cahiérs du Cinema*. While reviewing a book by US academics, Ben Brewster produces an article on 'Structuralism in Film Criticism'. Claire Johnston, who like Brewster would be an influential and long-term member of the SEFT Committee, surveys film journals in Britain and France.[82] At the back of the issue are to be found 'Education Notes', compiled by Diana Matias, the Editorial Assistant. This section

> ...has been introduced to provide a more direct link between the Society and its services on the one hand, and the teacher and the classroom on the other.[83]

Ominously a distinction is being made here between SEFT (which existed because of the teachers who subscribed to become its members) and the needs of those same teachers which are apparently to be addressed as an afterthought. Reassurance might be sought in the article which Rohdie himself contributed to the issue.[84] It is certainly possible to find something that reads like reassurance even if it is in a paragraph which plainly contradicts what the *Screen* Editorial Board had asserted about theory, only a few pages earlier.

The practical work of *Screen* is education. It is not primarily a journal for professional intellectuals, film critics, cinephiles, but for practising teachers. For it to be intellectualist would not only be sterile in itself, but it would not serve its supposed educational practice.[85]

But in the light of what would subsequently happen in *Screen*, Rohdie was perhaps protesting too much.

By appointing Sam Rohdie as its Secretary, SEFT was breaking with established practice. Previously those who had held SEFT's professional officer post had already served a lengthy voluntary apprenticeship on the Committee. Indeed in its early years gaining a position on the SEFT Committee itself had been regarded as a useful stepping stone. Rohdie was unusual too in that he came from higher education where he had taught film. SEFT's previous links with higher education had been substantial but always with teacher training. Only one of its previous officers, Don Waters, had experience of being employed in a specifically film teaching capacity. Consequently Rohdie was probably more at ease with the BFI Education Department than with the SEFT Committee. This is a view supported by Christopher Williams, BFI Education's Editor of Publications and Jim Cook who chaired SEFT 1971 – 72.[86]

The Briggs Committee

But closeness to the Education Department had its dangers. The Department had been under scrutiny for some years and when the BFI Governors began a policy review of the Institute, the Education Department was first in their sights.[87] Asa Briggs, Vice Chancellor of Sussex University, joined the Board in February 1970 and was almost immediately asked to chair a Governors' Sub-Committee to investigate the Education Department as part of the Governors' Policy Review Committee.[88] This committee consisted of Paul Adorian and Helen Forman whose criticisms of Whannel had first been recorded in 1968. No copy of the Briggs Committee Report appears to have survived. Its concerns have to be inferred from the responses it elicited, of which the most significant were the resignations of Whannel, Lovell and four other members of the department in August 1971.[89] The thrust of the Briggs Report seems to have been that the Department was developing a research/theoretical bias when it should have been supporting grassroots work in schools.[90] It is impossible to know whether the Report acknowledged that it was the previous 25 years of grassroots work in schools that had provided the platform for the theoretical work to begin.

The investigation of the Department's work was cursory. SEFT's appointment of Rohdie and his changed emphases in *Screen* were apparently included in the charges against the Department. Cook, then Chair of SEFT, remembers that he, Rohdie and Whannel attended a meeting, held before the BFI Governors' April meeting, with Briggs and Helen Forman on the 'neutral' territory of Granada's London headquarters.[91] Also present at that meeting was Denis Forman. His presence would suggest that he was already in the process of replacing William Coldstream as Chairman of BFI

Governors. This meeting probably took place on 6 April 1971 between the first circulation of the report to Governors and the point at which the Governors acted upon it.[92] The Governors' Minutes record that the Report was first circulated at the February meeting with the intention that it be discussed in March.[93] However at the subsequent meeting so many governors left early discussion was deferred until April.[94] At the April Governors' meeting there was a substantial item on the report. There was also consideration of SEFT and *Screen*.[95]

The Briggs group was initially styled as the Education Sub-Committee. Then its title was subsequently – and significantly – adjusted to become the Committee on Educational Services. Its report finally appeared as 'Report of the Review Committee on Educational Services', presumably to fit in alongside the other subsequent Governors' policy review papers. According to Briggs, his committee had produced 'a brief and practical report that purposely avoided involving itself at this stage in a detailed study of the work of individual members of staff'.[96] It was certainly easier for a committee to pass judgment if they exempted themselves from the necessity of examining detailed evidence but the Chairman remained confident that they had 'all the facts necessary to form a judgment'.[97]

Consequently Briggs told the Governors that his committee's aim was 'to see a more streamlined Department, playing a less independent role than hitherto.' The Governors' reaction was one of 'warm support'.[98] It is pertinent to remember that at this time the Institute's Governors were themselves under attack from the Members' Action Group which had been particularly effective in calling Governors to account at the previous December's Annual Meeting.[99] Two members of that group, Victor Perkins and Peter Wollen, were former employees of the Education Department and perhaps their presence helped to direct Governors' attention towards the department, some of whose other members were presumed to have left wing political affinities and against whom Governors' hostilities had been simmering for years.[100]

The Minutes record Whannel as vigorously defending the department.[101] Where the Governors had made incorrect assumptions, he was able to challenge them. His main problem was that, whereas he had a very clear idea about the need to establish that there existed a film culture which was as appropriate for study as a literary culture, his opponents only wanted to engage with film in a more nebulous educational context. Not only was the Institute's educational agenda to be broadened, but its implementation was not to be confined to the Education Department.

> The Committee were opposed to the concept that the educational function of the Institute should be solely conducted through the Education Department as it now existed.[102]

It would seem from the specific defence Whannel had to give to his department's involvement in the *Cinema One* book series, this aspect was one that particularly attracted criticism.[103] In 1969 two of the books published in the series were attributed to the Education Department. These had been written by two then current Education Department employees, Jim Kitses and Peter Wollen.[104] Both however had left the Department before the Briggs Committee was set up. Perhaps the implication was that they had spent BFI work time writing these books and that this was an inappropriate use of public money. Having not talked with individual members of the department, the Sub-Committee was possibly not aware that three then current employees, Lovell, Hillier and McArthur were producing *Cinema One* books which were duly published in 1972.[105] Certainly Whannel is recorded in the Minutes as having denied 'that members of the Department spent much time in lecturing and said that they did no sophisticated research themselves but made available the researches of others'.[106] The Governors supported the Report in full and its assertion that 'if the Education Department continued as it was now doing, the servicing aspect, which they regarded as important, would suffer'. Whannel was given a month in which to satisfy the Director 'as to the manner in which the recommendations contained in paragraph 8 of the Report would be implemented'.[107]

Under a later item of the same agenda SEFT came under separate scrutiny, initially as a result of reports from the Editorial Committee which had been considering *Screen*.[108] This Committee was recommending that the grant for *Screen* should be £500 per annum to bring it into line with other film journals. This was in fact the amount SEFT had received as a grant from the BFI in 1966, before the joint appointment had first been mooted. As this Editorial Committee meeting was held in mid April, it would seem likely that the only Rohdie edited issue of the journal the Editorial Committee might have inspected was the Spring 1971 issue. However Briggs intervened in this discussion of *Screen* and raised the wider issue of SEFT. His committee, following the meeting of 6 April, would recommend that 'the organisation should be gradually dissociated from the Education Department and become an independent body'.[109]

It is relevant at this point to consider what role Director Reed might have had in these developments. SEFT had for twenty years been an independent body but perhaps Rohdie's involvement with the Education Department had blurred the distinction between the two and Reed did not wish to disabuse the Governors of this. Those who resigned from the Education Department writing subsequently about these events alleged that Reed had stated publicly that Rohdie was not appropriate for the SEFT post, yet Reed had been on the joint SEFT/BFI appointing committee.[110] However, as Alan Lovell also on the committee recalls, Reed left the appointing meeting after all the interviews were completed but before the candidates were considered.[111] Reed had however concurred with the re-designation of the post so that both the SEFT element was increased and the Editorship of *Screen* was the key to a successful appointment. It is clear that at this point Reed was not voicing support for either Whannel or SEFT. Consequently that Governors' Meeting ended with SEFT being expected to operate independently with only a £500 grant from BFI from April 1972.[112]

Exit the Education Department

Whannel did not in the event attempt to satisfy the Director but, along with other colleagues, he resigned with effect from mid August.[113] Reed had found contact with the Education Department difficult in the face of hostility and had handed the task of dealing with the surviving rump of the department to his deputy Ernest Lindgren.[114] Reed then fell ill. In these circumstances SEFT decided that its best strategy for survival lay in direct contact with the new BFI chairman Denis Forman. History was to SEFT's advantage in that Forman, when he had been BFI Director two decades earlier, had publicly supported the newly formed Society of Film Teachers.[115] There was however a more fundamental card for SEFT to play. If the BFI wanted its educational staff to deal mainly with direct teacher enquiries, it would be more publicly acceptable for them to do so if other more research/theoretical areas could be seen as being addressed elsewhere.

Jim Cook as Chairman of SEFT, wrote to Forman in very strong terms.[116] There were two strands to the letter. The Governors' action meant that both Rohdie and Matias were implicitly being sacked from March 1972 since SEFT had no means of replacing the BFI funding. Yet in contractual terms both were BFI employees. This was a nicety which had eluded the Briggs Committee. Much of Cook's letter is highly critical of Reed who is accused of having declared publicly that Rohdie was unsuitable for the post and of telling a representative of the National Union of Teachers that SEFT would soon cease to exist. As evidence of Reed's hostility to SEFT, Cook cites Reed's provision of 'free films and services' to the Barry Summer School which was no longer a SEFT event.[117] Cook also claims that the newly founded National Association for Film Education (NAFE) is an anti-SEFT, anti-BFI Education Department organisation which is expecting a BFI grant. The letter hints that for these reasons NAFE may get a sympathetic response from the BFI. Finally Cook wants Forman to state where the BFI stands on this matter.

In his immediate reply Forman was able to avoid dealing with the issues concerning Reed, since the latter was still absent ill. Significantly Forman claimed that the area of the Institute educational policy where there had been disagreement 'is a small area; the Governors endorse the great majority of the work that has been done'.[118] The final paragraphs of Forman's letter are quoted in full below.

> The Governors and management do not regard it as the function of the Institute to 'shape a film culture'. This does not mean they are 'anti-intellectual'. On the contrary, they wish to promote theoretical and practical research into film appreciation and film education. But they wish to stimulate research through grant-in-aid bodies such as your own, in university departments and in other appropriate places.
>
> What they do not want to do is to support and perpetuate any single doctrine or dogma within the Institute about film to the exclusion of other schools of thought. They believe in a plurality of educational theories and methods. They

consider that as in the fields of textbooks, music and the arts, so in the area of film and television education it is the job of the central body to provide guidance, to stimulate educationalists, and to provide them with the tools for the job.

The notion of a 'film culture' appears to be the sticking point. This was the term that Whannel had long promoted and his repeated references to it seem to have been conflated in Governors' minds with what his department was up to – of which they were perpetually suspicious. It seems clear that in these two paragraphs Forman was trying to find room to manoeuvre.

In Cook's immediate reply he is able to identify the contradiction in the Governors' position.[119]

> On the one hand the Institute expresses concern at any charge against it of anti-intellectualism yet by an administrative formula defining the proper place for the generation of ideas it is in effect cutting off the two major areas where ideas on film education have been generated – namely SEFT and its own Education Department.
>
> The Education Department and SEFT have done precisely what you yourself ask for – 'promote theoretical and practical research into film appreciation and film education' – and yet the Governors sub-committee condemned them for doing just that.

He was also able to point to the problems that the BFI had created in another area of its responsibility by failing to provide any coherent context for its work:

> Perhaps the paradigms in your mind for what seems to SEFT a contradiction is the NFT and Regional Theatres which provide films but no context for their understanding or appreciation, a serious lack which in part may account for the financial distress in which these theatres now find themselves?

Forman took a slight pause before replying. When he did he proposed that, rather than continuing the correspondence, SEFT should meet with him in mid-September after he had returned from holiday.[120] A meeting was arranged for 21 September between Forman and Cook.[121]

In the interim Rohdie and Lindgren were in regular contact. Rohdie was preparing a case to be made at the October BFI Governors' meeting for SEFT to be properly supported. Lindgren was advising him to play down the significance of *Screen* and its demands on Rohdie's time and to 'establish that SEFT has other activities of a more practical nature'.[122] Consequently in a letter to Forman, Rohdie outlined a series of proposals and made a point of emphasising that it was only the uncertainty over SEFT's future that had prevented their earlier inception.[123] The two main proposals were the development of a SEFT regional policy and the introduction of *Screen Education Notes*.

The first innovation would be the organisation of a 'series of one-day schools in the regions as well as weekend conferences and seminars'.[124] The *Notes* was to be a new SEFT quarterly journal of 'practical film education'. Such were the changes of personnel on the SEFT Committee that the re-use of the recently discarded title *Screen Education* did not apparently cause concern. The implied trivialisation of the educational input by reference to it as *Notes* did cause some disquiet.[125] These particular moves clearly had a timely tactical value in that, given the previous attitude of the BFI Governors, these proposals were unlikely to be opposed. *Screen* does get mentioned and Rohdie is clearly determined not to diminish the importance of this particular SEFT project, the appeal of which was what had brought him to the Society. He does not mention *Screen*'s content but concentrates on its sales, pointing out that 'revenue now meets direct expenditure', presumably meaning printing and distribution. He claims that his first two issues have caused sales and subscriptions to rise by 150 per cent so that 2000 copies of both numbers 1 and 2 of Volume 12 have sold out.[126] Rohdie was probably being optimistic at this point.[127]

In a paragraph to reassure the Governors Rohdie states:

> In the future the Society will be devoting most of its efforts to the organisation
> of SEFT – the generation of a constituency of film teachers as a pre-condition
> for the acceptance and generation of ideas about film teaching.

Inevitably and understandably he makes the case for an end to the uncertainty surrounding his and Matias's employment situations. Lindgren was sympathetic and in a memo early in September is clearly seeing that SEFT's best bet is to go initially for a stay of execution and to get Governors to agree a full year's funding for SEFT for 1972/73 so that both Rohdie and Matias are secure for a further year at least.[128] At their September meeting the Governors agreed to this but wanted a detailed SEFT budget before their October meeting.[129] But the main deal was being worked out between Forman and Rohdie who alone had taken up the invitation for the meeting on 20 September. This seems to have been a particularly successful occasion. Cook had detected at the earlier meeting at Granada that Forman was not as hostile to SEFT as the Briggs Committee was.[130] Rohdie has described Forman's role in the proceedings as that of a 'gentleman'.[131]

In the event the outcome for SEFT was remarkable. It had in 1967 achieved a joint appointment where its Secretary would for half the time be a Teacher Adviser in the Education Department. By autumn 1971 it was being offered a grant to cover the salaries of two full-time SEFT employees. It had also been found premises in Old Compton Street which had been equipped and furnished at the BFI's expense. This additional generosity was not without advantages to the BFI who had sub-leased the Old Compton Street premises to a tenant who, while owing BFI money, was about to assign further his sub-lease.[132] The BFI felt justified in cancelling his debt and in paying him £400 for the furniture and fittings, which included four desks, four chairs, a large settee, carpets, curtains, light fittings, an electric heater and a safe. These were to be available to SEFT from 18 October. This advantageous outcome then came almost to a disastrous conclusion.

The Crisis in Film Education

Rohdie clearly had alternative strategies in place should the more conventional negotiations with the BFI fail. The first was to devote a considerable part of the Autumn issue of *Screen* to the events around the resignations from the Education Department. The second was to organise a SEFT all-day conference at the National Film Theatre called 'Crisis in Film Education' with speakers including Roy Knight, Alan Lovell, Peter Wollen and Colin Young.[133] The timing of events was such that *Screen* was published on 11 October, the Governors met to consider the detailed SEFT budget on 19 October and the Crisis Conference was on 23 October.

Rohdie had to act quickly. On publication day he sent a copy of *Screen* to Forman with a covering letter in which he had to explain why, when he had already achieved the best possible outcome for SEFT, he was devoting 42 pages of *Screen* to criticisms of the BFI. These were then followed by a seven page advertisement for the BFI Members' Action Committee.

> The issue was planned some time ago when both the Society and the Department felt their existence threatened; the Society's Executive and the SCREEN Editorial Board decided that we had no other choice but to print such an edition of SCREEN.
>
> Some six weeks ago I informed the Deputy Director that such an issue was at the printers but that we would be more than happy not to print it if the Institute could give us some positive guarantee about the future, but it could not.
>
> It was not until well after page proof stage that such a guarantee was forthcoming and hence the appearance of this crisis SCREEN.[134]

He then had to present the forthcoming conference as having a changed agenda 'now directed towards debating and defining policies for film education and strategies for their realisation'. He extends an invitation to Governors and Management to be present.[135]

Forman's response was to propose a meeting for 26 October – after the conference – with Rohdie and Cook.[136] Lindgren felt betrayed and wrote to Forman that 'personally I should like to see SEFT's grant cut immediately and *in toto*'.[137] Asa Briggs at the October Governors' Meeting stated that the *Screen* material might be defamatory.[138] Consequently Forman took legal advice and was told that

> *Prima facie*, I think that the articles and letters taken as a whole are defamatory of the Governors and Director of the Institute.[139]

This opinion does however hint at the considerable scale of any legal case that might be mounted:

...it would be necessary to consider the various changes in the composition of the Governing body which would have taken place over the years, since the criticism is not restricted to any particular period of time or to any one event.

In the event Forman took the matter no further.

Rohdie saw that the interest the Crisis Conference had generated might be used to SEFT's advantage. He wrote to Reed indicating that if BFI were shifting from the agreement that he had come to with Forman, he would have to inform the conference of this. Alternatively he held out the prospect of the conference providing 'a favourable opportunity for SEFT to both settle the disagreements of the past and the anxiety it has caused SEFT and the film movement clearly and publicly'.[140] Reed was not prepared to do more than state that Forman 'wants to continue discussion of the future relationship between our two bodies'.[141]

Reporting on the conference, Tom Ryall concedes that 'the discussion proceeded in a random fashion'.[142] It began with Rohdie presenting his official Report as Secretary. He blamed his predecessors in SEFT for 'the absence of a clearly defined constituency of film teachers' and for failing to organize such teachers into 'a coherent movement'.[143] Some antagonism was expressed from the floor toward SEFT as being focused on higher education. There was a call by some for a separate teachers' organization. David Lusted, then on the SEFT Committee, recalls that some teachers who attended were surprised to learn that there was a crisis.[144] Reed received reports from Thorold Dickinson and Kevin Gough-Yates.[145] Both had attended and were very critical of the proceedings. Rohdie tried to present the occasion to Reed as having been important in that over 200 people had attended.[146] But there had apparently been little agreement, which Rohdie had to concede. He chose to present the conference's disunity as inevitable, reflecting the fragmentation of the film education movement.[147]

Governors at their October meeting had noted that *Screen* 'contained numerous allegations and inaccuracies' but they were prepared to accept that the matter would be best dealt with by the Chairman meeting again with the Chairman and Secretary of SEFT.[148] At the November meeting Forman reported that a formal apology had been asked for and that a statement to this effect should appear in the next issue of *Screen*.[149] In a memo to Reed, Rohdie stated that he had written a letter of apology to Forman at the end of October.[150] It would appear that neither SEFT nor BFI wanted to risk losing what each regarded for separate reasons as an appropriate resolution. SEFT got total independence underwritten by substantial public funds (£9,994 for 1972–1973).[151] BFI was able to re-designate the Education Department as its Educational Advisory Service and thereby hope to demonstrate that theory and research were legitimately no longer part of its educational brief. Whannel was replaced by Douglas Lowndes, widely respected as an innovatory practitioner in both secondary schools and teacher training.[152] But the constraints imposed by Governors were to restrict the potential of EAS for a decade while SEFT was about to commence upon a period when the Society would become both prestigious and widely influential.

Notes

1. *SEFT Seventeenth Annual Report 1967–1968* dated 4 May 1968 is signed by T J Bolas as Acting Secretary.

2. An account of these activities is to be found in the Nineteenth Annual Report 1969–1970 published in *Screen* Vol 11 No 3 pp 96–111.

3. 'SEFT Conference May 3rd' *Screen* Vol 10 No 2 March/April 1969 p 4

4. 'SEFT 1970 Annual Conference' *Screen* Vol 11 No 2 March/April 1970 p 2

5. Terry Bolas 'Seft/Ilea Film Teaching Experiment' *Screen* Vol 12 No 1 Spring 1971 pp 87–92

6. See the Foreword to *Screen* Vol 10 No 3 May/June 1969 p 4 where it is indicated that the issue includes 'Paddy Whannel's annual report to the British Film Institute, which for the first time was partly conceived for publication in the SEFT journal'.

7. See the advertisement 'Twenty Regional Film Theatres are ready to help you' *Screen Education* 45 July/August 1968 p 71 including such centres as Petworth, St Austell and Street alongside those in Edinburgh, Manchester and Sheffield.

8. BFI Special Collections Box 89 Paddy Whannel *The Education Department: Policy and Role* BFI Governors' Minutes G381 Paper No 2, 4 November 1968

9. Ibid p 5

10. The papers considered at these seminars were subsequently made available as duplicated material by the Education Department.

11. Peter Wollen 'Towards a New Criticism?' *Screen Education* 41 September/October 1967 pp 90–91

12. Alan Lovell 'The Western' *Screen Education* 41 pp 92–103. This seminar was held jointly with the Birmingham Centre for Contemporary Cultural Studies.

13. Five of these seminar papers were edited by Wollen and reprinted as *Working Papers in the Cinema:Sociology and Semiology* London: BFI Education Department 1971.

14. Wollen 1967 op cit p 90

15. Alan Lovell 'The Aims of Film Education' Seminar paper 15 February 1968

16. BFI Special Collections Box 91 'Film Research' memo to Paddy Whannel from Peter Wollen 23 August 1968 p 2

17. BFI Special Collections Box 91 'Research Scholarships' memo to Paddy Whannel from Peter Wollen 3 September 1968

18. Whannel op cit p 5

19. British Film Institute Governors Meeting 4 November 1968 Item 5071

20. Ibid

21. Ibid

22. 'The British Universities Film Council – Past, Present and Future' *University Vision* No 11 April 1974 p 8

23. 'Ernest Lindgren OBE Obituary' *University Vision* op cit pp 6–7

24. Stuart Hall 'The Impact of Film on the University' *University Vision* No 2 October 1968 p 29

25. Liz-Anne Bawden 'Film Studies in the University' *University Vision* No 4 November 1969 pp 25–35

26. Ibid p 34.

27. Editorial in *Screen* Vol No 1 January/February 1969 p 3

28. See below endnote 31

29. David Gladwell 'Editing Anderson's *If* ' *Screen* Vol 10 No 1 January/February 1969 pp 24–33

30. Gillian Hartnoll's reading lists for *Screen*: 'Film History' Vol 10 No 4/5 pp 187–191; 'British Cinema' Vol 10 No 6 pp 108–109; 'Theory of Film' Vol 11 No 1 pp 101–102; 'Reference Books' Part I Vol 11 No 2 pp 96–98; 'Reference Books' Part II Vol 11 No 4/5 pp 133–136

31. Roy Armes 'Duplicated Materials' *Screen* Vol 11 No 3 pp 105–106

32. Alan Lovell 'Robin Wood's Criticism' *Screen* Vol 10 No 2 March/April 1969 pp 42–55; Robin Wood 'An Answer to Alan Lovell' *Screen* Vol 10 No 3 May/June 1969 pp 35–48; Alan Lovell 'The Common Pursuit of True Judgment' *Screen* Vol 11 No 4/5 pp 76–88

33. Andrew McTaggart 'Signs and Meaning in the Cinema' *Screen* Vol 10 No 6 pp 67–75; Roy Armes 'A Polemic' *Screen* Vol 10 No 6 pp 75–79

34. Peter Wollen *Signs and Meaning in the Cinema* London: Secker and Warburg 1969

35. Foreword in *Screen* Vol 11 No 1 January/February 1970 p 2

36. Edward Buscombe 'The Idea of Genre in the American Cinema' *Screen* Vol 11 No 2 March/April 1970 pp 33–45; Richard Collins 'Genre: A Reply to Ed Buscombe' *Screen* Vol 11; No 4/5 pp 66–75

37. See Alan Lovell *Anarchist Cinema* published by *Peace News* for which Lovell was the Film Critic.

38. Alan Lovell (1968) op cit p 1

39. Ibid p 7

40. Lovell (1970) op cit p 87

41. Ibid p 88

42. See for example: Christine Gledhill *Film and Media Studies in Higher Education* London: BFI Education 1981 p (i); Manuel Alvarado, Robin Gutch, Tana Wollen *Learning the Media* London: Macmillan 1987 p 24

43. Paddy Whannel 'The Problem of Film Availability' *Screen* Vol 10 No 1 January/February 1969 p 67–73

44. Terry Bolas 'Developments in Film Education' *Screen* Vol 11 No 3 May/June 1970 p 99

45. Whannel op cit p 68

46. Douglas Lowndes in interview with the author 5 June 2003.

47. Roger Watkins *CSE Examinations in Film* London BFI/SEFT 1969 on first of unnumbered pages following the Introduction.

48. Paddy Whannel 'Film Education and Film Culture' *Screen* Vol 10 No 3 May/June 1969 p 49

49. Ibid p 50

50. Ibid p 51

51. Ibid p 51
52. Ibid p 53
53. Ibid p 53
54. Ibid p 54
55. Ibid p 55
56. Ibid p 56
57. Ibid p 59
58. Ibid p 58
59. Paddy Whannel ' Servicing the Film Teacher' *Screen* Vol 11 No 4/5 1970 p 48
60. Ibid p 49
61. Ibid p 49
62. Ibid p 50
63. The author's recollections of meeting Young at the BFI in 1970
64. Ibid p 52
65. Ibid p 52
66. Ibid p 53
67. Ibid p 54 There is no record of any reaction on Whannel's part to Richardson's 1967 book
68. Ibid p 55
69. Roger Watkins 'Chairman's Foreword' *Screen* Vol 12 No 1 Spring 1971 pp 7–8
70. 'SEFT Nineteenth Annual Report 1969–70' published in *Screen* Vol 11 No 3 (pp 96–111) p 102.
71. The SEFT accounts for 1969–1970 have not been found. The 1970–1971 accounts show the costs of *Screen* consuming £2960 out of a total SEFT expenditure of £3780.
72. It was also agreed that relevant expertise of the new post-holder would be available to the Education Department to a limited extent.
73. When Sam Rohdie produced his first issue of *Screen* (Vol 12 No 1 Spring 1971), there was a nine person Editorial Board identified. Three members were from the BFI Education Department (Whannel , Lovell, Hillier), two SEFT Committee members (Buscombe and Cook) and three others (Terry Lovell, Jon Halliday, Peter Wollen). Rohdie would have made the SEFT representation up to three.
74. Watkins op cit p 8
75. Watkins op cit p 8
76. SEFT Nineteenth Annual Report 1969–70 *Screen* Vol 11 No 3 p 102; SEFT Annual Report and Accounts 1972 p 2
77. Christopher Williams in interview with the author 28 April 2005.
78. Gerald Cinamon was designer of the prestigious Allen Lane at the Penguin Press. He had designed the cover of *New Left Review* and the new SEFT logo.
79. Editorial *Screen* Vol 12 No 1 Spring 1971 p 4
80. Op cit p 5
81. See 'Soviet Film 1920s' *Screen* Vol 12 No 4 Winter 1971/72 pp 25–160

82. *Screen* Vol 12 No 1 Spring 1971 Jean-Luc Comolli and Paul Narboni 'Cinema/Ideology/ Criticism' (translated by Susan Bennett) pp 27 – 36; Ben Brewster 'Structuralism in Film Criticism' pp 49 – 58; Claire Johnston 'Film Journals: Britain and France' pp 39 – 46. Paul Willemen in interview with the author in July 2005 claimed that some of the article was his work, but that his position at the time as a BFI employee prevented his taking any credit.

83. 'Introduction to Education Notes' *Screen* op cit p 77

84. Sam Rohdie ' Education and Criticism – Notes on work to be done' *Screen* op cit pp 9–13

85. Rohdie op cit p 12

86. Christopher Williams in interview with the author 28 April 2005 and Jim Cook in telephone interview with the author 13 January 2007.

87. Colin McArthur in interview with the author 28 June 2005.

88. British Film Institute Governors' Minutes 17 February 1970 Section 5209.

89. Memo from Ernest Lindgren to all BFI Staff Office Notice No 28/71 20 August 1971 The other four were Eileen Brock, Gail Naughton, Jennifer Norman and Jim Pines.

90. British Film Institute Governors' Minutes 20 April 1971 Section 5338

91. Jim Cook in email to the author 10 January 2007

92. British Film Institute Governors' Minutes 20 April 1971 Section 5344

93. British Film Institute Governors' Minutes 19 January 1971 Section 5306

94. British Film Institute Governors' Minutes 16 March 1971 Section 5327

95. British Film Institute Governors' Minutes 20 April 1971 Section 5344

96. British Film Institute Governors' Minutes 20 April 1971 Section 5338

97. Ibid

98. Ibid

99. BFI Members' Action Committee 'A New Screenplay for the BFI' *Screen* Vol 12 No 3 Autumn 1971 p 44

100. Colin McArthur interview op cit and Jim Hillier in interview with the author 25 April 2005

101. British Film Institute Governors' Minutes 20 April 1971 Section 5338

102. Ibid

103. Ibid

104. Jim Kitses *Horizons West* London: Thames & Hudson 1969; Peter Wollen *Signs and Meaning in the Cinema* London: Secker & Warburg 1969

105. Colin McArthur *Underworld USA* London: Secker & Warburg 1972; Alan Lovell/Jim Hillier *Studies in Documentary* London: Secker & Warburg 1972

106. British Film Institute Governors' Minutes 20 April 1971 Section 5338

107. Ibid

108. British Film Institute Governors' Minutes 20 April 1971 Section 5344

109. Ibid

110. Eileen Brock *et al* 'Open Letter to the Staff of the British Film Institute' *Screen* Vol 12 No 3 Autumn 1971 p 5

111. Alan Lovell in interview with the author.

112. British Film Institute Governors' Minutes 20 April 1971 Section 5344

113. British Film Institute Governors' Minutes 21 September 1971 'The Future of the Education Department' Governors' Paper No 3 G413 p 1

114. Ernest Lindgren Office Notice to all Staff No 28/71 20 August 1971

115. See Forman's 'Foreword' to *School Film Appreciation* 1950 which was funded by the BFI soon after Foman's arrival as BFI Director.

116. British Film Institute Special Collections Box 117 Letter from Jim Cook to Denis Forman 17 August 1971

117. Ibid p 2

118. British Film Institute Special Collections Box 117 Letter from Denis Forman to Jim Cook 18 August 1971

119. British Film Institute Special Collections Box 117 Letter from Jim Cook to Denis Forman 19 August 1971

120. British Film Institute Special Collections Box 117 Letter from Denis Forman to Jim Cook 24 August 1971

121. British Film Institute Special Collections Box 117 Letter from Sam Rohdie to Denis Forman 9 September

122. British Film Institute Special Collections Box 117 Memo from Ernest Lindgren to Sam Rohdie 31 August

123. Letter from Rohdie op cit

124. The one-day schools were commenced immediately, followed by the SEFT/BFI seminars but the SEFT weekends did not start until 1975.

125. Jim Cook in interview with the author 13 January 2007.

126. Letter from Rohdie op cit p 3

127. SEFT accounts for 1970/71 put membership/subscription income at £1237 for the twelve months ending 31 March 1971 – an average income of £103 per month. The SEFT accounting year was then changed to the calendar year so that the next accounts cover only the subsequent nine months to 31 December 1971. In that period membership/subscription income amounted to £990 or £110 per month, an average increase of 6.8 per cent.

128. British Film Institute Special Collections Box 117 Memo from Ernest Lindgren to Sam Rohdie 7 September 1971

129. Minutes of BFI Governors' Meeting 21 September 1971 Paragraph 5380

130. Jim Cook in email to the author 11 January 2007

131. Sam Rohdie in email to the author 2 October 2005

132. British Film Institute Special Collections Box 117 Memo from Fred Gee to Vernon Saunders 15 October 1971

133. Advertisement in *Screen* Vol 12 No 3 Summer 1971 inside back cover

134. British Film Institute Special Collections Box 117 Letter from Sam Rohdie to Denis Forman 11 October 1971

135. Ibid p 2

136. British Film Institute Special Collections Box 117 Referred to in a memo from Sam Rohdie to Stanley Reed 20 October 1971
137. British Film Institute Special Collections Box 117 Memo from Ernest Lindgren to Denis Forman 21 October 1971
138. British Film Institute Special Collections Box 117 Letter from Denis Forman to Asa Briggs 28 October 1971
139. British Film Institute Special Collections Box 117 Letter from Alan Leighton Davis to Denis Forman 21 October 1971
140. British Film Institute Special Collections Box 117 Memo from Sam Rohdie to Stanley Reed 20 October 1971
141. British Film Institute Special Collections Box 117 Memo from Stanley Reed to Sam Rohdie 21 October 1971
142. Tom Ryall 'SEFT Annual Conference Report' *Screen Education Notes* Winter 1971 p 28
143. Ibid
144. David Lusted in interview with the author 16 May 2005.
145. British Film Institute Special Collections Box 117 Memo from Stanley Reed to Denis Forman 26 October 1971
146. Ryall op cit p 28 gives the attendance as 'over 170 film educationists'.
147. British Film Institute Special Collections Box 117 Memo from Sam Rohdie to Stanley Reed 25 October 1971
148. Minutes of BFI Governors' Meeting 19 October 1971 Paragraph 5394
149. Minutes of BFI Governors' Meeting 16 November 1971 Paragraph 5412
150. British Film Institute Special Collections Box 117 Memo from Sam Rohdie to Stanley Reed 9 November 1971
151. Sam Rohdie 'Foreword' in *Screen* Vol 12 No 4 Winter 1971/2
152. Lowndes's influential book *Film Making in Schools* had been published by Batsford in 1968.

By the 1960s the British Film Institute had shifted its main base away from the fringes of Bloomsbury to Soho. In its new home at Dean Street it was only a block away from Wardour Street which housed the offices of most of the UK's major film distributors.

There followed a further local dispersal, first of the BFI's Education Department and then of the Society for Education in Film and Television, into smaller offices in surrounding streets, often above commercial premises. Given the ways in which these organisations were developing their theoretical thinking with its Marxist and Gramscian inflections, they were to find themselves quite coincidentally in very close geographical proximity to landmarks connected with the sources of their inspiration. Similarly as television study was introduced and supplemented the original emphases on film study, they then discovered they were also working near where Baird had begun his early experimental work on television.

Theoretical and critical debates that had begun in BFI Education or SEFT offices were often re-invigorated subsequently in certain of the local public houses. These venues were embraced or shunned according to one's sympathy with or antagonism towards the faction that was known to dominate in a specific venue.

81 Dean Street, headquarters of the British Film Institute, as it was in the 1960s through to the 1980s. SEFT had an office here from 1969 to 1972. The top two rooms in the building at the extreme left hand edge of the picture housed the Gramsci Institute. The BFI building has subsequently been re-clad and re-furbished.

Summer School attendees shooting a 16mm film at a BFI Summer School in the 1950s. Precise date, location and personae are unknown. These students are involved in the production of a group-made film. This approach was routinely introduced at such events as the appropriate model for making films with children in schools.

From left to right, Lord Eccles (Minister for the Arts), Stanley Reed (Director of the BFI), Alan Lovell (Deputy Head of the Education Department) and the author at the reception for the biennial Young Screen event in the National Film Theatre in June 1971. Lovell was shortly to resign – along with Paddy Whannel and four other members of the Education Department – from the BFI.

70 Old Compton Street ('the University in Old Compton Street') where the BFI Education Department was housed from 1965 to 1969. SEFT was given office space within the Department from January 1967. The opticians are the latest occupants of the shop at street level; the exterior of the offices above is unchanged.

62 Dean Street was the building which housed BFI Education (then known as the BFI Educational Advisory Service) through the mid 1970s.

The first floor of 63 Old Compton Street (almost directly opposite No 70) was the first independent office of SEFT and was occupied by the Society from 1972–1976. It was 450 square feet in extent. Ownership of the café downstairs has changed.

Present day Soho from the air

The locations featured in the photographs on surrounding pages may be identified as follows:

Dean Street
81 British Film Institute HQ 1960-1977
31 The Crown and Two Chairmen
62 British Film Institute Educational Advisory Service 1973-1977

Old Compton Street
70 British Film Institute Education Department 1965-1969
63 Society for Education in Film and Television 1972-1976
29 Society for Education in Film and Television 1976-1989
23 Site of the Helvetia public house

Frith Street
23 Jimmy's Restaurant

Greek Street
29 Coach and Horses public house

Charing Cross Road
127 British Film Institute HQ from 1977-1987

Satellite view of Soho © 2008 Google – Map data © 2008 Tele Atlas

The first floor of 29 Old Compton Street was occupied by the Society from 1976 until its demise in 1989. It was 550 square feet in extent; the Amalfi Restaurant is unchanged. The SEFT office enjoyed unique internal access to the restaurant which was extensively used in the hot summer of 1976 because in those days it was one of the very few spaces in Soho that was air-conditioned. When David Bordwell and Kristin Thompson visited the SEFT office in 1976, they were so astonished at what a tiny operation the Society was they took the four members of staff here for lunch.

The Coach and Horses, on the corner of Greek Street and Romilly Street, has now become the most famous of the pubs frequented by SEFT activists in the 1970s. In those days it was a quiet 'tucked away' pub frequented by famous actors, the *Private Eye* team and the painter Francis Bacon. It has now become a tourist attraction partly as a result of the play about Jeffrey Barnard (one of the notorious habitués of the pub).

If 70 Old Compton Street provided home for the 'film academy-in-waiting' in the 1960s, it was the public bar of the Crown and Two Chairman that provided informal refuge for the BFI Education Department-in-exile in the 1970s. So substantial were their bar-room debates around film theory that the ambience of this venue was invoked by Geoffrey Nowell-Smith in 'I Was a Star*Struck Structuralist' (*Screen* v14 n3 Autumn 1973 pp 92-99). The exterior of this pub in Dean Street is largely unchanged but the interior has been gutted and no longer has a separate public bar. It is on the other side of the street from where the BFI's offices were located for three decades and just three doors away from where Karl Marx and his family lived while he was writing *Das Kapital*.

The Bar Soho (or Soho Brasserie) has long replaced the Helvetia pub which occupied this site in the 1970s and was regularly used by the SEFT Executive/Editorial Board members of *Screen/Screen Education* following highly fraught and contentious meetings. The Helvetia was a very large, empty and dilapidated public house frequented by 'off-duty' sex-workers. The SEFT activists would repair there after meetings but sit in cabals at different tables in order further to continue the arguments of the meetings or to 'lick their wounds'.

Jimmy's is a long-established Greek Cypriot restaurant located in a Frith Street basement which was a favoured lunchtime haunt of BFI Education and SEFT colleagues/activists. The blue plaque to the left above the Bar Italia (an equally long-established and popular coffee bar) indicates that John Logie Baird first demonstrated television in a room at the top of the building in 1926.

7

The Felt Intervention of *Screen*

The first two 1971 issues of the British journal Screen *published a translation of essays by Comolli and Narboni, Leblanc and Fargier. Their impact was immediate. They at once initiated an open battle, which led* Screen *to play a major role for several years both as a participant in the debate and as a battlefield.*

Francesco Cassetti, 1999

While Screen *embarks upon a trajectory of pursuing theory, from its back pages emerges* Screen Education Notes. *This modest quarterly publication not only chronicles the quickening pace of educational developments around film but begins to develop its own stable of writers. Then in 1974 it metamorphoses into the second SEFT journal bearing the title of* Screen Education. *The BFI Summer Schools are re-structured to provide a key transmission route for* Screen's *theories. Film teachers in favoured areas have access to substantial self help projects and even an O level in film. Meanwhile* Screen *recruits from the intelligentsia.*

The changes that came about in SEFT in the 1970s were extraordinary. What had been a marginal grouping of teachers rapidly had at its core an intellectual cell. Film study which had persistently found itself able only to worm its way into gaps in the curriculum of schools and colleges, became the intellectual standard behind which a whole cadre of young graduates were marshalled. What had been perceived as appropriate fodder for the less able or for those on courses with spare time to be filled, became the territory for displays of intellectual experiment around the translation and transmission of European thought.

A new meaning for *Screen Education*

If the nucleus of this activity was to be *Screen*, its partner journal, the revamped *Screen Education*, would turn its focus on to the educational implications in its title. The original *Screen Education* had been so titled in order to allow SFT to become SEFT, the term 'screen' enabling the accommodation of television into the Society's remit. The emphasis in the shift then had been on 'screen'. 'Education' was merely the appropriate afterthought. The writers of the new *Screen Education* saw that if they were to consider those elements of the visual culture implied by 'screen' then the educational context for that consideration was the key determinant.

For two decades SFT then SEFT had in turn presented themselves as the professional subject association for film and television teachers. But these were unlike other subject associations. None of the members had been trained to teach about film or television; and an even tinier fraction of them had been employed specifically as teachers of film and television. Most SFT/SEFT members were likely to belong to other subject associations that represented their commitment to the subject which they spent most of their time teaching. Thus in 1966, at the stage when SEFT was to make its first joint appointment with the BFI, its Chairman taught Chemistry, its Secretary taught Geography and its Treasurer, History.[1]

A consequence of this loose alliance of teachers who were enthusiastic about film was to diminish controversy. For many the involvement with this aspect of their teaching was subsidiary and film/television teaching was only an enjoyable phase on a career path that had to lead elsewhere. For two decades SFT/SEFT had encouraged those who wanted to develop 'screen education' to do whatever was possible in each individual situation. From the experience of those who had been around longer, an accumulation of information was made available. If a beginner wanted to share her/his first attempts with others, both *Screen Education* and to a lesser extent BFI Education Department would facilitate the dissemination. Nobody was to be deterred. Everybody was compromised.

Thus when SEFT found itself staffed, housed and independent while the remnants of the BFI Education Department had instructions principally to service teachers' queries, a unique situation had been created which reversed the roles that each had traditionally played. The voluntary body had a secure flow of public money on a far larger scale than before.[2] The thinking Whannel had fostered in his Education Department was no longer acceptable within the BFI. The thinking had to go somewhere. And there were certainly thinkers about to enter territory where there had not been much intellectual investigation. It was undiscovered territory and that was to be its greatest attraction.

When Rohdie became Secretary of SEFT, he inherited the constituency of established SEFT members, though he did not perceive them as forming a coherent group.[3] But he brought with him another constituency – one that might best be summarised as New Left. The potency of this constituency was first demonstrated at the Crisis Conference Rohdie called in October 1971 when 170 people attended and from among whom Rohdie was to recruit several new Committee members, some of whom were also new to SEFT.[4] Those teachers who were pre-existing SEFT members were probably those whom Lusted remembers as being surprised to find themselves in a crisis. Cook's view is that perhaps Rohdie's determination to go ahead with the conference, despite having settled SEFT's future with Forman, was fuelled by the need to recognise and respond to the significance of this new constituency.[5]

Screen Education Notes

There is no doubt that following SEFT's move to 63 Old Compton Street, the Society set in motion a number of ventures which would reassure BFI Governors that SEFT was indeed more than simply the body that published *Screen*. This chapter will in the main consider these non-*Screen* ventures in the period up to the end of 1975. *Screen*'s history will feature in the next chapter though, as will be shown, *Screen* was influential in a range of related SEFT and BFI activities during this period. The most important of these non *Screen* ventures was *Screen Education Notes*, of which there were nine quarterly issues between Winter 1971 and Winter 1973/74. The 'Notes' had begun as a section at the back of *Screen* in 1971 called 'Educational Notes'.[6] The first issue was typed and duplicated; subsequent issues were offset litho printed at generally around 40 pages per issue. Additionally there was a one-off *International Edition* that followed the October 1972 Ludwigshaven/Mannheim Conference. This conference on aspects of screen education was an annual event which had featured in the previous year's first issue of *Screen Education Notes*. The international edition was 'only a gesture on the part of SEFT, and does not have any official backing' stated the Editorial.[7] The published accounts of various European perspectives on screen education revealed – as had always been the case with previous SEFT international publishing ventures – a great variety of different approaches, some of which would have not been considered appropriate for any United Kingdom specific publication, hence the need for the disclaimer about official backing. Since the UK had been represented by Jim Hillier from the Educational Advisory Service of the BFI, rather than by SEFT, publication may have been a goodwill gesture to EAS on the Society's part.

Throughout its two-year existence the *Notes* was edited by Edward Buscombe and also for most of the period by Tom Ryall. They were supported by an active Editorial Board whose members regularly contributed items to the journal. Three members, Richard Collins, Jim Hillier and Chris Mottershead remained on the Board throughout. The change-over of other members was gradual and the continuity of approach was maintained. But the greatest significance as viewed from today's perspective is the subsequent durability within the film teaching movement of those involved with *Screen Education Notes*. Previous generations of SEFT activists had served their time and then found career progress outside film and television teaching. Here and now was the first cohort who would develop long-term careers within screen education. Those involved with *Screen* might subsequently attract more attention and rise more visibly into the posts that would become available in higher education. But it was the group which produced *Screen Education Notes* that would be more influential for a longer period in determining the evolution of media education.[8]

The SEFT Committee may have considered that, given the turmoil which surrounded the setting-up of SEFT's new found independence, there was a need conspicuously to address the established teacher audience within SEFT, since this was the grouping some claimed had been disenfranchised by the 'New Left takeover'. Indeed an alternative body, the National Association for Film Education (NAFE), had been created which sought to replace SEFT as the institutional home for those teachers. SEFT's response was to shift 'Screen Education Notes' from its location at the back of *Screen* and to make it a separate publication. Ultimately the *Notes* would become *Screen Education* in 1974 and that journal would then establish its own distinctive identity. But for the period the *Notes* existed it addressed a teacher audience and performed a crucial task. Events of the early 1970s in the arena of film and television education were occurring at a much faster rate than ever before and were beginning to demonstrate a shape and structure that would definitively replace what had gone before. *Screen Education Notes* took on the tasks both of detailing what was happening and of providing a commentary on its significance. The journal was able to fill its pages, to be current and yet repeatedly focus on developments that would prove to have long-term implications. There were sufficient of these for each issue of the *Notes* after Number 1 to focus on a discrete area.

The second issue dealt with students' film-making. It is clear that such was the controversy created at the October 1971 Crisis Conference around the separation of theory and practice that it was felt that if *Screen* was about to devote its first post Conference issue to Soviet Film in the 1920s, *Screen Education Notes* was the appropriate publication to redress the balance.[9] Buscombe's editorial makes clear that, given how widely views on film making ranged, 'this journal can do no more than hope to open up the area of discussion'.[10] He is equally clear that any previously assumed connection between the experience of student film-making and the same students' abilities in studying film must be open to question. The debate about this relationship has persisted ever since and has on occasions assumed fundamental importance in the construction of many courses at all levels. The shape of the debate has constantly been remodelled as the facilities offered by advancing technology have been absorbed by each generation of students at a younger age.

Thereafter the *Notes* managed to monitor contemporary developments. Its television issue in Summer 1972 coincided with the publication of veteran screen educationist Groombridge's book, the influential Penguin *Television and the People*.[11] Issue 4 was able to demonstrate how current substantial courses in higher education – in Art and Design and teacher training – were anticipating the introduction of 'a fully fledged degree level course in film'.[12] Issue 5 on film courses outside higher education gave space to the introduction of two initiatives that would have enormous influence in secondary schools: the Inner London Education Authority (ILEA) Film Study Course for Sixth Formers and the proposals for a GCE Mode III O level in Film Study.[13] These were complemented by a student's review of the long established but evolving Certificate in Film Study under the auspices of the University of London Extra- Mural Department. Issue 6 faced the reality that other curriculum areas were using film as part of the delivery mechanism for their subjects and, following a cautionary editorial questioning how far this might restrict the development of film study itself, *Notes* features film in modern languages courses. It is ironic that film would eventually come to subvert some of the language departments that were ready to embrace it. When certain language departments could no longer recruit postgraduate students to enrol for MA language courses, they switched and offered Masters degrees in film.[14]

But Issue 6 addressed a more pressing reality: the raising of the school leaving age to 16 which was to follow later in 1973. Len Masterman, having moved from teacher training to in-service teacher education and having chosen as part of this move to teach a group of secondary school students who were in that first generation to stay until 16, writes a polemical piece.[15]

> The problem thus created by the raising of the school leaving age, will, I believe, give substance to the view that for many children film ought to become the principal medium for the transmission of cultural values within school.[16]

The significance of Masterman's timely article is that he challenges the educational context in which the leaving age is being raised. This challenge would be one that the successor to *Notes*, *Screen Education*, would see as central to its mission. Here Masterman echoes the familiar attack on training in 'discrimination and taste' that had gathered momentum in the late 1960s.[17] But he goes beyond this to argue for the displacement of literature from the curriculum of those students most affected by the raising of the school leaving age.

> This kind of approach will almost certainly cut no ice with lower stream pupils. Perhaps the most potent reason why literature is able to say so little to them is that it is filtered down to them via middle-class sensibilities. The experience of watching film however is a lateral rather than hierarchical process. A filmic tradition has been experienced directly without the interference of an intermediary; it has been absorbed without being taught, transmitted without any moral overtones.[18]

The references in his text are to educationists and thinkers beyond the small comfortable world of film study: Freire, Postman, Weingartner, Illich and Reimer.

Issue 7 focused on the manner in which film was gaining acceptance in a particular facet of higher education: American Studies. It also had an article by Richard Dyer on 'Stars', the significance of this being that it was work he had undertaken at the Birmingham Centre for Contemporary Cultural Studies, an institution which would parallel in its investigations issues that SEFT would also subsequently explore in each of its journals. The final two issues of *Notes* looked closely at the detail of film courses. Issue 8 attempted an evaluation of the now established ILEA course for Sixth Formers. Its assumptions were investigated by some of those teachers who had participated. This critiquing was extended to two very well established screen education events: the Young Screen Conference and the BFI Summer School. Manuel Alvarado questioned the whole basis of the Young Screen event, with its showing of school made films on the big screen for the benefit of a child audience. He advocated a replacement teacher only event with the focus being the educational case for film-making in schools. Bazalgette was equally radical in her assessment of the 1973 Summer School, which had been attended by 121 students coming with a very wide range of levels of knowledge about the cinema. Like Alvarado, she identifies an unwieldy event, trying to be as welcoming and inclusive as possible, with the consequence that the potential in each case for exploring fundamental issues was awkwardly evaded.

The last *Screen Education Notes* marked another significant start-up: the Diploma in Film Study at the Polytechnic of Central London (which would ultimately be converted to a Masters degree). It was however put into a very precise context in *Notes*: dissatisfaction with the London University Extra-Mural Certificate and Diploma. *Notes* published two accounts: the revised scheme for the Extra Mural Course and an introduction to the Polytechnic's proposal by Richard Collins who saw the new diploma as a considered response to the 'unsatisfactoryness of the scheme of study and structure of the University certificate classes'.[19] More recently Collins has claimed that the Diploma came out of the SEFT problematic.[20]

Other SEFT Ventures

Rohdie had promised Forman that in addition to *Screen Education Notes* SEFT would work both at developing regional groups and at extending the screen education message beyond the metropolitan area. In 1972 energy did go into these projects with SEFT-run courses at among other places: Ormskirk, York, Sheffield, St Austell, Exeter, Birmingham, Leicester, Bristol and Grimsby.[21] The venues were self-selecting in that each had an institution or an individual with SEFT connections. This was a demanding schedule and Rohdie complained to the SEFT Committee of the additional workload this imposed.[22] Perhaps it was unsurprising that by the end of 1972, the direct responsibility passed to the Educational Advisory Services with the setting up of a BFI/SEFT Regional Committee to oversee the process.[23] Delivering a one-day course in the regions was a straightforward, if time-consuming operation; establishing a permanent regional group was a task of a different order. In the Summer 1972 issue of *Notes* ten potential regional groups are listed, most in places where a SEFT course had taken place.[24] The named contacts were usually individuals in colleges or local education authorities, but the distribution across England was irregular and uneven. There was a plea to SEFT members to come forward and to participate in these embryonic groups or to start up their own groups. In the event none of these groups persisted. Only later would a small number of SEFT regional groups take shape.

The SEFT Summer School modified its ambition and from 1972 to 1974 took place annually in London, first at Stockwell College of Education and then at the Polytechnic of Central London. After this, as key SEFT members' involvement with the BFI Summer School increased, the SEFT summer school – which had always been scheduled to run at a similar time during the summer school holiday period – ceased. It was however to be replaced by quarterly SEFT weekend schools, starting in spring 1975 and by the Easter residential schools for teachers starting in 1974.[25]

If there is a moment in the brief history of *Screen Education Notes* that marks the separation of the film education movement of the 1970s from what had gone before, it is to be found in the two reviews it published of *Film in English Teaching* which had been edited by Roy Knight for the newly re-branded Educational Advisory Services of the BFI, though published elsewhere as its Governors had insisted.[26] The book had been commissioned by the Education Department when it was still able to operate as an independent publishing house. The book's long period of gestation and the changing fortunes of the Education Department meant that it was not published until late 1972. These delays had served to ensure that the book, the ideas of which were embedded in the 1960s, would not match the needs of the 1970s.

If a book receives two simultaneous reviews in the same publication, it is usually an indication that it is controversial and therefore it becomes appropriate for it to receive one hostile and one sympathetic review. *Film in English Teaching* however came under sustained attack from both Len Masterman and Jim Cook.[27]

> Helpful as *Film in English Teaching* is in chronicling the movements of the past decade, it could well hinder the teacher who wishes to catch a whiff of the future.[28]
>
> If *Film in English Teaching* attracts newcomers to the idea of using film in their work and provides them with some basic information – well and good; if its ideological assertions are left unchallenged and become assimilated into an orthodoxy – less good.[29]

The problem for both reviewers is that they recognise that the publication of this material in book form will serve only to reinforce precisely the kind of unreflective personal experience the old-style *Screen Education* had regularly promulgated. For Masterman in particular it is no longer appropriate to make a facile link between the study of English and the study of film as equal elements in a shared culture.

> *Film in English Teaching* represents an attempt to assimilate film into a cultural heritage which has itself been called into question by Freire, Marcuse and others who have shown us the ways in which it has become an instrument for domination in both school and society.[30]

While it is possible to claim that Cook and Masterman have in effect jointly written an obituary for the work of their predecessors, it is relevant to indicate that the momentum the screen education movement had gained by 1973 had only been possible because of what had gone before. The book's editor Roy Knight was well-placed to acknowledge this in his dedication.

...and finally to the various editors of *Screen Education* and *Screen*, and to the officers and members of the Society for Education in Film and Television over two decades – to their persistence and devotion to the causes of film and teaching this book is gratefully dedicated.[31]

If *Film in English Teaching* was out of date before it was published, there were soon indications that the BFI was finally prepared to give proper recognition to the importance of television in its educational brief. Although EAS was no longer a book publishing body, it nevertheless retained a member of staff responsible for publications, Christopher Williams (until 1973) and then Ed Buscombe. Williams began a series of monographs on television by different authors. The series of thirteen ran until 1981. Williams was aware that the only previous publication about television to emerge from within the BFI's education remit had been *Talking about Television* a decade earlier. This had done little beyond demonstrate that children might be encouraged to transfer to their discussions about television programmes the approaches already familiar to them when they discussed feature films. The first four monographs were published in the period 1973–75 and these, as Paterson observed, were disproportionately focused on television's current affairs output.[32]

Rohdie recruits

The SEFT that Knight had acknowledged in that dedication no longer existed as he must have known, since he had addressed the 1971 Crisis Meeting as SEFT's President, a role that had no constitutional input into the Society. However as a consequence of his success in the dispute with the BFI over SEFT, Rohdie had become a powerful and independent figure in the Society, the Committee of which had become seriously depleted in membership. Collins who joined the Committee in 1972 describes Rohdie as having 'energy, charisma, authority' while having to relate to 'a rump of people with stronger roots in schools and further education'.[33] Rohdie took it upon himself to find recruits both for the SEFT Committee and for the *Screen* Editorial Board. Rohdie's methods were *ad hoc*. Alvarado recalls being recruited to the Committee as a result of a chance encounter with Rohdie at a screening.[34] If the SEFT committee still maintained a regime of regular meetings it seems that the *Screen* Editorial Board was a much more casual arrangement with little formality as Willemen recalls.[35] Lovell identifies Rohdie's readiness to recruit to the Board without seeking its approval as an early cause of the SEFT Committee's dissatisfaction with its General Secretary/Editor.[36] The Associate Editors seem never to have met together. Neither Perkins nor Barr who were listed as such editors can recall any formal meeting. Their contact with *Screen* was always via its editor.[37]

In recruiting to the Editorial Board Rohdie used his London contacts and quickly involved Brewster and Willemen. But he extended his searches when, following the publication of *Signs of the Times*, Stephen Heath and Colin MacCabe were contacted in Cambridge. MacCabe recalls how he learned from Heath that 'some people' in

London were interested in contacting them.[38] This led to a Soho lunch with Rohdie and Wollen in 1973 and invitations to join the *Screen* Board followed. MacCabe who had found it impossible to get funding for *Signs of the Times*[39] and had paid to publish it himself, found the enticements of the *Screen* set-up irresistible, like an invitation to the best ever party. He could see how the staffing and funding SEFT had achieved would provide a unique opportunity to promote the theories he had found so attractive when researching in Paris. What is particularly significant about MacCabe's involvement was that he claims to have no special interest in the cinema at that point. What he perceived was the scope to take theories that were already well developed in the abstract and to test them out in a territory where little previous serious thinking had taken place. Indeed Rohdie's strength as an editor seems to have been his readiness to act as a facilitator for the expression of other people's priority ideas. He wrote little himself for *Screen*. Geoffrey Nowell-Smith believes that Rohdie modelled his editorship on that of Perry Anderson, Editor of *New Left Review*.[40]

It had been the Education Department seminars in the late 1960s which first provided a regular focus for the discussion of theoretical ideas. Given the prohibition from its governors, the BFI was not in a position to revive these. They were however reintroduced but with the label SEFT/BFI seminars on the unexceptional organisational rationale that SEFT would provide the intellectual leadership and the BFI the seminar spaces. The first tranche of the seminars in the spring of 1973 was designed to be 'a preparing ground for the 1973 Institute Summer School, "Concepts in Film Criticism"'.[41] They followed the pattern of the previous seminars where papers were circulated in advance and then presented at each seminar.

The next series of seminars were to be much more heavy duty:

> It is suggested that each session a different member of the group summarise the content of the reading for that session; however, every member should prepare for the session in such a way that he could introduce the session himself if called upon to do so. Hence it is essential that every participant commit himself to carry out the reading for every session. The readings for each session are relatively short, amounting to less than 100 pages per session...[42]

A further refinement was that the one large seminar group was now split into three groups, each with its own leader: Ben Brewster, Colin MacCabe and Kari Hanet. The seminars were to be 'more formalised and pedagogic, presenting a basic introduction to the concept of semiology or semiotics'.[43] It seems that for those able to attend and put in the work these seminars were welcome and productive events, as Douglas Lowndes, then the newly appointed Head of the Educational Advisory Services, recalls.[44] If those involved with *Screen* felt the need to set up these preliminary briefing sessions for their immediate contacts, there can be little doubt as to their assessment of the scale of the intellectual heave they were about to attempt in the pages of *Screen*.

Rohdie was a tough if idiosyncratic editor. A succession of controversial editorial decisions began with the Autumn 1972 issue when Rohdie published an article on English Hitchcock by John M Smith but pre-empted the reader's response by using his introductory editorial to undermine Smith's article by labelling him as someone who 'relates to an older and I think incorrect aesthetic position, but one nevertheless in the mainstream of British Film Criticism'.[45] It seems that part of the decision to print Smith's article was to set it against the collective text of the Editors of *Cahiers du Cinéma* on *Young Mr Lincoln*, translated in the same issue. Smith's contribution was apparently an example of how not to do it. Then Rohdie quotes from V F Perkins's *Film as Film* as evidence of what constitutes this 'species of Romantic aesthetics'.[46] In fact Rohdie was preparing for his next attack when in the following *Screen* he printed a savage review of *Film as Film*. Perkins recalls that he was unprepared for the onslaught of Rohdie's review, having previously had amicable meetings when he had offered to help Rohdie. It seems that Rohdie's only concession to Perkins was to let him see the review in advance so that Perkins had his right of reply published immediately after Rohdie's hostile review.[47]

Most of Rohdie's offending review is taken up with an attack on the recently published *Movie Reader* where he makes an attempt to locate its writing as a feature of the 1960s which had now been superseded, presumably by *Screen*.[48] Rohdie then sets out to discredit *Film as Film* by association. Rohdie claims that Perkins's book 'only makes sense in the context of the *Movie* tradition'.[49] Rohdie however begins his review by conceding that in *Film as Film* Perkins presents 'a rigorous, coherent explication and rationale of his own critical position'.[50] Given that Rohdie so assaults Perkins's position, this praise may be inferred as being extremely patronising to an author who allegedly offers a theory which relates 'only to a handful of directors'.[51]

Perkins's reply is eloquent and thoughtful but it elicited no further response from Rohdie.[52] Indeed the editorial to this issue of *Screen* written by Alan Lovell, while making no direct reference to the book reviews, writes in a context which is more sympathetic to Perkins.[53] Lovell reminds readers how in its first Editorial (*Screen* Vol 12 No 1) Rohdie had stated

> Auteurs are out of time. The theory which makes them sacred makes no inroads on vulgar history...The primary act of auteur criticism is one of dissociation – the auteur out of time and history and society is also freed from any productive process...[54]

In this *Screen* auteurs are put back into history with a substantial article on 'The Cinema of the Popular Front in France', as Lovell acknowledges. However what Lovell has to face up to, given Rohdie's previous claims for *Screen* to be a theoretical journal, is the obvious absence of theory from the issue which he is introducing.

We can only say in our defence that the production of theory is not as easy as we first thought, not so much a matter of pulling rabbits out of hats as, perhaps, we have made it seem. We have also become increasingly conscious that knowledge is needed as well as theory.[55]

Knowing their material well was a quality *Movie*'s editors and writers had always manifested.

In January 1973 Rohdie planned to publish later that year (as Volume 14 Number 2) an issue of *Screen* containing a series of articles on experimental cinema. Film-maker Malcolm Le Grice was hired to be in charge of this section and he set about commissioning articles from others with expertise in this area. Copy was expected by 1st April and was delivered by that deadline.[56] At the beginning of June Le Grice received a letter from Rohdie which rejected the material.[57]

Each member of the Editorial Board read all of the copies submitted and we all felt as a group that the material did not fulfil the function for which it was commissioned and we have therefore decided not to publish it.[58]

By way of explanation Rohdie continued:

We felt that much of the copy submitted constituted propaganda and advertisement; that aesthetic problems were raised in only a vague way; that a fetish of technology, of alternative, was endlessly invoked, rather than analysed and constituted therefore more aesthetic ideology than aesthetic understanding.[59]

An acrimonious exchange of correspondence followed.[60] Christopher Williams who had joined the Editorial Board in late 1971 and had had the task of representing the Board in discussions with Le Grice during the early spring of 1973, confirms that it was a decision by the whole Editorial Board.[61] The acrimony arose not simply from the Board's rejection of the work but also from the fact that, having paid the contributors a fee for their work, Rohdie then claimed copyright of the material, despite not considering it fit for publication. A consequent editorial decision was made to compensate SEFT members for the missing issue by producing a double issue of *Screen*. This was achieved by increasing the amount of content in the 'Metz' issue to cover for the missing experimental cinemas issue.[62]

There were other delegated projects which proved to be more successful. Rosalind Delmar recalls that Rohdie took the initiative in facilitating a women's cinema group which met to view and discuss films.[63] Claire Johnston who was associated with the group then wrote *Notes on Women's Cinema* which drew on the debates that had taken place within the group.[64] This was published as a *Screen* Pamphlet and sold out very quickly. Earlier Ed Buscombe's *Films on TV* had started the series.[65] However these specifically *Screen* publishing ventures were to cease after Rohdie's departure.

Rohdie appears to have related more effectively to his Editorial Board than to the SEFT Committee. Perhaps for this reason he involved the Editorial Board, but not the SEFT Committee, in an expensive decision which led to a further controversy. Paul Willemen who joined the Editorial Board in autumn 1972 and Claire Johnston, who would later join the SEFT Committee, were principal figures in the organisation of the 1973 Edinburgh Film Festival which focused on the films of Frank Tashlin. It was the Festival's practice to publish a small paperback book to support its screenings. Previously such books had been published in association with outside bodies who contributed financial assistance. On this occasion a book was published 'in association with *Screen*'.[66] This was a decision apparently taken by Rohdie who then chose to inform only the Editorial Board. Quite how expensive this venture finally became may only be approximately detected by comparing the total publication cost of 1972 (£7,086) with that of the following year when *Frank Tashlin* was published (£9,029).[67] An official SEFT link with the Festival was subsequently made in 1975 for what became known as the Brecht Event, transcribed in *Screen* a few months later.[68] Lynda Myles became Director of the Festival in 1974 and Laura Mulvey identifies Myles as the key figure in establishing this link.[69]

Rohdie departs
There was increasing dissatisfaction with Rohdie which led to the Committee in late 1973 seeking legal advice as to its position, given that it had been Rohdie's employer since April 1972. Detailed letters were sent to Rohdie setting out the causes of the Committee's dissatisfaction to which he responded with equally detailed replies.[70] What emerges from these documents is that there were issues which arose around Rohdie's personal style – a style that had enabled him first to stand up to the BFI and then effectively and confidently to recruit his own Committee and produce a transformed version of SEFT in just over two years. Nevertheless, having recruited to the Committee people who had responded to his crisis call two years earlier, Rohdie was now confronted by these same people who were taking their responsibilities very seriously, recognising that as members of the Executive Committee of SEFT they were personally answerable for the substantial income both from members' subscriptions and public funds via the BFI.

When the 1973 AGM took place in November of that year, some Committee members were prepared and, having read the report that Rohdie had written for the occasion, they raised a motion from the floor which proposed that 'the Annual Report be rejected on the grounds that it did not represent a real reflection of the work, policy and position of the Society over the last 12 months'.[71] The motion was eventually passed after much discussion, as was another motion that a Special General Meeting be called before 31 May 1974. The pressure increased on Rohdie who resigned on 28 February. As part of the deal worked out with the Committee his name stayed on *Screen* as editor for the Spring and Summer and the Autumn 1974 issues. Most of the editorial work for these issues fell to Brewster and MacCabe who took on the task with relish and enthusiasm, although they were not in favour of Rohdie's departure.[72]

SEFT reorganises

Following Rohdie's departure, the SEFT Committee was able to complete its thorough review of the Society's work and organisational priorities. It had to hold a Special General Meeting in the summer of 1974 as it had promised at the abandoned AGM in November 1973 and it needed to have substantial proposals for that meeting. Changes were already under way even before the meeting. What SEFT members would have noticed first were the changes to *Screen Education Notes*. Its Contents page for the Spring/Summer 1974 double issue still appeared under the banner of 'Screen Education Notes' but its cover had a different emphasis. The new cover design like its predecessor had been borrowed from *Screen* but it now resembled the other journal even more closely. But on the new cover the name was now *Screen Education*. The 'Introduction' stated

> The board feel that the term *Notes*, carried over in the title of the journal is no longer appropriate to the publication which has developed, so from this issue the journal will be called simply *Screen Education*.[73]

Screen Education would now have different editors for each issue. This first issue had Cook, Hillier and Mottershead as editors, a consequence of the collaboration of both SEFT and the BFI Educational Advisory Service for this particular issue, which was on CSE courses. SEFT's grant from the BFI was channelled through the EAS and Douglas Lowndes, who was very supportive of SEFT, found additional money specifically to finance this issue of *Screen Education*.[74]

Further developments were manifested in the document produced for the Special General Meeting which eventually took place on 6 July 1974.[75] No longer were the tasks of General Secretary SEFT and Editor *Screen* to be combined. Editing *Screen* was now to be a paid half-time post. A new full-time post was to combine the Editorship of *Screen Education* with the new role of SEFT's Education Officer. In practice this post was much closer to what the SEFT Committee of 1970 had envisaged when it combined the Editorship of *Screen* with the role of General Secretary SEFT, in that under the new arrangements SEFT would have its own full-time professional officer overseeing a regular educational publication. But after the three years of Rohdie's involvement SEFT had not only gained its 1970 ambition but also now had its independence and additionally was the publisher of an influential intellectual journal that was avidly exploring new territory. What the document recognises is the need for SEFT to identify its position in the rapidly evolving world of 1970s film and television education. What is also implicit in the following quotation (which makes no specific mention of *Screen*) is the Society's caution about what its involvement with *Screen's* promotion of European theory might be likely to entail. There are separate references in three of the four proposed aims to SEFT's engagement with British culture.

The Executive Committee proposes to utilise the reformed structure of the Society and deployment of staff outlined in order to put into practice the following basic aims:

- to promote the study of film and TV and the identification of their disciplines within the context of British culture;
- to work towards the growth of a British film and television culture;
- to encourage the development of film and television education within the context of the British cultural and educational scene;
- to ensure the closest links between the prosecution of these three interrelated areas, in particular by re-dressing the present imbalance through putting more staff and financial resources into the journal *Screen Education* and related education work.[76]

The Committee, having got the agreement of the Special Meeting, was then in a position to make appointments to each of these posts. They selected two individuals who had demonstrated proven qualities: Alvarado, an established member of both the SEFT Committee and the *Screen Education* Board, became Education Officer/Editor *Screen Education* from 1 January 1975. Brewster could now be properly recognised from 1 December 1974 as Editor of *Screen*, a task he had already been discharging on a voluntary basis for nearly a year.[77] There were two further posts which were already in place: a part-time Business Manager (Ann Sachs) and a full-time Editorial/Administrative Officer (Elizabeth Cowie).

Film Study developments beyond Old Compton Street
Screen Education Notes had kept a record of developments beyond SEFT. For many teachers in the early and mid 1970s these would be of more direct consequence than the institutional changes within SEFT. The BFI/ILEA Sixth Form Film Study Course which originated in 1972 was unlike any previous project in screen education for several reasons.[78] It was on a large scale; it evolved over many years; its materials were produced as part of a collective enterprise focused around the BFI Educational Advisory Services; an advisory teacher was appointed by the ILEA specifically to support the teaching and the participating teachers were to be continuously involved in its evaluation.[79] There were to be further benefits which would extend beyond ILEA: the supporting documentation was publicly available and could be used by teachers not participating in the course while through their involvement in the course, numerous London teachers began the process of becoming trained film and media teachers.

The origins of the course were modest. Michael Simons, a teacher at Wandsworth School, who also ran a local ILEA centre for Teachers of English had in 1970 arranged to hire the National Film Theatre for the screening of three versions of *Hamlet* to A level students studying English. Seeing how successful the screening of films to students under such near ideal conditions had been, Simons contacted the Inspectorate to see if there was support for a film study course.[80] Leslie Ryder, the Aural and Visual Aids Inspector, who had supported the earlier SEFT experiment in one ILEA division and now presided over an expanding Learning Resources community in the authority, supported the proposal. He set up a preliminary investigative course in autumn 1971 for teachers in secondary and further education who might be interested in teaching film.[81] Ryder's subsequent commitment extended to the appointment of Chris Mottershead as Advisory Teacher to support the work from January 1973. In the following year Mottershead would become Chairman of SEFT. The authors of the materials in the early years of the project were Jim Cook, Cary Bazalgette, Christine Gledhill, Michael Simons and Jane Clark.[82] Jim Hillier who committed much of his time at EAS to the ILEA Project felt that in doing this he was in practice involved in a much more substantial project of designing a transferable approach to film teaching. He had a particular involvement in the production of slides which he felt was introducing a new focus of study: the detail of *mise-en-scène*.[83]

The project was expensive but very successful, with 500 students from 37 London schools participating in the first year.[84] Such was the enthusiasm of schools that the original single screening in NFT 1 was supplemented by a second in NFT 2 on a different afternoon.[85] The course was offered as a contribution to sixth form General Studies.[86] There was no particular expectation of written work from the students and no examination at the end. However over time the course was to change. It ran for some thirteen years and eventually a smaller group of some dozen schools was attending when the course was geared specifically to the requirements of the CEE (Certificate of Extended Education) Examination, as the composition of ILEA sixth form groups changed.[87]

Whatever benefits individual students may have received from the course, probably its most lasting importance would be in the scale of on-the-job training it offered to would-be film and media teachers. There were specially prepared materials for students, but more significantly substantial Teachers' Notes were produced simultaneously. The screenings were fortnightly and in each alternate week the teachers had the task of using the materials in the classroom. When a major review of the course was undertaken in 1976, teachers were supplied with a version of the students' material into which the notes for the teacher had been incorporated.[88] Previously the teacher had had to juggle two booklets. However, the extracts from texts to which the students were referred were no longer in in a single student booklet but were now produced separately, so each student had two booklets: Study Notes and a Study Guide. At this stage of the development, documentation was the work of Cook and Hillier from the BFI together with Mottershead.[89] A substantial part of the course now focused on the use of specially chosen slides made specifically for the course from frame enlargements.[90]

Like the long-term support by the BFI for the London University Extra-Mural Course, this was another metropolitan venture where the location of BFI facilities determined that the population of the capital would be the beneficiaries. There was a previous history of such ventures in that the National Film Theatre had been the venue for BFI Film Appreciation Department/London County Council joint lectures for students since the 1950s. But on this occasion there were additional favourable factors. The BFI Governors wanted to see their educational staff directly servicing teachers and that desire justified large scale BFI involvement in the course. The ILEA had introduced in 1968 training for the first holders of the posts of Media Resources Officers. These MROs wanted to have responsibilities around media which clearly defined them as being more than AVA technicians. Supporting film study fitted into the desired category of additional expertise.[91]

What linked the ILEA course to almost all previous developments in screen education was its grass roots origin. It had started from the initiative of a single teacher who saw an opportunity to replicate in a larger arena what individual teachers had done for years in their own school or college situations. Simultaneously another teacher-led initiative was to have long-term consequences. David Lusted, then a lecturer in further education who had developed a CSE syllabus, decided to approach all the GCE O level boards with a proposal for an examination in film at that level.[92] Only the Associated Examining Board responded positively, albeit saying in effect 'very interesting but not yet'. However when one of their examiners subsequently had a letter published in the *Times Educational Supplement* calling for the media to be studied in schools, Lusted seized the opportunity and got the Board to call a meeting of interested parties. Subsequent progress was rapid with Lusted appointed convener and then moderator when the first group of about a dozen schools and a further education college in the London and South East area submitted candidates for the examination in 1972. The film O level (or more accurately OA level) went national in its third year.

The ILEA project and the O level were similarly constructed to contain in their syllabuses the emphases of film study then current: authorship, genre and an understanding of the film industry. However the teachers who were pioneering these developments had a problem. They saw that these projects offered opportunities to be seized by teachers in order to secure a firmer place for film study within educational institutions. At the same time they were also aware of the momentum that was building around the development of film study. In designating specific elements for inclusion in the structure of syllabuses, they were indicating a degree of certainty as to the nature of these elements, whereas the reality was that they were giving authenticity to areas that should more appropriately have been labelled as work in progress.

Defining the 'subject' of Media
By the autumn of 1975, with Alvarado now established as Editor of *Screen Education*, the journal signalled recognition of the tentative nature of the concepts it was addressing.

Thus the present situation is one in which members of the editorial board see the need for a continuing re-examination of how the field of film, television, media might be conceptualised and for a reconsideration of how the 'subject' ought to be presented.[93]

In a series of articles around teaching about the Film Industry, the scale of the shift in thinking that might be required of film teachers is made much clearer. In the leading article Cook looks critically at the way that teaching about the industry had been justified in the Teachers' Introduction to the original Industry Unit on the ILEA course.[94]

> The industrial context, therefore, is presented as one of organisation – obtaining and financing personnel and plant; conceiving of an audience and appealing to them by particular forms of presentation; while the work itself is justified to the teacher on the assumption of some sort of relationship between it and 'the wider critical issues and problems involved in studying film', and to the student on the assumption that it will enable him/her 'to become more aware of film as a specific medium which requires understanding and might therefore be worth studying'.
>
> As with the metaphorical descriptions referred to in Nos 10/11 of *Screen Education*, at the time such a generalised justification was sufficient to get the work established, and given the fact that so few coherent models for work on the industry existed prior to this course, it is perhaps inevitable anyway that it should be justified in these terms. Now however with such work more firmly established, there is a need to try and refine the description of what it might set out to do, and to examine more rigorously justifications for it – bearing in mind that this is not an attempt to put a brake on such work but rather to attempt to assess more precisely what, if anything, the nature and outcome of such work might be.[95]

The scale of the potential task of *Screen Education* becomes clearer as Cook develops his thinking. He identifies the gap that exists between the level of theory being advanced by *Screen* in the work of writers such as Althusser, Benjamin and Williams and the more detailed investigations also published in *Screen* from Barr, Ellis and Buscombe. The writings of the first group of writers, he suggests, did not provide a clear theoretical perspective that was applicable to the study of the industry while the latter's researches are too specific to allow for meaningful generalisations about the industry to be inferred.[96]

Cook then has to accept that the level of concern he is recording has different implications for different student groups. The rather simplistic recognition of the functional role of the film industry in the production of texts that the original ILEA course had accommodated clearly needs to be challenged. But he can offer little by way of how to develop it. He has to acknowledge that

…at the secondary and further level it is probably enough to endorse the general concern of broadening the perspectives in which film is considered and we should work towards devising material which generally (and perhaps intuitively) seem to help achieve this…[97]

But it is at the higher education level that the changes are imperative where

…one ought to embark on the production of more substantive research analogous to Barrs's and Ellis's and more generally to subject existing substantive material on the industry…to an ideological scrutiny of the extent to which they do or do not recognise some determining role for the industry.[98]

This instance has more general applicability. Until the 1970s it was the case that the impetus for film and television study came from the grass-roots. Whannel, in his determination to get film study established in higher education, realised there were limits as to how far the grass-roots might continue to be the engine driving the movement. He therefore consistently called for developments to be set up in higher education. Now that *Screen* existed to push ahead with theoretical developments and *Screen Education* had the distinctive role of connecting the emerging area of theoretical film study with its delivery in classrooms, it was evident there was a problem. The subject specific expertise which most teachers acquired in higher education before being required to perform in the classroom had not been there for film teachers. Provision of more resources of intellectual stimulation for would-be film teachers was now on the agenda. This would be met in a number of ways.

Courses for Teachers

While the BFI collaborated with ILEA to deliver the film study course for sixth formers, another long-term player in the development of film study, the National Union of Teachers, collaborated with SEFT to provide week-long Easter schools in 1974 and 1975.[99] These were targeted specifically at teachers and allowed wider scope for the investigation of the ideas that were being explored in *Screen Education*. In 1975 Philip Simpson, a lecturer at Alnwick College of Education, attended with some of his students and as a group they reported on the experience.[100] Unlike the substantial recruitment for the BFI summer schools, attendance here was much smaller (24 students). Most of those who came were familiar with the concepts involved. Alvarado, having taken over the organisation of the event when he became Education Officer three months earlier, reported back to the Executive that the attendance had been disappointing. Thirty students had attended in 1974 and more had been expected. Among his reasons for the low turnout was the fact that NAFE had run 'a much cheaper, shorter course at exactly the same time'. [101] The significance of the Alnwick report lies in its questioning of the centrality of film study. During the week students had spent time both looking at carefully selected images – such as those proposed in the work of

Golay and Gauthier – and also had participated in photoplay exercises.[102] These activities had given rise to questions about the wider relevance of image study. Simpson and his students felt that the question 'Why teach film?' which had opened the first session of the week (and had been resurrected unanswered at the end of the course) avoided wider issues.[103]

> But the raising of this question in a final seminar showed how arguments stemming from film as 'popular culture' or from the need for developing understanding of the way images, with or without sound, work make at least as much sense in the context of media studies generally and are by no means specific to Film Study.[104]

Perhaps the most influential of the mechanisms by which potential film teachers outside the ILEA were to be trained was the annual BFI Summer School.[105] Lusted considers that there was a definite progression route for teachers, who would transfer from the Easter Schools to the Summer Schools.[106] In the 1960s these schools had followed a pattern common to much of the wider summer school movement. They provided the opportunity for a learning holiday, with formal sessions usually occupying only a part (albeit large) of each day. In the 1970s BFI Summer Schools changed to become events that, in the descriptions of many who attended them, were both exhilarating and exhausting.[107] The intensity of the events was in part a result of the Educational Advisory Service having been restricted in what it might do. Philip Simpson is clear that the Summer Schools were the way in which the EAS was able to define itself at a time when its contribution in other areas had been restricted.[108] Planning for each subsequent summer school would begin in the autumn and the use of the two weeks would be constructed with great care since the school now represented the main opportunity for BFI's educational staff to address teachers and lecturers.[109] But alongside this circumstance was the existence of SEFT and in particular of *Screen*.

The organisers of the BFI Summer School saw an important part of its function as being the interface between the theorists of Old Compton Street and the teacher in the classroom. The rapidity with which the summer school's organisation was changed is reflected in how events were recalled in the booklet *BFI Summer Schools '71–'79* published after the Education Department was given back its old status in the 1980s.[110]

> However, in general terms it is worth signalling the moves from a 1971 school which was in effect constructed before the new *Screen* began publishing (Spring 1971) through to those of 1972 – 1976 where in varying ways attempts are made to describe and understand formal semiotic approaches to cinema and particularly to assess the ways in which they developed and/or displaced more traditional critical notions such as authorship, genre, *mise-en-scène*.[111]

The pace of change may be detected in a number of ways. In 1971 the Summer School was held at Eastbourne College of Education. 16mm film-making was still a feature of the course with obligatory end-of-course screenings for the student made films. The reading list and checklist of texts supplied to the students in advance of the fortnight occupied only a single sheet of A4.[112] By 1975 film-making had disappeared, its demise preceded in the intervening years by a shift first to 8mm and then to video. The 1975 reading and checklists now amounted to nine sides of A4.[113] The school found a more congenial and permanent home from 1972, being based in Scotland at the University of Stirling, a location which had the added advantage of being backed by financial support from the Scottish Film Council. In its advance publicity prospective students were advised that 'priority is given to applicants such as film teachers'.[114]

The 1971 school, 'Realism: Theory and Practice' had been built around the British Documentary Movement, Italian Neo-realism and the writings of Bazin. In doing so it was not that different from summer schools of the 1960s when a title like 'The Western' was a draw for students and sufficient justification for staff.[115] By 1972 the title was 'Technique/Style/Meaning' and *Screen* articles made up half of the checklist of texts. Both Rohdie and Perkins featured on the list of staff.[116] The latter recalled how out of place he felt at the event, where it appeared that semiotics and Marxism were to be presented as the new critical normality. By default he found himself to be 'the voice of the opposition'. He recalls that when he challenged the apparently unquestioned acceptance of Marxism, he felt he was being identified as part of the enemy.[117] It seems that the charge of ' intellectual terrorism' which was subsequently to be levelled at *Screen* started in Stirling. For different reasons neither Rohdie nor Perkins would be on the summer school staff again.

Of the 120 students present in 1972, 45 were from overseas, the largest single contingent being from the USA. The great majority were working or studying in educational establishments.[118] From the list of all the students it is possible to identify numerous participants who would become very influential in the subsequent development of film and media teaching.[119] If the 1972 list functions as a snapshot because it is available, nevertheless the pattern would persist in subsequent years, as successive cohorts arriving at the BFI Summer School would routinely contain a core of dedicated enthusiasts who would subsequently be involved with film and media teaching in the long-term.

In 1973 'Concepts in Film Criticism' were on the agenda. Perhaps the experience of disjuncture that Perkins had experienced led to the school being introduced thus:

> The course assumes that film criticism and film theory are at a crucial juncture which demands that questions which have been raised and debated, particularly over the last ten to fifteen years in magazines like *Cahiers du Cinéma*, *Sight and Sound*, *Movie*, *Screen*, etc, be reviewed and re-examined.
>
> The course will concern itself both with general attitudes to the cinema and to film criticism and theory, and more particularly with some of the concepts which

have been used in critical and theoretical writing, for example concepts of *mise-en-scène*, authorship, genre. The course will also take account of the way semiology and ideology have been discussed in relation to the cinema and examine attempts to approach cinema more scientifically on the basis of these concepts.[120]

By the following year, 1974, 'Critical Theory and Film Analysis' has a reading list not dissimilar to that of 1973. However the design of the event had changed with the first week 'a concentrated introductory study of certain areas developed in criticism and critical theory over the last decade'. Given the disparity in student backgrounds that Bazalgette had noted in her review of the 1973 course, the planners had recognised there needed to be some preliminary preparation before week two with its 'intensive analyses of particular films'.[121] Roy Stafford, a summer school regular, considers this to have been the first '*Screen* theory' Summer School.[122]

In 1975 the school subject was 'Genre: Problems and Approaches' where the films under scrutiny would be American film noir. But the context had changed from that in which the Western had been considered in the 1960s. Now it was the concept of genre itself that was under investigation.

> Despite widespread use of the concept, particularly in discussions of film as popular art, genre has remained uncertain in definition and problematic in application. The school will aim to assess the nature and usefulness of the concept of genre in the development of film study and criticism, looking at areas such as generic approaches in other arts, relations between art and society, conventions of narrative, style and subject matter, the intersection of genre with other critical approaches such as authorship.[123]

Demonstrative of the intensity of this inquiry was the re-scheduling of the students' day. As practical work had disappeared the free time available to students in the afternoon had been curtailed.

The authors of *BFI Summer Schools 71–79* consider the 1976 Summer School (Film: Image and Analysis) to be the last in the sequence of those that were heavily indebted to *Screen*. Important in its content were the days devoted to 'Psychoanalysis and the Cinema'.[124] These sessions would have been planned in late 1975 when four members of the *Screen* Editorial Board had written a statement questioning the significance *Screen* was giving to psychoanalysis.[125] By the summer 1976 issue of *Screen* and the timing of the summer school, all four had resigned. Thereafter the delivery of BFI Summer Schools would be less influenced by the theories coming out of Old Compton Street.[126]

SEFT's weekend schools were designed for a more specialist audience than the BFI summer schools. The weekends were advertised in such a way that they were likely to attract those who read *Screen* and/or *Screen Education*. If the summer schools were facilitated by the BFI and if as a consequence the BFI's staff were to form the transmission mechanism for certain of *Screen*'s theories, the weekend schools provided a more direct address from SEFT rather than from *Screen* to its membership and to others during 1975 and 1976. The sequence of schools was: Narrative and the Cinema; *Mise-en-scène*; Women and Film; Television Fiction: the Series; *The Searchers*; Pleasure, Entertainment and the Popular Culture Debate; Realism and the Cinema; British Independent Cinema/Avant-Garde.[127] Christine Geraghty who joined the SEFT Executive in 1975 believes that the significance and strength of these events derived from their being seminar driven, without the formality of lectures.[128]

The regularity of the weekend schools was a direct result of SEFT now having its own Education Officer, part of whose remit was to develop these events. Costings for the four 1975 schools exist and show that two schools made a profit. The total deficit for the year was £27. The full fee per student was £4.32 which divided into the figures for receipts would suggest that attendance for each event was in the range of 50 to 80 students.[129] These were intensive weekends, running from Friday evening to late Sunday afternoon, with students receiving in advance substantial documentation.[130] At this time, weekend events were usually held at the then London International Film School. Unlike the series of seminars which preceded them, these were open to all.

Funding Film Teaching posts in the Universities

One major development was totally within the remit of the BFI. Whannel had always argued for film in higher education and had indeed been directly approached by Warwick University in the late 1960s about the possibilities of the funding of a film teaching post there being provided by the BFI.[131] After the re-organisation of the Education Department, the BFI Governors established an Advisory Committee on Grants to Higher Education and in 1972 began to offer funding for which universities might apply.[132] This was one of the last decisions to be made by Reed who retired from the BFI in June 1972. Williams and McArthur believe that Reed's decision to proceed with this proposal was a direct consequence of the upheavals in the Education Department.[133] Reed, it is suggested, felt the need to demonstrate recognition of those calls from within the BFI for film to have a place in higher education and, by giving money to selected universities, he might ensure that these developments could be definitively outsourced.

The task of approaching the universities fell first to Williams and then to Buscombe as part of the Publication Officer's brief. The project was designed to be enticing. The BFI would pump-prime a full-time post for three years, after which the intention was that the university would take over the funding. Each year starting in 1973 a new post would be created at a different university, so that by 1975 and thereafter BFI would be funding a total of three such lectureships annually. The Governors under Forman accepted these arrangements, but were reluctant still to shift their basic position and went on record as having schools as their priority.[134]

The BFI offer was specific to universities, not polytechnics. Consequently whereas there were developments in some polytechnics into which such lectureships might have been suitably fitted, with the universities there were no automatic connections to be made. The task for BFI therefore was threefold: first to find an appropriate niche in a sympathetic university, then to define the job to be done there and finally to appoint someone to fit the post. Finding a niche in the system where film study might flourish had some similarities with what had been happening in schools during the three post-war decades. In different institutions film would find a different home but the underlying justification would be that, for whatever reason, student numbers were increasing and meeting the needs of a greater number of students simply by offering more of the same was becoming less and less sustainable.

The first lectureship went to Warwick which had campaigned longest. But a solitary lecturer can only provide a modest offer to students. To maximise recruitment, Warwick offered a single option open to students in all departments of the university. The post itself was attached administratively to the Theatre Studies Department. The postholder was Robin Wood who saw his long-term task as developing a full Single Honours Degree in Film Studies.[135] In succeeding years posts were established at Keele (Richard Dyer, 1974) and Essex (Peter Wollen, 1975).[136] At Keele the post was divided between the undergraduate American Studies Department and the university's adult extra-mural work where film had had an established position since film study there had first been encouraged by Roy Shaw in the 1950s. At Essex Wollen was in the Department of Language and Linguistics where his classes formed no part of any degree scheme and as he observed 'my work is somewhat marginal to the concerns of the University'.[137] He did however establish a class in Semiotics within his 'home' department.

From the contemporary observations of these pioneer post-holders, it is clear that, even with BFI funding, the early years of the pump-priming operation did not initiate a period when film study took a firm hold within the host universities. Again there were echoes of what had happened in schools where, when courses began, only a small number of students benefited but found themselves to be learning in the context of the improving expertise and knowledge of their teacher/lecturer. When *Screen Education* published accounts from each of these early lecturers it is clear that each was able to use the scope of his post to develop his own particular research and teaching interests. As for the students, their interests were partly determined by what reference material was available for them, when so few texts had been published. There was however scope for initiative. At Warwick two students in Wood's first intake started the journal *Framework*; for Keele students there was the option of participating in a successful local SEFT group; while at Essex Wollen in his first year offered the Semiotics specialism drawing heavily on *Screen* material.[138]

Viewpoint on Schools Television

In the Educational Advisory Service Douglas Lowndes did not attempt to reproduce the charismatic leadership that Whannel had given. He gave his staff scope to develop their own work within the reduced remit now given to EAS. But he was at heart a practitioner rather than an administrator or a manager. He needed to find an outlet for his expertise. Lowndes had established a reputation as an innovator when involved in teacher training at Hornsey College of Art in the 1960s. There his work had challenged long established ideas about children's film-making as a group exercise, albeit he had done this from a situation where he was able to experiment with children's creativity outside the constraints of the school curriculum. Subsequently while at the BFI, Lowndes collaborated with Thames Television Schools Department and produced in Autumn 1975 a series of television programmes called *Viewpoint*, targeted at students aged 14 and above. The ten programmes and their associated notes for teachers provided 'a 10 week course on mass communications which could be used by teachers of English, Art and History either within their separate disciplines or as an interdisciplinary study'.[139]

The programmes combined observations made direct to camera by the presenter, Lowndes, with illustrated visual material from advertisements, films and television. Commentary on both this material and on the assertions of the presenter was provided by specially written music and lyrics, performed to camera by actors. A Monty Python-esque quality was inserted into some of the graphics. Each episode usually ended either with a small number of students from a selection of schools commenting on the issues raised in the preceding programme or with students participating in a further experiment to test out *Viewpoint*'s hypotheses. At the conclusion of each programme Lowndes cautioned the audience with the proviso that the views they had seen and heard were those of the presenter; the challenge was for them to continue the debate in the classroom when the programme was over.[140]

There were clear parallels between the work that Lowndes had done at Hornsey and was then developing in collaboration with Thames Television. Although always involving school students in the experimental situation, in neither place was Lowndes working within the constraints of a given school's curriculum or organisation. This had the advantage of foregrounding in the experiment what might be possible when circumstances changed within schools. Thus his 8mm film work in the 1960s, which celebrated the individual student's creativity, did become a model for work in schools in the 1970s when simple portable equipment became cheaper and more plentiful. *Viewpoint* proved to be more controversial.

The problem for *Viewpoint* was not that the teachers using the programme complained about it. They simply did not organise to support it, because it had no dedicated audience.[141] Had *Viewpoint* been received by teachers of Media Studies, if they had existed at that time, then its innovative use of television to inquire into the mechanisms of the media would have been recognised and commended. What did happen was that the Independent Broadcasting Authority intervened to prevent any repeat broadcasting of the series in the following school year.[142] The grounds for the intervention were bizarre and followed objections by the Board and Management of Southern Television.

The company have informally advised IBA staff that they do not wish to transmit the repeat of the series in autumn 1976, since the programmes could cause offence to the general audience in the home.[143]

The Head of Education Programmes at the IBA who found himself at the centre of events in 1976 was Brian Groombridge. Groombridge, who only fifteen years earlier had represented the radical edge of screen education thinking, now found himself in opposition to one of the next generation of radical screen educators. This situation would become not untypical of the upheavals within the movement generally that would follow in 1976. Much had been achieved in the half decade that followed the BFI Governors' decision to behead their own Education Department. But if it seemed that the programme of events and publications seen in 1975 would represent a new normality, 1976 was to demonstrate otherwise.

Notes

1. Recollection of the author.
2. For the calendar year 1973 (which became SEFT's published accounting year at this point) the BFI grant total was £11,392.
3. See the account of the 1971 SEFT Annual Conference in the previous chapter.
4. At the May 1971 AGM Jim Cook was elected Chairman and Ed Buscombe Treasurer. No listing is given for Committee Members in the Minutes of the 1971 AGM. Chris Mottershead (in interview with the author 9 November 2005) remembers that he volunteered for the SEFT Committee as a direct result of the conference, as did Richard Exton, Christine Gledhill, Geoff Goldstein and Felicity Grant. By the time that the 1972 AGM was called in November Jim Cook had taken up a post at the BFI and resigned; Les Reynolds was in the Chair and Mark Nash was Treasurer. A further twenty two individuals are listed as members of the Committee. Of these only four were survivors from the Committee elected in 1970.
5. Jim Cook in telephone interview with the author 22 January 2007.
6. *Screen* Vol 12 Nos 1–3
7. *Screen Education Notes* International Edition October 1972 p 1
8. Among those who made up the Editorial Board between 1971 and 1974 were: Manuel Alvarado, Cary Bazalgette, Ed Buscombe, Richard Collins, Jim Cook, Elizabeth Cowie, Christine Gledhill, Jim Hillier, Chris Mottershead, Tom Ryall.
9. *Screen* Vol 12 No 4 Winter 1971/2
10. It is important to clarify the numbering of *Screen Education Notes*. The first issue in Winter 1971 was not numbered. The second issue in Spring 1972 was identified as No 1. The third issue in Summer 1972 was correctly identified as No 3. For the sake of clarity, the first and second issues will always be referred to here only by their publication dates. Therefore the reference for this quote is: Ed Buscombe 'Editorial' *Screen Education Notes* Spring 1972 p 2
11. Brian Groombridge *Television and the People* Harmondsworth: Penguin 1972

12. Tom Ryall 'Editorial' *Screen Education Notes* Autumn 1972 No 4 p 2
13. When the course was re-written in 1976 it became the BFI/ILEA Film Study Course.
14. For example in London University the Italian Department at University College and the Spanish Department at Queen Mary College offer such MAs.
15. Len Masterman in interview with the author 15 September 2006.
16. Len Masterman (1) 'Film and the Raising of the School Leaving Age' *Screen Education Notes* Spring 1973 No 6 p 21
17. Ibid p 23
18. Ibid p 23
19. Richard Collins 'A Diploma Course in Film Study at the Polytechnic of Central London' *Screen Education Notes* Winter 1973/74 No 9 p 11
20. Richard Collins in interview with the author 24 May 2004.
21. SEFT Annual Report and Accounts 1972 p 6
22. Chris Mottershead in interview with the author 9 November 2005.
23. SEFT Annual Report op cit p 7 and see also SEFT Archive Bretton Hall BH /PL/ 132 (2) 1973 SEFT Annual Report and Accounts.
24. *Screen Education Notes* Summer 1972 No 3 p 48
25. British Film Institute Special Collections O/16/2 Box 117 SEFT Annual Report and Accounts 1974 p 5
26. Roy Knight (Ed) *Film in English Teaching* London: Hutchinson Educational November 1972
27. 'Film in English Teaching' Len Masterman (2) 'Review One' and Jim Cook 'Review Two' *Screen Education Notes* Spring 1973 No 6 pp 29–35
28. Masterman 1973 (2) p 31
29. Cook op cit p 35
30. Masterman 1973 (2) p 31
31. Roy Knight op cit p 9
32. The four monographs (all published by British Film Institute Educational Advisory Services) were: Nicholas Garnham *Structures of Television* 1973, Richard Dyer *Light Entertainment* 1973, Trevor Pateman *Television and the February 1974 General Election* 1974, Ed Buscombe (Ed) *Football on Television* 1975. These were reviewed by Richard Paterson in *Screen Education*19 Summer 1976 'Review of EAS publications' pp 45–50.
33. Collins interview op cit
34. Manuel Alvarado in interview with the author 15 July 2003. The screening was of Murnau's *Sunrise* in the basement of the BFI.
35. Paul Willemen in interview with the author 18 August 2005.
36. Alan Lovell in interview with the author 7 June 2005.
37. Victor Perkins in interview with the author 19 April 2005 and Charles Barr in interview with the author 15 June 2005.
38. Colin MacCabe in interview with the author 11 December 2006.
39. Stephen Heath, Colin MacCabe and Nick Prendergast *Signs of the Times – Introductory Readings in Textual Semiotics* Reprint London: BFI 1978
40. Geoffrey Nowell-Smith in interview with the author 30 June 2003.

41. British Film Institute Special Collections May 2005 BFI Education File Memo from Christopher Williams to Douglas Lowndes 24 November 1972

42. British Film Institute Educational Advisory Service/Society for Education in Film and Television Joint seminars flyer November 1973

43. Ibid

44. Douglas Lowndes in interview with the author 5 June 2003.

45. Sam Rohdie 'Editorial' *Screen* Vol 13 No 3 Autumn 1972 pp 2–3

46. Ibid p 3

47. Perkins interview op cit

48. Sam Rohdie ' Review: *Movie Reader, Film as Film*' *Screen* Vol 13 No 4 Winter 1972/3 pp 135–145

49. Ibid p 141

50. Ibid p 141

51. Ibid p 143

52. Victor Perkins 'A Reply to Sam Rohdie' *Screen* Vol 13 No 4 Winter 1972/3 pp 146–151

53. Alan Lovell 'Editorial' *Screen* op cit pp 2–3

54. Sam Rohdie 'Education and Criticism' *Screen* Vol 12 No 1 p 10

55. Lovell op cit p 3

56. Independent Film and Video Producers' Association Archive, Sheffield Hallam University Letter from Sam Rohdie to Malcolm Le Grice 12 January 1973

57. Independent Film and Video Producers' Association Archive, Sheffield Hallam University Letter from Sam Rohdie to Malcolm Le Grice 7 June 1973

58. Ibid

59. Ibid

60. Independent Film and Video Producers' Association Archive, Sheffield Hallam University Letters from Le Grice to Rohdie on 10 June and 20 June 1973; letter from Rohdie to Le Grice 15 June 1973

61. Christopher Williams in email to the author 20 March 2006.

62. Ibid

63. Rosalind Delmar in interview with the author 30 June 2003. She recalls that other members of the group included Jean McCrindle, Laura Mulvey and Margaret Walters.

64. Claire Johnston *Notes on Women's Cinema* SEFT Pamphlet No 2 London: SEFT 1973

65. Ed Buscombe *Films on TV* SEFT Pamphlet No 1 London: SEFT 1971

66. Claire Johnston and Paul Willemen (Eds) *Frank Tashlin* Edinburgh Film Festival in association with *Screen* 1973

67. Figures from SEFT's Annual Report and Accounts for 1972 and 1973

68. *Screen* Vol 16 No 4 Winter 1975/6

69. Laura Mulvey in interview with the author 24 July 2003.

70. The documents are identified as Document One and Document Two and are unsigned and undated. Each is a response to the 'Document from SEFT Committee to the General Secretary'. Document One is a response to 'crises' that the SEFT document revealed.

Document Two is a response to 'rules and procedures affecting the General Secretary' that the SEFT document had detailed.

71. British Film Institute Special Collections O/16/2 Box 117 Minutes of the AGM of SEFT held on 17 November 1973

72. MacCabe interview op cit The information concerning the attitude of the replacement editors to their predecessor was provided by Manuel Alvarado 2 July 2007

73. Introduction to *Screen Education* Nos10/11 Spring/ Summer 1974 p 3

74. Lowndes interview op cit

75. British Film Institute Special Collections O/16/2 Box 117 A statement of policy from the SEFT Executive Committee to the membership of the Society for Education in Film and Television 15 May 1974

76. Ibid Note 4 p 3

77. SEFT Annual Report and Accounts 1974 p 1

78. British Film Institute Education Archive Bretton Hall PL/133 (2) Chris Mottershead 'Some Background Notes on the BFI/ILEA Film Study Course' March 1978

79. Mottershead interview op cit

80. Michael Simons in email to the author 1 February 2007.

81. Mottershead interview op cit

82. Ibid

83. Jim Hillier in interview with the author 25 April 2005.

84. 'Inner London Education Authority Film Study Course for Sixth Form Students' *Screen Education Notes* Winter 1972 No 5 p 12

85. Mottershead interview op cit

86. Christine Ridge 'Reflections on the ILEA 6th Form Film Course' in *Screen Education Notes* Autumn 1973 No 8 p 11

87. 'Teachers' Introduction to Teachers' Guide to Narrative' *ilea:bfi 6th form film studies course 1983–1984*

88. BFI/ILEA Film Study Course Teachers' Notes Introduction 1976

89. Mottershead 1978 op cit

90. Hillier interview op cit

91. Recollection of the author who was Lecturer in Educational Technology at Wandsworth Technical College when the first intake of Media Resources Officers was trained there.

92. David Lusted in interview with the author 16 May 2005.

93. Manuel Alvarado, Jim Cook, Geoff Goldstein, Chris Mottershead 'Editorial' *Screen Education* No 16 Autumn 1975 p 1

94. Jim Cook 'Teaching the Industry' *Screen Education* op cit pp 4–18

95. Ibid p 6

96. Ibid p 16

97. Ibid p 17

98. Ibid p 17

99. Planning had already started on the 1976 school when the NUT withdrew. SEFT continued on its own but teamed up with the BFI Educational Advisory Service subsequently.

100. Karen Brumer, Mike Hagen, Josie McDonough, Will Scurlock, Philip Simpson 'Report of the NUT/SEFT Easter School "Approaches to the Teaching of Film Studies" York, 1975' *Screen Education* No 15 Summer 1975

101. SEFT Archive Bretton Hall ME/PL/133 (2) Manuel Alvarado 'NUT/SEFT Easter School Report 1975' April 1975

102. Bremer et al op cit p 48

103. Ibid p 47

104. Ibid p 50

105. Williams interview op cit

106. Lusted interview op cit

107. This has been a consistent theme in many of the interviews conducted for this investigation.

108. Philip Simpson in interview with the author 4 September 2006.

109. Williams interview op cit

110. Jim Cook, Nicky North *BFI Summer Schools 71–79* London: BFI Education Department April 1981

111. Ibid p 1

112. Ibid pp 3–8

113. Ibid pp 38–51

114. Leaflets advertising the Summer Schools in 1974 and 1975

115. Cook and North op cit p 4

116. Ibid p 9

117. Victor Perkins interview op cit

118. List of students 1972

119. Manuel Alvarado, Cary Bazalgette, Andrew Bethell, Stephen Crofts, Christine Geraghty, Felicity Grant, Robert Lapsley, Chris Mottershead, Steve Neale, Tom Ryall, Philip Simpson

120. Cook and North op cit p 16

121. Ibid p 28

122. Roy Stafford in interview with the author 11 May 2005

123. Ibid p 39

124. Ibid p 55

125. Edward Buscombe, Christine Gledhill, Alan Lovell, Christopher Williams 'Statement: Psychoanalysis and Film' *Screen* Vol 16 No 4 Winter 1975/6 pp 119–130

126. Edward Buscombe, Christine Gledhill, Alan Lovell, Christopher Williams 'Statement: Why We Have Resigned from the Board of *Screen*' *Screen* Vol 17 No 2 Summer 1976 pp 106–109

127. SEFT Archive Bretton Hall ME/PL/133 (1) Stephen Crofts 'SEFT Weekend School Papers' 20 June 1977

128. Christine Geraghty in interview with the author 2 August 2005

129. Weekend Schools Costing 1975/76

130. Narrative Cinema Weekend School 11–13 April 1975 Students' Advance Programme

131. Lovell interview op cit

132. British Film Institute Governors' Meeting 21 March 1972 Paragraph 5453 contains a reference to University Research Centres upon which Douglas Lowndes is to liaise with Asa Briggs.

133. Williams interview op cit and Colin McArthur in interview with the author 28 June 2005.

134. British Film Institute Governors' Meeting 9 May 1972 Section 5471

135. Robin Wood 'Film Studies at the University of Warwick' *Screen Education* No 19 Summer 1976 pp 51–54

136. Richard Dyer 'Film Studies at the University of Keele' and Peter Wollen 'Film Studies at the University of Essex' *Screen Education* op cit pp 54–60

137. Wollen ibid p 57

138. Ibid pp 59–60

139. *Viewpoint* 'Teachers' Notes' London: Thames Television 1975 p 1

140. The author is grateful to Bob Ferguson of the London University Institute of Education for the loan of video recordings of the *Viewpoint* series.

141. Manuel Alvarado and Richard Collins 'The *Viewpoint* Controversy' *Screen Education* No 19 Summer 1976 pp 74–81

142. Ibid p 75

143. Ibid p 80

8

Screen Saviours

The SEFT Committee, concerned about how far Screen *was being understood, organised a regular series of events (one-day conferences, week-end schools) which aimed to explicate and explore the kinds of issues dealt within* Screen *and* Screen Education. *The majority of the* Screen *board were noticeable for their absence from these events and have been censured for this by the committee.*

Edward Buscombe, Christine Gledhill,
Alan Lovell and Christopher Williams, 1976

On a wintry campus in early 1976 film teachers meet to take stock and start to expand their remit into the study of media. The intellectuals producing Screen *propose psychoanalysis as the theory to complement its Althusserian structuralism and for some SEFT stalwarts this becomes a resigning matter. The first* Screen Reader *will appear in 1977.* Screen Education *is less troubled by factionalism and is increasingly confident in its pursuit of a theoretical understanding of both education and media. It will achieve 96 pages by 1978. The Society's membership divides at its 1976 Annual General Meeting where, despite some decisive voting, it seems that nobody will win in the long term.*

1976 started for some screen educationists with their attendance at a unique event. Early in January a conference was held at York University entitled 'Film and TV Studies in Secondary Education'. The joint organizers, SEFT and the BFI/EAS Regional Committee, had determined to invite as many practitioners as possible. If they were limited in the success of their targeted recruitment, the overall attendance was impressive. 'Of the eighty six delegates listed for the conference only thirty four were actually teaching at secondary level, and the remainder included inspectors, advisers, film officers and lecturers in tertiary education.'[1] Once assembled they had none of the consolations usually provided at such events by screenings, apart from *Invasion of the Bodysnatchers* which was shown on the Saturday evening. They had to stay focused on the issues for some six days. That such a lengthy and specific event was possible in 1976, which would have been unthinkable five years earlier, is a measure of the pace of development that film study had undergone in the preceding five years. 1976 and subsequent years would prove to be significant in the history of screen education for a number of reasons.

SEFT and 'The Left'

Later in 1976 Prime Minister James Callaghan would start his 'Great Debate' around educational issues which was designed to curtail educational experimentation and thereby begin to counter the influence 'the left' was assumed to be gaining within education. For the general public, the intensive press coverage of such proceedings as the ILEA inquiry into the events at the William Tyndall Junior and Infant Schools had provided a dramatisation of such claims. The inquiry had reported in July 1976. In higher education individuals would be targeted in the following year when Julius Gould produced his report on Radical and Marxist Penetration.[2] George Foster recalls that SEFT was implicated in its findings.[3]

Victor Perkins had found himself out of step at the 1972 BFI summer school when he observed that Marxism seemed to be the orthodoxy of belief for the new generation of screen educationists. In preparing participants for the York conference Jim Cook and Jim Hillier had produced an introductory paper detailing the growth of film and television studies. Its bibliography was very selective containing only four works, all demonstrating Marxist thinking and influence. When the paper was reprinted a year later the list had been extended to include *Screen Education 22*, the 'Popular Culture' issue, published in Spring 1977. By the mid 1970s the consensus of interviewees is that most screen education activists, whether in SEFT or BFI, were positioned politically on the Left. In early 1977 Robin Wood's move leftwards is revealed in an account of his work at Warwick University.

> The question of ideology – the urgent necessity for examining and evaluating all our acquired and inherited assumptions at a time when bourgeois capitalism, and civilisation as we know it, may be entering its final phase of disintegration – has become increasingly prominent on all my courses, as in my published criticism.[4]

SEFT had two journals; both were part of what may be considered a New Left project. Interviews with the participants in the project have demonstrated SEFT was a very broad church and that even for the most politically active, its publications were not the preferred location for their activism. What all those who wrote for *Screen* and *Screen Education* did share was a sense of being in pioneer thinking territory. Previous generations of SFT and SEFT activists had succeeded in demonstrating that a wide range of film and television activity was possible with students of all ages. Whilst having reservations about what others might be doing under the heading of screen education, there was little criticism between those in the movement, probably because they were all accustomed to being on the receiving end of antipathy from those outside it. Again a feature of the interviews for this investigation has been how, at all levels of education, many of those who had ventured into screen education even during the 1970s and 1980s reported encountering persistent institutional opposition to their work. The presence of two substantial SEFT journals was to be a decisive factor in changing this situation, not by displacing the opposition but by developing solidarity among screen educationists.

External hostility lost its capacity to unify screen educationists once there was scope for proper debate within the screen education arena. What each of the SEFT journals did was not only to legitimise controversy within screen education but also to demonstrate it might be very productive. They did this in completely different ways. For *Screen* the task was the more straightforward. It wanted to create and apply a body of theoretical thinking where previously theory had been largely absent: to investigate the nature of film and its reception. For *Screen Education* it was a more complex task. Manuel Alvarado has defined it as a tripartite enterprise. 'This was to try and link: (a) film theory (b) educational theory and (c) educational practice/pedagogy.'[5] If the 1970s was a time when film theory was evolving rapidly, it was also a time when educational theory was controversial. Thus the educational perspectives underlying the articles in *Screen Education* are probably more variable than the film theory with which they engaged. The particular problem for *Screen Education* was to find a body of educational theoretical work which would provide an analysis compatible with the stance that the Editorial Board wished to take.[6] There was however an explicit recognition of the significance of these debates within SEFT by winter 1976 when the first eighty eight page issue of *Screen Education* could now be perceived to be an equal partner to *Screen*.

Evidence of a new found readiness on the part of SEFT to take risks was demonstrated in Summer 1976. Chapter Seven ended with the refusal of the IBA to sanction the repeat screenings of *Viewpoint*. Background documentation about the refusal had been leaked to *Screen Education* from inside the Independent Broadcasting Authority. The Editors decided to publish it.[7] The justification for the IBA's refusal was a curious one: they argued they had a duty to protect the adult daytime television viewer. This was the basis of the case put forward to the IBA by Southern Television, apparently the prime mover in opposing the repeats. Southern argued the IBA risked being in breach of Section 4 (1) (f) of the relevant Broadcasting Act. The thrust of their argument appears to have been that in the classroom the teacher was present to take up the issues raised by the programme and deal with them immediately. The home viewer, however, might be left floundering, confronted by 'matters of political and industrial controversy' without the guaranteed safety mechanism available in the classroom. If the programme had this potential to disturb the adult viewer, we must assume the IBA felt confident that the teacher would be both willing and able to neutralise Lowndes's critiques. One can only infer that the television company, in objecting to Programme 8, was resisting what appeared to be a view of society from a left perspective and one which consistently referred to the non transparency of television broadcasting. The *Viewpoint* series in a revised form was eventually transmitted again in 1977.

Independent Practitioners

An unexplored aspect of the *Viewpoint* events is the context in which the programme came to be produced. The creative energy for the series came from Douglas Lowndes, who happened to be the head of BFI/EAS at a time. Lowndes's involvement with film and media had begun in the 1960s when he had been working in initial and in-service teacher training at Hornsey College of Art. He had found, in that situation, ways of working directly with school students and had experimented with a range of creative film, photography and recording techniques. These practitioner instincts were still there when he was at the BFI, where he was able to use a comparable freedom to that he had enjoyed at Hornsey to involve groups of students in the work he would then show on *Viewpoint*. He recognised that if you could demonstrate to students and their teachers that the ideas within the programme might be translated into effective classroom practice, this would make the strongest case to doubtful teachers for looking critically at the media.

Lowndes was not the only 'independent' practitioner to become strongly influential in the development of media education. The IBA did not allow a repeat of Lowndes's *Viewpoint* in 1976, but they did also that year give an IBA Fellowship to another experienced teacher trainer, Len Masterman, who was responsible at the University of Nottingham Education Department for in-service teacher training over an extensive area covering most of the East Midlands. Masterman voluntarily took on a regular secondary school teaching commitment after taking up the Nottingham post in 1971. He rapidly revised the views he had earlier espoused in *Screen Education Notes* about the importance of film as the language of communication for school students. He discovered that his students in a mining village almost never went to the cinema. He switched to television and in another school from 1972 – with the prospect of the raising of the school leaving age in 1973 – designed and taught a CSE TV Studies Mode III syllabus.[8]

With his subsequent year's Fellowship Masterman was able to consider what TV studies might look like as a disciplined area of study. From these deliberations he produced in succession, a report for the IBA, a thesis for a PhD and finally *Teaching About Television* for which he eventually found a publisher, after many rejections, in 1980. It was, Masterman believes, 'a book of its time'. The first print run of 3000 copies sold out within three months. Fourteen impressions were to follow with some 60,000 copies sold in all.[9] Until the widespread take-up of Media Studies examinations for GCSE and A-level caused textbook sales to soar, no screen education publication had approached the success and widespread dissemination of *Teaching About Television*.

Masterman's book takes as its starting point the 1976 York conference where the four commissions into which participants divided for the duration of the conference were: Television, Film CSE, Film O-level, Images. The trajectory of their deliberations led toward a recognition that what was beginning to emerge was 'media studies'. This was the conclusion of Philip Simpson, attending as a teacher training college lecturer, who subsequently wrote up the event for *Screen Education*.[10] Jim Hillier suggests it was implicit in the nature of this event that it would demonstrate to BFI Director, Keith Lucas, the momentum of this move toward media studies.[11] To argue in response, as Lucas did, that the BFI's remit did not include such media as advertising, the press and radio, seems now to have been a serious misreading of the situation, as much subsequent work initiated by the educationists within the BFI was to demonstrate. However in 1976 the case for media education was not proven. Masterman, while clearly sympathetic to the issues raised about considering the media, draws attention to 'the epistemological fuzziness surrounding media studies' and decides that he can more convincingly argue that 'the medium of television itself can offer to the teacher a framework for disciplined study'.[12] The four year interval before his book's publication would have an unplanned benefit for its author. By 1980 schools were beginning to consider video recorders to be standard equipment.

SEFT'S influential journals

In the mid 1970s it was undoubtedly the two SEFT journals, *Screen* and *Screen Education*, which made the greatest contribution to the evolving disciplines of film theory and screen education. Other developments were inevitably shaped by what these journals did. It has been noted how BFI Summer Schools responded to *Screen* by adapting their programme structure to its current thinking. Events organised by SEFT at Weekend Schools or in regional groups became the means of transmitting these new ideas.

A recurrent observation from interviewees who were one-time SEFT activists has been how very young they were at the time. This has been said both by those in their fifties who were the 1970s activists and by those in their forties who were involved with SEFT in the 1980s. But it is essential to distinguish between the two cohorts in a fundamental way. By the 1980s SEFT activists had usually come to the Society via some academic pathway which had involved them in a formal encounter with film or media. Those of the 1970s were different in that they had almost all had involvement with the academy, but film and media had been excluded from their formal university experience. One of the outcomes of having so many young graduate activists involved in the 1970s was that they were prepared and able to devote a great deal of time to the SEFT enterprise. The essential way in which commitment was expressed was in attendance at meetings of the SEFT Committee and Editorial Boards. The boards of the two journals had separate memberships with almost no overlap of personnel. Those who served on the *Screen* Board have recollections of a less harmonious enterprise than those who met to plan *Screen Education* where Richard Collins recalls a constructive, collaborative atmosphere.[13] While both journals did demand the same level of involvement from Board members, Roy Stafford identifies a particular characteristic of the *Screen Education* Board which facilitated its coherence: everyone on it had at that time a London teaching connection.[14]

For the purposes of this chapter, the period under examination ends in 1978 when there was a change in the editorships of both journals. *Screen* had been edited by Ben Brewster until the end of 1976 when he was replaced by Geoffrey Nowell-Smith who was in post until the end of 1977. Nowell-Smith's successor was Mark Nash who started in 1978 at approximately the same time that James Donald replaced Alvarado as Editor of *Screen Education*. These new editors approached their tasks differently from their predecessors and their work will be explored in the next chapter.

Screen and Theory

Following Sam Rohdie's departure and SEFT's setting up of a new structure, the *Screen* Editorial Board had become a much more formal body with clear rules about eligibility and attendance. It met in a three-weekly cycle, with the SEFT Executive and *Screen Education* Board following a similar cycle in the intervening weeks. *Screen* Board members were involved in reading everything in advance of publication, usually in a troika arrangement.[15] Sometimes during Nowell-Smith's editorship, the Editorial Board readers would have not only the article in manuscript but also an initial report on it by the Editor.[16]

The Editorial Board – frequently at odds over many issues – was however united in seeing *Screen* as something very different from an academic journal.[17] On one level this soubriquet of 'academic' could be denied on very simple grounds: there was in the UK no academy for film study to be grounded in, so no British journal could properly be styled 'academic'. But much more fundamental was the way in which the people involved in *Screen* regarded themselves. Nowell-Smith points out that the *Screen* agenda had very deliberately to do with cultural politics in Britain.[18] *Screen* offered a home to non-academic intellectuality according to Nowell-Smith where engagement with popular culture became a mechanism for challenging academic traditions and for 'blowing up the Humanities'.[19] Laura Mulvey is also clear about the status of those involved with *Screen*: 'we didn't think of ourselves as being academic – much more being an intellectual and a cinephile – certainly not an academic'.[20] Peter Wollen summarises it thus: 'The first generation were freelance intellectuals who were interested in laying the foundations of film study'.[21] John Ellis is more specific. People arrived at *Screen* perceiving it as 'a surrogate for wider political activity, feeling in the post 1968 world that the realm of ideas was important but that there was no place for intellectuals in the Left political process at that time'.[22] Alvarado's view complements this. He saw the *Screen* experience as a 'coming-together of a group of deliberately independent people who had no power or influence'.[23]

The role of *Screen* in the mid-1970s was hugely important in demonstrating that film study could become a disciplined area for investigation. Such was its impact that a succession of *Screen Readers* was published and many of the original *Screen* articles were reprinted in the *Readers*.[24] The same articles were also to be included in successive generations of film theory editions. The 1970s' readership of *Screen* was founded particularly on the buying power of universities in the United States of America. *Screen* became influential in the USA because there were many departments of film within American universities, a situation not to be found in the UK for some two decades. David Rodowick, a postgraduate student in the US at this time, remembers the considerable influence *Screen* was to have there. Indeed he believes that the American understanding of what French writers were thinking about the cinema was simply what was 'filtered' through *Screen*. The journal's 'Marxist approach' was very controversial at first. He instances his own *Screen* influenced thesis which attracted marks from different examiners which ranged from the top to the bottom of the marking scale.[25]

Although *Screen* was created by intellectuals outside the academy, its survival and success depended on it being valued in higher education. Indeed it would eventually become an academic journal with a readership in UK universities. Though important in this role *Screen*, with its emphasis on film, became less significant in the development of screen/media education at other levels in the UK education system. *Screen Education* however had a wider brief and would interact more readily with its educational constituency. Both journals were produced in the same SEFT office and this interconnection where each editor understood what his colleague was attempting to achieve undoubtedly provided an inbuilt monitoring mechanism to the benefit of each journal during the period up to 1978. Ellis recalls 'the strong personal dynamic of two editors in a small office'.[26]

The *Screen Education* of the 1970s unlike *Screen* did demonstrate continuity with work in screen and media education from earlier decades. Several of its authors had been active screen educationists in the 1960s. *Screen* however, while dipping very selectively into the past, was creating a legacy rather than responding to one. It was the pace of its perceived dedication to creating a new critical and theoretical forum that triggered the split within its Editorial Board and which subsequently led to four members resigning. Two distinctive aspects of *Screen* need some examination here: *Screen* language and '*Screen* theory'. There was also the associated charge of 'intellectual terrorism' which was subsequently to be levelled at *Screen* at the end of the decade.[27] Each of these descriptions originated as a response to the level of difficulty that for many became associated with reading the journal. If *Screen Education* would see its task as one of engaging with its readers, *Screen* sought to challenge its readership.

There was a different attitude to translation evident during Brewster's editorship which reinforced notions of there being a '*Screen* theory'. The earlier translation from the original French of 'Cinema/Ideology/Criticism' by Comolli and Narboni in spring 1971[28] had been done at Rohdie's request by Susan Bennett who worked as a translator within the BFI Education Department.[29] Her strategy as a translator was to find an English formulation which was as close as possible to what had been expressed by the French. Her aim was to make the translation comprehensible, given the novel nature of what was being introduced. Bennett was however aware that the translation mode of the period was to use the French word or a neologism based on it. She recalled that her approach was well received by the Editorial Board at the time, though the reaction of

Cahiers du Cinéma was perhaps ambivalent, saying that her work was in accord with the *ésprit anglais.*[30]

Bennett's approach was very different from that of Heath and Brewster three years later. Alvarado maintains that theirs was a strategy of trying to create a language for theory. Brewster believed that the translation should retain in the English formulation the complexities of the original language, so his translation of Althusser maintains an essentially French structure. Heath's style similarly avoided 'neat, easy' prose. His non-transparent style is designed deliberately to make the reader think.[31] *Screen* readers were not immediately faced with the contrast between the Bennett and Brewster styles, in that other translators, especially Diana Matias, were involved during the interim. Nevertheless the Brewster/Heath style was very distinctive and in its foregrounding of stylistic complexity gave additional credence to the notion that there was a '*Screen* theory'. Ellis also confirmed that, during his involvement on the Editorial Board, there was a structured policy toward translation in support of the Brewster/Heath agenda.[32]

Paul Willemen argues that the adoption of an 'experimental' language for all the articles in *Screen* was essential to the project.

> There was a feeling that if you were to write in the kind of language that the BFI would find agreeable, it was impossibly restrictive. You could not think of different ways of understanding film in that language which was so heavily, heavily invested with other meanings. One had to find a language and that other language was going to be almost by definition at the time unacceptable to the advocates of good journalistic English. It didn't bother us that it wasn't good journalistic English. It couldn't be any way. It had to be one that reflected the fact we were still searching for a way of understanding.[33]

'*Screen* theory' is a term referred to by numerous writers looking back at the period of the 1970s when *Screen* was at its most productive in developing theory. Though much used, there is considerable confusion as to what it might mean. Both Anthony Easthope[34] and Janet Bergstrom[35] state that there never was a '*Screen* theory'. Others refer to what *Screen* presented in a way which suggests there was some unity around its theoretical pronouncements, but then do not feel it appropriate to use that particular term. In 1990 Kaplan writes of 'a set of approaches'[36] where earlier Lapsley and Westlake had talked of '*Screen's* project'.[37] More recently Nicholas Tredell would go no further than to see *Screen* as having provided 'a major forum'.[38] The term '*Screen* theory' was apparently first used by Hall in 1980 when he specifically identified it as a 'convenience term' to cover the variety of theoretical approaches the journal had promoted.[39] Although the term has tended to be avoided by scholars when going into print, on less formal occasions the term has undoubtedly enjoyed a currency. In their introduction to the most recent of the four *Screen Readers*, Annette Kuhn and Jackie Stacey acknowledge that '*Screen* theory' has in effect become common shorthand.[40]

While some of those interviewed have very different understandings of what the term might imply, Christine Geraghty observes that 'it wasn't a label anyone would want to dispute'.[41] Alvarado, who was probably more involved than anyone with SEFT, with *Screen* and with *Screen Education* as distinct institutions in the mid 1970s, is adamant that any notion of there having been '*Screen* theory' is misleading.[42] The commitment of both SEFT journals to the prime importance of theory in their respective projects was what distinguished them. Laura Mulvey, on the other hand, whose involvement with SEFT and *Screen* was very much more limited, takes a different view. For her '*Screen* theory' is specific to the period of Brewster's editorship when the ideas of Althusser, Freud and Lacan were introduced. She sees the intellectual overlap with the journal *New Left Review* (with which Brewster had previously been involved) as marking his editorship of *Screen* out from the others.[43] Willemen looking back now detects a 'filter of selection through a *New Left Review* political agenda'.[44]

Whereas use of the term might be problematic, there is general consensus as to the identity of *Screen*'s key theoreticians: Colin MacCabe (on realism), Stephen Heath (on narrative space) and Mulvey (on visual pleasure). These may be directly nominated – as by Easthope in 1988[45] – or their stature may be deduced by the inclusion of their work in edited collections – as by Rosen in 1986.[46] These three may be the most anthologised but interviewees have acknowledged the importance of Willemen writing on ideology and particularly of Brewster as a constructively interventionist editor, working closely with authors on the shaping of their work. Mark Nash however considers Brewster to have applied 'heavy filtering to the articles he intended to print'.[47] Despite drawing heavily on *Screen* for articles in *Narrative, Apparatus, Ideology* Rosen gives no currency to the notion of '*Screen* theory' by saying that 'what requires repetition and emphasis is that it would be a distortion to hypostasise this discursive network into an easily unifiable theoretical entity'.[48]

Resignations

For some members of the *Screen* Board elements in *Screen*'s content were becoming disturbing. They felt there was an important and significant section of the readership, notably teachers, which *Screen* was in danger of alienating. The particular issue which triggered a more organised opposition from the group was the journal's decision to explore a psychoanalytical dimension to the theories with which film was to be examined. There are three key statements published in *Screen* around these issues which led to the resignations of Ed Buscombe, Christine Gledhill, Alan Lovell and Christopher Williams from the Editorial Board.[49] It is clear from references within these pieces that there were many documented discussions within SEFT and the *Screen* Editorial Board over some three years. Geraghty recalls that the arguments over the language of *Screen* were taken up quite separately from the dispute over psychoanalysis.[50] The articles published in *Screen* provide evidence but they do not represent the whole picture[51] of which readers would first have become aware from the editorial in Spring 1975 when Brewster trails the journal's impending involvement with psychoanalysis.[52] The strategic importance of psychoanalysis was that it might solve the problem of the perceived lack in Marxism of any theory of subjectivity or individual agency.

Several of those interviewed made it clear that the resignation issue around psychoanalysis affected not only the *Screen* Editorial Board but also the SEFT Executive Committee. There was some overlap of personnel between the two, but significantly by 1975, there were influential members of the Board who had almost no connection with SEFT and who have subsequently betrayed their ignorance of the parent organization in retrospective writings where confident references to SEFT as a part of the BFI from its inception are simply inaccurate.[53] It was perhaps significant therefore that those who were resigning were those who had been active not only in *Screen* but also in the SEFT Committee since 1971.[54] Buscombe is clear that the leader of the quartet was Lovell.[55]

The original statement on psychoanalysis and film in *Screen* Winter 1975/76 concluded by offering itself as a way of opening up a discussion.[56] Although it must be noted that this offer was not taken up – a brief mention in the editorial notwithstanding – it did offer *Screen* readers who might otherwise have been struggling to follow some of the arguments a concise analysis of some of the issues. The invitation to discussion was however taken up by the journal *Framework*. Stephen Crofts, whose byline makes it clear he is writing in *Framework* as a member of the SEFT Executive (to which he had recently been elected), led the debate.[57] His stance was very clear. He attacked the four who had produced the statement by arguing that they were still attached to 1960s' notions of popular culture and were not prepared to shift their position, whereas Crofts saw only progress:

> In the final analysis, the statement amounts to a refusal of psychoanalysis and a retrenchment in the popular culture position logically displaced later in the 1960s by classical semiotics, which in turn has been logically displaced in the mid 1970s by a semiotics recast within terms of psychoanalysis.[58]

Alvarado recalls how divided the various bodies were at this point.[59] While the resignations apparently offered a resolution to one issue, there was a legacy of factionalism in the board so that by the time of Nowell-Smith's editorship, there were frequent disagreements which were often highly personalized.[60]

Although addressing the manner in which *Screen* was becoming involved in the detail of debates around psychoanalysis and film, the statement by the dissenting four begins by identifying the two distinct areas of concern. Firstly they claim there is a lack of critical distance, so that controversial intellectual choices are made to appear unproblematic. The ideas of Althusser and Lacan are evidenced as being controversial. Secondly there is the issue of intelligibility: 'we do not think that obscurity is a guarantee of profundity'.[61] The obscurity is demonstrated by quotations to show how this may result both from the compressing of complicated ideas and from the adoption of precise terms from other disciplines, combined with an interest in the play of language.

It is clear that, given their SEFT credentials, the writers are concerned about the reception *Screen* is having among SEFT members. Not only are the members' subscriptions fundamental to *Screen's* survival but it is the work these members are undertaking in educational institutions which underpins the reasons for SEFT's existence. A rival organisation to SEFT was in existence in the 1970s – the National Association for Film Education (NAFE). This Association was in practice relatively short-lived but it drew its legitimacy from teacher dissatisfaction with SEFT's changing priorities.[62] It had been founded with the change in direction of *Screen*. Alvarado recounts how the SEFT Executive felt it appropriate to maintain contact with this potentially rival organization,[63] but at this stage he acknowledges SEFT was no longer seeking to be identified as a subject teachers' professional organisation.[64] In practice NAFE concentrated its attack on the BFI where Director Keith Lucas came under constant pressure from it, as Hillier recalls.[65] When David Lusted joined EAS, he was instructed by Lucas to try to set up a joint BFI/NAFE project in order to improve relations.[66]

The more specific concerns which these dissenting authors have about psychoanalysis still seem today to have been worth addressing. There is the questionable acceptability of seeing the film as a patient under analysis. In relation to Heath's analysis of *Touch of Evil* attention is drawn to the over-emphasis on drawing conclusions from insignificant detail.[67]

> It seems that in this analysis one of the worst 'popular' effects of psychoanalysis is at work, the encouragement it is taken to give to ingenious interpretation where the ingenuity is thought to guarantee the interest of the exercise.[68]

Questions are then asked about the relationship between spectatorship and film. The writers show how, in different articles, Heath, Metz and Mulvey take the same Freudian concept of the fetish and yet use it, each in a different way. Similarly they compare how Metz and Mulvey differ in the use they make of the ideas around the Lacanian 'mirror image'. These are such obvious discrepancies that the Editorial Board does acknowledge them eventually when responding to the authors' final resignation statement by stating that the discrepancies emanate from a 'process of understanding'.[69] The other key point with which the four authors took issue was Mulvey's argument about the construction of classic narrative films specifically for a male spectator. How then do women relate to films?[70] The Editorial Board did not respond to this. Rather there were clearly different political agendas at work and it was these which divided the Board. Specifically, the authors of the statement argue that psychoanalysis is being used to maintain a high bourgeois position and this provides a problem for educationalists working with working-class children.

The subsequent resignation letter in summer 1976 invokes more deliberately the audience *Screen* is addressing when it draws attention to the 'serious' film/television study which is now in place and that there is a 'serious' audience for *Screen*. Plentiful examples are cited. Additionally attention is drawn to the Centre for Contemporary Cultural Studies in Birmingham and to other groups now becoming involved in film study and associated areas. The four allege that the 'positive contribution that *Screen* had made initially is now being counter-balanced by other factors'. *Screen* it seems may now be doing more harm than good. The charges against *Screen* are now more specific:

1. *Screen* by its obscurity and inaccessibility handicaps SEFT's efforts to develop film study and make contacts with other groups.
2. By taking a high bourgeois position *Screen* advocates the *avant-garde* against the popular cinema with which education also has to engage.
3. The Editorial Board has no interest in educational matters and does not attend any SEFT events.[71]

In responding the Board predictably deals most severely with the second of these. Someone had clearly researched past issues of *Screen*, so that the authors of the resignation statement might have their own words quoted back at them. The details of the parrying of the attack are not relevant here. What is clear is that this is where the issues become most personal. On the charge of obscurity and lack of interest in educational matters, there is much less said. It is those political differences that separated these four from the rest of the Board and which would be played out at the SEFT AGM in the following November.

Screen Education and Teachers

The 'Introduction' to *The Screen Education Reader: Cinema, Television, Culture*, published in 1993, puts into context the work of the journal which had ceased publication ten years earlier. It is a useful retrospective, though curiously does not distinguish between the two very different editorships of Alvarado and Donald and the shift toward a cultural studies emphasis under the latter's regime. What cannot emerge so clearly from it however is the sequential manner in which *Screen Education* addressed its readership, particularly in the early years as the new identity of screen education/media studies emerged as a specific area of the curriculum. The importance of considering the issues in sequence is that through this procedure it is possible to demonstrate both the level of activism and intellectual commitment surrounding each publication and the sense of the participants sharing an engagement with a progressive trajectory.

The editorials in *Screen Education* functioned in several ways. Until 1977 all SEFT members and institutional subscribers received both its journals. Only in 1977 did it become possible to subscribe to either or both journals, though in practice most readers kept receiving both. *Screen Education* had emerged from *Screen* and needed to establish what it stood for with its inherited readership. It clearly needed to be perceived as fundamentally different from the predecessor *Screen Education* published in the 1960s. The practice of identifying which Board members had edited each issue acted as a signal to readers that the contents, even if individually authored, had undergone group scrutiny.

SEFT membership had originally been composed mostly of teachers in secondary schools and lecturers in further education. So it would probably be *Screen Education* rather than *Screen* which, on first inspection, they would have found more immediately useful. *Screen* with its single but multi-faceted task of developing theory was less constrained by the expectations of its readership. In practice it would acquire an additional readership widely distributed in higher education, as academics in established disciplines realised the applications of *Screen*'s theories went beyond the confines of film study. But it was vital to *Screen Education* that it was not perceived as a teacher's version of *Screen*, where difficult ideas were simplified. In practice *Screen Education* had the more complex task: to find a means of simultaneously addressing film theory, educational theory and pedagogy. The Editorials regularly re-assured the readership the journal had a definite sense of direction. During the period when Brewster edited *Screen* and Alvarado *Screen Education* the two journals did succeed in projecting a unity of purpose for SEFT by complementing each other. In effect the presence of each validated the existence of both. Geraghty's view is that *Screen* at this time would have more closely represented *New Left Review* had *Screen Education* not existed.[72] Collins believes that the distinctive character of each journal might not have evolved without the other.[73]

Where *Screen Education* sought to become radical was in its engagement with educational theory. It was not promoting a particular theory necessarily, but as a first step it needed to identify that theory was implicit in all practice. It did however resist the more extreme child-centred theories of the 1970s, since the very nature of the enterprise in which SEFT was engaged demonstrated the impracticability of child-centredness. Here was a group of educated committed adults seeking to shape an area of the curriculum which might at the time have variously been defined as screen education or media studies. If this dedicated group was struggling with the process, but was nevertheless convinced this was an area of such importance that school students should engage with it, it was clearly a territory where the students even more than their teachers were going to be in need of guidance. Neither teacher nor student could discover and interpret it successfully alone. It was of necessity a subject-centred rather than child-centred enterprise.

If members of the *Screen* Board were influenced by Gramsci into perceiving themselves as organic intellectuals rather than academics, for *Screen Education* it was another aspect of Gramsci's thinking which supported their stance. To support working-class students effectively, teachers should not be tempering their methodology nor finding ways of making learning more palatable. Only by teaching such students with rigour were teachers providing them with the necessary knowledge and skills to operate in the students' own best interests, or rather, as it would more predictably have been justified then, in the interests of the working class. Soon after Alvarado became the paid Editor, the editorials began to detail the parameters of the journal's various quests which lacked the apparent investigative precision which *Screen*'s concentration on film theory apparently ensured for that publication.

> We will give particular attention to education, to the way in which a subject area is defined; to the way in which study, teaching and learning are performed and the resultant social relations that this generates. This activity of thinking of media education as part of a social totality and the call that makes for us to investigate that totality in order to define the shape and purpose of media education is an emphasis very different to the one that has distinguished the development of film studies in Britain. In that field there has been a pronounced (and understandable) tendency to insist on the subject area's authenticity and to construct and defend strict parameters for the young body of knowledge.[74]

Surprisingly this same issue on 'Media Studies, Methods and Approaches' then includes an example of the sort of personal account of practice which had been so familiar and which had so limited the usefulness of the 1960s' *Screen Education*. Written under the pseudonym John Pearce its inclusion is justified in the Editorial as an article which 'provocatively suggests ways of studying mass communications and of restructuring the classroom relations that other, traditional teaching procedures enforce'.[75] Pearce, it turns out, is in his first term of teaching and the article, based on a diary record he kept, is explicitly critical of his teaching colleagues. Puzzled readers, some of whom had written to SEFT to protest, had to wait for the Editorial in the next *Screen Education* for the explanation of its publication and even then the rationale is a curious one. The Editors criticise Pearce on several grounds, all of which are essentially for making the sort of mistakes experienced teachers would expect a beginner to make.[76] Even if the readers were to accept the argument that Pearce's inexperience was specially revealing of the problems faced when putting classroom practice under scrutiny (because the potential in those circumstances for making mistakes was compounded), the situation in which a beginner was so exposed was never justified. A more substantial considered and thoughtful collaboration piece is printed as part of the issue focusing on 'The System and Classroom Practice'.[77]

The Autumn 1975 issue 'Teaching the Film Industry' needs fewer explanations in the Editorial. But there is underlying that Editorial – as with all the Editorials at this time – a determination to find an appropriate intellectual format into which articles of each issue might be fitted. The Editorial Board met once every three weeks and, given that *Screen Education* appeared only quarterly, there is a sense when reading the Editorials that they emerged from lengthy and controversial debates, the implications of which the reader can only infer from the contents of each issue and the format the relevant Editorial proposes to erect around it.[78] There is no mistaking the journal's political stance. 'The Education Cuts' sets out to rally teacher support via their unions, on the grounds not only of the impact of the cuts on education generally but more particularly on the vulnerability of this emerging area of film and media studies with its need for specialised hardware. It concludes by attempting to define more precisely the position from which its authors are coming.[79]

Yet this process of reflection, of theorising and developing new educational practices is subject to more than its own internal dynamics. *Screen Education*'s project is also governed by the determination of consciousness by being: as Marx formulated it, 'Universal consciousness is only the theoretical form of that whose living form is the real community, society...' (Economic Philosophical Manuscript 1844). Our project of understanding and formulating a programme of educational activity in film and media studies takes place within a social context which decisively influences the shape and possibilities of that project.[80]

The next four issues are presented to the readership as having a specific unity underpinning each one: *The Searchers*; Media Education in Europe; a reflection on work established by SEFT/BFI and *The Sweeney*. Unfortunately no records survive of the Editorial Board meetings of this period. There was a troika approach to the consideration of articles, which paralleled that of *Screen*, so that the implications of publishing each article were thoroughly debated and there were legacies of these debates to be detected in the Editorials. In Summer 1976 it is possible to detect an effect which this was having on the Board members' perspective of the readership. Each Board member had to defend her/his position not just about the relevance of the article under consideration, but about her/his stance generally. Consequently there was a perceived need to caution the readers who would be tackling the articles without the benefit of group mediation.

The need for a theoretical investigation of our work as teachers becomes clear when we begin to confront the problems of *what* the teachers are going to teach and, having decided that, determining *how* to communicate that knowledge. We are aware that to respond pragmatically to educational problems and to support a position that suggests each individual teacher knows best how to deal with teaching situations through empirical observation is to encourage a form of experimentation that is positively dangerous if we are really concerned with the *needs* of the people we teach. That is why we argue for the importance of developing a better theoretical understanding of the processes of education as well as constructing a theorised body of knowledge about film and media.[81]

Screen Education 18 in spring 1976 was timely in its content. Susan Bennett had been employed as a researcher by UNESCO to survey 'the situation and aims of media studies in Europe'.[82] The project had developed from the Ludwigsheim/Mannheim conference in 1972 following which *Screen Education Notes* had produced its special edition.[83] Bennett's survey in abbreviated form, with an additional summary of the British situation, forms the bulk of *Screen Education* 18. Her introductory article is useful in that it positions the British experience within European wide trends.[84] A legacy of 1968 is still to be detected in the countries surveyed, where educational reform has worked to make curricula less rigid. As a result there has been a limited recognition of the necessity for media education in secondary schools.[85] But the provision of training for the teachers is always informal and usually only available in the teachers' own time as with the BFI and SEFT provision in the UK.

At the same time, as was already noted with reference to the UK, the spread of educational technology often worked to obscure developments in media education. Bennett points out how such innovations actually work against the introduction of media education.

> Technology in order to justify its existence, is supposed to 'do' something. The only material that technology can 'do' something to is the student. But this conception does not readily accord with that inherent in media education that the student picks apart what is presented *via* the technology (and not *by* the technology).[86]

When media educationists were able to intervene in these situations and subvert at an institutional level, there would be scope for media to begin to be studied and the assumed neutral status of media apparatus might then be contested. *Screen Education* 21 has an interesting account of the beginnings of such an intervention at the University of London Institute of Education following the appointment there of Bob Ferguson who had worked with Douglas Lowndes at Hornsey College of Art.[87] Bennett's conclusion is that the major problem faced by media education is the opposition presented to it 'by the social context within which it is contained'.[88] Certainly the treatment of *Viewpoint* by the IBA provided a convincing example of her claim. What is also clear from her survey as presented in *Screen Education* is that nowhere was educational theory underpinning the introduction of media education. She does however identify certain 'marginal' institutions within European countries where such thinking was beginning. One of these was the Birmingham Centre for Contemporary Cultural Studies.

Screen Education 22
The Editorial of *Screen Education* 22 is important in tracing the journal's development. It is explicit in defining what needs to happen if there is to be an agreed theoretical position among the *Screen Education* Editorial Board which goes beyond the shared recognition of the need to connect film/television with education/pedagogy. Such an agreed position, it is argued, is both desirable and essential. The previous absence of such an agreed position had been because

> ...we have not so far really opened up for examination many of the covert assumptions which, though rarely expressed, determine our own various practices and critical/theoretical evaluation of them. This issue therefore attempts to

correct this error by considering less aspects of the conjuncture 'screen + education' directly – broadly *Screen Education*'s practice to date – and more some of the underlying assumptions/ value judgments which have been associated with our formal concerns – film and television – ever since their inception: namely that they are *mass* media and *popular* forms.[89]

Like the NUT Conference some decade and a half earlier 'Popular Culture' is the area which is seen as providing a productive locus for investigation. But that is as far as the similarity may be pushed. In 1960 the expectation had been that, by bringing together the producers of popular culture with the teachers and the critics before an *ad hoc* but concerned audience, some beneficial interaction would emerge, if everyone were to respond responsibly. The debates of the 1970s were not being played out before an *ad hoc* audience but were directed specifically at the readership that was assumed to share a commitment to the *Screen Education* project.

Perhaps because of the charge of difficulty and inaccessibility that had been levelled at *Screen*'s articles, the Editorial here repeatedly seeks to justify an issue that may be perceived as 'potentially difficult and contentious'. Clearly for the Editorial Board this was a defining moment in their enterprise. The case for this move toward theory had been under discussion for some time. In a statement from the *Screen Education* Editorial Board to the SEFT Executive Committee in March 1976 the following was highlighted:

> *Screen Education* cannot afford to not engage in theoretical work and inquiry, particularly in the area of education and mass communications but also, when necessary, even in the area of film theory.[90]

When the *Screen Education* policy statement was subsequently promulgated by SEFT in May it was expressed more emphatically:

> *Screen Education* must engage in theoretical work and inquiry, particularly in the area of education, mass communications and film theory.[91]

Where *Screen Education* 22 differed from previous ones was in the four articles identified as specially commissioned for it. Two authors, Jim Grealy and Richard Collins, were members of the Editorial Board, the third Geoffrey Nowell-Smith was the recently appointed Editor of *Screen* and the fourth Colin Sparks was a lecturer in media studies from the Polytechnic of Central London.

The introductory article by Grealy, called 'Notes on Popular Culture', is actually very closely focused on film teaching. [92] This focus was probably a decision made in order to connect more directly with the experience of the majority of the readership. Provided that the film teacher he addresses is ready to align her/himself with the identity of 'socialist teacher', Grealy's position is straightforward.

Here I am not arguing that teachers must 'politicise' education but that they recognise the ideological roles that the school plays in society, and that their teaching explicitly confronts the problems which arise when this ideological functioning of the educational apparatuses is recognised. School plays a crucial part in the production and diffusion of 'popular culture'. The function of socialist teachers is to work at the contradictions which arise in the culture at the educational level. [93]

Nowell-Smith's article on Gramsci is also essentially introductory, given that Gramsci's writings were only then becoming available in translation.[94] He uses the model of Gramsci's investigation into 19th-century Italian Culture to suggest the nature of the questions which need to be asked in relation to British popular culture. He identifies the limitations of current writing on popular culture as having no perspective 'other than that which is supposed to emanate from the forms themselves and the attitude taken by the writer towards them'.[95]

Sparks writes of the evolution of cultural studies, a term which was only at this time acquiring common currency, most often within references to the Centre for Contemporary Cultural Studies at the University of Birmingham, where he had been a post-graduate student. It is some of the work of the Centre that Sparks describes in his article.[96] But the greatest importance of the article lies in its attempt to explain how Marxism in a variety of manifestations had, via *New Left Review*, come to influence the thinking of a generation of intellectuals. The distinguishing features of this generation were their increased access to Marxist influenced thinking, the greater proportion of university graduates among their number and their connections with the events of 1968 and its aftermath. He then indicates where that cohort might currently be found, some ten years later and what influence they might be having. Though Sparks does not specify it, among that cohort would be included the activists within the SEFT Committee and the Editorial Boards and a significant number of the journals' readers.

Collins in the final piece of the four revalues the contribution of Leavis.[97] As has been shown the legacy of Leavis in film study had been considerable both directly in the attitudes of Whannel, the work of Robin Wood and *Movie* and more indirectly as a consequence of the transfer of a Leavisite methodology from the study of literature to the study of film by the great many English teachers who had been trained to follow Leavis's approach. It was of course these teachers who had been attracted to the teaching of popular culture by the arguments advanced by Hall and Whannel who had demonstrated that it was possible to discriminate within popular culture. 'Revaluation' for Collins means abandonment of the Leavisite model completely.

The absence in Leavis' model of a notion of the reciprocal determination of base by superstructure left none of the space for action, and we need rather an analytical model that is adequate to the totality of social relations in which culture, its primary object for study, is located; one that, to put it modestly, attends to the absence of free play in culture, that recognises the dominance of ruling-class ideology in mass communications, and the function of mass communications in propagating and naturalising the world view of the ruling class.[98]

An aim of *Screen Education* was to stimulate debate beyond those who constituted its Editorial Board. This began to happen in 1975 with the formation of first a North Staffordshire SEFT Group and then a North Eastern Group. By the end of 1976 SEFT began to approach the task more systematically by making available a list of its members, organised regionally, to anyone who wanted to take the initiative and form such a group.[99] There was an irony in these arrangements in that though it was in *Screen Education* that reports of these groups' activities were carried, it was a pre-occupation with *Screen* that usually shaped these groups' activities. In January 1977 the SEFT Glasgow group was set up, though as its first report makes clear, it was essentially a *Screen* reading group.[100] At about the same time a Manchester group was formed from members of the North by North West Film Society and specifically from subscribers to *Screen*.[101] Such was the influence of *Screen* on this group that its journal, *North by North West*, rapidly became a mechanism for the transmission of *Screen* theories. This regional expansion was made more substantial later in 1977 when the first SEFT Weekend School outside London was held in Glasgow in June.[102] This was followed by the SEFT Potteries Group holding their first Weekend School in Manchester in December.[103] Both schools were focused on television study: realism in Glasgow and the soap opera *Coronation Street* in Manchester.[104]

The *Sweeney* Debate

If the Editorial to issue 22 had looked for debate it had arrived by *Screen Education* 23. SEFT groups were forming in the regions and London was not to be left out. Not styling itself as a SEFT regional group, but meeting as an informal reading and study group, the London group's members included some of those on the *Screen Education* Editorial Board. Seven London members wrote to the journal.[105] They were not however responding directly to the major issues raised by the previous *Screen Education* but were concerned about *Screen Education* 20 which had focused on *The Sweeney*. Despite including Richard Exton and Chris Mottershead from the Editorial Board, some of their complaints were basic and perhaps representative of the concerns of some of *Screen Education*'s readers who were finding it difficult to keep up-to-date with reading either or both of the two SEFT journals. To the present reader their resistance seems to have been both against the rapidity with which the world of screen education was being propelled and against the level of generalisation that this momentum seemed to encourage. It was also perhaps relevant that some of the signatories had stood for, but failed to get elected to, the SEFT Committee at the 1976 AGM.[106]

They contested some of the assumptions of *The Sweeney* issue under four headings. They felt that the methodology of the issue was assumed rather than explained. Ideology, they claimed, was used without explanation and consequently they were forced to conclude that as a concept it was 'all pervasive, infinitely devious and totally inescapable'.[107]

> We are not convinced that because we live in a capitalist society within which bourgeois ideology is dominant that it follows that this ideology expresses itself in a clear, uncontested way through film or television, or that these art forms are primarily ideological weapons.[108]

Their third challenge was to the use of the term 'realism' where they maintained that they detected confusion, while MacCabe's writing on this topic had been rapidly subjected to his own substantial revision.

> Whereas MacCabe is putting forward ideas in a journal, *Screen*, not directly concerned with the formal educational system, and can therefore argue a position in an abstract way, it is a matter of concern to us that such ideas can be taken up in a journal, *Screen Education*, which does have a direct concern with the formal educational system, in such a way as to encourage a kind of carelessness and assertion of generalities which does not lead to understanding, but rather to confusion and an actual lack of theory.[109]

Writing mostly from the perspective of classroom teachers they claim that the approach to *The Sweeney* downgrades problems of aesthetics, entertainment, genre and teaching.

> We do not see the construction of teaching approaches and of theoretical work as being two different activities, nor that the former follows naturally from the latter. The relationship between them is not so simple. If we are interested in, concerned about, or committed to, educating people about a TV series, in this instance, then our knowledge of education has to inform the way in which we construct the theoretical work. We are involved in such work not simply to increase our own understanding, but to provide opportunities for anyone to be able to learn and understand. This process depends on the contribution of our actual, or potential, students whose opinions and knowledge of television already exists, is not waiting for us to formulate the discipline. If we want to teach cultural studies then we must take account of the fact that it is a 'live' area of knowledge and that members of that culture participate in its development. To suggest that we try to suspend the production of teaching materials whilst we try to sort out what to teach them is to overrate our own role in this field and to ignore, even deny, the importance of our students.[110]

A fundamental problem that was to bedevil SEFT for the remaining decade of its existence was an increasing separation of its constituencies into higher education on the one hand and schools/further education colleges on the other. The reply to their complaints is made by Phillip Drummond, one of the contributors to *The Sweeney* issue, who mostly limits his response to a defence of his own piece. Rather than examine what deeper concerns might be underlying their antagonism to *The Sweeney* issue Drummond, a polytechnic lecturer, is dismissive of their arguments.[111] He asserts that '*Screen Education* and the Society as a whole needs stronger and more rigorous opponents if it is to progress within that circuit of undeniably difficult and intricate problems over film, TV and media studies which forms its necessary trajectory.'[112]

The subsequent Editorial in *Screen Education* 24 recognises there may be a problem for the journal as it addresses an expanding constituency.[113] It is not going to be able to promote the development of screen education practice substantially if the readers are alienated by being told they are not worthy of the journal. Recognising too that individual readers will be at the very different stages of accessing screen education knowledge and practice when first coming into contact with the journal, the Editorial determines to adopt a more flexible approach. This had been a long-term problem that *Screen Education* of the 1960s had solved by having a series of topics, such as Film Making or Higher Education, and within an erratic cycle each topic would in turn dominate a specific issue. Therefore if a reader remained a subscriber for just a few years, s/he would have covered all the territory and the articles would then become repetitive. Such was the pace and intensity of developments in screen education in the 1970s that even if such a mechanistic device had seemed justifiable, it would have served only to exclude the readership further.

For the remainder of Alvarado's editorship until mid-1978, *Screen Education* ceased to group articles into specific issues in order to achieve a topical coherence.[114] The expectation was that if issues appeared less monolithic, readers would not find the journal so daunting. It was clear that if an account were presented as work in progress and accompanied by other unrelated articles also of other work in progress, readers might find it easier to seek out their own individual points of accommodation. The previous chapter demonstrated there had been significant growth in film and television teaching by the mid 1970s; however while many teachers might have access to the SEFT journals, what they lacked was up-to-date material for use in the classroom.

The Arrival of Textbooks
Indeed one of the persistent problems for film and television teachers had always been around issues of contemporaneity. The reliance on, for example, BFI selected extracts in teaching inevitably meant that what was chosen for use in the classroom might be dated by the time it became available. The gradual introduction of video recorders into schools and subsequently a relaxation in copyright law on broadcast material began to change this in as much as a greater range of visual texts became accessible. But as the nature of film and television study shifted from the study of the text in isolation to investigations of how texts were produced, teachers lacked information. Two books coming from authors who were key figures in the *Screen Education* project addressed this directly: *Making Legend of the Werewolf*[115] and *Hazell – the making of a TV series*.[116]

The former by Buscombe was a detailed account of the making of a 'typical' British feature film of the period, where the author had been allowed access to the various stages of production and promotion of the film. A 16 mm print, extracts and slides from the film were available for hire to accompany the use of the book. Valuable for teachers, *Making Legend of the Werewolf* had the additional advantage of being usable by students and was priced so that a set of textbooks might be ordered. Not all teachers were convinced of the book's usefulness as a text book. Foster in reviewing it found much to complain about, both in terms of its accessibility for students and in its theoretical stance, which he saw as extending the territory of the auteur theory to cover many of those working as specialists in various subsidiary film crafts.[117]

Hazell – the making of a TV series was by Alvarado and Buscombe. They did have a specific readership in mind.

> The book is intended for all with an intelligent interest in television, though within that audience we have particularly addressed ourselves to teachers at secondary and further education level who may be teaching television, possibly in the context of a media studies course. We hope that for them this book will provide some basic material on the television production system, material which is difficult for them to obtain by themselves.[118]

The series of TV monographs published by the BFI had tended to concentrate on the non-fiction output of television. This book deliberately addressed that omission and more significantly it engaged with the complexity of the enterprise that it sought to describe. The monographs had generally been concerned with the consumption stage of the television process; this book addressed the production stage.

A comparable journal partnership

It is useful to consider the phenomena that were *Screen* and *Screen Education* against that of the earlier journals *Scrutiny* and *The Use of English*. The backdrop to *Scrutiny* has been examined in detail by Mulhern in his book *The Moment of Scrutiny*.[119] Comparing their operational context with that of *Screen* and *Screen Education* is valuable in that what emerges are revealing contrasts and similarities between them. *Scrutiny* in the 1930s grew out of the recently established English School at Cambridge. Cambridge University had been late in setting up such a school which thereby removed English from its previous home in Anglo-Saxon Studies. *Scrutiny* reflected the energies of a group of university teachers and their ex-students who wished to promote a particular approach to literature through practical criticism. *Screen* operated at an earlier stage in the evolution of film study. There was no established place in the academy apart from the Slade School of Art (within University College, London) and the extra-mural courses also offered by London University.[120] With the effective dismantling of the BFI Education Department as the 'embryonic academy', *Screen* had no academy to play to and, as argued elsewhere, it was deliberately non-academic.

But *Scrutiny* and *Screen* were in turn connected with a particular generation of the intelligentsia. For *Scrutiny* it was the grammar-school scholarship boys who entered Cambridge between the two world wars and probably saw themselves as spearheading an attack on the classical tradition of teaching English.[121] They were however still advocating an essentially conservative approach in their recognition of a 'great tradition'. The SEFT journal provided a base for a differently motivated post-1968 student generation who saw themselves as disenfranchised. In practice they represented a range of left positions and were the intellectual legacy of various political parties. What they had in common was a belief in the inescapability of politics in the theories they wished to develop.

It was axiomatic given their political beliefs that those involved with either of the SEFT journals would avoid the formation of any hierarchical situation in their working together. *Scrutiny* however had had as its focus F R Leavis, who, though in many ways marginal to the academy at Cambridge, was nevertheless unusually influential as a teacher. *Screen* and *Screen Education* were ultimately the journals of SEFT and answerable to its Executive Committee which in turn was answerable to members at the AGM.[122] Nevertheless both groups were distinguished by their conviction and unity around their respective projects. One notable area of similarity is that both *Scrutiny* and *Screen* had partner 'educational publications'; for *Scrutiny* it was *The Use of English*[123] and for *Screen*, the 'revised' *Screen Education*. In each case the educational journal operated independently and in practice found itself addressing a different constituency with a separate group of authors contributing to each magazine. This pattern of repetition some forty years on does seem to reveal an inherent distinction in British education where it is considered proper that the practical needs of teachers should be addressed separately. In its final years this would become an even bigger issue for SEFT.

Scrutiny and also *The Use of English* had as their readership the disciples of Leavis in many classrooms. A whole generation of post-war English teachers contained many who were taught or influenced by Leavis. These teachers passed on their enthusiasm for the Great Tradition to the generation of students that were then to be so affected by the failed student revolution of 1968. It has been shown that the debates in the 1969/70 *Screen*[124] involving Robin Wood and Alan Lovell demonstrated how persistent the Leavis influence was beyond the study of English literature.[125] The 'disenfranchised' who were involved in *Screen* found themselves in a different situation. They were on the attack yet they were state-subsidised. Their chosen area of interest was not accepted in the academy, yet by their efforts it would be. They resisted being labelled academics yet they were all academics-in-waiting.[126] According to Alvarado they all agreed at the time on the Gramscian distinction between the 'academic' and the 'intellectual' and saw themselves in the latter category.[127] Mulhern writes of the small circle around Leavis:

> They cast themselves as 'outlaws' whose purpose was to save 'the essential nature' of the Tripos from a narrow academicism that now threatened to extinguish it.[128]

Some would contest that whereas *Scrutiny* and *The Use of English* transformed English studies, SEFT both created a new subject area and transformed other disciplines in the humanities, including English studies. But it is in the very different political stance of the two journals that the greatest discrepancy is to be observed. As Mulhern remarked in the year after *The Moment of Scrutiny* was published, he had tried to demonstrate in the book that *Scrutiny*'s commitment to notions of culture and community had the determinate effect of a 'categorial dissolution of politics as such'.[129] *Screen* came with a very different stance. As Alvarado explained, 'We saw ourselves as the cultural arm of the *New Left Review* ie independent left and not doctrinaire. We were interested in thinking aesthetics politically'.[130]

The comparison of *Screen Education* with the *Use of English* reveals instructive differences. Film and television study and the emergence of media studies were grass roots, bottom-up enterprises. The 1970s intellectuals were not the first group of dissatisfied learners to see screen education as an enterprise worth pursuing. The Society of Film Teachers had been started by those who were involved in the post-war emergency teacher training programme, whether as mature students or lecturers. Their dissatisfaction was partly with the abbreviated courses that the exigencies of the post-war situation imposed, but it also had some similarity with those of the 1970s' graduates. Both groups saw film as something more significant in society that needed recognition in the education system beyond its instrumental use as an audio-visual aid. What the pioneers of the 1940s could not anticipate was that they were creating in SEFT an entity which a later generation would inhabit and transform. By the mid-1970s, it was the journal *Screen Education* that still connected with the grassroots. *Screen*'s contribution has continued to be celebrated in the anthologies of film theory designed for university students and its theoretical writings have thereby achieved a landmark status. However, to trace the evolution of the transition from screen education into media studies and the transmission of those ideas through the education system then it is *Screen Education* which more adroitly documents the legitimate history of the 1970s.

The Battle of the Constituencies

Various issues that had been contentious within the SEFT Committee and *Screen* Editorial Board were confronted at the Society's Annual General Meeting in November 1976. Normal AGM procedure was to request from each candidate standing for the SEFT Executive a 300 word statement in support of that candidate. On this occasion eight members of the Committee who were standing for re-election produced and circulated to only part of the electorate a 'Provisional Policy Document for the SEFT'.[131] Covering five A4 pages of closely typed documentation, the signatories argued that they were addressing 'a lack of consistency in the Society's policy during the past year'. A further five who were also standing for the Committee had joined the eight, so that there was in effect a 15 strong ticket.

The minutes of this AGM (taken by Brewster) provide an unusually detailed record of the discussion.[132] On the basis of this account, the meeting would appear to have been divided between those who were schoolteachers and those in higher education. But there were schoolteachers among the 13 signatories, so whilst the secondary/higher split was undoubtedly a feature of the Society's make-up, there were broader issues which had their origins in divisions within the *Screen* Editorial Board where that journal's promotion of a psychoanalytical dimension to film theory had become the focus of dispute. The importance of the policy document was in its careful construction, so that its thrust would not be that contentious for a generally left leaning constituency, provided of course that when it came to the vote, there would be an organised core of support for the agreed ticket. In practice, of the 130 members present, it seems that some 90 had come prepared to back the document.[133] Both the contents of the document and how it had been selectively circulated were discussed acrimoniously and at length during the meeting.

If the document was designed to provide a mechanism for separating the factions within the Society, the timing and the targets were carefully chosen: schoolteachers who might already feel uneasy at the pressure then being exerted on left sympathisers within state education following the Great Debate. It was the perceived neglect of the needs of teachers that the four who resigned form the Editorial Board had used in part to justify their resignations. Lovell and Williams were present at the AGM and vocal in their support for the teacher constituency.[134] SEFT was about to announce plans to produce teaching materials for classroom use in schools. It had previously acted as a distributor for ILEA materials, making them available to teachers outside London but SEFT had never produced any of its own. Here was an area where the Society had produced nothing yet, so there was no one directly responsible whose work would be implicitly criticised. Thus the nature of the proposal might be framed in such a way in the policy document as to impinge only on those schoolteachers who were not of the 'hard left'. It would produce a defensive reaction from them, since such teachers would inevitably see agreement with its implementation as likely to place them in a very exposed position. Therefore they would consider that they must oppose the stance of the Provisional Policy Document.

It would seem that the authors of the Policy Document had devised a carefully constructed strategy to isolate those teachers who were hesitant about the unrelenting politicisation of the Society's projects. Thus in support of SEFT's production of teaching materials the following statement was included.

The decision of the Executive Committee to investigate the production of educational materials is an important innovation in the Society's work. A tremendous void exists in this area, and our work here could be of real value to teachers, but we feel that one danger must be avoided, namely the production of materials on a simple technical basis, without taking into account the ideological use to which they are necessarily subject in the school context. Therefore we propose that materials should be considered which allow the progressive teacher to use them in the context of ideological contradictions within the media, and that their technical production should not be separated from considerations of their potential political use in schools.[135]

Willemen recalls how careful preparations had been made for the AGM with planning meetings involving selected members from the SEFT Committee and from both Editorial Boards.[136] The first stage of the manoeuvre at the AGM was to replace Mottershead as Chairman. Steve Neale, one of the Policy Document's signatories, was elected Chairman, achieving an almost two to one majority.[137] Mottershead maintains he was unaware that this coup was about to happen and only subsequently realised there had been 'a conspiracy to take SEFT down a radical road'.[138] Foster agrees that the retiring committee was unprepared for this 'orchestration of the opposition' though he acknowledges the signatories were not a 'tightly knit group'.[139] Geraghty's view is that the Policy Document group succeeded in their objective of replacing a committee that had been sympathetic to teachers.[140] Williams describes the result succinctly: 'We lost'.[141]

Neale had produced his own 'discussion document' in support of his candidature which had a three-point agenda for future SEFT priorities.[142] These were: mutual co-operation with the Independent Film Producers' Association (IFPA); a clear and coherent socialist theory of education; and a coherent socialist analysis of the ideological apparatus that television represented. The poor condition of the SEFT archives is a particular problem here in that Neale under his third priority area states that 'Colin MacCabe's proposals should be taken seriously'. No trace of these proposals has been found. Of greatest significance in Neale's manifesto is the prominence he gives to co-operation with the IFPA. This group would form in the 1980s the basis of a third constituency within SEFT.

In the subsequent SEFT Committee elections after Neale had taken over as Chairman, all remaining Policy Document signatories were elected, filling twelve of the top fourteen places in the members' poll. As a consequence there were only four remaining committee places to be filled and three of these were taken by the re-election of previous committee members, presumably those who were considered least objectionable by the Policy Document group.[143] In interview MacCabe made reference to 'the Grealy/Wollen document', the genesis of which followed the 1976 AGM. This too has not proved traceable. MacCabe's recollection was that the Grealy/Wollen document laid down the parameters for the subsequent SEFT/*Screen*/*Screen Education* relationship and how it would in future be formally manifested.[144]

Notes

1. Philip Simpson 'Film and TV Studies in Secondary Education Report of the BFI/SEFT York Conference 1976' *Screen Education* No 19 Summer 1976 p 35
2. Julius Gould *The Attack on Higher Education: Marxist and Radical Penetration* London Institute for the Study of Conflict September 1977
3. George Foster in interview with the author 18 November 2003.

4. Robin Wood 'Film and Television Studies in the UK' *Visual Education* April 1977 p 21
5. Manuel Alvarado in a letter to the author 16 February 2007.
6. Manuel Alvarado in email to the author 1 March 2007.
7. Manuel Alvarado, Richard Collins 'The *Viewpoint* Controversy' *Screen Education* No 19 Summer 1976 pp 74–81
8. Len Masterman in interview with the author 15 September 2006.
9. Ibid
10. Philip Simpson op cit pp 35–44
11. Jim Hillier in interview with the author 25 April 2005.
12. Len Masterman *Teaching About Television* London: Macmillan Press 1980 p 7
13. Richard Collins in interview with the author 24 May 2004.
14. Roy Stafford in interview with the author 11 May 2005.
15. Manuel Alvarado in interview with the author 15 July 2003.
16. Geoffrey Nowell-Smith in interview with the author 30 June 2003.
17. As were the members of the *Screen Education* Editorial Board.
18. Nowell-Smith op cit
19. Nowell –Smith op cit
20. Laura Mulvey in interview with the author 24 July 2003.
21. Peter Wollen *Signs and Meaning in the Cinema* Expanded Edition London: BFI 1998 p 155
22. John Ellis in interview with the author 4 July 2003.
23. Alvarado interview (2003) op cit
24. *Screen Reader 1: Cinema/Ideology/Politics* (1997) and *Screen Reader 2 Cinema and Semiotics* (1981) were published by SEFT. *The Sexual Subject A* Screen *Reader in Sexuality* (1992) was published by Routledge.
25. David Rodowick in interview with the author 9 June 2004.
26. Ellis interview op cit
27. Andrew Britton 'The Ideology of *Screen*' *Movie* No 26 Winter 1978/79 pp 2–28
28. *Screen* Vol 12 No 1 pp 27–36
29. Susan Bennett in interview with the author 5 June 2003.
30. Op cit
31. Alvarado op cit
32. Ellis op cit
33. Paul Willemen in interview with the author 18 August 2005.
34. Anthony Easthope 'The Trajectory of *Screen*, 1971–79' *The Politics of Theory* Ed Francis Barker *et al* Colchester University of Essex 1983 p 121
35. Janet Bergstrom (Ed) *Endless Night Cinema and Psychoanalysis – Parallel Histories* Berkeley: University of California Press 1999 p 4
36. E Ann Kaplan (Ed) 'From Plato's Cave to Freud's Screen' *Psychoanalysis and Cinema* New York: Routledge 1990 p 8
37. Robert Lapsley and Michael Westlake *Film Theory An Introduction* Manchester: Manchester University Press 1988 p 10

38. Nicolas Tredell (Ed) *Cinemas of the Mind: A Critical History of Film Theory* Cambridge: Icon Books 2002 p 131

39. Stuart Hall 'Recent Developments in Theories of Language and Ideology: A Critical Note' *Culture, Media, Language: Working Papers in Cultural Studies* London Hutchinson 1980 p 157

40. Annette Kuhn and Jackie Stacey (Eds) *Screen Histories A Screen Reader* Oxford: Oxford University Press 1998 p 2

41. Christine Geraghty in interview with the author 2 August 2005.

42. Manuel Alvarado interview (2003) op cit

43. Laura Mulvey in interview with the author 24 July 2003.

44. Willemen interview op cit

45. Anthony Easthope *British Post-Structuralism* London Routledge 1988 pp 43–59

46. Rosen op cit. In this volume of articles collected mostly from Anglo-American film journals, reprints from *Screen* account for seven chapters while five other journals together contribute a combined total of eleven chapters. What is significant for a study of *Screen* is that only three of the reprinted articles were written specifically for it. Four were in fact translations of Bellour, Barthes, Metz and the Editors of *Cahiers du Cinéma*. Apart from the last, the translations all appeared during Brewster's editorship and were the work of Heath (on Barthes) and Brewster. The *Screen* originals were MacCabe on 'Theory and Film: Principles of Realism and Pleasure', Heath on 'Narrative Space' and Mulvey on 'Visual Pleasure and Narrative Cinema'.

47. Mark Nash in interview with the author 21 April 2005.

48. Rosen op cit p viii

49. See *Screen* Vol 16 No 2 Summer 1975 pp 5–6, Vol 16 No 4 Winter 1975/76 pp 119–130 and Vol 17 No 2 Summer 1976 pp 106–116

50. Geraghty interview op cit

51. The present state of access to SEFT archive materials is such that one can only make inferences from the published material and from what was recollected by those interviewed.

52. *Screen* Vol 16 No 1 pp 5–6

53. Thus Stephen Heath is quoted by Nicolas Tredell (*Cinemas of the Mind: A Critical History of Film Theory* Cambridge: Icon Books 2002 p 13): '*Screen* had a marginal institutional position as a subsidiary part of the Society for Education in Film and Television which was itself an outpost of the British Film Institute'; Colin MacCabe writes (*Theoretical Essays: Film, Linguistics, Literature* Manchester: Manchester University Press 1985 p 4): 'Originally *Screen* and its parent body SEFT (Society for Education in Film and Television) were set up at the end of the fifties by teachers interested in bringing film into the classroom, and it was practical questions about the teaching of film which dominated the magazine for its first twelve years. Throughout this period both the Society and the magazine were located within the offices of the BFI, which was the Society's funding body.'.

54. SEFT Archive Bretton Hall BH/ME/PL/132 (2)The supporting evidence for this is drawn from the rather inadequate record in the Minutes of the November 1972 AGM.

55. Ed Buscombe in interview with the author 13 June 2003. Lovell had also been Whannel's deputy from 1969–71; he became a SEFT committee member after his resignation from the BFI.
56. *Screen* Vol 16 No 4 p 130
57. Crofts ibid p 16
58. Ibid p 16
59. Manuel Alvarado interview (2003) op cit
60. Geoffrey Nowell-Smith in interview with the author 30 June 2003.
61. *Screen* Vol 16 No 4 Winter 1975/76 p 121
62. NAFE was founded in late summer 1971. In 'A Letter from the Chairman' dated November 1975 it is stated 'At that time relations between the British Film Institute and SEFT were not at their best and the appearance on the scene of another body of film teachers seemed not altogether unwelcome in some quarters' SEFT Archive Bretton Hall BH/ME/PL/132/1.
63. Alvarado op cit
64. Manuel Alvarado in interview with the author 11 July 2005.
65. Jim Hillier in interview with the author 25 April 2005.
66. David Lusted in interview with the author 16 May 2005.
67. *Screen* Vol 16 Nos 1 and 2
68. *Screen* Vol 16 No 4 Winter 1975/76 p 125
69. *Screen* Vol 17 No 2 Summer 1976 p 113
70. These issues have of course been taken up by women writers subsequently, including Mulvey herself. See in particular 'Afterthoughts on "Visual Pleasure and Narrative Cinema" inspired by King Vidor's *Duel in the Sun* (1946) in Laura Mulvey *Visual and Other Pleasures* Basingstoke: Palgrave 1989.
71. *Screen* op cit pp 107–108
72. Geraghty interview op cit
73. Collins interview op cit
74. Manuel Alvarado, Richard Collins 'Editorial' *Screen Education* No 14 Spring 1975 pp 2–3
75. Ibid p 2
76. Manuel Alvarado, Cary Bazalgette, Jim Hillier 'Editorial' *Screen Education* No 15 Summer 1975 pp 1–2
77. *Screen Education* op cit pp 19–42
78. Manuel Alvarado, Jim Cook, Geoff Goldstein, Chris Mottershead 'Editorial' *Screen Education* No 16 Autumn 1975 pp 1–3
79. Richard Collins, Jim Grealy 'The Education Cuts' *Screen Education* op cit pp 41–46
80. Ibid p 46
81. Manuel Alvarado, Richard Collins 'Editorial' *Screen Education* No 19 Summer 1976 p 1
82. Manuel Alvarado, Cary Bazalgette, Felicity Grant 'Editorial' *Screen Education* No 18 Spring 1976 p 1
83. See previous chapter.

84. Susan Bennett 'Mass Media Education – Defining the Subject' *Screen Education* op cit pp 15–21

85. Ibid p 17

86. Ibid p 20.

87. Bob Ferguson, Robert Stephens 'Media Studies and Media Usage in an Institute of Education' *Screen Education* No 21 Winter 1976/77 pp 20–31

88. Bennett op cit p 21

89. Manuel Alvarado, Richard Collins, Jim Cook, Roy Stafford 'Editorial' *Screen Education* No 22 Spring 1977. p 1

90. SEFT Archive Bretton Hall BH/ME/PL/133 (2) '*Screen Education* Statement to the SEFT Executive' March 1976

91. SEFT Archive Bretton Hall BH/ME/PL/133 (2) '*Screen Education* Policy Statement from the Editorial Board' May 1976

92. Jim Grealy 'Notes on Popular Culture' *Screen Education* No 22 Spring 1977 pp 5–11

93. Ibid p 11

94. Geoffrey Nowell-Smith 'Gramsci and the National Popular' *Screen Education* op cit pp 12–15

95. Ibid p 15

96. Colin Sparks 'The Evolution of Cultural Studies…' *Screen Education* op cit pp 16–30

97. Richard Collins 'Re-evaluating Leavis' *Screen Education* op cit pp 39–47

98. Ibid p 37

99. Statement in *Screen Education* No 21 Winter 1976/77 p 86

100. John Caughie 'Glasgow SEFT Group' *Screen Education* No 22 Spring 1977 p 76

101. Anthony Easthope, Rob Lapsley 'Manchester SEFT Group' *Screen Education* No 23 Summer 1977 pp 71–72

102. John Thompson 'Report – SEFT Glasgow Group Weekend School "Television and the Real World"' *Screen Education* op cit pp 69–70

103. Advertisement in *Screen Education* op cit p 68

104. Alvarado recalls that there was also a SEFT group based in Amiens, France.

105. Richard Exton, Christine Geraghty, Ian Gilman, Harry Lyons, Stephanie McKnight, Chris Mottershead, Christopher Williams 'Statement: *Screen Education* and *The Sweeney*' *Screen Education* op cit pp 59–64

106. Exton, Geraghty and Mottershead had been re-elected. Gilman, and Lyons had failed to be re-elected. McKnight and Williams had also failed to be elected.

107. *Screen Education* op cit p 60

108. Ibid

109. Ibid p 62

110. Ibid p 63

111. Phillip Drummond 'Reply to Critics of *Screen Education* 20 *The Sweeney*' *Screen Education* op cit pp 65–68

112. Ibid p 68

113. Manuel Alvarado, Felicity Grant Editorial *Screen Education* No 24 Autumn 1977 pp 1–3

114. Alvarado left after editing *Screen Education* 27. However he had commissioned articles for the next two issues.

115. Edward Buscombe *Making Legend of the Werewolf* London: BFI/EAS 1976

116. Manuel Alvarado and Edward Buscombe *Hazell – the Making of a TV Series* London: BFI in association with Latimer 1978

117. George Foster 'Review of *Making Legend of the Werewolf* *Screen Education* No 24 Autumn 1977 pp 57–60

118. Manuel Alvarado and Edward Buscombe op cit p 9

119. Francis Mulhern *The Moment of Scrutiny* London: New Left Books 1979

120. It has been shown that film study was established in certain teacher training colleges eg Bede and Bulmershe, but these were not then considered university level.

121. Mulhern op cit p 32

122. Such a lineage could result in marked policy shifts in the SEFT journal's trajectory, as happened in 1969 when *Screen* replaced the first version of *Screen Education*. There were other shifts. In 1971 *Screen* turned emphatically toward the development of theory and then in 1979 under Mark Nash a more journalistic approach was undertaken.

123. *The Use of English*, originally *English in Schools*, was started in 1939 and edited by Denys Thompson. It continued into the 1960s.

124. *Screen* Vol 10 No 2 pp 42–55 and Vol 10 No 3 pp 35–48

125. A decade later Britton, attempting to demolish 'Fortress' *Screen* in *Movie* No 26 (See Chapter 7) uses Leavis on several occasions as a fixed point of reference.

126. The six who joined the Editorial Board in 1976 following the resignations of Buscombe, Gledhill, Lovell and Williams were at the time of writing this account professors of film, as indeed were the then Editor, the Editorial Assistant and the surviving members of the board which they joined.

127. Manuel Alvarado interview (2003) op cit

128. Mulhern op cit p 33.

129. Francis Mulhern 'Notes on Culture and Cultural Struggle' *Screen Education* No 34 Spring 1980 p 32

130. Alvarado op cit

131. Stephen Crofts, Phillip Drummond, Jimmy Grealy, Claire Johnstone, Mark Nash, Steve Neale, James Pettifer, Peter Wollen *Provisional Policy Document for the S.E.F.T.* Undated but circulated before the 1976 SEFT AGM.

132. SEFT Archive Bretton Hall BH/ME/ PL/132 (2) Minutes of the Twenty Fifth Annual General Meeting of the Society for Education in Film and Television held on Saturday 6th November 1976

133. Ibid as revealed in the voting pattern of the various elections.

134. Ibid

135. Crofts et al op cit p 4

136. Willemen interview op cit

137. Minutes op cit Item 4

138. Mottershead interview op cit

139. Foster interview op cit
140. Geraghty interview op cit
141. Williams interview op cit
142. Steve Neale *Discussion Document for SEFT Policy Statement* Undated
143. Minutes op cit Item 4 (continued)
144. Colin MacCabe in interview with the author 11 December 2006.

9

SEFT Limited

As Screen *got locked into bitter internal debate, much of the original energy and excitement of the original project was refound in the society's new magazine* Screen Education *where concern both with secondary teaching and popular culture were very much to the fore.*

Colin MacCabe, 1985

Screen, *under new editorship, becomes less committed to theory and more to exploring a broader perspective on associated arts while* Screen Education's *new editor regularly features the emerging area of cultural studies. In 1980 a change of personnel in key positions at the BFI forces a review of SEFT's situation since both journals have changed course and the Society's role beyond publishing the journals is unclear. A resurgent Education Department wants SEFT to have an identity distinctive from the Department's. The new BFI Director sees SEFT in a campaigning role and producing only one journal. SEFT, swayed by the prestige which* Screen *still holds and the income it produces, keeps* Screen *and abandons* Screen Education.

Repercussions
Douglas Lowndes left the Educational Advisory Service at the end of 1976, shortly after the SEFT Annual General Meeting. He wrote a substantial document for his BFI colleagues, which had been occasioned by the events of the AGM. He presumably felt justified in his frankness by his imminent departure. What he wrote is indicative of the relative status of SEFT and EAS at the time. Lowndes clearly believed that the ability of some SEFT members to organise and dominate the Society would have repercussions at the BFI.

This situation forces the department into a crisis situation because distribution of the SEFT document coincides with the imminent appointment of a new head of EAS and the governors' seminar on BFI policy.[1]

He was aware that members of EAS who had, as SEFT members, opposed the SEFT policy document might wish to pursue the production of an oppositional document. Lowndes is against such a move, as any BFI statement in the circumstances 'would suffer from the historically confused status of the SEFT/EAS relationship and lack of clear policy, agreed, on what should be their priorities'.[2] Instead he feels the Department should write its own policy to 'end any fears both within the department and in SEFT that some institutional intervention might be attempted by myself or other members of the department regarding the future of SEFT'. Lowndes clearly felt that he must be seen to be ruling out any such action.[3]

At the heart of Lowndes's paper is his articulation of concern at the potential for problems in SEFT's relationship with teachers. He detects 'the inherent contradiction between radical theory and formal education as represented by curriculum projects, O-level consortia and regional curriculum initiatives'.[4] He indicates that he has some sympathy with those who had taken charge of SEFT at their AGM and yet is specific as to the inherent dangers. 'SEFT must know the dangers of a policy that runs the risk of alienating traditional, or even progressive, teachers'.[5] Lowndes was aware of the damage that had been done to the Education Department in 1971 when a very questionable distinction had been made between giving support and advice to teachers on the one hand and the development of theory on the other. He fears that a similar rift now threatens SEFT. 'What however is not acceptable is the setting up of a critique of SEFT on the ideological dichotomy of teachers work being opposed to intellectual activity.'[6]

He clearly feared that those activists who attended the SEFT AGM would have expectations that EAS should follow suit. He argues that EAS will be in a better position to support SEFT if it is not perceived within the BFI as simply following a SEFT initiative. He specifically cautions that 'departmental work must be clearly marked out from that of SEFT'.[7] As to the role of the SEFT journals his views are very specific.

> It should be apparent that I envisage *Screen Education* as the radical arm of screen education practices and it should not be associated with formal LEA classroom projects. By advocating that role [as a politically active journal] for *Screen Education* I envisage its life, in that form, being not more than two or three years.[8]

Screen is perceived as less of a problem. 'I consider their project a correct one, the introduction of psychoanalysis, semiology and social theory into film and TV study.'[9] The BFI records contain several subsequent drafts for an EAS Policy Statement proposed by the remaining members of the department during December 1976 and January 1977.

Whether a final agreed version of such a draft ever emerged, it is, at the current stage of consolidation of the BFI Document Archive, impossible to say.

Of more immediate importance to SEFT was the reaction of the BFI Governors to developments in the Society. Jim Hillier, the Acting Head of the Educational Advisory Service after Lowndes left, had to defend SEFT.[10] He produced a very convincing document which was incorporated into the Director's 1977 Report on Grant-in-Aid Bodies. In the minutes of their meeting at which the report was received, the Governors were recorded as being very positive about the Institute's support for SEFT.[11] Hillier had presented the Society as 'a professional society of educators' which had produced 'one of the foremost journals in the English speaking world'. He argued that *Screen* had 'unjustifiably' become the main activity by which SEFT was noticed. Accordingly he drew attention first to *Screen Education* which had 'a very substantial international reputation' and then to SEFT's Weekend Schools, Easter School and its Regional Groups.[12] What Hillier was able still legitimately to do was present SEFT as 'the only major national professional society representing the interests and concerns of teachers and lecturers involved in film and television study in secondary and higher education'.[13] While such a professional body might expect BFI's support, it would be increasingly difficult for SEFT in the 1980s to continue to match up to Hillier's description.

Lowndes has claimed that he and Director Lucas, sharing an art college background, were not dissimilar in their assessments of situations.[14] It is possible that Lucas was influenced by Lowndes's document, as the Director's response to the latter's departure was to take time in appointing a replacement. Interviews were set up in late spring 1977, but there were clearly still unresolved issues.

> During the course of interviewing for a new Head of the BFI's Educational Advisory Service, a number of issues arose about the BFI's educational role which I felt worth airing more widely before an appointment was made.[15]

Lucas then decided to consult widely on the purpose and function of the Educational Advisory Service. This included the setting up of a series of seminars with BFI's contacts representing the different sectors of education.[16] Given the numbers of teachers, lecturers and other educationists invited to offer their opinions, the consultation produced a very long list of proposals which the increasingly cash-strapped BFI was in no position to address.[17]

The one definite proposal was for a new post of Research and Higher Education Officer. Though the title was new, two of the proposed post's main duties were ones that EAS staff had been familiar with for some time: advising higher education institutions on film and television study and promoting in-service courses for teachers. Only 'the supervision and administration of a research programme' was novel.[18] To describe it as 'new' is misleading. Whannel had seen this as a desirable function of his Education Department. Indeed several of his staff had researched books, albeit without anyone being officially recognised as a researcher. It was the Governors' antipathy to such a theoretical and research emphasis that led to Whannel's resignation and the redesignation of the Education Department as the Educational Advisory Service. A research post was a particularly inappropriate outcome from the consultation since Lucas's starting point had been the aftermath of the 1976 York conference. In his letter inviting participants to the seminars, Lucas referred to 'film/TV/media studies' and asks of the move to media studies 'is this a productive shift?'[19] Unsurprisingly therefore the research post never materialised and Lucas retired at the end of 1978.

The appointment of Lowndes's successor was unexpected. Richard Sherrington was not known in screen education circles; he was an audio-visual aids specialist from the British Council. Sadly Sherrington never took up the post. He was killed in an airplane hi-jack in the final weeks of his British Council employment. The post of head of EAS was then offered to and accepted by Geoffrey Nowell-Smith, who had recently resigned as Editor of *Screen*. During the interregnum the Deputy Head, Jim Hillier, had again taken over as Acting Head of EAS. It fell to Hillier not only to defend the BFI's grants to SEFT but also to intercede on behalf of Lucas when the latter was under persistent pressure from the National Association for Film Education (NAFE), which by 1977 had been in existence for six years.[20]

NAFE was sufficiently well established to merit inclusion alongside SEFT when *Visual Education* ran a group of articles on 'Film and Television Studies in the UK' in April 1977.[21] NAFE's distance from SEFT's thinking may be deduced from the NAFE contribution to the articles. NAFE welcomes the 'Great Debate' and sees it as a helpful intervention and believes that Callaghan's curriculum reform will embrace film and television. As a consequence these areas will be retrieved from their isolation from the curriculum, an isolation produced by the action of many film teachers who 'have contributed to this situation in some measure either through their own lack of vision, or through their prior commitment to other goals, such as political change (or sometimes their own academic advancement).'[22] It is clear from the article that NAFE had taken over two of SEFT's successful enterprises begun in the 1960s – the fortnight Summer School at the Glamorgan College of Education and the London Co-operative Society's 'Let's Make a Film Festival'. Indeed these are the only two NAFE events identified in the article. There is no evidence available of NAFE after 1977, though the 'Let's Make a Film Festival' survived into the 1990s when, as the 'Young People's Film and Video Festival', it celebrated its 25th anniversary at the National Museum of Photography, Film and Television.[23] The Co-op was still the primary promoter, but NAFE had long before been replaced by the BFI.

Post-graduate qualifications

SEFT and BFI together had been the most influential bodies in the slow evolution of film appreciation into media education during the post war decades; however this leadership would be challenged in the 1980s particularly by institutions which were able to deliver courses directly to full-time students. The University of London Institute of Education's Department of Educational Media had become significant in the evolution of media education by the end of the 1970s. Previously the only screen education offered at the Institute had been within its Teachers' Centre, run by David Johnstone, an early advocate of film teaching. In spring 1959 the Centre had offered a one term evening course on 'Film Appreciation in Secondary Schools'. The course tutor had been Paddy Whannel and his guest lecturers had come from both BFI and SEFT.[24] A similar arrangement had supported 'The Cinema and the Teacher' in spring 1968. This too had been a joint BFI/SEFT arrangement but with a later generation of personnel from those organisations, with Victor Perkins as course tutor. The synopsis in the Teachers' Centre leaflet reflects the period:

> This course has been designed to introduce teachers to the practicality of the study of film in all senses, including the consideration of feature films and the use of film as a liberal catalyst helping to break down the rigours of traditional subject barriers.[25]

With Johnstone's initial encouragement Bob Ferguson, the new departmental head, had been able to move what was essentially an audio-visual aids support section into a training department for media teachers. The first step had been to offer those studying for the postgraduate certificate in education (the PGCE teacher training qualification) the option of taking a combined English and Media course. Then with the recruitment of Alvarado and Phillip Drummond to its staff, the department was able to offer from 1981 an MA in Film and Television Studies for Education, on both a full-time and part-time basis.[26] Almost simultaneously the Post-graduate Diploma in Film Study at the Polytechnic of Central London was modified so that it became the first stage qualification *en route* to an MA. Those in the metropolitan area therefore, by the early 1980s, had the choice between two Masters degrees. The Institute provided for the teacher or further education lecturer looking for an in-service qualification; the Polytechnic perhaps attracted more of those with ambitions to teach in higher education.[27]

The Institute's MA required students to submit a dissertation and to sit three examination papers of three hours each with a student answering three questions per paper. The papers were:

Paper 1: The Theory and Practice of Film and Television Education.
Paper 2: Film and Television History and Theory.
Paper 3: Children, Education and Television.

After the first year an alternative Paper 3 was made available: Realist and Anti-Realist Theory and Practice in Film and Television.[28]

The question papers in the early years were demanding, perhaps less so for those who were regular readers of *Screen* and *Screen Education*. A question from the 1982 paper provides a convincing example.

> To what extent do you think it is desirable and possible to utilise 'structural analysis' of film and television narrative in the classroom? Answer with reference to: either Levi Strauss's work on myth; or Metz's syntagmatic analysis of film; or Barthes' work on the codes of narrative.[29]

As Ferguson, Alvarado and Drummond were all at this time members of the *Screen Education* Board, students were no doubt advised as to the advantages of their joining SEFT. SEFT itself would benefit as students from the PGCE course, when taking up teaching posts, would be available to be recruited to play volunteer roles within SEFT. Those who joined SEFT from the Institute would have been subscribing at a time when the Society was beginning to face financial pressures. These would not have been immediately apparent since the Institute's Library had shelves stacked with volumes of *Screen* and *Screen Education* from the 1970s. Close inspection of the issues around the end of the 1970s would have revealed evidence of the transitional processes both journals were undergoing.

Changes at *Screen Education*
Perhaps the main article of interest in *Screen Education* 26 (published in Spring 1978) was that on 'Examinations and Strategies' by James Donald.[30] There are two reasons for this interest. Firstly Donald would shortly be appointed Editor in succession to Alvarado and secondly because the issue of examinations highlighted a dilemma for SEFT. The wider society valued examinations and for working-class students examination success had for decades provided the route that enabled them to achieve. On the other hand 'the examination system is bound to determine and limit subject areas, and must ultimately stifle the radical potential of the space that any new subject area may create'.[31] Among the journal's readers were those members of the various consortia who were teaching the GCE O level in Film Study who would have wished to counter the argument. For them the recognition and money that teaching film had now achieved at institutional level was directly attributable to the status that being able to offer a GCE examination conferred.

The most significant part of Donald's article for the purposes of this investigation is when he poses 'the sensitive question of SEFT's own location in the social formation – it is, after all, funded mainly by the State (although at third or fourth hand). How long will its privileged license [sic] as an oppositional clerisy be secure?'[32] Donald then contrasts SEFT with the Media Studies Association. The latter was a short lived attempt to have a professional body for media teachers whereas Donald clearly sees SEFT, long established as such a body for teachers of film and television, as something very different. He asks 'How can SEFT most effectively intervene in the current debate (the struggle between ideologies about education) -- crucially at the level of theory, but also politically?'[33] He wants to put on the agenda 'the question of SEFT's relationship to the organised working class'.[34] The questions around SEFT's status and role would stay unresolved for the remainder of the Society's existence.

A response to Donald is provided by 'Reading the Realist Film' which is the most extensive article in the issue.[35] Taking up a debate that had been running in *Screen*, the author Tony Stevens, having engaged with the theoretical arguments, enquires as to the role that this theory of realism plays in the teaching of film. For Stevens the class struggle is at the heart of the realism debate because 'For the ruling class film language is transparent, communicating or expressing a world of meaning which confirms its rule'.[36] Teaching 'realism' therefore means engaging with the class struggle and demonstrating to working-class students that realism is 'the very term of the involvement of film in that struggle'.[37]

Screen Education 27 (the last to credit Alvarado as Editor) has an editorial which seeks to identify the problems confronting both BFI and SEFT in the development of a British film culture. The BFI is perceived as making a virtue of its reluctance to adopt a political stance, since in so doing it avoids being targeted by those who might take a different stance. But *Screen Education* argues that not taking a political stance is by default the adoption of a political stance. It argues that pre-1971, SEFT too had avoided taking a political stance but had subsequently decided that 'financially and institutionally, it was in a key position to attempt to make a more serious and sustained intervention into the existing British film and TV culture'.[38] To assist in the widening of the horizons of the Society's work, 'education' was defined in its widest sense. 'As all practices are political so too are they educational'.[39] Alvarado was joined in the editing of this issue by Roy Stafford and Elizabeth Cowie. The established practice was for Alvarado to draft an editorial and for the issue editors then to comment.[40] Given that Alvarado was on the point of leaving SEFT, perhaps here he was concerned to redefine the Society's fundamental task and the distinctiveness of its status in relation to the BFI. However it is clear that, whatever means are to be employed, both organisations have a fundamental responsibility to film culture. It would become increasingly apparent in the succeeding years that the territory which the BFI and SEFT had once occupied in isolation would be increasingly impinged upon as higher education expanded and academics saw the potential for developing courses in a wide range of new study areas (Communications/ Culture/Media/Film). These would necessarily include the study of film and television.

Although *Screen Education* 28 was the first to have Donald credited as Editor, its editorial is signed by Donald, Alvarado, Collins and Ferguson. It reads as a continuation of the thinking of the previous editorial and attempts to define 'the central concern of *Screen Education*' or at least to identify the kinds of questions which need to be asked if someone is to 'teach about film and television against the grain of both the media and the education system'.[41] In the light of how *Screen Education*'s priorities were to change under the new editorship, it is less important to list here what the questions were than to note how *Screen Education* still clearly saw its role as being in the arena of teaching film and television. There was then an assumption that those choosing to engage in this arena were politically progressive. If *Screen* had championed certain theorists, here *Screen Education* would promote Antonio Gramsci and Pierre Bourdieu.

By *Screen Education* 29 there were two new members of the editorial board: Simon Frith, a lecturer in sociology at Warwick University and Irene Payne, a London teacher. The issue's innovation was to foreground articles on sexuality, the principal ones being by Frith and Angela McRobbie, who was a research student at the Birmingham Centre for Contemporary Cultural Studies and who would succeed Donald to become *Screen Education*'s final editor for its closing issues. McRobbie's involvement together with Frith's being on the board, were indicative of Donald's intention to seek contributions from institutions that had previously not had an effective connection with SEFT. Another contributor was Jo Spence, co-founder of Photography Workshop, whose article explored how class was insufficiently considered in the representation of women. The third contributor on sexuality was Gregg Blachford, a member of Gay Left collective, who wrote on pornography and its potential for subversive readings. Given the new territory which these articles were introducing to *Screen Education*, the editorial refers back to the beginnings of the revived *Screen Education* and to its declaration that the journal had to be involved in the construction of theoretical work which would support the film and television teacher. The editorial concedes that the articles may be read as provocative but argues that together they change the way in which much of the then current teaching about stereotyping was being effected. Simply to deplore the use of stereotypes as demeaning to individuals who might be thereby identified was to miss the fundamental point that stereotypes were 'ideological constructions with determinate political outcomes'.[42]

Birmingham Centre for Contemporary Cultural Studies

At this period, Donald, as both Education Officer and Editor of *Screen Education*, established closer contact with the Birmingham Centre for Contemporary Cultural Studies.[43] There had been limited contact between it and SEFT for most of the 1970s, despite the broad similarity of their projects. It might be assumed that the BCCCS, housed within the University of Birmingham's English Department, would have been the better funded organisation. It seems however that SEFT with its two printed journals and four staff was in the stronger position. The Birmingham Centre for many years had only duplication facilities by which it published the papers of its research graduates. *Screen*'s contributors had access to a more prestigious form of publication. Notably absent from the Centre's research programme were papers on aspects of film. The reason was simple. While *Screen*, through its BFI connection, had easy access to screening facilities, the Birmingham Centre could not even afford a 16 mm projector.[44]

Stuart Hall (Acting Director of the Centre from 1968–72 and then Director till 1978) welcomed Donald's involvement of researchers and staff from the Centre in writing for *Screen Education* and he subsequently regretted its ceasing publication since he regarded it as the more accessible of SEFT's journals.[45] The Centre's relationship with *Screen* had been rather different. The contacts between them had been limited. *Screen* had published an article by Rosalind Coward to which the Centre had responded.[46] Coward had attacked both *Screen* and the Centre. In his editorial introducing Coward's article, Nowell-Smith had summarised her attack on *Screen*, where he considered she was claiming that the journal had 'failed to develop adequately certain implications of its work on representation'. Her onslaught on the Centre was more severe,

> ...arguing that its theory of culture as an expression of class and class interests fails to recognise, in fully Marxist terms, the complexity of the way 'cultural' representations are produced and the determining action of the means of representation (with its attendant possibilities of subject position) on the represented.[47]

In its defence, the Centre sought first 'to repudiate the sectarian manner in which this attack was conducted'.[48] The authors from the Centre felt that Coward had picked only two of its papers and generalised her attack from these. Hall now concedes Coward was correct in demonstrating that the Centre whilst 'always at a distance from a full-blown theoreticist paradigm' retreated into 'an anthropological class-based version of culture'.[49]

It is useful to compare the Birmingham Centre for Contemporary Cultural Studies and SEFT/*Screen*/*Screen Education* as 1970s institutions. There were several notable similarities. Each was regarded as potentially subversive by a larger 'parent' institution, respectively the University of Birmingham and the British Film Institute. This reputation for subversiveness then served to attract graduate students to Birmingham and activists to SEFT. Marxist thinking was fundamental to both but, as John Ellis discovered when joining SEFT after time spent researching at Birmingham, each answered to a very different kind of Marxism.[50] Each had survived an attempt to close it down: SEFT when Whannel and his colleagues resigned from the BFI in 1971 and BCCCS when it became clear Hoggart would not return to continue as Director of the Centre when he left his secondment to UNESCO in 1972. Both organisations survived these attempts, though by different mechanisms: Rohdie deployed the activism of the New Left against a vulnerable BFI management; Hall called on the academic reinforcements of Raymond Williams and James Halloran.[51]

The legacy of Leavis impinged on both SEFT and BCCCS and the shared intellectual quest was for a more theoretical and less intuitive approach to their non-literary investigations. In neither case would the search be for a home-grown replacement theory; the choice was considered to lie between European and US alternatives. Both took the European option. *Screen* defined itself by being outside the academy. The Centre, despite its physical location within the Birmingham University Campus, was effectively also operating outside the academy. It had, from its inception in 1964, gathered together graduates engaged in collective research at a time when such a phenomenon had no formally agreed status within the academy.[52] Perhaps it was this uncertainty around its position within the University which resulted in the Centre neither approaching nor being approached by the BFI when there was the offer of funded film lectureships. The Centre would certainly have welcomed both the funding which the lectureship would have brought and the novel intellectual stimulus that film study might have provided. Hall now regrets no such overture was ever made by either party. 'It would have been an inspired move but it never happened.'[53]

There were differences between SEFT and the Centre, as Hall acknowledges. Since it was he rather than Hoggart who had recognised the need to go beyond Leavis in the search for theory and had therefore taken the Centre in that direction, Hall is perhaps being rather self-effacing when he describes the Centre's approach as 'always bringing a low-flying pragmatism to these over-elaborated questions'.[54] Nevertheless there was a fundamental difference specifically between *Screen* and the Centre in that *Screen* sought to develop theory while the Centre wanted to find a methodology for applying theory to society. Hall's assessment is similar to that which Willemen would make.

> Occupying Marxist theory at a very advanced level was for *Screen* the only justification needed for their politics...Theory was operating in a realm of theory which generated theory.[55]

SEFT had two journals. Each needed to meet publication deadlines and to have copy ready for the printers. This regime imposed its own discipline which was absent from the Centre where individual postgraduates worked at their own pace on their own projects. Each journal wanted to demonstrate a collective authority in its publication, rather than individual authorship. The Editorial Board meetings were therefore experienced very differently by board members from the way in which the Centre's graduates were able to move between a selection of 'work in progress' seminars. But some of the work presented at these seminars found its way into the later issues of *Screen Education*.

Donald's Editorship

By *Screen Education* 30 two additional members had been recruited to the Board. They were: Philip Simpson, who was the newly appointed Adult Education Officer in the BFI's Educational Advisory Service, and Madeleine McDonald, a member of the Faculty of Education at the Open University. This issue would have reached members in the run-up to the 1979 General Election. The tone of the editorial with its references to cuts, to the declining school population and to the wide circulation of 'a coherent critique from the radical, populist Right' reflects what must have been the mood of many SEFT members.[56] The *Screen Education* project is defined. The statement takes on a political urgency and is expressed with a precision of language which suggests the involvement of Jim Grealy, one of the joint editors for that issue.

This project remains the elaboration of the theoretical bases of critical teaching about film and television and an investigation of the relationship of these strategies to the developing knowledge about the mass media's place in the social formation.[57]

As a statement of intent it is wide ranging, but by virtue of its generality it will enable the inclusion by the end of the next paragraph of 'socialists working within the educational and cultural apparatuses' who can 'try to transform the relations of the State…in the interests of dominated social classes'.[58]

There follows the only piece Donald would write for *Screen Education* during his editorship, a response to the 1977 Green Paper *Education in Schools*, in which he calls for 'a theory of ideological struggle'.[59] A role in this struggle is envisaged for SEFT, here redefined as 'a cultural organisation' and associated with (among others) the Socialist Teachers' Alliance. Such organisations should, Donald suggests, follow Gramsci and produce 'a series of ideological, religious, philosophical, political and juridical polemics, whose concreteness can be estimated by the extent to which they are convincing, and shift the previously existing disposition of social forces'.[60] However since SEFT, Donald concedes, is not a political party he is then somewhat constrained in what he proposes the Society may offer. What he does in the article is to prescribe a course of action for teachers. Those in state education 'should be using all the resources available to them to create an expanding layer of "organic intellectuals"'.[61]

In the same issue Philip Simpson (a former college of education lecturer) writes about the closure of many colleges of education (as the teacher training colleges had been re-designated). This had a particular resonance for lecturers in film where during the 1960s and early 1970s film and television study had found its only higher education niche. Now it seemed that the small number of colleges offering such a specialism was threatened. Simpson's case is that even though the consequences of the imminent fall in school pupil numbers which had triggered the closure programme had been resisted by those working in the colleges, this resistance had had almost no effect since decisions were being taken on a simplistic numbers basis at a very remote governmental level. Readers of this issue would have had to confront the disparity between what Donald was proposing as a potentially influential role for SEFT (in the opening pages) and what Simpson was identifying as the reality dominating the lives of those who were college of education lecturers (at the back of the journal). Perhaps this was an inevitable outcome for SEFT where the boards of its journals were increasingly occupied by those furthest from the educational front lines.

Another new board member, John Tagg, then an art historian from Leeds University but formerly at the BCCCS, had joined by *Screen Education* 31. He had previously contributed to *Screen Education* 28 where he had continued the interest the journal had been showing for several issues in photography. The poor quality of photographic reproduction in *Screen Education*, consequent upon the type of paper on which it was printed, would soon be remedied with the introduction of a section printed on glossy paper, starting with *Screen Education* 34.[62] Issue 31, with its contents generated entirely under Donald's editorship, has a range of articles covering areas which had been addressed in the previous sequence of issues. Their diversity is used as justification for the re-orientation of *Screen Education* which returns to the recently abandoned practice of having a title for the issue. This one is 'Interventions'.

> The logic of *Screen Education*'s shift from its original limited concern with teaching about film and television to engagement with broader cultural questions is made clear by the way that certain issues cut across these articles.[63]

The rebranding it seems is now a *fait accompli*, though a specific announcement is made to the effect that the next issue is going to include 'a new look at some of the central terms in the field of film studies'.[64] However, when *Screen Education* 32/33 appeared its title was 'History/Technology/Culture'.

Francis Mulhern's book *The Moment of Scrutiny* had just been published.[65] This was an account of the intervention by Leavis into the teaching of English. *Screen Education* engages with the book's publication and *Scrutiny* is exhibited as an example of effective journalistic intervention into cultural practice. However the editorial has to concede that 'such journalism can only become effective if it fits in with a range of other – often more direct – tactical engagements with educational practices and institutions'.[66] By which one must infer that the effectiveness of Leavis was probably more the result of cohorts of Cambridge English graduates going into school teaching, than simply through the publishing of *Scrutiny*. What appears to be happening in this editorial is a retreat from its previous hard-line position on the class struggle: 'we do not see a strategic perspective in terms of donning a set of political certitudes like the team colours before a football match'.[67] Mulhern had argued that *Scrutiny*'s flaw had been its attempt to ignore politics. The lesson that *Screen Education* had taken from the *Scrutiny* experience seemed to be that it might be in danger of going to the other extreme. If avoiding politics was one danger, the other would be to retreat from 'a concern with specific cultural struggles into a notion of politics as nothing but the clash of pre-given, economically defined class interests'.[68]

Screen Education 32/33 despite its cover designation of 'History, Technology, Culture' is divided into three different sections: 'On Photography', 'Studies in Film' and 'Culture and Communication'. Another recruit had joined the Editorial Board: Hazel Carby, a researcher at the Centre for Contemporary Cultural Studies. At 100 pages the 'Studies in Film' section dominates the issue. The editorial is more reflective and considered than some of its immediate predecessors. This might have been stimulated by the arrival of Anthony Smith as Director of the British Film Institute and his immediate intervention in order to discover what the three grant-in-aid bodies did for the money the BFI allocated for them. The editorial of this *Screen Education* is important for several reasons. Firstly the issue's editors were members of the Educational Advisory Service. Simpson would soon take over as Head of what would be once again known as the Institute's

Education Department. Bazalgette, having joined the BFI in 1979, would remain in the Department until 2007. Secondly it addresses the issues raised at the 1979 conference 'Film and Media Studies in Higher Education'. Thirdly it identifies the question that must have perplexed readers who had been long-term SEFT members: how was film study regarded in relation to the ever extending variety of discourses that now preoccupied *Screen Education*?

Simpson's interventions at the BFI will be discussed subsequently. Undoubtedly his style of management of the Department and his engagement with the Boards of both *Screen Education* and then *Screen* would indicate he was prepared to operate as Head of the Department very much as Whannel had done. At this stage Simpson was notable for being a long time SEFT member, an activist in the North East Film and Television Teachers' Association and a former lecturer in film at Alnwick College of Education. He had a very different pedigree from the other new recruits to the *Screen Education* Board where Bazalgette had been a member since joining *Screen Education Notes* in 1973. Quite apart from their commitment to film study, both BFI personnel would have been very aware of how closely the SEFT journals were read and interpreted inside the British Film Institute.

The Introduction of Media Studies in Higher Education

The 1979 Conference had been a very different event from that in York three years earlier. The differences reveal how rapidly the world of screen education within the UK was changing. 'Film and Media Studies in Higher Education' had been held at the University of London Institute of Education in summer 1979, promoted by both the EAS and the Institute's Department of Educational Media. 'Media Studies' now shared equal billing with 'Film' in the conference title. Only three years earlier at York, the status of Media Studies had still been in question. The York conference had been aimed at secondary school teachers, but in attendance they had been outnumbered by other interested parties. The 1979 conference had been for those in higher education and the attendance had reached 170.[69] Indeed it seems that the expectation of the organisers had been such that initially two separate conferences were envisaged to cope with the potential numbers.[70] At the event numbers were so great that each individual seminar group contained around thirty people.

Simpson had delivered a paper at the conference where he had drawn on research he had carried out before joining the BFI. He revealed that the study of film was offered on courses in fourteen colleges/departments of education, twenty two universities and seventeen polytechnics. In five of the polytechnics, film was offered in more than one department.[71] The attendance figures at the conference confirmed Simpson's research which indicated that some fifty eight higher education departments already had staff teaching film. There were undoubtedly numerous other conference participants about to start such courses. A key paragraph in his report is revealing.

...lectures and seminars are structured around perspectives opened up by film theory in the last few years. Ideology and cinema has already been mentioned as an important concern, but the more recent work on film derived from structural linguistics and psychoanalysis also tends to be introduced in courses where the teachers recognise an obligation to ensure that students who have committed most of their final year to Film Studies have an awareness of the current issues in the field. Meeting this sense of obligation can often present difficulties since few film teachers would claim competence in those disciplines from which much film theory is currently derived.[72]

This huge expansion had been carried out by lecturers who had only minimal – if any – training in what they were teaching. Some students might be taught by lecturers who were current recipients of the BFI funded university lectureships. Seven were in place at the time, either directly BFI funded or formerly funded lectureships which had been taken over by the universities. But most students were probably taught by lecturers who were aware that film study was now supported by theory, but a theory of which they had only a limited grasp. The conference might have assisted/alarmed them when they saw how many others shared their predicament.

It was in this environment that, as the *Screen Education* editorial reports, an atmosphere of disenchantment was discernible. Given the background to the conference outlined above, it is not surprising negativity was to be found at the event. Clearly expectations of the new subject area had been high in some quarters since the editorial reports that the accusation which had been voiced about Film and Media Studies was that 'it has not only failed to undermine traditional academic hierarchies and practices but has even become "just another discipline" itself'.[73] The editors suggest that the responsibility for this state of affairs was judged by the dissatisfied participants to be the consequence of two flaws: a tendency to be ahistorical and to fetishise the film text. The editors refer to articles in the journal which they consider demonstrate that film study does not necessarily possess these flaws and may therefore be read as a refutation of such claims.

A common implication of all these articles is that the 'object' of Film Studies is *not* the film text as a unique object, but film-making practices (technological, industrial and semiotic), bodies of films conceptualised generically or according to their conditions of production, the history of film theory, and so on – in short, the apparatus cinema.[74]

Rather, they turn the argument back on the protesters at the conference and the protesters' failure to conceptualise with equal rigour the institutional context in which Film and Media Studies has been put to work – the education apparatus. Clearly the editors were determined to resist the level of dissatisfaction which had been directed against film study. Some share of the responsibility lay with the institutions that had in effect directed a largely untrained workforce to teach in an emerging discipline, a discipline known for its engagement with difficult theory. Most importantly the editors seize the opportunity to commit the now wide-ranging *Screen Education* to a definition of the specific version of film teaching that it wished to endorse. It

> ...has a different and perhaps more precise educational purpose. This is to show students how films produced within determinate socio-economic conditions themselves produce *meaning* through systems of signification – meaning which by its modes of representation in turn sustains social identities and categories. Film Studies, in this view, is a way of challenging the ideological power of the cinema; it can interrogate the nature and effectivity of the pleasure derived from films and can give conceptual coherence to audiences' resistances to them.[75]

Screen Education and Cultural Studies

Nevertheless *Screen Education* was being moved, by Donald, towards Cultural Studies. At the end of the editorial there is a trail for the next issue, *Screen Education* 34. It would focus on 'parallel growth in recent years of activities given coherence by notions of 'cultural struggle' and 'cultural studies'.[76] Therefore there needed to be a clear link from the statement of endorsement about the nature of film study to cultural studies articles with which the readers would not already have been familiar. This is approached diplomatically, given how the editors had reacted to the conference.

> Although the magazine occupies a space bounded neither by 'film culture' nor by the context of school, college or university, it has to be responsive to what is actually happening in those institutions. Because the journal's work is by definition theoretical, it strives to be consistent and systematic in its analysis and the strategic perspectives. But because it is precisely this theoretical work that makes it *useful* and *effective*, *Screen Education* will continue to be intellectually accessible and open to the expression of different positions.[77]

To demonstrate that it would deliver on this claim *Screen Education* 32/33 included an article by Claude Bailblé which was designed to relate technical knowledge to broader considerations of film theory.[78] Its translator was Susan Bennett whose expertise in rendering difficult French constructions into accessible English had resulted in her falling out of favour with *Screen*. But her style clearly fitted *Screen Education*'s agenda and was particularly appropriate for Bailblé's writing which involved concepts from biology, physics and mathematics and sought to connect the approach of the theorist with the knowledge of the technical practitioner. Thus for example he challenges the long established notion that the spectator's engagement with the film was analogous to her/his reading it. Instead he offers insights into what might be involved in the process of looking.

In February 1980 SEFT organised a weekend conference on 'Culture and Politics'.[79] The speaker invited to start the event was Francis Mulhern, Editor of New Left Books. Among the other speakers were Stuart Hall, then recently arrived at the Open University, and Ernesto Laclau, Lecturer in Politics at Essex University. Mulhern recalls that the main interest generated by the event was how Hall and Laclau would interact.[80] It seems probable that *Screen Education* 34 had been expected to publish papers from the conference and space in the journal had been provisionally allocated accordingly. Only Mulhern's introductory paper is printed as evidence of the conference.[81] There are pieces by Hall and Laclau but unrelated to the conference. The former reviews Raymond Williams's *Politics and Letters* while the latter is represented by a paper delivered in Montréal in 1979.[82] Mulhern's contribution is a model of good practice in getting a conference off to a controversial start but without the publication of any of the responses, it serves only to whet the appetite for what no longer follows.

As advertised in the preceding double issue, *Screen Education* 34 engages with cultural studies. It begins by referring back to *Screen Education* 22 where the editors had contested the separation of the elements 'screen' and 'education' and had instead placed screen education 'within the nexus of politics/ideology/culture'.[83] These circumstances are considered to have changed in the intervening three years and the editors now seek a mechanism to underpin oppositional education. A redefinition of 'culture' is sought which will admit 'the social relations that have been excluded from education'. In negotiating the incorporation of 'culture' this issue of *Screen Education* seeks substantial contributions from Richard Johnson, who had succeeded Hall as Director of the Birmingham Centre and Tony Bennett, the Course Chairman for the Open University's forthcoming undergraduate course on Popular Culture.[84] Increasingly a feature of the journal is the mode of address adopted towards its readers. Their engagement with, and commitment to, an oppositional practice is assumed, but if they happen to be teachers they may be found wanting. Johnson writes 'the teacher must take, or be capable of taking, the standpoint of the oppressed'.[85] Hazel Carby writes 'the anger evoked by texts representing the oppression of black women could not be separated from anger directed at the white teacher, herself implicated as a direct source of oppression'. Making its annual report to the BFI earlier in the year, the Society had felt it appropriate to reassure its funder that it was 'by no means merely a professional association for teachers and lecturers'.[86]

Readers of *Screen Education* 35 on Television Drama may have felt that they were back with a more familiar version of the journal. Some older readers might have become nostalgic for the 1960s' version in that the final fifteen pages contain listings of reference material and resources available for teaching television drama.[87] The editors of this issue were Alvarado, Cowie and Grealy who had elicited contributions from well established writers such as Buscombe, Murdock and McArthur. The editorial deals directly with anomalies of the copyright law. As more video recorders were being purchased by schools for the sanctioned (temporary) recording off-air of educational television programmes, teachers were becoming aware of the prohibition on their recording of any other material. The editorial concludes 'it should surely be possible to negotiate agreements that protect the interests of authors, performers and technicians without perpetuating the absurd anomaly of outlawing television studies'.[88] The listings are preceded by an article by Vincent Porter detailing the many legal limitations in force that constrained the use of video recording equipment in schools.[89]

The final issue produced under Donald's editorship had Bennett and Tagg as its joint editors.[90] Their editorial is revealing of the shift the journal had undergone during the two years of Donald's editorship. Increasingly it had shared with *Screen* an impetus to explore a specific area of theory. Here there are references to Althusser, Lacan, Derrida, Gramsci and Foucault. But where *Screen* had primarily sought to develop theory in order better to understand the nature of film, *Screen Education*'s priority had become the understanding of the politics of culture. This had supplanted the search, under the previous Editor, for theories that might facilitate a better understanding of the problems faced in education. Consequently the journal's 'advocacy of media teaching' is quoted in this editorial as simply one example of how *Screen Education* is now approaching the politics of culture.

> If culture is thus defined as the complex unity of practices and institutions that produce sense – if 'experience' is always experienced, organised and expressed through linguistic and other semiotic representations – there is a clear political significance to struggles around the hierarchies of institutions in which representation are [sic] produced, circulated, regulated and have their effects.[91]

The editorial then justifies its interest in media teaching because such teaching intervenes within 'the education and entertainment apparatuses'.[92] The intervention is important because it elaborates terms for 'reading' modes of representation 'within film, television and other popular cultural forms'.[93]

At this time 2000 copies of *Screen Education* were being printed per issue of which 1300 were going to subscribers.[94] No records survive of who these subscribers were. Some presumably were long time SEFT members, but the composition of the remainder may only be guessed at. Even the most dedicated and assiduous reader of *Screen Education* would have been aware of the intellectual distance between those who wrote for it on the one hand and most of its readership on the other. Donald had recruited authors from the Centre for Contemporary Cultural Studies and from the Open University's Popular Culture team. These were the people with the time, commitment and responsibility to develop their thinking, to follow through their ideas and then to deploy the results of this thinking within articles and degree level teaching materials. Simultaneously higher education teaching institutions, as Simpson demonstrated in relation to film alone, were promoting courses around culture, media and communication that would necessarily incorporate this thinking. It is pertinent here to refer again to the reactions of some of those who attended the higher education conference.

Those who had kept pace with *Screen Education* would recognise its fundamental premises. They would therefore perhaps accept that it was now the politics of culture which preoccupied the attention of academics and that consequently screen education was but an aspect of media teaching, which was itself but an instance of a range of mechanisms for engaging with culture. Some articles in the journal were clearly commissioned to assist in this process, particularly Colin Mercer's 'After Gramsci' and Iain Chambers's 'Rethinking Popular Culture'. [95] Those who were reported as voicing a protest at the conference were possibly those who were maintaining their reading and keeping up with the thinking. They were dissatisfied both with the limitations imposed on them at work and then had to listen to papers at the conference which they interpreted as insufficiently engaged with recent developments in theory. Despite their acceptance of these innovative approaches this dissatisfied cohort worked in institutions where they had to construct syllabuses and award qualifications. In these tasks too they would have found themselves constrained by 'old' thinking. But there must have been other conference participants who found the pace of developments daunting and whose professional profiles matched those, as identified by Simpson, who struggled to keep themselves informed about theoretical developments.

Screen's New Editor

There were important changes taking place simultaneously at the other SEFT journal. Mark Nash became Editor of *Screen* with the Summer 1978 issue. He was able in some measure immediately to signal he had taken over by changing the colour of the cover paper to a vibrant green.[96] The next four Nash issues would have covers made distinctive by their brighter colours. The interregnum between Nowell-Smith and Nash had been covered by Elizabeth Cowie as 'Interim Editor'. For his first three issues Nash drew heavily on the *Screen* old guard: Brewster, Heath, MacCabe, Wollen, and Nowell-Smith. The editorials which he signed personally were generally brief exercises in contextualising the articles that followed in each *Screen*. The Editorial Board was unchanged from that which had operated when Brewster was Editor.

With the first *Screen* of 1979, Nash and Steve Neale wrote the editorial jointly for an issue that had a more unified shape with three major articles on authorship. The editorial confronts an obvious reality. Despite there having been much examination of the concept of authorship in the *Screen*s of the early and mid-1970s, the journal had subsequently moved to other theoretical preoccupations. But if notions of authorship had been displaced from *Screen*, the editors were now recognising that these notions were still dominant not only in film criticism but also in film production, distribution and exhibition. As a first step a ten year old article by Foucault is printed.[97] Nash was maintaining the *Screen* procedure of transmitting French theory to the English-speaking world, though in this case the article had previously appeared in book form having been translated for publication in the USA.[98]

Big changes for *Screen* are anticipated in the next editorial where five new members are listed as joining the Editorial Board.[99] Subscribers are alerted to the fact that they will have to wait six months for the next issue, but it will be a double issue. When it appeared in Winter 1979/80, *Screen* Volume 20 Number 3/4 had a larger format and had been completely redesigned by Julian Rothenstein. The substantial editorial, signed on this occasion by the Editorial Board, attempts to make an assessment of what *Screen* has achieved and, recognising that 1980 is the 30th year of SEFT's existence, states that the journal has 'a revised project and a new format'.[100] *Screen's* achievements are summarised both by identifying the particular theories it has advocated and by listing those categories of its English-speaking readership which it has influenced, whether in education, filmmaking or aesthetic practices more widely. It concludes the section on its influence thus.

> Finally, *Screen* has offered to cultural and literary theory, and to theories of the place of 'ideology' in the social formation, a constant insistence on language in its specificity as signifying practices rather than as communication; in the light of this insistence it has worked to examine the nature of the text as systematic process and to explore the subject, as conceived by psychoanalysis, as an area of political struggle.[101]

The debate then concerns *Screen* and its relationship with the academy. Previously it had determined not to be an academic journal. This editorial is therefore an exercise in careful diplomacy. It sets out to facilitate the transition from the *Screen* of the 1970s, but without appearing to dissociate itself from the achievements of that decade. Those who were activists around *Screen* during the editorships of Rohdie, Brewster and Nowell-Smith have, when interviewed for this research, been emphatic that the *Screen* of their period was not an academic journal. It was the vehicle in which intellectuals committed to theorising film study were able to put their thinking into print. Here the editorial comments that *Screen* 'is sometimes mistaken as the academic journal of film studies'.[102] Since there had been almost no 'film study academy' for most of the 1970s, this had not been a difficult position to maintain. However, as Simpson's research had revealed, by the end of the decade there were the strong beginnings of such an academy in the UK. *Screen's* subscription income had, since Brewster's time, been buoyed up by the contributions from United States university libraries where there was a substantial film academy. Thus there were practical economic reasons why the journal might need to modify its position. This is effected in the editorial by distinguishing between how the term 'academic' had been interpreted in the 1970s and how it might now be reinterpreted.[103]

For the *Screen* authors of the 1970s regular academic practice entailed 'an essentially reflective mode of thought and writing', whereas the *Screen* strategy had been designed to recognise that deploying such a practice changed 'the object it analyses by virtue of the systematisation it imposes on it'.[104] Certain articles had been written to make explicit this displacement. However, there was now an emergent film study academy and *Screen* inevitably had become part of the discourses circulating within it. Thus while still seeking to be oppositional to the academy, *Screen* was 'simultaneously within and against academic institutions'. The consequence of these manoeuvres was to see *Screen* as 'extremely vulnerable' to the pressures of the academy.[105] By professing vulnerability, perhaps the Editorial Board was acknowledging they might need a cover story for any modifications in approach which might be adopted in order for *Screen* to survive. John Ellis recalls that the aim was very deliberately to move *Screen* towards a more journalistic engagement.[106]

The *Screen* Editorial Board would have been as aware as the *Screen Education* Board that the new BFI Director would be perhaps their most diligent reader. In January 1980 it was reported to BFI Governors that Smith had required the three grant-in-aid bodies to provide the Governors with evidence to justify the continuation of BFI support.[107] Smith was being approached by numerous other bodies which wanted BFI funding and he needed to be convinced that the BFI's support for SEFT, the British Universities Film Council (BUFC) and the British Federation of Film Societies (BFFS) continued to be appropriate. Other organisations were discovering, as had NAFE, that only those which had grant-in-aid status had any security of income.

Having dealt with this transitional sequence, the editorial lists the new *Screen*'s priorities. Firstly, though its primary commitment to film and television remains, 'all practices of representation' will now be included in its remit.[108] As with previous *Screen* statements of intent there is recognition of the need to provide space for the consideration of independent film. This would prove to be a better indication of commitment at this point than previously, when stated good intentions toward independent filmmaking had produced little in *Screen*. SEFT had recently committed itself to supporting independent filmmakers as a third constituency alongside its subscribers in schools and higher education.[109]

A further issue to be addressed was that of the difficulty represented by the style of writing which had become an essential characteristic of *Screen*. First there needed to be a justification for this difficulty, which is ascribed to the specific requirements of the *Screen* project up to this point. These included

> ...first the need to introduce a number of unfamiliar terms, drawn from the discourses of semiotics and psychoanalysis, whose use was justified by the precision with which they enabled certain arguments to be handled; and secondly the need to promote arguments in a way which broke with traditional (and for the most part liberal-academic) formulations and modes of address.[110]

Academic writing was perceived as 'essentially reflective'; much critical writing as 'bourgeois journalistic'. *Screen* therefore needed to have a style that prevented the reader from 'being given the chance to be confirmed in one's position of already knowing what one has just been told'.[111]

But as with the circumstances surrounding its status as an academic journal, so too with the concerns about a *Screen* style, the editorial had to find room to manoeuvre. It had to concede that '*Screen* does not disturb the film and television establishment as it ought to: it merely irritates it'.[112] Thus if it is to extend both its readership and its influence, *Screen* must be more reader friendly. Here a deliberate tactic is deployed: find some real villains to attack who just happen to be few in number. They are neither the readership nor even the non readers among critics and broadcasters. Instead they are revealed to be other film magazines which allegedly criticise *Screen* 'as though it were what it has never claimed to be: a marxist journal in the traditional sense'.[113] The two writers then targeted are Andrew Britton and Kevin Robbins, writing in *Movie* and *Media, Culture and Society* respectively.[114]

Britton's article, though printed in *Movie*, was essentially a personal response to *Screen*, not an official *Movie* rebuff.[115] It was nevertheless written from a film theory perspective. Britton introduced the term 'intellectual terrorism' to describe the attitude adopted by *Screen* towards its readers. This was a term which, although not in currency until the end of the decade, might have first been applied to the atmosphere of the 1972 BFI Summer School.[116] Robins, a sociologist, was in the process of using the material in the article to shape a chapter for the forthcoming publication *Recovering Marxism*. Both writers are dismissed on the grounds that they have criticised *Screen* for not adopting whatever set of 'marxist postulates a particular author might at that moment have espoused'. 'Such pieces are evidence of an obstinate foreclosure of understanding for which *Screen* need bear no responsibility.'[117] Today MacCabe considers the Robins article to be the best analysis of the mid-1970s *Screen*, since Robins identified *Screen*'s selective linking of Althusser with Lacan as the nub of its project.[118] Perhaps it was impossible for this jointly produced editorial to take up the challenges of its critics, since to do so would almost certainly have exposed divisions within the Editorial Board. Britton's article presented particular problems for joint editorial comment in that he was prepared to identify some *Screen* authors as writing more effectively and consistently than others. Nash has conceded that he found, as Editor, he was answerable to a great many strong-minded individuals.[119] This is corroborated by MacCabe who concedes that Nash 'had a dreadful time dealing with all us monsters'.[120]

It is surprising how little impact was felt at *Screen* during the 1970s as a result of the emergence of feminism.[121] One influential feminist, Claire Johnston, was a long-term activist within SEFT and indeed the second of the Society's two occasional pamphlets was written by her.[122] However, despite SEFT's publication of this early pamphlet in 1973, during the editorships of Rohdie and Brewster, few women ever wrote for the journal. Laura Mulvey, whose 'Visual Pleasure and Narrative Cinema' has been reprinted in almost all English-speaking film theory editions, was not a *Screen* regular.[123] This celebrated article was the only piece she ever wrote for the SEFT journal. Linda Williams, who also wrote for *Screen* at this time, must have been considered to have had a strong claim for inclusion, in that she had worked with Metz in Paris.[124] Other articles contributed by women tended to be either reprints or collaborative pieces written with men.

During the Nash editorship, there was a stated commitment to recognise and include the contributions being made by feminists. However compared with *Screen Education*, there were very few women writers employed, though women were a substantial part of the attendance at SEFT Weekend Schools, notably at the 1976 Weekend School on Feminism. Willemen considers that such events were important as a means of recruiting new writers.[125] Among those he identifies as having been enlisted in this way was one woman: Claire Pajaczkowska. In fact Pajaczkowska's experience was not one of being recruited. She had attended the Weekend School on Pornography in May 1980 as a filmmaker. Having made a number of interventions from the floor in response to the succession of male speakers, she felt sufficiently exercised to want to write up her reactions more comprehensively. This was completed over several months while supervising independent film exhibition, after which Pajaczkowska turned up speculatively at the SEFT office and handed over her article to Mark Nash. It was duly printed in *Screen* without any amendments being made.[126] In turn her article was reprinted along with Mulvey's in the *Screen Reader in Sexuality*.[127] These were the only two articles written on that subject by women to be published in *Screen* before its first woman editor, Mandy Merck, was appointed in 1982.

In the 1970s there had been several relatively short lived film journals that had circulated in the UK.[128] Apart from *Screen*, the other survivors by the end of the decade were the intermittently produced *Movie*, *Afterimage* and *Framework* which had been started by undergraduates at Warwick University, some of whom had attended Robin Wood's early film classes there. In certain respects, if early issues of *Framework* were compared with *Screen*, *Framework* might have been considered to be the more academic journal.[129] Subsequently *Framework* moved from Warwick to the University of East Anglia and then became independent. One of its most active contributors and then Editor was Paul Willemen, who had been a very influential force on *Screen*. In part Willemen's move to *Framework* was triggered by his increasing disillusion with *Screen*, about which he wrote at length.[130] In Willemen's view by 1979 *Screen* was 'politically and intellectually vacuous'. In particular he blamed (unnamed) 'post-structuralists' who dominated the Editorial Board.

> By the time meetings started, heads had been counted, positions regarding issues to be discussed were known in advance and the rest was just a painful ritual to be endured.[131]

Willemen, who worked within the BFI for a long period, ascribes his engagement with film theory in Britain to his initial involvement with the BFI Education Department seminars starting in the late 1960s where he had first encountered Peter Wollen.[132]

Willemen considers the outcome of the 1976 SEFT AGM to be a victory that went wrong, leading to 'theoreticism'.[133] For him *Screen*'s concern with theory was appropriate when theory was developed in order to be relevant to the cultural struggle; instead he considers that the production of theory became a self sufficient activity: 'the journal set itself up as a Laboratory of Pure Theory'.[134] He considers that the abandoning of the section on Film Culture (when Nowell-Smith became Editor) accelerated *Screen*'s 'trajectory towards the deep space of academia'[135] which occurred at a time when government financial cuts constrained the 'marginal spaces available for oppositional practices' which had previously been accessible in educational institutions. Willemen is brutal in his assessment of just why theoreticism became attractive

> One result of this development was the re-emergence of theoreticism as a credible doctrine enabling academics to maintain a radical rhetoric which in no way would interfere with the serious business of careerism.[136]

Nevertheless Willemen remained on the Editorial Board until the two SEFT journals merged. He had always seen the role of *Screen Education* as subsidiary to *Screen*: 'cutting edge theoretical work on the one hand and transmission belt work on the other'.[137] At this point he saw no possibility of a return to a *Screen* committed to the cultural struggle.

Another SEFT Reorganisation

While appearing to its members as successful, with two substantial journals in regular publication, SEFT was facing problems by 1979. Already at this time, Donald recalls that the Society was being challenged as to the viability of its having two journals. They were clearly not functioning as complementary publications as Brewster's *Screen* and Alvarado's *Screen Education* had been. Once Smith was in post at the BFI, he and Donald had conversations in which Smith made clear that the BFI expected to be supporting a membership organisation with a single journal, not two journals each with a separate subscription list.[138] Although Donald would leave the Society before the final decision had been made, it was clear to him that *Screen* had the more survivable reputation for SEFT's future. He was replaced as Education Officer by Rod Stoneman but the editorship of *Screen Education* went to Angela McRobbie as caretaker editor,[139] albeit her editorship lasted for the last five issues until the Winter/Spring *Screen Education* in 1982. BFI Governors were told that SEFT was ceasing publication of both journals and starting a new one.[140] The new journal was however to be styled *Screen incorporating Screen Education*.

Strong support for SEFT had come in June 1980 from Colin McArthur, Head of the BFI's Distribution Division, through whose department the grant to SEFT was channelled.[141] McArthur's report had been presented to the Governors when they scrutinised the case made to them for the continuation of SEFT's grant-in-aid status. The Society's Officers had then to convince the BFI that they were prepared to take strong measures and subsequently they had to convey this to the membership. These measures included changing the legal status of SEFT into that of a company limited by guarantee. This was agreed at the AGM following the divisive 25th AGM in 1976.

Delayed until early 1978, at this 26th AGM those nominated for the Executive Committee were elected unopposed.[142]

A short term measure was the appointment of Steve Brockbank to a temporary new SEFT post of Publications Sales Officer at the end of 1978.[143] By this stage SEFT was offering for sale a wide range of periodicals and books from its small offices now at 29 Old Compton Street. These publications were available to callers, but mostly they were dispatched by mail. What had started as a service to members seeking copies of 'hard to find books', had grown substantially. A list of what was available went out as a regular insert in the journals. Storage of stock became a problem, which was resolved first by some space being found at the BFI and then by the hiring of a lock-up garage in Docklands.[144] In the event Brockbank's temporary post was not renewed after a year.[145]

During 1979 further economies had to be found. *Screen's* contributors were no longer paid and both journals made savings by simultaneously producing double issues for the winter 1979/80.[146] 1980 would be the year when hard decisions had to be taken, including that of running on a small deficit. It was also the occasion of facing up to other realities. An Interim Report at the end of 1980 spells out that membership of SEFT consisted ' of little more than a subscription to one or both journals'.[147] Whereas in the 1970s, the different roles of *Screen* and *Screen Education* had been such that each might be perceived as validating the existence of the other, currently in 1980 it was becoming evident that 'the two journals, envisaged as complementary within SEFT's project, were now the only visible part of the Society, and their twin concerns were seen as potentially polarising and factionalising tendencies'.[148]

Not only had the Executive Committee decided in July 1980 to publish only one journal but, as a further element in this re-organization, there were to be three new full-time posts of Education Officer, Editor and Clerical Officer. These posts were to be offered on a three-year contract basis, justified as giving SEFT as a 'part-time voluntary employer' more control over its staff.[149] Nash, as part-time Editor of *Screen*, and Susan Honeyford, the full-time Editorial Assistant to both journals, were faced with redundancy. Although their individual situations were eventually resolved and they left with compensation, there had been an Emergency General Meeting in June 1981, called because of the manner in which these employees had been treated.[150] Both journals continued until early 1982. The replacement journal would revert to bi-monthly publication and would have a 'proselytising role' so that it might achieve a wider readership. Its remit would be to cover 'Film and Television Culture and Education'.[151] As part of this new project the proposed Education Officer would be expected to recruit members and would have a 'substantial budget' in order to achieve this.[152]

The Goldsmiths Conference

While the SEFT Executive attended to this internal reorganization, the Society's role and influence in media education generally was in danger of disappearing. In November 1981, BFI Education and a new partner organisation, Goldsmiths College, organised a two-day event: 'Media Education Conference 1981'. It attracted 117 teachers and lecturers, but despite this attendance the event was described as being 'far from the euphoria of 1976'.[153] Like the 1979 conference for those in higher education, the very process of gathering teachers together had stimulated the articulation of a range of concerns. If the inclusion in its title of 'film and television' and 'secondary education' had been crucial in defining those for whom the earlier event in 1976 might have been appropriate, 'media education' had been deliberately chosen on this occasion for its vagueness.[154] 'Media studies' had been considered too specific a reference to an already existing curriculum subject. In the event such a wide range of participants turned up that

> ...some who were about to take their first steps in media teaching found themselves in seminars with teachers of considerable experience in the field and so it was difficult to pursue questions about the definition and institutionalisation of media education *and* retain everyone's involvement.[155]

There were thirty four group leaders at Goldsmiths, some of whom had connections with SEFT, but although each leader is identified by her/his professional involvement with media teaching, none is listed as having a role within SEFT When the report of the conference was published, it became clear how marginal to such proceedings SEFT as an organisation was becoming. There had been a debate about the need for a national body to protect and foster the interests of media educationists. SEFT, in the opinion of Philip Simpson, the new Head of the BFI Education Department, 'already had an ill-defined role in this field'.[156] This is re-emphasised subsequently in the independent report commissioned by the BFI from two group leaders.[157] In the section of their report dealing with the need for such a national body they comment that 'SEFT has too wide a brief to allow it to function in this way'.[158] In the same paragraph they regret the imminent disappearance of *Screen Education*, so SEFT's wide brief was clearly perceived as impinging on its effectiveness, even if this brief no longer included the Society's producing an educational/pedagogic journal or its involvement in an important conference for media teachers.

The conference had a dual function – to provide a retrospective of the 1970s and to offer a planning opportunity in which to develop a strategy for the 1980s. David Lusted had the task of reviewing the previous decade. He makes no mention of SEFT's contribution during the period, even though he had been on the SEFT Executive for several years. There is a single mention of *Screen Education*.[159] When the conference came to look forward, anxiety among participants focused on the imminence of the plans for a new 16 plus examination structure to replace 'O' level and CSE. Such was the level of concern that the conference organisation was modified and Len Masterman, who had been the speaker scheduled to lead on 'Media Education in the 1980s', was allowed to introduce background information around the proposed examination structure as an additional emergency presentation.[160] A working party was set up to take the topic forward and to lobby the Joint Council of GCE and see CSE Boards. The immediate outcome was a letter to the Boards from the Conference.[161]

Murdock and Phelps a decade earlier had surveyed teacher attitudes to media; they had not targeted those involved in teaching media. This conference set out to attract those who had some interest or involvement in media education, yet there was evidence of the same hostility to media that the earlier researchers had detected in teachers generally. The divisions among the participants were categorised.

> For instance, many came from a broad left perspective, with particular concern over questions of gender, race and class in the media. Some had a concern with teaching practical media skills in their own right, while others had a Leavisite, high/low culture perspective, concerned with protecting students from the dangerous influences of the mass media.[162]

It would seem that the 'vagueness' of the term 'media education' had tempted some of those who were generally hostile to the mass media to turn up.

The invitation to Masterman to present the keynote speech at the conference was no doubt in recognition of the influence that his book *Teaching about Television* was having.[163] If *Teaching about Television* had a predecessor, it was *The Popular Arts*. Hall and Whannel had attempted to combine for a teacher audience a reference book, a theoretical justification for studying popular culture and demonstrations of classroom expertise that might be copied. In order to authenticate the authors' credentials, the dust jacket of the book had made reference to their having been teachers in secondary modern schools. Masterman's book, published sixteen years later, employed the same combination of ingredients, but had the advantage of an educational audience that was much better briefed about media issues. The imminent arrival of Channel 4 and its potential for difference had generated a focused interest and expectation which had eluded the arrival of BBC2 just before *The Popular Arts* was published.

Josephine Langham who researched the outcomes of the Independent Broadcasting Authority Fellowship scheme has high praise for Masterman, albeit it is *Teaching About Television* that she considers, rather than the report that he wrote for the Fellowship.[164] Nevertheless, as he acknowledged, his book was the final stage of a lengthy research process. Her assessment is quoted in full

> What Masterman did in *Teaching About Television* was not simply provide practical ideas about the way to approach television education in the classroom but he engaged in a major debate about the nature of education and confronted key philosophical issues about teaching and learning. It was not just the book that was important for television studies: it had everything to say about education too. Television Studies attracted scholars who were interested in the problems of society, they were concerned about the alienation of working-class students from the educational system and they were prepared to confront conventional pedagogy.

Teaching children about television stimulated many of these teachers to challenge accepted teaching practices and syllabuses. They accepted the significance of popular culture and developed a corresponding suspicion of elitist assumptions and indoctrination. They began to uncover what they saw as the spurious mystique surrounding the educational machine in order to reveal the hypocrisy which lay behind much of the cant about democratic societies. In short, they began to use the language of revolution and made many traditional educators, broadcasters (and politicians) not just merely uncomfortable but ferociously angry.[165]

It might be inferred from this paragraph that Masterman did it single-handedly, which is not a claim he would make. Certainly the issues Langham identifies in Masterman had received much attention in *Screen Education* and undoubtedly many of that journal's readers would have bought and valued the book. What Masterman had done was to make very particular use of the freedom that being a teacher trainer in the 1970s allowed. He linked theory and practice and tested the outcomes over time in the school situation. It was different organisationally from what Lowndes had done in *Viewpoint* in that Lowndes had tried out different ideas but with different student groups on a short time scale. But both were focusing on the need to develop an educational response to the impingement of television.

SEFT without *Screen Education*
SEFT became a very different operation from 1982. It was not just that it now published only one journal; the basis of its organisation was changed. For the first time *Screen* had a full-time Editor: Mandy Merck, an experienced journalist from *Time Out/City Limits* with a commitment to film and a determination to position the journal within the Academy.[166] The post of full-time Education Officer fell vacant when Rod Stoneman resigned in July 1983. Discussions with the BFI about the nature of his replacement delayed any appointment until the post was re-designated as National Organiser with a brief extending far beyond education. Sean Cubitt, subsequently appointed in spring 1984, was a community activist with experience of teaching in higher education.[167] Not only was SEFT now seeking to operate in a fundamentally different way, it was doing so in the changed political circumstances of the Thatcher government years. An almost unavoidable consequence was, as succeeding chapters will seek to demonstrate, the closure of the Society in 1989. What this investigation has attempted to demonstrate is how SEFT and the various SEFT/BFI collaborations had, by the start of the 1980s, provided a lead in transforming a grass-roots movement which had started in schools and further education colleges into a discipline increasingly gaining status in higher education. Once the momentum for entering the Academy was established and with *Screen* committed to the same enterprise, SEFT then failed successfully to engage with other, perhaps less prestigious, projects. It would become increasingly an enterprise that lacked an identity at a time when education involving media was expanding in many institutions.

Chapter 9

1. British Film Institute Special Collections May 2005 Education Department File Douglas Lowndes 'The SEFT Provisional Policy Paper and the Policy Situation in EAS – A Personal Statement by Head of EAS' 9 November 1976 p 1
2. Ibid p 2
3. Ibid p 2
4. Ibid p 3
5. Ibid p 3
6. Ibid p 3
7. Ibid p 6
8. Ibid p 8
9. Ibid p 8
10. British Film Institute Governors' Minutes 13 December 1977 Confidential Governors' Paper 'Grant-in-Aid Bodies' G463/4.77
11. British Film Institute Governors' Minutes 24 January 1978
12. Ibid G463/4.77 Section A 'Society for Education in Film and Television'
13. Ibid
14. Douglas Lowndes in interview with the author 5 June 2003.
15. British Film Institute Special Collections May 2005 BFI Education File Letter from Lucas 10 June 1977 inviting BFI contacts to attend seminars
16. Ibid
17. British Film Institute Special Collections May 2005 BFI Education File List of participants in Secondary and Further Education Review Seminar 12 July 1977
18. British Film Institute Special Collections May 2005 BFI Education File Keith Lucas 'Educational Advisory Service Review Seminars' Section 6.4 September 1977
19. Letter from Lucas op cit
20. Jim Hillier in interview with the author 25 April 2005.
21. Graham Baines 'The National Association for Film Education' *Visual Education* April 1977 pp 30–31
22. Ibid p 31
23. Chris Mottershead and Tricia Jenkins *Children Moving Images* London: BFI 1992 p 1
24. Archive of the Institute of Education University of London *Institute of Education Teachers' Centre Short Courses 1959*
25. Archive of the Institute of Education University of London *Institute of Education Programme of Courses for Practising Teachers Spring 1968* p 4
26. Leaflet from University of London Institute of Education: *Master of Arts Degree 'Film and Television Studies for Education* 1981
27. The Certificate/ Diploma offered by the London University Extra-Mural Department had expanded with the setting up of a parallel course offer at Goldsmiths College. The Slade School now offered its tiny postgraduate intake in film the opportunity to acquire an M Phil.

28. Archive of the Institute of Education University of London University of London MA Examination September 1982 Film and Television Studies for Education Paper 3

29. Archive of the Institute of Education University of London University of London MA Examination September 1982 Film and Television Studies for Education Paper 2

30. James Donald 'Examinations and Strategies' *Screen Education* 26 Spring 1978 pp 3–11

31. Manuel Alvarado, Cary Bazalgette, Edward Buscombe 'Editorial' *Screen Education* 26 p 1

32. Donald op cit p 11

33. Ibid

34. Ibid

35. Tony Stevens 'Reading the Realist Film' *Screen Education* 26 pp 13–34

36. Ibid p 34

37. Ibid p 34

38. Manuel Alvarado, Elizabeth Cowie, Roy Stafford 'Editorial' *Screen Education* 27 Summer 1978 p 1

39. Ibid p 1

40. Manuel Alvarado in conversation with the author 8 March 2007.

41. James Donald, Manuel Alvarado, Richard Collins, Bob Ferguson 'Editorial' *Screen Education* 28 p 1

42. Editorial *Screen Education* 29 Winter 1978/79 p 1

43. James Donald in interview with the author 4 January 2006

44. Stuart Hall in interview with the author 17 March 2005

45. Ibid

46. Rosalind Coward 'Class, "Culture" and the Social Formation' *Screen* Vol 18 No 1 Spring 1977 pp 75–105; Iain Chambers, John Clarke, Ian Connell, Lidia Curti, Stuart Hall, Tony Jefferson 'Marxism and Culture' *Screen* Vol 18 No 4 Winter 1977/78 pp 109 – 119.

47. Geoffrey Nowell-Smith 'Editorial' *Screen* Vol 18 No1 p 6

48. Iain Chambers *et al* op cit p 109

49. John Ellis in interview with the author 4 July 2003.

50. Hall interview op cit

51. Ibid

52. Ibid

53. Ibid

54. Ibid

55. Ibid

56. 'Editorial' *Screen Education* 30 Spring 1979 p 1

57. Ibid

58. Ibid

59. James Donald 'Green Paper: Noise of Crisis' *Screen Education* 30 pp 13–49

60. Ibid p 48

61. Ibid

62. See Bob Long 'Photo Practice 1' *Screen Education* 34 pp 106–112

63. Ibid p 3

64. Ibid p 2

65. Francis Mulhern *The Moment of Scrutiny* London: New Left Books 1979.

66. Ibid p 2

67. Ibid

68. Ibid

69. Film & Media Studies in Higher Education Conference 1979 Listing of Seminar Groups (8/9 June)

70. Advertisement in *Screen Education* 30 Spring 1979 p 50

71. Philip Simpson Appendix I 'Film and Media Studies in Higher Education 1977–79' in Christine Gledhill (Ed) *Film & Media Studies in Higher Education Conference Papers* London: BFI Education September 1981 pp 153–160

72. Philip Simpson op cit p 159

73. Editorial *Screen Education* 32/33 Autumn/Winter 1979/80 p 1

74. Ibid p 2

75. Ibid p 1

76. Ibid p 4

77. Ibid p 3

78. Claude Bailblé 'Programming the Look' *Screen Education* 32/33 pp 99–131

79. An Advertisement for SEFT Weekend School *Screen Education* 32/33 p 134 'Culture and Politics' London February 9–10 1980

80. Francis Mulhern in conversation with the author 15 March 2007.

81. Francis Mulhern 'Notes on Culture and Cultural Struggle' *Screen Education* 34 Spring 1980 pp 31–35

82. Stuart Hall 'The Williams Interviews' pp 94–104 and Ernesto Laclau 'Populist Rupture and Discourse' pp 87–93 *Screen Education* op cit

83. 'Editorial' *Screen Education* 34 p 1

84. Richard Johnson 'Cultural Studies and Educational Practice' *Screen Education* op cit pp 5–16; Tony Bennett 'Popular Culture: A Teaching Object' *Screen Education* op cit pp 17–29

85. Richard Johnson op cit p 16

86. Hazel Carby ' Multi-Culture' *Screen Education* op cit p 69

87. Compiled by Ian MacDonald, the BFI's Television Information Officer

88. 'Editorial' *Screen Education* 35 p 2

89. Vincent Porter 'Video Recording and the Teacher' *Screen Education* 35 Summer 1980 pp 87–90

90. *Screen Education* 36 Autumn 1980

91. 'Editorial' *Screen Education* 36 p 1

92. Ibid

93. Ibid

94. Figures from SEFT Annual Report for 1978/79 written by Phillip Drummond for the AGM 26 January 1980

95. Colin Mercer 'After Gramsci' pp 5–15 and Iain Chambers 'Rethinking Popular Culture' pp 113–117 *Screen Education* 36

96. Mark Nash in interview with the author 21 April 2005

97. Michel Foucault 'What is an Author?' *Screen* Vol 20 No 1 Spring 1979 pp 13–29

98. Translation by Donald F Bouchard Ithica Cornell University 1977

99. *Screen* Vol 20 No 2 Summer 1979 p 10

100. *Screen* Vol 20 No 3/4 p 7

101. Ibid

102. Ibid p 8

103. Ibid

104. Ibid

105. Ibid

106. John Ellis interview op cit

107. British Film Institute Governors' Minutes 22 January 1980

108. *Screen* op cit p 9

109. See Chapter 8

110. *Screen* op cit p 11

111. Ibid

112. Ibid

113. Ibid p 12

114. Andrew Britton 'The Ideology of *Screen*' *Movie* No 26 Winter 1978/79 pp 2–28; Kevin Robins 'Althusserian Marxism and media studies: the case of *Screen*' *Media, Culture and Society* 1979 No 1 pp 355–370

115. Victor Perkins in interview with the author 19 April 2005.

116. Ibid

117. *Screen* op cit

118. Colin MacCabe in interview with the author 11 December 2006.

119. Nash interview op cit

120. MaCabe interview op cit

121. There was a Weekend School on Feminism in 1976.

122. Claire Johnston *Notes on Women's Cinema Screen* Pamphlet 2 London: SEFT 1973

123. Laura Mulvey 'Visual Pleasure and Narrative Cinema' *Screen* Vol 16 No 3 Autumn 1975 pp 6–18

124. Linda Williams 'Hiroshima and Marienbad – Metaphor and Metonymy' *Screen* Vol 17 No 1 Spring 1976

125. Paul Willemen in interview with the author 18 August 2005.

126. Claire Pajaczkowska in interview with the author 31 March 2007.

127. *The Sexual Subject: A Screen Reader in Sexuality* London: Routledge 1992

128. For a useful summary of the 1970s' cinema journals see Paul Willemen 'Introduction' Paul Willemen and Jim Pines (Eds) *The Essential Framework* London: Epigraph 1998 pp 1–11.

129. This is the view of Geoffrey Nowell-Smith (Editor of *Screen* 1976–77) in interview with the author 30 June 2003.
130. Paul Willemen 'Remarks on *Screen* A Spiralling Trajectory' *Southern Review* Vol 16 No 2 July 1983. The references given here are to a typescript version of the article distributed by Willemen to students on the BFI MA course in the early 1990s.
131. Willemen (1983) op cit
123. Paul Willemen interview op cit
133. Ibid
134. Willemen (1983) op cit p 9
135. Ibid p 8
136. Ibid p 20
137. Willemen interview op cit
138. James Donald in interview with the author 4 January 2006.
139. Editorial *Screen Education* 37 Winter 1980/91 p 2
140. British Film Institute Governors' Minutes 24 February 1981 Item 6227 Grant-Aided Bodies p 3
141. British Film Institute Governors' Minutes 24 June 1980 Colin McArthur 'BFI Funding and the Grant-in-Aid Bodies' G486/7.80
142. Minutes of the 26th SEFT AGM 21 January 1978
143. SEFT Annual Report for 1978/79
144. George Foster in interview with the author 18 November 2003.
145. SEFT Interim Report April – December 1980
146. SEFT Chairperson's Report for 1979/80
147. SEFT Interim Report op cit
148. Ibid
149. Ibid
150. Minutes of the 29th SEFT AGM 31 January 1981
151. Report to SEFT Emergency General Meeting June 1981
152. Ibid
153. Myra Connell and Michael O'Shaughnessy Report in *Media Education Conference 1981* London: BFI Education 1982 p 7
154. Philip Simpson Introduction *Media Education Conference 1981* London: BFI Education 1982 p 7
155. Ibid
156. Ibid p 2
157. Connell and O'Shaughnessy op cit p 10
158. Ibid
159. David Lusted 'Media Education and the Secondary/FE Curriculum' in Connell and O'Shaughnessy op cit pp 13–26
160. Len Masterman in interview with the author 15 September 2006.
161. Connell and O'Shaughnessy op cit Appendix 1 pp 57–60
162. Connell and O'Shaughnessy op cit p 6

163. Len Masterman *Teaching about Television* London: Macmillan 1980
164. Josephine Langham *Teachers and Television: The IBA Educational Fellowship Scheme* London: John Libbey & Company Ltd 1990
165. Ibid p 220
166. Mandy Merck in interview with the author 16 June 2004.
167. Sean Cubitt in e-mail interview with the author 14 January 2006.

10

A Moral Panic Averted

When can we expect media studies A levels? Why are there new parallels between technology education and teaching the media? And why should media educators be cautiously optimistic?

All these questions are discussed – if not definitively answered – in the new edition of Initiatives, *the Society for Education in Film and Television's termly journal, whose jaunty redesign signals more of the new spirit of hope in the media studies camp.*

A positive comment on the publication of Initiatives *9 in* The Times Educational Supplement *July 1988*

There is great potential for a moral panic as the new Secretary of State for Education deliberately selects a group of teachers with no media education expertise to watch television and comment on how it deals with representation. Careful management by the combined energies of HMI and BFI can't prevent the Press from having a field day but they do find institutional mechanisms for taking forward the educational debate. SEFT does not get involved. Meanwhile SEFT's new journal Screen *tries unenthusiastically to address the* Screen Education *agenda – which it was to have incorporated when the two journals merged.* Initiatives *is introduced to help fill the gap. For teachers the face of SEFT becomes a series of national conferences, staged outside London. In 'the Office' the accounts begin to tell a sad story.*

As the BFI increasingly applied pressure on SEFT to define its role and then staff itself accordingly, the Society's relationship to current educational developments became more disengaged. During the period when the full-time paid officer role was in transition from that of Education Officer to that of National Organiser, it seems that the Society lost momentum. It did of course have *Screen* as a regular bi-monthly product and this may have rather disguised inactivity elsewhere.

HMI looks for Allies

In January 1982 the recently appointed Secretary of State for Education, Sir Keith Joseph, became concerned about television and its potential influence on children. He approached HMI with his disquiet and 'asked HMI to convene a group of teachers to report on the values and images of adult life presented in a series of popular evening BBC and ITV programmes'.[1] In fact this is exactly the form of words used to introduce the resultant report *Popular TV and Schoolchildren*.[2] The precision with which the request is framed would suggest that HMI had worked to focus Joseph's more generalised concern. The potential for a disastrous political intervention was averted by a series of manoeuvres. James Learmonth HMI, a former London headteacher sympathetic to film and television education, was in operational charge of setting up the mechanics of the project. One of his first tasks was to check out the BFI. Philip Simpson, now heading the Education Department, recalls how Learmonth turned up unexpectedly and asked to see him.[3] This appears to have been the first formal contact between HMI and the BFI since the early 1960s.

The scale of the project was kept very small. Fifteen teachers were swiftly recruited to watch television for a limited period of five weeks in March/April 1982. The teachers came from a very wide range of sectors and had a national distribution geographically. Since a third of them were headteachers, it seems that their selection was precautionary, possibly chosen via the teaching unions.[4] When *Popular TV and Schoolchildren* was published there is a disclaimer about the panel of teachers, to the effect that 'none was chosen as an expert or because of a lifetime teaching television appreciation'.[5]

The conclusions of the group were cautious and designed to be non-inflammatory. There was an implicit recognition of the need for more media education, but expressed as the desirability of teachers finding ways of addressing popular television programmes in a range of classroom contexts.

> But specialist courses in media studies are not enough: all teachers should be involved in examining and discussing television programmes with young people.[6]

Both BFI and SEFT are acknowledged as having been 'offering advice and in-service training to teachers for many years'.[7] There is also recognition of the imminent changes in the viewer experience which will stem from cable channels and the spread of video recording. The implications of these changes in the home environment led the group to conclude that in future parents will need to become more involved both in a domestic supervisory role and in formal liaison with teachers and programme producers. The engagement of parents in their children's viewing of television would become a feature of the later 1980s.

Despite all the precautions, the national press reaction was, according to Learmonth, 'hysterical'.[8]

The teachers did not intend the Report as an attack on television. The vocabulary used in press coverage however 'slam', 'lash', 'accuse', 'target', 'condemn', 'attack', 'slapped wrists' and inevitably 'TV stars get a caning' suggested that the teachers categorised programmes into 'good' and 'bad' and judged the majority to be the latter. In fact the structure of the Report was chosen to consider themes, not individual programmes.[9]

When the Report appeared in late June 1983 and gained distorted coverage in the press, the BFI Education Department saw the need to shape a response. For SEFT, however, the publication came at a time when the Society had limited scope for response as its Education Officer, Rod Stoneman, was due to leave in July and the BFI wanted SEFT to reconsider its staffing before proceeding to make a replacement. Significantly when the retiring Chairperson George Foster reported to the AGM in December, his account concentrates entirely on describing how the Society is dealing with BFI pressure and makes no mention of the DES Report.[10] Eventually at the end of 1983 there was a response in *Screen*, albeit written by BFI Teacher Adviser David Lusted, who examined how the press reception of the Report had manipulated the contents to feed into a moral panic about television.[11] Lusted observes

> *Popular TV and Schoolchildren* is not, however, yet another alarmist contributor to the long march of useless moral panics as its press coverage overwhelmingly represents it. It is important to build on the positive possibilities its publication affords to develop cultural debate and media studies.[12]

Perhaps if the timing of its publication *Screen* had been otherwise, SEFT might have paid more attention to the contents of the Report. Earlier generations of SEFT activists would have interpreted the careful prose of the Report's conclusions as being as positive a signal as was possible from the DES under the Thatcher regime and have found a way of signalling this to the membership. Perhaps the SEFT volunteers were becoming too dependent on their paid staff to take necessary initiatives. At the BFI Philip Simpson deduced that as the report had received 'overwhelming public exposure', here was an opportunity for the media education world to make an intervention which might both address its own interests and be seen by the DES to be supporting the original intentions of HMI.[13]

A conference was consequently organised by the BFI Education Department with the University of London Institute of Education in November 1983 which attracted 300 delegates, an attendance at a 'media education' event on a scale only previously recorded at the NUT Conference in 1960.[14] There was, as Lusted subsequently pointed out, a very significant difference between the concerns of the two events.

> Where the Reports differ is in their focus. For the NUT report, the issue was the *effects* of television, a very familiar theme. For the DES report, the focus is on the

'images of adult life' on television. That shift from a set of worries about television's effects to a set of questions about television's representation of the social world is central and absolutely crucial. It must be held to as a direction for the future of schooling about television.[15]

Indeed Lusted views the outcome represented by the conference and the book *TV and Schooling* which resulted from it as a 'negotiated settlement with the Government and the DES'.[16] A further distinction between the two conferences may be observed. In 1960 BFI Education had depended on SEFT to shape the practitioner response in the debate; in 1983 SEFT had no presence at the conference or in the subsequent publication, where the credit is shared between the BFI Education Department and the Department of English and Media Studies at the Institute of Education. Writing in *TV and Schooling* Learmonth gives a cautious go-ahead to the development of media education rather than to the specific subject of media studies.

Specialist courses in media studies represent one approach, but all teachers should be involved in examining and discussing television programmes with young people.[17]

Simpson understood the importance of Learmonth's position as a sympathetic HMI and would subsequently invite him to join the new BFI Education Committee when it was formed in the following year.

SEFT loses its Roots

SEFT had survived the initial impact of Smith's directorship and his investigation of its roles. In early 1982 when BFI Governors were approving the 1982/83 budget allocations they were reassured that

SEFT has totally reorganised its management structure very much in line with the Institute's recommendations. A new editor, who combines commercial experience and flair with a solid educational background, has been appointed for SEFT's new publication, and an education officer, in whom Institute officers have confidence, will take up his post in the new financial year.[18]

The Society perhaps assumed that Smith's intervention had been a one-off event at the start of his directorship. Subsequently, although not bringing the issue to Governors' attention, Smith and Colin McArthur continued to monitor and pressure SEFT Following the news of Stoneman's resignation and his imminent departure, McArthur, by this time Head of Film Availability Services and responsible for overseeing the grant to SEFT wrote to the Society with some precisely focused questions.

1. What is the present role of the society and does it need redefining?
2. What are its membership catchment and recruitment policies?
3. How effective are its structures, particularly the relationship between full-time officers and Executive?
4. What is the relationship between *Screen* and the work of SEFT as a whole?
5. What is the relationship between the work of SEFT and that of the BFI Education Department?[19]

According to the report of SEFT's Chairperson the opportunity for SEFT's response was first subsumed into informal meetings set up by the BFI with 'a range of people in the educational constituency both in and around SEFT' before Executive Committee representatives were able to meet directly with the BFI.[20] Director Smith then wrote to SEFT making it clear the kind of SEFT that he wanted.

The BFI would like to support an organisation which seeks to represent the interests and aspirations of everyone involved in film and TV education, (taking the term to refer to the education system as well as education in the widest sense) and would expect such an organisation to have a significant visibility in the media culture and to lobby appropriate bodies in the interests of its cause and of its members. Within this very broad statement the precise questions in Colin's letter to you of 15 June need to be addressed.[21]

A 3000 word response was prepared by SEFT to which, after consideration, Smith replied at the end of October.[22] His fundamental point was that SEFT was receiving a large sum of public money from the BFI at a time when there were many other potential recipients for such funding. SEFT needed to have a distinctive voice which would substantiate its claim to be a recipient of BFI money. Smith was prepared to guarantee SEFT's funding only until the end of September 1984, pending the Society's transformation into a version of SEFT that met BFI criteria of acceptability.

Today we feel we should be supporting an organisation with an authoritative voice on matters of media education, and with a view which is sought by Government and others whenever this range of questions is at issue. As you know, we want SEFT to be an organisation which seeks to bring together <u>all</u> of the formal and informal media education constituencies. It ought also to act as a source of pressure on official bodies to help improve the standards and availability of media education.[23]

Members were informed of the situation in the Chairperson's Report of November 1983 which encouraged them to attend the AGM in the following month.[24] At that AGM various pieces of BFI documentation were discussed and a tactically appropriate motion was passed unanimously.

This AGM therefore recognises that the following points are central to their negotiations with the BFI:

1. that while more stress should be laid on campaigning in the coming period, the Society's educational and campaigning functions cannot be separated. It therefore seeks adequate resources to employ staff with responsibilities and expertise across both areas, to implement the Society's policies in this field.
2. that the work of *Screen* and the Society's other publishing and distribution ventures represent a key area of SEFT's education work. While accepting the desirability of an enlarged campaigning policy, the AGM reaffirms SEFT's commitment to the current policies and concerns of *Screen*.[25]

Two further motions were passed which committed the Executive Committee to 'a more campaigning role' and the Society to a Special General Meeting in 1984.[26] In practice the Executive would need to act before any SGM could be organised. A letter went to the BFI in early February 1984 outlining a confident five-year plan whereby SEFT would develop into 'a campaigning and educational organisation with a much wider range of influences and connections'.[27] SEFT was telling Smith what he needed to hear – probably in order to guarantee continuation of the BFI grant to SEFT beyond September 1984.

SEFT had always operated successfully for three decades by intervening selectively in appropriate arenas. For much of that time it had been comfortable with its identity as a subject association for teachers who were engaging with aspects of film/media education. It had never offered to be all things to all men. Now it was dangerously close to doing just that.

Our aim will be to heighten public awareness of media education in all its senses and of SEFT as an appropriate agency through which to secure that objective. This will be facilitated by substantial campaigning activities in regard to media education at all levels, in partnership with like-minded organisations. These activities will be organised by an Officer/Officers with a wide-ranging familiarity with the personnel and concerns of such organisations, from NATFHE to IPPA, from IDEA to the DES. Their work will stretch from journalistic interventions in the UK educational media and general press to organising special discussion in events and a regular national media education conference, to direct contact with relevant teachers and academics, civil servants, councillors and MPs, art officers and film and television producers and exhibitors.[28]

This response was so wide-ranging and inclusive that it may have been composed with assistance from someone in the BFI who was sympathetic to SEFT. It worked to the extent that by the time of the Special General Meeting, BFI had agreed to maintain the grant for the full financial year 1984/85. A significant decision had by this time already been taken in that Sean Cubitt had been appointed National Organiser, a completely new role within SEFT.

Members at the SGM had to vote in some technical changes introducing a rota-style election to membership of the Executive Committee so that half would retire in alternate years. It did this at the same time as redefining the Executive Committee's role as one of overseeing the *Screen* Board and Education Board. It remains unclear why an Education Board was needed when it left the Executive Committee without a proper role.[29] SEFT was also taking on a new constituency by becoming the umbrella organisation for the Television Users' Group with its National Organiser playing a central role. The decision was also taken to organise an annual National Media Education Conference, the first being scheduled for 1985. Anticipating 'the advent of cable, direct broadcasting by satellite and interactive information technologies' there was on the agenda a policy motion on the 'New Technologies' notionally addressed to Parliament but also effectively flagging up the kind of issues that would dominate media developments in the late 20th century. The motion was withdrawn because of lack of time and referred to the next AGM.[30]

The final motion to be debated was proposed by David Lusted and Barry Curtis:

> That a strategy be developed re-establishing SEFT as a professional body representing the interests of teachers, film and media studies.[31]

Curtis recalls that the aim of the motion was to encourage teachers to 'rally round' and support SEFT. If teachers might be encouraged once again to become an important part of SEFT, this would strengthen SEFT's remit if it came increasingly under threat as Government cuts impacted on the BFI. Despite the Society's new-found enthusiasm for taking on additional tasks, this motion, unlike those taken earlier in the meeting, was not passed unanimously. Instead it was amended:

> That the SEFT Education Board develop strategies to heighten SEFT's campaigning role to represent the interests of teachers of film, television and media studies.

Shedding its origins as a teachers' organisation had been a characteristic of SEFT for some time, as demonstrated in the previous chapter. Here the Executive is delegating to its Education Board the task of developing strategies to accommodate teachers who presumably should take comfort from the fact that SEFT's campaigning will apparently be 'heightened' by their inclusion.

The resistance to endorsing SEFT as a subject organisation for teachers was all the more extraordinary in that the Society was already engaged in setting up the beginnings of a national network of media teachers. The first practical step in establishing this network had begun at the BFI Easter School for teachers in April 1984, attended by SEFT's new National Organiser. By the time of the Chairperson's Report in December

1984 5000 copies of the first issue of *Initiatives*, an eight page newsletter, had appeared, produced by members of the Education Board.[32] These copies had been distributed free to schools in addition to those going to SEFT members. They carried details of the first regional organisations to be included in what was to become the Media Education Initiative.

A Resurgent BFI Education Department

Philip Simpson would play a much more interventionist role in relation to SEFT than had his predecessors in the 1970s. Simpson had been an active and appreciative SEFT member during the 1970s and had been involved with the North East Film and Television Teachers' Association, one of the successful regional groups connected to SEFT. He had joined the BFI as Adult Education Officer in 1979 and at that point had become more aware of the disparity in prestige between SEFT and what was then still called the Educational Advisory Service. There were, he felt, very talented people working in BFI Education who should have been getting recognition for what they were doing and should have been able to make a greater contribution to media education.[33] Once he became Head of Department, he determined to raise the status of his department. He understood that inevitably this would impinge on SEFT. He also a found himself with roles to play in SEFT, first taking a place on the Editorial Board of the new *Screen incorporating Screen Education* and then being invited to full membership of the SEFT Executive. It was important to him that he would be seen to play no direct part in the SEFT funding process, which was handled elsewhere within the BFI. McArthur, heading Film Availability Services, was a long time champion of SEFT and his Department controlled the process by which the SEFT grant was channelled. McArthur would take early retirement in 1985.

Simpson was on the 1981 selection panel for the post of Editor of *Screen* to which Mandy Merck was appointed. He recalls at the time that he thought – in sequence – 'but she's a journalist' and then 'good'.[34] The importance of Merck's appointment for Simpson was that it helped to begin the process of differentiating SEFT from BFI Education. Merck as Editor would have a clear agenda for *Screen*. Simpson would develop an agenda for his department. The problem that would ultimately destroy SEFT (but not *Screen*) was that the Society failed to have a clear identity for itself.

As Head of Department, Simpson began a series of changes about which he had to convince BFI Governors. In the 1970s the BFI had pump-primed film lectureships in various universities; some of these had proved to be very successful and had been maintained by the host universities. Simpson now argued for a similar funding model to be offered to local education authorities to support advisory teacher posts for media education.[35] He additionally argued for the funding of the film teaching posts in the universities to be redirected to pay for lectureships specifically in teacher education institutions. There had been only one such appointment during the first decade of the programme: Phillip Drummond's post at the University of London Institute of Education. In the event a compromise of the two proposals was achieved. The university funding was diverted to fund advisory teacher posts.[36] Simpson also realised that the BFI needed to move strategically as media education was gaining wider recognition.

> Bringing the need for urgent action about media education to the DES's attention is, perhaps, the most difficult strategic task but one which only the Institute can undertake.[37]

When his proposals were discussed by the Governors there was, for Simpson perhaps, a surprising, but pleasing, outcome in that the Governors went on record as expressing that they 'were deeply interested in the subject of media education in schools and colleges'.[38] In practice this resulted in the setting up of a Governors' working party 'to consider alternative strategies for developing media education'. Two governors who were prepared to be involved were Baroness Birk and Christopher Frayling.[39]

With the discontinuance of the funding of university film lecturer posts, the BFI's Grants to Higher Education Committee had been replaced by an Education Committee which was chaired by Trevor Vibert, a BFI Governor. This committee would now be responsible for appointing to the new BFI funded teacher adviser posts.[40] When it first met in November 1984, its membership included several with a SEFT connection, including the new Chairperson, Tana Wollen. A significant recruit to the Committee was HMI James Learmonth who was able to report that, following the reception given to *Popular TV and Schoolchildren*, HMI were setting up 'a new network of contacts'.[41] With the reformed Education Committee and Governors' Working Party, Simpson had ensured a status for his department that Education in the BFI had lacked for years.

Screen's New Identity

When Mandy Merck became Editor of the new *Screen* in 1982, her position was very different from that of editors of previous SEFT publications. She was a full-time editor. Her predecessors had either been part-time or had been full-time but with additional SEFT duties. Alvarado and Donald had been Education Officers first and editors of *Screen Education* second, and thus also part-time editors. Since so much of SEFT's resources were to be directed to *Screen*, now that it incorporated *Screen Education* having a full time editor was a necessary consequence.

At the time of the planning for the new journal, a less practicable judgment had been made: *Screen* would be published bi-monthly. If *Screen* were to accommodate some of the writing that had appeared in *Screen Education*, then having two extra issues a year offered a compensating mechanism. However SEFT had a history of never quite managing successfully to produce a bi-monthly journal. In the 1960s *Screen Education* as edited by Ray Wills had apparently maintained a bi-monthly regime throughout the decade. The reality was however than it was bi-monthly only from January to October. The November/December gap had been filled by the annual *Screen Education Yearbook* which had been edited quite separately. When *Screen* started in 1969 it was planned as a bi-monthly publication. However the practicalities of the regime meant that in each year only five issues were actually produced, with one being a double issue. The need for editors, writers and production staff to have a break at some point in the summer defeated the bi-monthly routine and Sam Rohdie from the start of his Editorship in 1971 made *Screen* a quarterly journal. Merck maintained the bi-monthly regime for five years from 1982 to 1986, but always had to resort to a combined issue around the middle of each year to cope with the exigencies of staff having time off. In 1987 *Screen* would once again become a quarterly at Merck's prompting.[42]

The Editorial Board for the new *Screen* was different. Brewster, MacCabe, Willemen and Nowell-Smith had departed from the journal's board with the last Nash edited *Screen* appearing at the end of 1981, though Brewster remained active within SEFT. The new Editorial Board had 16 members, half of whom were inherited from the previous journal.[43] By the start of 1984, the board had 18 members of whom 12 had not been there the year before.[44] Being on the Editorial Board involved members in editing specific issues of *Screen* and the Board itself controlled the recruitment of new members. There was no longer any input from the SEFT Executive Committee. Merck recalls that invitations to join the Board were usually set in train when the Board wanted to develop an issue of *Screen* on topics where existing Board members were lacking in expertise.[45] As a result the style of Board meetings was very different from the days of the set piece confrontations that Willemen recalled. Ginette Vincendeau, who was invited to join the Board in 1986 after *Screen* had published her article on Film History, remembers *Screen* meetings as very positive occasions.[46]

Given her background as a journalist, Merck saw the need for *Screen* to attempt to operate more commercially. She needed a detailed breakdown of *Screen's* circulation. Figures for 1984 revealed that of the 1245 members who subscribed to the journal almost half were categorised as being based overseas. 259 of these were higher or further education institutions as compared to 189 such institutions in the United Kingdom.[47] Merck wanted to sell copies in stores by making the content sufficiently attractive to speculative buyers. Since some of *Screen's* biggest subscribers were already in the USA, Merck wanted to be able to sell additional copies in that huge potential market. She set about finding distributors both in the States and in Australia.[48] There were inevitably practical problems in such an exercise which she encountered. But these aside, she was concerned about the presentation of the product itself. Issues would sell best if they consisted of articles on related areas and had an appropriate cover designed according to the content of each issue.[49] This was a break with the cover design that had been based on variations on a single geometric pattern established in the Nash editorship. However the cover design of those early 1980s *Screens* was still to be found miniaturised on the back cover of the new journal. There were two particular constraints which the content could have on the success of such casual sales. An issue that had a particularly British focus was inevitably going to have only a parochial reception. An issue that dealt with media education might prove even less appealing.[50]

Merck has acknowledged that she was resistant to publishing articles about pedagogy because she found that they generally lacked the rigour that was being demonstrated elsewhere in the journal.[51] The nub of the problem was that *Screen* had incorporated *Screen Education*. SEFT could have reversed the priorities and kept *Screen Education*, but *Screen* was the journal that had recruited the substantial American University library subscriptions. *Screen* was still a vanguard publication, introducing major debates around race and gender and becoming more enterprising in the range of photographic work that it was publishing, notably introducing the work of Cindy Sherman.[52] As such it was not an obviously appropriate environment for the incorporation of media education material.

Screen Education Incorporated

There were some occasional education related pieces published in *Screen* as when the proposals of the SEFT working party on the debates around the 16 plus examinations were printed under the title 'What every 16-year-old should know about the mass media'.[53] But only two issues of *Screen* in this period were essentially devoted to screen education – in May/June 1983 and September/October 1986. Each had a substantial editorial contribution from BFI Education, Philip Simpson in 1983 and David Lusted in 1986.[54]

The Editorial to the first of these issues 'Teaching Film and TV' opens disarmingly:

> When *Screen* incorporated *Screen Education* last year a journal was created whose field of reference was impossibly large and complex.[55]

The Editorial of the first issue exactly a year before had not been so frank. The hope then had been to 'preserve the continuity of SEFT's two previous publications' and 'to add new readers and concerns to those already addressed by these publications'.[56] By Spring 1983, the Editors felt it necessary to explain why they had an impossible task,

> A journal of advanced screen theory with an international readership and a legacy of debate that sometimes resembles an incubus was supposed to assimilate a journal of advanced educational theory, in relation to popular culture, which had developed a national reputation and a range of regular contributors many of whom neither knew nor cared much about *Screen* and its history. Outside pressures had determined the incorporation, and only a left pluralism of cultural theory and practice, legitimately and reciprocally representing the membership of SEFT and the readership of the journals, and a certain optimism of the will provided the bases upon which the new magazine could be founded.[57]

Nevertheless – with references to the scope of *Screen Education* which had addressed teachers without patronising them – the Editors are determined for this issue to resume the *Screen Education* project and promise that it will be 'sustained regularly over the next year'.[58] Subsequent issues did carry at least one article that addressed this brief, but it might only occupy a very few pages.

For the 'Teaching Film and TV' issue, the legacy of *Screen Education* is pervasive. The most substantial piece by Alvarado and Ferguson examines the workings of the school curriculum, which the authors propose, is the most important contributory factor in the education system's functioning as an 'agency of social control'.[59] Acknowledging the influence of Foucault, they take issue with Michael Young's concept of knowledge. If Young is stating that teachers teach in such a way as to 'perpetuate a class stratified social formation' and that by their teaching differently, there might be different outcomes for students, then the authors seek to present the teacher, too, as essentially compromised.[60]

> What they teach however is not knowledge. It is *preferred discourses*. These are not necessarily chosen by the teacher, nor must the teacher necessarily be aware of what is taking place.
> The teacher's task should be to *de*naturalise various discourses rather than to endlessly invalidate them by a complicity with the unspoken norms of a powerful ideological state apparatus.[61]

The second *Screen* to have a media education emphasis was produced in autumn 1986 and styled 'Pedagogy -- Critical Accounts of Media Education'.[62] Pressure had probably come from the SEFT Executive for *Screen* to produce such an issue. The existence of this one-off serves to demonstrate why there needed to be more of the same. A long introduction by Lusted, 'Why Pedagogy', provides *Screen*'s readers with a context.[63] This contexting was necessitated by the introduction of media education matters into a journal which existed to address other priorities. The infrequency of issues of *Screen* devoted to media education inevitably meant that the content would be reactive rather than proactive. Since by the mid-1980s, there had been considerable expansion in the provision of media education, there was much to react to. Inevitably this meant that a substantial part of the issue was taken up with reviews of the important publications and materials which were appearing. Gillian Swanson reviewed *The Power of the Image: Essays on Representation and Sexuality*; Cary Bazalgette examined *Making Sense of the Media*; Simon Watney considered *The New Art History*; David Buckingham responded to *Teaching the Media* and Len Masterman wrote a reply to Buckingham's criticism of his book.[64]

The range and variety of these review items is striking, yet all could legitimately be included. It is perhaps more significant for the purposes of this investigation to consider the reviewers and the positions that they held in relation to media education: Bazalgette (like Lusted) was in the BFI Education Department; Swanson and Watney taught in higher education; while Buckingham and Masterman were based in institutes of education. It was perhaps inevitable that as media education became more professionalised, the classroom teacher would be a less frequent participant in the debate. The debate between Buckingham and Masterman, where each was presenting a fundamentally different approach to media education, was curtailed in a single issue. Buckingham was not expecting Masterman's necessarily condensed response to be printed in the same issue as his review article. *Screen* in an earlier manifestation had seen the Wood/Lovell debate conducted in substantial articles over several issues. Given *Screen*'s priorities by the mid 1980s, such a commitment of space and continuity was no longer possible. There was no appropriate UK arena in which this important debate might be accommodated. In the decades that followed both Masterman and Buckingham have become leading international representatives of UK media education.[65] Their respective positions have been repeatedly inferred, but the debate between them has not been resumed.

> Buckingham, more than Masterman, operates within the cultural studies paradigm wherein the idea of "interpretative communities" and the pleasures attending media experience are privileged and where the alleged negative and dangerous "effects" of media – especially on children and youth – that so consume the debate over media in the United States are either ignored or actively eschewed. The effects question is not even a question for Buckingham – indeed, it is the "wrong" question. Masterman (1997), too, extolls the pleasures that attend media use – as one might hope any media teacher would – but unlike Buckingham, he also still thinks in Frankfurt school terms wherein commercialism of the media presents particular problems.[66]

The National Organiser

When the post of SEFT's National Organiser was advertised in 1984, the wording of the advertisement and the job description it contained were very different from what had been expected of any previous applicant for a job with the Society. Whereas the previous comparable post holder had been styled as Education Officer, the National Organiser's proposed relationship with education was to be more distant. The experience which applicants might bring was described thus

> Candidates should have a good knowledge of current debates in Film and Television theory. S/he should have experience of Film and Television education in both the institutional and informal sectors. If this is not the case, the officer must be prepared to familiarise her/himself with the educational field quickly.[67]

Presumably drafted as a compromise in committee, the expectation that anyone might 'familiarise her/himself with the educational field quickly' seems both to demonstrate the inexperience in recruiting staff of the members of the SEFT Executive at this stage and a dismissive attitude towards the complexities of the 'educational field'.

Under pressure from BFI it seems that the SEFT Executive felt obliged to demonstrate its difference from the BFI by distancing itself from education as formally delivered in schools and universities.

> We are now embarking on new directions and wish SEFT to develop into a campaigning and educational organisation with a much wider range of influences.[68]

The first of the nine major responsibilities listed for which the National Organiser would be responsible was 'the smooth functioning of the Society, with the exception of *Screen*, which is the responsibility of its Editor'.[69] Thus while giving the Editor of *Screen* a clearly defined and limited responsibility, the other full-time professional officer employed by SEFT was expected to manage a huge portfolio of tasks in which was identified only one education related activity: 'to initiate preparations for a national education conference to be held early in 1985'. Much more specific were playing 'a central role in the formation and continuance of a Television Users Group' and 'planning for effective campaigns in 1985–1986 around Copyright, Censorship and New Media'.[70]

While the Editor of *Screen* had an Editorial Board to support her work and a part-time Deputy Editor to assist, the National Organiser was expected still to report to an Education Board, though Education was barely mentioned in his brief. The Board was responsible for producing *Initiatives*, so inevitably some very specific tasks around the production of that magazine – not mentioned in the job description – fell to the Organiser as Sean Cubitt has confirmed.[71] The challenges set for the National Organiser may be compared with the tasks envisaged for an Education Officer in 1980 when the Executive Committee first planned to have one journal with an editor and a full-time Education Officer, who would be responsible 'for the development and organisation of a full programme of educational events, for promoting the educational aspects of SEFT's work as well as its work in the regions and for generally encouraging an active membership.[72]

An insight into the compromised position of SEFT following the National Organiser appointment may be deduced from the record of the meeting of the BFI Regional Consultative Committee in October 1984, at which a report on SEFT was given by Mike Clarke, a member of the SEFT Executive Committee.

> Sean's appointment was an attempt to reconcile the need for an educational worker, a political worker and an administrator.[73]

Clarke also mentions that SEFT now had a 'renewed thrust towards political activity' and that as a result of the 'reorientation of emphases' SEFT was having problems 'in the projection of a recognisable image'. As a result of this 'there was still a tendency for people to mis-recognise it in its former guise' – presumably as a teachers' organisation. His comments must have been considered appropriate by BFI Director Smith, also at the meeting, who added

> ...that he hoped that the inception of the TV Users Group would prove an influential force, for it had the potential to provide motivation as great as the Whitehouse movement.[74]

In the event the TV Users Group did not survive long as a SEFT supported independent body. In 1986 it was amalgamated with the Campaign for Press and Broadcasting Freedom.[75] By late 1987 there was an attempt to redefine the National Organiser post when a possible job share arrangement was being discussed.[76] The discussion document demonstrates that there clearly had been an examination of what the post holder was actually doing. The largest single item, taking a quarter of his time, was the production of *Initiatives*. Lobbying now accounted only for 5% of the time. But as Cubitt remembers telephone callers with educational inquiries were a constant but unscheduled impingement on the working day.[77]

The Bradford Conference
The original job description for the National Organiser had given prominence to the organisation of an annual conference. In July 1985 SEFT (supported by additional BFI funding) organised a National Media Education Conference in Bradford. Presented as the successor to the Goldsmiths Conference of 1981, it was a large scale attempt by SEFT and its National Organiser to place the Society once again centre stage at a major media education event. This residential conference was very well attended and its programme was deliberately designed to attract practitioners from Primary, Secondary, Further and Continuing Education, with scope for participants to be involved in sector specific workshops.[78]

Once again a key speaker was David Lusted who produced a 'Timetable of Landmarks' in his account of how Media Studies and Media Education related to each other.[79] Taking the theoretical description of cultural evolution proposed by Raymond Williams, Lusted grouped together the decades from the 1950s to the 1970s and he depicted their legacy as representing the residual aspects of approaches to teaching the media. The 1980s were inevitably the dominant period and Lusted projected the 1990s as a radically different emergent phase. The significant differentiation of the 1980s from previous decades was the theme of the conference, as those working in education had come to recognise the pervasive influence of radical conservative thinking. Lusted allowed his fanciful projection of the emergent phase into the 1990s to foresee a very different regime where the presentation of knowledge would be transformed. Cultural Studies would replace the traditional humanities and Language and Representation would extend across the curriculum. He offered no explanation of how this metamorphosis might be achieved.

Lusted's Timetable, in differentiating the 'dominant' 1980s, depicts a decade where the entries under each of his chosen headings (Knowledge, Curriculum, Pedagogy, Education and Culture) demonstrate a distinctive break with earlier decades. The curriculum is dominated by 'new vocationalism', pedagogy by 'instrumentalism', education by the appearance of TVEI and culture is now the territory of 'radical conservatism'. It was probably inevitable, given the break with consensus that Thatcherism represented, that the conference should need to be more politically engaged. A subsequent speaker, David Buckingham, framed his paper as a response to a speech by Secretary of State,

Joseph. Addressing 'The Technology of Control' Buckingham is wide-ranging in summarising the kinds of changes that he predicts are imminent.

> The demise of the Schools Council may thus be seen as further evidence, firstly of a shift from a concern about *learning* to a concern about *testing*, and secondly of a shift towards greater central control.[80]

Buckingham depicts the possible implications for media education by referring to the DES publication *Curriculum Matters: English 5 – 16*. He identifies that document's emphasis on the use of objectives and criteria as being at the core of teaching. He argues that their deployment is misleading since there is an assumption that terms such as these are neutral and non-contentious. Buckingham therefore demonstrates the questionability of these assumptions and argues that there must be a challenge to them. In particular his argument is that a version *Media Education 5 – 16* which replicated the objective model of *English 5 – 16* would counter all that teachers of media were seeking to achieve.[81]

Other conference speakers, including Valerie Walkerdine and Tim Blanchard, also mounted political challenges.[82] It was therefore unsurprising that at the conclusion of the conference, many resolutions were passed. It must be noted that the conference had no authority to pass any motions which extended in remit beyond the conference itself, but nevertheless there was a succession of motions proposed by the various working groups in the closing session. These, in theory at least, instructed SEFT to take action.[83] There was recognition that these 'instructions', should the SEFT Executive agree to them, would require additional funding and SEFT was accordingly urged to lobby the BFI for more money to carry out the tasks.[84] One motion however had only five supporters:

> To carry out even a small proportion of the recommendations made by Conference, SEFT needs to generate new income.
>
> Conference urges SEFT to establish a paid membership scheme to an organisation equivalent to Scotland's AMES, an equal partner to TUG, with higher subscription fees to *Initiatives* to meet that need.[85]

This was evidently an emergency motion which may help to account for its curious wording. Nevertheless it has to be noted that the enthusiasm of conference participants for SEFT to act, was greatly diminished at the prospect of their having to pay more to support the Society. But the motion demonstrates several confusions in its final three lines. AMES (Association for Media Education in Scotland) had been founded in the early 1980s and was what SEFT had for decades by then already been. The implications of this motion are that the status of those who paid subscriptions to SEFT was perceived as either subscribers to *Screen* or to *Initiatives*. No one, it seemed, believed that s/he had any longer the status of being a SEFT member. The Society was beginning to be viewed as something other – a body which presided over activities but had no part in them. The style of reference to the TV Users' Group seems to suggest that it had become a dominant part of the SEFT organisation and that teachers now apparently needed to have their status raised to that of the TV Group.

The editorial in the November 1985 issue of *Initiatives* attempts to address the confusions that had emerged at the conference and therefore includes the following account of 'what SEFT's roles actually are'.

> First and most relevant to *Initiatives'* subscribers, SEFT organises and assists those on the ideological chalk face of education, through the work of the education board and the MEI groups. Secondly it lobbies, not only for media education but on wider media issues through the Television Users' Group and through SEFT's well established relationship with the independent sector. Moreover, SEFT has organised a wide range of events concerning the media which are 'educational' but not necessarily related to formal education. Finally there is publishing and distribution; this includes a firmly established and well-known contribution that *Screen* makes to film and television theory.[86]

Whether the inclusion of this vague paragraph convinced the readership is debatable. Nevertheless, in an attempt to tidy up some of SEFT's arrangements, *Initiatives* subscribers are urged to come to the February 1986 AGM where it was intended to give them full SEFT membership.

Initiatives and the Regions

To a very limited extent the gap left by *Screen Education* had been filled by *Initiatives* which was produced termly from early 1985. *Initiatives* was intended to provide a link between the various Media Education Initiatives associations. These were either new groups being directly set up as such or associations developed around existing groups which were prepared to be identified with the MEI network. The total number of these groups increased rapidly, peaking at 36 in Spring 1987.[87] An arrangement that was seen as offering a mechanism for these individual groups to become involved with SEFT was that each issue of *Initiatives* would be produced by a different MEI group. The first to be outsourced was Number 3 in February 1986, produced by North West England MEI. Number 4, perhaps because it contained articles anticipating the 1986 SEFT Conference to be held in Birmingham, was produced in London by the Education Board. Subsequently there were to be only four issues between Autumn 1986 and Spring 1988, each was produced regionally, but the difficulties of delegated regional production meant that 1987 had only two issues of *Initiatives*.[88] An account of the background problems is to be found in the National Organiser's confidential report to the Education Board.[89]

Though the issues of *Initiatives* provide a useful source of information about SEFT's final years, it is an incomplete history in part because of the spasmodic production schedule. It had also become essentially a house journal and assumptions were made that its readers would know the references, so that for example in *Initiatives 6*, members of West London SEFT (who were editing the issue) each submitted a separate report on the 'TRIST/SEFT Conference' without making any attempt to identify where and when the conference had been held and under whose auspices.[90] Each issue provides a snapshot of what were the priorities and preoccupations of the SEFT Committee and the Education Board. Reviewed in sequence, there seems to have been little continuity of enterprise between what is reported in successive issues. The procedures of delegated editorship that dominated the production of the issues would have militated against continuity But it seems also that the number and range of activities with which SEFT sought to engage meant that the Society presided over an unwieldy agenda of well intentioned commitments. Early in 1986 the Society published what would be the last of its occasional pamphlets specifically for teachers: *Media Studies and the GCSE*.[91] The text was based around the responses SEFT had received from the nineteen English and Welsh examining boards then preparing, within five Examining Groups, for the introduction of the new GCSE examination. However only one actual Media Studies syllabus had become available by the time the pamphlet was published. SEFT saw that for Media Studies as an examination subject, GCSE would provide a flexible framework; what it would not do was to 'provide some form of Media Education for all'.[92]

Following the Bradford 1985 Conference, there were other annual conferences, but on a smaller scale. In 1986 a one-day event 'Watching Media Learning' was held at BBC Pebble Mill, Birmingham. Billed as the SEFT/HMI conference the intention was

> …to bring together parents, teachers and broadcasters to establish an agenda for media education for the age range 3 to 19.
>
> The brave new addition of pre-school education, and the long neglected opportunity to address parents makes this conference markedly different to other media education conferences.[93]

The inclusion of parents as a constituency interested in media first gained recognition at a conference in 1980, the International Year of the Child, which was followed by a related publication *Television and the Family* later in the year.[94] Then there had been *Popular TV and Schoolchildren* in 1983. Simpson at the BFI believed that his department's work on media education should include this area and as part of that project he edited *Parents Talking Television* in 1986.[95]

Initiatives 5 carried accounts of the Pebble Mill Sector Workshops. Like many conference workshop accounts, their particular emphases and partiality may be ascribed to those who became the reporters for the groups. The publication of these rather disorganised accounts was justified in the hope they might provide a stimulus for readers

...with the aim of consulting the *Initiatives* readership on the development of a document on Media Education 3 – 19.[96]

No trace of the production of such a document has been found. Tana Wollen was to produce a 'skeleton' document to be circulated for comment. It would seem that her leaving SEFT for a post at the BFI in Autumn 1986 probably delayed the project, which was disrupted subsequently by the constraints of the National Curriculum proposals.[97]

In April 1987 SEFT was involved with BFI in organising a major conference on 'Teaching Alternative Media'. Since SEFT had convinced the BFI in 1984 to continue funding the Society on the basis of what was to be its wider campaigning role, SEFT was centrally involved in this conference which had been set up to address what might be the gaps left in London's moving image culture by the abolition of the Greater London Council.[98] Certainly the conference agenda was different from that of previous SEFT events. The conference dossier contained

> ...a variety of papers on educational policy and practice, exhibition, distribution and production from the smallest video community project to the big plans for inter-sector work. The whole of Saturday will be given over to one long workshop, addressing such issues as word processors, using tapes in the classroom, feminist pedagogies, organising events, student placements, artists in residence, training, and the future for our students.[99]

The emphasis in the conference was planned as

> ...a working conference in which delegates from the two sectors of Education and Independent Production/Exhibition/Distribution can meet and share experiences; debate issues; and hopefully forge alliances[100]

To prepare themselves for the event those attending were sent a conference dossier of Briefing Papers, some seventeen in all with a suggested running order in which they might productively be read.[101]

The next issue, Summer 1987, *Initiatives* failed to appear and by the time of the Autumn issue, it was perhaps considered too late to publish reports of the April Conference. Organisational details of the event are to be found in a report from the National Organiser which records that 142 people attended.[102] Two reports written by conference delegates for their own organisations do survive.[103] Both comment on the novelty of the event in bringing together teachers and independent production personnel, emphasized by the organizers construction in advance of 'mixed' groups to address issues on the first day. The reporters suggest that the success of these experimental groupings depended on the effectiveness and preparation of individual group leaders. On the second day self-select groups tended to have topics that appealed differentially to the two categories of participants. The conference seems to have begun with the assumption that the coming together of the teachers and the producers would be mutually beneficial and to have ended with that thesis still being asserted rather than proven.

Later in 1987 there was the annual SEFT conference, following the previous events in Bradford and Birmingham. This was held in September and based at Liverpool Polytechnic to which the National Organiser refers in his regular report where he states simply that the event made a loss of some £260.[104] When the conference was discussed at the October Executive meeting, many criticisms were noted. Long-standing issues were demanding to be addressed.

> It was agreed that part of the problem lies with the job description of the National Organiser's post. If the priorities are fund-raising and new premises, little time is left for *Initiatives* and conference organisation, to say nothing of the continuing pressure of individual requests for advice and information.[105]

A further critical account of the event is to be found in a report for the North West Regional Arts Association, written by one of its Assistant Directors who had attended the conference.[106] His presence at the event was a result of his organization having been a principal funder of this SEFT conference. Unlike previous SEFT conferences held in the regions but planned from London, the Liverpool event had been planned in the North West.[107] The ambition displayed in order to get regional funding had not been understated, as the claimed purpose of the event had been

> ...to explore teaching and learning methods, resources and concepts suitable for teaching in media studies, and in particular to indicate areas of 'good practice' in the development of regional networks for media education involving local employers and workshops as well as more traditional partners in the education process such as local education authorities and regional arts associations.[108]

Perhaps, unsurprisingly, given this level of promotion, about a hundred delegates attended. However, the visitor from the funding body was disappointed, both with the choice of venue and with the organization of the day.

> The purpose of the Conference was vague and unfocused. Various issues were hinted at though not pursued and the major issue of the national core curriculum rather over-powered the discussion.
>
> It is suggested that future conferences should be much more specifically geared towards one particular area of interest and a target market identified accordingly.[109]

For an educational conference in 1987 to be preoccupied with the Conservative Government's proposals for a National Curriculum was only to be expected. It was the absence of any externally imposed curriculum that had facilitated the growth of film and media education in the UK and therefore the construction of such a national framework was likely to have the greatest impact on areas like media education. SEFT was in danger of neglecting its home territory in its ambition to extend its influence. There is a reference that 'an initial [SEFT] response has been delivered to the DES' in an Education Policy discussion paper, but no copy is currently extant.[110] The BFI Education Department however was adopting a much more directly interventionist approach and had since 1986 been involved in a BFI/DES National Working Party for primary education.

> With the passing of the 1988 Education Reform Act and preparations of the National Curriculum, the working party feels that it is essential to make a contribution to these developments and argue for a place for media education within the new curriculum.[111]

The Education Department followed this primary statement with a secondary media education statement in 1991.[112]

In July 1988 SEFT held that year's annual conference as a two-day event at the Cambridgeshire College of Arts and Technology, for which *Initiatives 9* was the 'conference edition'. Perhaps in an attempt to address the problems encountered at Liverpool, this conference was designed 'with the National Curriculum in mind' and like its predecessor it too was to be workshop based.[113] It received an extensive report in *The Times Educational Supplement*.[114] The reporter, Nick Baker, was inclined to be positive in his assessment of what he describes as a summer school which appears to have drawn heavily on the expertise of a local teachers' group, the Media Initiative for Norfolk Teachers (MINT). The event was on a large scale:

> The huge exhibition of media education work from across the country stood as further testimony to the diversity of the subject.[115]

Indeed it seems that the variety of enterprise encompassed by media education was the dominant message coming from this conference/summer school attended by 150 participants. Yet again the keynote address at a SEFT event came from David Lusted of the BFI Education Department. Lusted, like previous generations of SEFT activists, saw that media educators had to find imaginative ways of working within the constraints of the educational system.

> Lusted's conviction that media educators could exploit apparent contradictions between increased centralization and the liberality of GCSE and TVEI extension work was well received.[116]

It seems clear from Baker's description of the variety of the workshops on offer that SEFT was engaged in displaying the scale of the venture which might be possible through the Media Education Initiative movement. One must infer from Baker's account that much of the energy came from activists within the local groups for which *Initiatives* had been designed to cater. The reporter's reaction to the diversity on display was cautionary.

> However, the writing on the classroom wall, urging teachers to constantly examine how, where and why their activities might fit into the curriculum was the most important. The SEFT event showed how, given careful thought, media education's sword can be usefully double-edged. It can cross the primary and early secondary curriculum and be offered at GCSE and A level. However, its diversity of application (creative, evaluative, analytical, archival, recreational) means it will always be in danger of having identity problems. Clarity of intention is paramount.[117]

It is significant that, in researching what was clearly an important SEFT event, the source of evidence should be, not a SEFT publication but a newspaper cutting. There was an item scheduled for a report back from the conference on the agenda sent out for the Executive Committee meeting in August 1988.[118] However it is not clear whether this meeting took place. While it appeared that the National Organiser was delivering effectively on this aspect of his extensive brief, at the Executive Committee level there was a very different take on SEFT's situation which would cause routine activity like Executive Committee meetings and the publication of *Initiatives* to stall.[119] Shortly before the Cambridge weekend, a new Chair and Vice-Chair of the Society had written to the BFI with a very particular request.

Notes

1. James Learmonth 'Organisation and Aftermath' of *Popular TV and Schoolchildren* p 19 in David Lusted & Phillip Drummond (Eds) *TV and Schooling* London: BFI Education Department 1985
2. *Popular TV and Schoolchildren The report of a group of teachers* London: Department of Education and Science April 1983 – inside front cover
3. Philip Simpson in interview with the author 4 September 2006.
4. Learmonth op cit p 19
5. *Popular TV and Schoolchildren* p 1
6. Ibid p 27
7. Ibid
8. Learmonth op cit p 19
9. Ibid p 20
10. British Film Institute Special Collections 0/17/3 Box 104 Chairperson's Interim Report on the Period April 1 to November 14 1983
11. David Lusted 'Feeding the Panic and Breaking the Cycle – *Popular TV and Schoolchildren*' *Screen* Vol 24 No 6 November/December 1983

12. Ibid p 93
13. Editor's 'Preface' in Lusted & Drummond op cit p vii
14. Lusted & Drummond op cit p v
15. David Lusted 'A History of Suspicion: Educational Attitudes to Television' p 11 in Lusted and Drummond op cit
16. David Lusted in interview with the author 16 May 2005.
17. Learmonth op cit p 23
18. British Film Institute Governors' Minutes 26 January 1982 G500/4.82 Budget Allocation 1982/83 Appendix B p 4
19. British Film Institute Special Collections 0/17/3 Box 104 Society for Education in Film and Television AGM held on 10 December 1983 Chairperson's Interim Report April 1–November 14 1983 p 5
20. Ibid
21. Ibid
22. The author has been unable to trace a copy of the SEFT document.
23. Ibid p 6
24. Ibid p 7
25. *Screen* Archive University of Glasgow Box 11 1985 Society for Education in Film and Television Minutes of 32nd AGM held on 10 December 1983 Chairperson's Report p 1.
26. Ibid p 2
27. *Screen* Archive University of Glasgow Box 11 1984 Attachment to Agenda of Special General Meeting of Society for Education in Film and Television 23 June 1984 Condensed Version of letter sent to BFI 7/2/84 p 2
28. Ibid
29. *Screen* Archive University of Glasgow Box 11 1985 Minutes of the Special General Meeting of the Society for Education in Film and Television 23 June 1984 p 3
30. Ibid p 5
31. Ibid
32. *Screen* Archive University of Glasgow Box 11 1985 Minutes of the 33rd AGM of the Society for Education in Film and Television 9 February 1985 Chairperson's Interim Report April 1984–December 1984 p 9
33. Simpson interview op cit
34. Ibid
35. British Film Institute Governors' Minutes 18 October 1983 G516/4.83 Item 3.3
36. Simpson interview op cit
37. G516/4.83 Item 5.3
38. British Film Institute Governors' Minutes 18 December 1983
39. British Film Institute Governors' Minutes 29 November 1983
40. British Film Institute Governors' Minutes of the First Meeting of the BFI Education Committee 2 November 1984 Item 4
41. Ibid
42. Mandy Merck in interview with the author 16 June 2004.

43. *Screen* Vol 23 No1 May/June 1982 p 1
44. *Screen* Vol 25 No 1 January/February 1984 p 1
45. Mandy Merck in telephone interview with the author 25 April 2007.
46. Ginette Vincendeau in interview with the author 25 April 2006.
47. SEFT Archive Bretton Hall BH/ME/PL/133 (2) Membership Breakdown 17 May 1984
48. Mandy Merck in interview with the author 14 February 2006
49. Ibid
50. Ibid
51. Ibid
52. *Screen* Vol 24 No 6 November/December 1983 pp 102–116
53. SEFT working party 'What Every 16 Year Old Should Know about the Mass Media' *Screen* Vol 24 No 2 March/April 1983 pp 91–95
54. *Screen* Vol 24 No 3 May/June 1983 and Vol 27 No 5 September/October 1986
55. Editorial in *Screen* Vol 24 No 3 op cit p 2
56. Editorial in *Screen* Vol 23 No 1 May/June 1982 p 2
57. Editorial in *Screen* Vol 24 No 3 op cit p 2
58. Ibid
59. Manuel Alvarado, Bob Ferguson 'The Curriculum, Media Studies and Discursivity' *Screen* Vol 24 No 3 p 28
60. Ibid p 29
61. Ibid
62. *Screen* Vol 27 No 5 September/October 1986
63. David Lusted 'Introduction – Why Pedagogy?' *Screen* Vol 27 No 5 September/October 1986 pp 2–14
64. Gillian Swanson 'Rethinking Representation' pp 16–28; Cary Bazalgette 'Making Sense for Whom?' pp 30–36; Simon Watney 'Canvassing *Screen*' pp 50–53; David Buckingham 'Against Demystification – *Teaching the Media*' pp 80–95; Len Masterman 'A Reply to David Buckingham' pp 96–100
65. Robert W Kubey 'Why US media education lags behind the rest of the English speaking world' *Television and New Media* Vol 4 No 4 November 2003 p 362
66. Ibid
67. *Screen* Archive University of Glasgow Box 11 1984 SEFT Limited 'National Organiser – Job Description' March 1984 p 2
68. Ibid p 1
69. Ibid
70. Ibid p 2
71. Sean Cubitt in e-mail correspondence with the author 14 January 2006.
72. 'A Report to the Executive Committee From the Ad Hoc Sub Committee on the Future Structure of SEFT' September 1980 p 5
73. British Film Institute Governors' Minutes of Regional Consultative Committee 5 October 1984 Item 19.8

74. Ibid
75. *Initiatives* 5 Autumn 1986 p 24
76. *Screen* Archive University of Glasgow Box 11 1988 'Report of a Meeting to redefine the National Organiser's Job Description' 9 December 1987
77. Cubitt e-mail op cit
78. *Papers from the Bradford Media Education Conference* London: SEFT 1986
79. Ibid p 28
80. David Buckingham 'The Technology of Control' *Bradford Conference Papers* op cit p 50
81. Ibid pp 53–54
82. Valerie Walkerdine 'Progressive Pedagogies' pp 2–8; Tim Blanchard 'The Centralisation of Education' pp 32–41 in *Bradford Conference Papers* op cit
83. Op cit pp 135–141
84. Ibid p 142
85. Ibid
86. Editorial *Initiatives* No 2 November 1985 p 1
87. *Initiatives* 6 p 26
88. *Initiatives* 5 Avon Media Teachers; *Initiatives* 6 West London SEFT; *Initiatives* 7 Clwyd Media Studies Unit; *Initiatives* 8 North East Communications Teachers Association
89. *Screen* Archive University of Glasgow Box 11 1987 Sean Cubitt 'The Saga of Initiatives 7' Undated document
90. *Initiatives* 6 pp 3–5
91. Tim Blanchard *Media Studies and the GCSE* London: SEFT January 1986
92. Ibid – on final unnumbered page
93. *Initiatives* 6 p 22
94. Rick Rogers (Ed) *Television and the Family* London: University of London Extra Mural Department 1980
95. Philip Simpson (Ed) *Television and the Family* London: Comedia 1987
96. *Initiatives* 5 pp 19–21
97. *Screen* Archive University of Glasgow Box 5 1986 Sean Cubitt 'Pebble Mill Post Mortem' 12 June 1986
98. *Initiatives* 6 p 34
99. *Initiatives* 6 p 22
100. *Screen* Archive University of Glasgow Box 11 1986 Letter from Steve Brookes, Jim Cook, Sean Cubitt to Conference delegates Date as Postmark p 1
101. *Screen* Archive University of Glasgow Box 11 1986 Conference Briefing Papers: Checklist of authors and titles
102. *Screen* Archive University of Glasgow Box 11 1987 Sean Cubitt National Organiser's Report 15 April 1987
103. British Film Institute Special Collections Box 141 Steve McIntyre and Lindsey Hall are the authors.
104. *Screen* Archive University of Glasgow Box 5 1986 Sean Cubitt National Organiser's Report January 1988

105. *Screen* Archive University of Glasgow Box 11 1987 'Minutes of the Joint Meeting of the SEFT Executive and the Education Board' 17 October 1987

106. British Film Institute Special Collections Box 141 Duncan Fraser 'Society for Education in Film and Television Limited Conference' This was an internal report dated 17 February 1988, a copy of which was forwarded to Steve Brookes at the BFI for information.

107. Ibid p 1

108. Ibid

109. Ibid p 2

110. *Screen* Archive University of Glasgow Box 11 1987 Jane Arthurs 'SEFT Education Policy: A Discussion Paper' October 1987. At the 1987 AGM one of the working groups was charged with examining the consequences for Media Studies of the National Curriculum.

111. Cary Bazalgette (Ed) *Primary Media Education: A Curriculum Statement* London: BFI 1989 p 1

112. Julian Bowker (Ed) *Secondary Media Education: A Curriculum Statement* London: BFI 1991

113. *Initiatives* 8 p 24

114. 'Double-edged' *The Times Educational Supplement* 15 July 1988 p 31

115. Ibid

116. Ibid

117. Ibid

118. *Screen* Archive University of Glasgow Box 11 1988 Agenda for Executive meeting 13 August 1988

119. *Screen* Archive University of Glasgow Box 5 1986 'Important Notice' Undated circular to the Executive stating that there would be no Executive Committee meetings until November 5th.

11

Comedia delves arbitrarily

But the days are long past when SEFT was in the vanguard of film education and Screen was a necessary expression of this vanguard role.

Geoffrey Nowell-Smith, 1988

The BFI finally looks closely at SEFT and apparently can't decide what to do, so it funds a consultancy report on the Society. The consultants arrive in late summer. By September they have decided that SEFT must go. SEFT finds it has few supporters, even on its own Executive Committee. The Society's plans for a fortieth Birthday party are in ruins. But BFI will pick up the bills from SEFT's creditors and pay the employees their redundancy money. There is one legacy that people are prepared to fight over: who will give Screen *a new home. Finally it is decided and* Screen *goes to the John Logie Baird Centre in Glasgow.*

SEFT members whether attending or reading about the Cambridge conference in the *Times Educational Supplement* might reasonably have deduced that the media education movement was becoming firmly established in the UK. Indeed the study of media had achieved a much higher profile in secondary, further and higher education than many would have thought possible ten years earlier. But SEFT which had done so much to promote that expansion was now itself in trouble.

At the BFI: the Assessment of SEFT
By the mid-1980s the meetings between SEFT and BFI were logged by the Institute as 'assessment meetings' and were at this stage conducted at the Institute with officers from the Funding and Development Department. SEFT's representation was by the Chairperson (Andrew Higson), the Treasurer (George Foster) and the National Organiser (San Cubitt).[1] *Screen* – the production of which took the bulk of the Society's money – was not represented in the meetings. Mandy Merck as Editor was content not to be involved in these negotiations which she considered to be an issue for the Society's

wider management.[2] No specific SEFT records of the assessment meetings have survived (if they ever existed). Some BFI accounts are available.

Negotiations with BFI in the 1970s had been conducted in a more favourable environment than that of an assessment. Alvarado recalls that it was then seen as essential to the Society both to host the event on SEFT premises and to use the opportunity to present the Society in a positive context.[3] The impression as assessed by the BFI representatives at the December 1987 meeting was not a positive one; the minutes taken by Steve Brookes do not flatter the Society. SEFT's 'Priorities' and 'Desirable Activities' were listed as separate but sequential items on the joint agenda. In recording the discussion of the second of these items, Brooke's writes:

> If the previous discussion could be described as muddled and inconclusive then the same terms must be applied to this one.[4]

Matters had deteriorated further by the final agenda item 'SEFT 5 Years Hence'.

> This was the least productive phase of the assessment discussion, rendered ineffective by the complete lack of specificity. We were left with broad aspirations such as '...to have an impact on the future shape of the curriculum' or '...to establish Media Education across the curriculum'.[5]

If the conclusion was that there were 'no grounds for any serious adjustment to the funding of SEFT at present' this probably was a reflection of the BFI's assessment of the competence of SEFT's Treasurer: 'the financial control exercised by George Foster is good and tight'.[6] Nevertheless:

> The focus of many problems remains the National Organiser's post with its impossibly broad brief and highly energetic postholder...Meanwhile, most of the resources continue to go to a *Screen* which is holding its own but no longer represents the social/cultural/political cutting edge of the Society and certainly does not represent an expanding membership base.[7]

Brookes's conclusion is ambivalent. It may be read as offering SEFT time to revamp both its intentions and its presentation of them or alternatively as simply a stay of execution.

> Serious thought needs to be given to its future over the next twelve months, but there are in the writer's view, no grounds for any serious adjustment of funding to SEFT at present. Before any such action should be taken, Funding and Development must be clear about what it wishes to see achieved within the next five years in the field of audio-visual culture and then to assess precisely what

place should be reserved for SEFT (as it is now or rehabilitated) within its policy and strategy.[8]

By early 1988 it was clear BFI had recognised that its 'benign neglect' of SEFT was unsustainable.[9] Irene Whitehead, Deputy Head of Funding and Development, wrote to Cubitt in March referring back to the December assessment meeting.[10] She identified five areas of concern about SEFT, most of which related to the Society's apparent inability to answer simple organisational questions about the job descriptions of its staff and the relationship between the constituencies of *Initiatives* and *Screen*. In particular the post of National Organiser is said to need redefinition, being 'impossibly broad and detailed in its scope'.[11] Her frustration targets the 'somewhat hazy picture of the future offered by SEFT representatives' and the absence of 'a clear set of aims and objectives over time with resources earmarked against priorities'.[12]

When the group next met in mid May 1988 the record was kept by Whitehead. SEFT was deeply in trouble as 'due to problems with the dollar and unrealistic sales targets, SEFT will finish 1987/88 showing a £11,000 deficit'.[13] The Society's responses were to propose possible ways of raising money. Potential options included selling more books and charging fees for the advice given to teachers and lecturers, which had for the previous four decades been given free. Additionally the post of Vice-Chair was to be created which would be taken by Dave Morley, who would be charged with the specific task of 'looking at staff management and financial planning'. Higson had been seeking to resign from the role of SEFT Chair for some time and had signalled his intention to the SEFT Executive on a number of occasions. As part of his withdrawal strategy he had been courting Morley and Caroline Taylor with the notion that the duties of Chair might usefully be shared.[14] Despite their concern over SEFT's finances, the BFI representatives were still at this stage apparently ready to leave SEFT to sort out its own affairs and the next assessment meeting was scheduled for the following September.[15]

Meanwhile in Old Compton Street

While the prospect of facing a large deficit may have served to concentrate the minds of the SEFT Executive in 1988, there had been determined if unsuccessful attempts during the previous two years to make the running of the Society more comprehensible and efficient. Andrew Higson, who had taken over the Chair between AGMs in mid 1986, recognised that SEFT's survival depended on its being made to operate more professionally. During his two year spell as Chairperson he produced a succession of papers in an attempt to define and then address the issues that had to be resolved if SEFT were both to establish a coherent identity and to survive in the changed circumstances of the late 1980s.

One of these documents – of which no copy is now to be found – was *Screen's policy: the Present and the Future*. It forms the subject of a lengthy letter sent in response from David Buckingham to Higson in late August.[16] Buckingham, a teacher trainer at the

University of London Institute of Education, was an established member of both the SEFT Executive and its Education Board. He had contributed to the current 'Pedagogy' issue of *Screen*.[17] The document to which he responded had probably been triggered by the production of that issue of *Screen* which was only the second under Merck's editorship to engage with teaching issues. The 'policy' document on which Buckingham comments had raised issues about *Screen*'s relationship with the 'compulsory education sector'. He describes how greatly approaches to media education have changed from the previous decade.

> *Screen Education* in the mid and late 1970s was largely a vanguardist journal: it was the vehicle by which a small group of pioneers were able to generate new theory and (in my view, particularly usefully) to make links with radical developments in educational theory more generally. The situation today is very different: Media Education is expanding rapidly, and is now far more broadly-based. Insofar as it involves greater numbers of people, there is significantly greater consensus: but at the moment at least, there is much less concern with theoretical debate. This means that teachers' needs may well be more immediate: there is a greater emphasis on generating practical strategies for the classroom, and on making interventions in specific curriculum sites. To this extent, then, there is perhaps a greater need for a journal to provide 'tips for teachers' than major theoretical contributions.[18]

Recognising that *Initiatives* is addressing these needs, Buckingham is clear where a part of *Screen*'s priorities should lie: with theory relevant to the educational experience.

> In my view, the role that *Screen* should play in this situation is to ensure that new developments in Media Education continue to be informed by theory, rather than degenerating into the 'act first, think later' rhetoric of AMES.[19]

What Buckingham sought was 'research which is carried out by teachers in their own classrooms, and which examines in detail the teaching and learning which is taking place'.[20] This would be an approach that he would subsequently develop at the London Institute. Here he is concerned to involve SEFT in addressing the task directly by setting up 'a teachers' research group', since the greatest problem for teachers as opposed to academics is their difficulty in finding the appropriate opportunity to write analytically about their experiences.[21] Buckingham was aware of Merck's hostility to publishing educational contributions to *Screen* on a regular basis because the quality of such contributions compared unfavourably with those coming from academics. The letter to Higson was a deliberate diplomatic attempt on Buckingham's part to try to connect the different SEFT constituencies.[22]

Whereas Buckingham had a clear sense of the history of SEFT and its longer term agenda, many of those whom Higson wished to engage in the debates that he was generating had no such perspective. The Chairperson's task which was both necessary and appropriate would prove to be particularly difficult for, in the mid 1980s, those who became involved with SEFT, as opposed to those only on the *Screen* Editorial Board, found themselves in an organisation with apparently a very fluid identity. It was possible to participate in the governance of SEFT and yet to have little knowledge of both its past and its present. It would seem that some recruits to the SEFT Executive and Education Board in the mid 1980s had only a hazy sense of the nature of the organisation with which they were becoming involved. The legacy of the SEFT brand so strongly reinforced during the 1970s was still alluring. Thus in October 1987 in the Minutes of a joint meeting of the Executive and the Education Board is the following statement, recorded as representing a consensus in the discussion.

> SEFT used to be a vanguardist political party. Now it has acquired a movement which, because of its diversity of needs and interests, is difficult to satisfy.[23]

SEFT had never been sanctioned as a political party, nor in the 1970s had it pretended to be such. It had always been a movement. For Higson, who had a longer history of involvement with SEFT than most of its other volunteers, this statement would have been in conflict with his own experience of the Society. He recalls that when he moved to the University of Kent in 1980

> SEFT and *Screen* were the things to be involved in if you were on the Left. They were organising things you had to be at.[24]

However Buckingham recollecting the period of the mid to late 1980s would endorse the spirit at least of that record in the minutes, considering SEFT to have been 'a cultural/political organisation like SWP or IMG, but state funded'.[25] Eight years later when he resigned from the Chair, Higson recalls that he had to recognise that SEFT had changed. At that point he was of the opinion that

> SEFT was in effect two separate organisations that didn't have much to do with each other: a very successful journal that could operate as an international academic journal for a discipline that was becoming increasingly professional and didn't have much to do with the broader field of media education.[26]

Higson had begun his period as Chairperson by attempting to address directly the policy issues facing SEFT. At the point when he had taken on the role, the public face of the organisation may be inferred from the promotional leaflet that was prepared in August 1986.[27] In order of priority the activities of the Society are presented as: Publications, Distribution, Events, Research and Lobbying. It puts a gloss on each of these aspects; in some instances rather an unrealistic one. Under Publications, while the descriptions of *Screen* and *Initiatives* are accurate, the claims made around the publication of Occasional Papers are somewhat exaggerated. It is also stated that SEFT hopes to expand into video production after first making available in Autumn 1986 'a show reel of independent film and video of interest to teachers'.[28]

Distribution begins with the statement that 'SEFT operates a bookshop at its offices' and concludes that 'all titles are also available through our mail order distribution service'. The mail order service was very active; however to describe SEFT's cramped accommodation as including a bookshop was inaccurate. While the account offered in the Events section is uncontroversial, the Research paragraph makes exaggerated claims.

> SEFT supports and actively engages in research into all aspects of the media and media education, especially with those engaging against racist and sexist representations and practices, publishing its findings in the Society's publications and in related journals. Extensive holdings in published and unpublished materials make us a major centre for research consultancy, advice on courses, careers and organisational questions from members. SEFT also works as a consultant on matters falling within its areas of expertise, and can provide speakers on a wide range of topics for a range of audiences in the UK and abroad. Our membership, numbering in the thousands, is extremely active, notably in Media Education Initiative groups throughout the UK, in academia and in independent film/video production. Among our members are holders of key positions [in] media education, advisory services, and mainstream as well as independent film and video production. It is an active membership locally, nationally and internationally, especially through the pages of the Society's publications, and through local networks of media education activists.[29]

The reality was that, apart from the production of *Screen*, the dispatch of mail order items and the maintenance of book keeping records, it was only the single National Organiser who was employed to organise and discharge the activities of SEFT. The task facing the new Chairperson was a daunting one. He and the Treasurer began by meeting with the staff in September 1986 with the intention of planning ahead for the period until April 1988, thus covering the two financial years until the end of March 1988.[30]

Underlying the findings of this internal scrutiny was the relationship of SEFT with the BFI which had since the late 1960s been a substantial if occasionally demanding and unpredictable funder of the Society. It was also as the meeting recognised the funder which 'was able to influence SEFT policy to a degree that was unacceptable'.[31] It was after all pressure from the BFI that had encouraged SEFT to adopt its new unwieldy identity. The solution of finding other funders seemed to be a priority for the meeting, albeit no obvious potential benefactors were identified. As each aspect of SEFT's achievement was scrutinised in relation to its ambition, the gap between what its staff actually could deliver and what the Society claimed to be able to do was revealed. Most fundamental was the discrepancy between the range of duties expected of the National Organiser and any one individual's ability to discharge them. The meeting produced two alternative if still-to-be-funded proposals for employing an additional full-time professional officer who would be either a regionally funded and regionally based Education Officer or a London based General Secretary with responsibilities for fund raising and financial management. A key conclusion was about the SEFT Executive Committee itself.

> It was felt necessary that the Exec should be made into a much more active body, with members having specific areas of responsibility. This should be reflected in recruiting new members, with nominees indicating areas of interest and expertise.[32]

For the Executive's meeting later that month, Higson developed these ideas further. He saw the need to find a way of managing the seemingly *de facto* regionalisation of SEFT that had followed the linking together of regional groups under the MEI umbrella.[33] The problem then raised at the meeting was that many of these groups pre-existed MEI, had specific constitutions and should not be presumed to be bodies coming within the SEFT constitution. Little seems to have been resolved on the other issues. Perhaps the imminence of the 1986 AGM and the consequent elections to the Executive diminished enthusiasm for reform.[34]

Consequently at the January 1987 Executive Higson had to reiterate the issues facing SEFT for the benefit of several newly elected members.[35] For the February meeting he produced a substantial Chairperson's Report, spelling out in detail his concerns.[36] A disturbing matter had been raised by members at the AGM when concern had been expressed that 'very few of those standing for election to the Executive actually attended the AGM'.[37] Their absence from this key annual event of would-be Executive members may be interpreted in retrospect as evidence of the process of partial disengagement of many SEFT volunteers from the organisation. It seems they wanted others to vote for them and make them responsible for a Society with which in practice they sought to have only a casual relationship. Higson was nevertheless able to report that one pressure on the Society had been relieved. The lease on the Old Compton Street premises was about to expire and finding new premises had been about to become a priority. SEFT was now being offered a three year lease with the rent frozen. With this security the Executive planned its meetings for 1987 so that other urgent areas for decision-making might be tackled systematically throughout the year at identified single issue meetings. A by-product of the renewal of the lease was that the office was re-organised. Some of the historic SEFT records unearthed during this process were handed to former SEFT Chairperson Phillip Drummond at the University of London Institute of Education who would set up the official SEFT Archive there.[38]

The March meeting was dedicated to 'Fund Raising, Accommodation and New Projects'. However, despite the positive note implied in the agenda heading, the feeling of the meeting would have been gloomy. The Treasurer had to report that the impending deficit would be greater than first projected and by March 1987 the accumulated deficit would reach £5,241, almost £3,000 more than in 1986.[39] Consequently the book distribution section had no money to re-order books from publishers while the National Organiser's attempts at seeking potential funders had produced no outcome beyond his agreement to providing 'a tabulated list of funding and commercial bodies for the next meeting'.[40] Staffing considerations now focused on the proposal for a regional education officer. It was thought that if s/he were to be located in one of the English regions, the post might thereby attract significant funding from regional bodies. Executive members Gordon Eaton and Caroline Taylor would respectively explore the potential for a Wolverhampton or Manchester based post.[41]

For the following months until July, the SEFT records are incomplete and it is impossible to infer subsequent developments during the first half of 1987. By the Autumn, Higson had a clear ally in Jane Arthurs, Chairperson of the Education Board, who produced a thoughtful and comprehensive discussion paper.[42] At the end of her lengthy and detailed analysis she concluded 'Administrative Procedures and Structures' by stating unequivocally that '...the present structure of SEFT has the effect of marginalising education which should be the primary concern of the Society'. She recommended that each member of the Executive 'should have a specified responsibility' and that 'the paid officers should be set clear, realistic objectives by negotiation, with periodic reviews of the extent to which they have succeeded in meeting these objectives'.[43]

Her paper was written for the joint meeting of the Executive and the Education Board on 17 October. The timing of the meeting had also been scheduled to follow an assessment meeting the previous day at the BFI. However the weather intervened and following the hurricane on the night of 14/15 October the BFI meeting was postponed until December. A further complication for the meeting was that it followed the Liverpool conference at which a new Education Board had been elected. This represented a shift in SEFT practice. Previously Education Board members had been elected at the AGM. The conference had also produced a crop of resolutions including one to amalgamate the Executive and the Education Board. At the joint meeting in addition to the two Chairs and the Treasurer were just four elected members of the Executive and ten members of the Education Board of whom several had been newly elected just three weeks previously. Perhaps inevitably with such reduced attendance from the Executive, though much was discussed, few decisions were taken other than to set up agenda items for the next Education Board meeting, though working parties were put in place to review the Job Descriptions of the National Organiser and the Future of *Initiatives*.[44] However it was agreed that the three key items of Arthurs's paper identified above went forward to the 1988 Executive whose members were to be elected at the December 1987 AGM.

The AGM however produced its own problems in that the election of the Education Board at the Liverpool conference was seen as 'the marginalisation of the Education Board and its concerns'.[45] Such a reaction would have fitted Higson's long-term strategy and so with the assistance of Chris Vieler-Porter, a member of the Education Board, a new structure was proposed where nine individual Executive members would be responsible for nine working groups including separate editorial boards for *Screen* and *Initiatives*.[46] A more manageable model was agreed at the February 1988 Executive where it was agreed there would be just four sub-committees: *Screen*, *Initiatives*, Conference and WIMEN.[47] Two new officers were envisaged: Vice Chair and Deputy Treasurer.[48]

When the Executive met in late May 1988 it was a very poorly attended meeting. Those present were: the Chairperson (who intended on that occasion to carry out his long announced intention of retiring from office), the Treasurer, George Foster, the Chairperson of the Education Board, Caroline Taylor (who by the end of the meeting would have agreed to become temporary Chair), David Morley (who would take on the role of Vice Chair) and just three other elected members of the Executive. This small group heard the bad news from the Treasurer that 'the predicted deficit of £2,760 had become an actual deficit of over £10,000'.[49] The meeting had to look for ways of saving money and a number of small-scale measures was settled upon. At the end of this list of agreed Action Points, the minutes record that Foster and Morley would draw up a brief for a consultancy to advise SEFT on its options. Since no discussion had apparently preceded this proposal, the idea must have been hatched outside the meeting in order to be produced as a solution at the point when other measures seemed only to amount to a delaying of the inevitable – SEFT's becoming insolvent.

Briefing the Consultants

It would appear the BFI was then approached by SEFT with its first attempt at a consultancy brief in the expectation that the BFI would be prepared to fund such a move on the Society's part. This assumption would only have been feasible if some informal discussion had already taken place between representatives of the Society and its principal funder. This brief was however rejected by the BFI. Taylor in her new role then wrote to the members of the Executive to the effect that the BFI was prepared to continue funding SEFT only if there was a 'prompt investigation of the full range of SEFT's activities and current problems'.[50] A revised brief was circulated with the letter, Taylor and Morley having taken 'Chairpersons' action'. The Executive would meet in July to discuss the new brief. The mood within the BFI is revealed in a confidential memo from Simpson to new BFI Director Wilf Stevenson on receipt of the Taylor/ Morley letter.

> As an ex-officio member of SEFT's Executive I hope to attend this meeting and would welcome advice on the enclosed. The document also shows that SEFT is in yet another crisis: is this the last one?[51]

The brief to the consultants chooses to place SEFT at a 'crossroads' and identifies many aspects of its performance that are to be scrutinised. Significantly *Screen* is mentioned only once – when certain operational issues are identified. *Screen* and its production – which took the bulk of SEFT money – had it appears by this stage acquired a ring-fenced status which would ultimately be reflected in the stance taken by the consultants' report. The brief did however identify numerous other issues which were impinging on the SEFT volunteers. Five were highlighted: 'the financial crisis', 'the problem of cramped premises', 'an ideological shift in the grant-aided sector', 'a management vacuum' and 'the allocation of human and material resources'.[52]

When the Chair and Vice-Chair wrote of the financial crisis, their focus was apparently sharpened by what they perceived as the threat of personal liability proceedings being taken against individual board members under 'the new insolvency act'. How real this threat was is unclear since SEFT had earlier in the decade finally become a company limited by guarantee in order to restrict individual liability. The problem of a cramped building was still an issue albeit made less urgent by the temporary extension of the lease on the Old Compton Street premises, which when first occupied a decade earlier had been considered ideal for SEFT's tighter operation in the 1970s. The Society had already begun to explore options, one of which was to share premises with other voluntary or media organisations. These explorations, started in 1987, had not to date been successful.

It was however the final three identified items that contained the core of the Society's problems. These were the later years of the Thatcher Government and the brief refers to the general climate where voluntary organisations were expected to 'move towards greater economic self-sufficiency'. SEFT's 'management vacuum' was defined for the benefit of potential consultants thus:

> The executive and other voluntary boards are not equipped with the right expertise, and are too remote both geographically and in time available, presently to give adequate advice and to take clear sighted decisions on the Society's problems.[53]

There were several contributory factors here. The above description certainly did not apply to one voluntary group – the *Screen* Editorial Board. Its function was clear and members of the *Screen* Board were recruited specifically to meet the requirements of that agenda. But the Executive Committee and the Education Board were two quite distinct bodies that – once the *Screen* operation was discounted – had not a great deal to administer. It had not been clear to Higson why the Executive Committee of an educational body needed a separate Education Board to look after the annual conference and the intermittently produced *Initiatives* when professional members of staff were employed to address those issues on a day-to-day basis. Where the management vacuum probably did exist, albeit this was not spelled out, was in the lack of adequate control of staff (referred to in the brief only obliquely as the 'allocation of human and material resources'). Higson recalls the youth and inexperience of the volunteers at the heart of SEFT which had the result that

> …the Executive was not sufficiently experienced to take control; staff just had to get on with their work.[54]

There was a SEFT Council of Management composed of the Directors of SEFT Limited, the company limited by guarantee that provided SEFT with its legal identity. These were the trustees who formally presented the SEFT Limited accounts at the Company's annual meetings, events which were usually incorporated into the Society's AGMs. The Council was in practice made up of two elements. There were individuals who had previously been active in the Society (such as Ben Brewster and Christine Geraghty) and who had a longer term perspective on its performance. They were joined by the currently elected Chair and Treasurer. The evidence suggests that many who became involved with SEFT's other bodies were not introduced to an understanding of the relationships between the Society, the Boards, the Executive and the Council. There was no formal attempt by the Society to train its new volunteers nor was there sufficient accumulated expertise in the running of SEFT for newcomers to absorb the rudiments of an understanding of the basis of a voluntary operation. A consequence of this was the extended period during which George Foster discovered he had become irreplaceable as the Society's Treasurer. Foster's role in SEFT was considerable. Merck credits him with having successfully kept the whole SEFT enterprise afloat for so long in the 1980s.[55] In such circumstances the employees inevitably developed individual survival strategies. The combination of these factors would make the Society very vulnerable when exposed to the consultancy.

By the next meeting in July, three consultancies had submitted tenders to the Executive: Comedia, CAG Consultants and Simon Blanchard.[56] Again it was a very poorly attended meeting. In addition to the Chair, Vice-Chair and Treasurer were the four members of staff, Simpson who was ex officio BFI and just four elected members, one of whom resigned at the end of the meeting 'because of impending employment at the BFI'.[57] The predicted deficit now approached £13,000. When it came to deciding which of the three tenders to accept, two members present had to rule themselves out of the decision-making. Simpson was representing BFI the funder and Morley was a significant partner in Comedia. Consequently six elected members would select the consultants and thereby set in train the process which would decide the fate of SEFT. The meeting settled on Comedia as the chosen consultancy. An unrealistic air of optimism seems to have pervaded the meeting once that decision had been taken. The minutes record as follows:

> The consultancy should come up with a series of strategy options for SEFT, one of which should be based on a no-BFI-funding scenario.[58]

A small steering group was set up to liaise with Comedia and then it was back to business as usual with proposals for new subscription rates for 1989 and new budgets tabled for 1987/88 and 1988/89.

Observing the pressures mounting on grant-aided bodies some of those previously involved with the voluntary sector had engaged with the self-help spirit of the 1980s by becoming consultants and offering a sympathetic input into these pressures. SEFT was now about to be scrutinised by such an organisation. Merck (who had been granted unpaid leave of absence from April 1988 to work on a project at Channel 4 while Jenifer Batchelor became Acting Editor of *Screen*) was not impressed with Comedia.[59] She regarded their operation as that of

> ...foolish fantasy entrepreneurs who thought they could correct the failings of the Left on a consultancy basis.[60]

Buckingham saw the whole process as symptomatic of the 'beginnings of the culture of consultancy. BFI brought in consultants to justify a decision they had already made'.[61]

Value for the BFI's Money

If key BFI staff were by 1988 becoming alarmed as a result of their routine dealings with SEFT about the Society's apparent lack of direction, they were very aware of the amount of money that SEFT now received by way of BFI grant – by this stage around £60,000 a year.[62] It had been the practice of the Society since the 1970s to generate an amount at least equivalent to the BFI grant from other sources, but as its turnover increased, the amount SEFT received was now substantial in absolute terms. Significantly it was no longer only the Institute's Education Department that might have alternative uses for the money. The recent BFI Corporate Plan was envisaging an important expansion into research and this would require 'at least £30,000 in 1988/89'.[63]

In June 1988 Geoffrey Nowell-Smith, Head of BFI Publishing, wrote a confidential memo to both the departing Director Anthony Smith and his successor Wilf Stevenson. A decade previously Nowell-Smith had been Editor of *Screen* before becoming BFI's Head of Educational Services. Given this pedigree, his lengthy memo entitled 'Thoughts on funding for Research, Research Publications and Journals' would probably have carried particular authority. Despite its wide-ranging theme, much of the document's three A4 pages is concerned with the future of SEFT. The future of *Screen*, however, is presented at the outset as an issue quite distinct from the future of the Society that published it.

> It would be mad to kill off *Screen*. There are few enough journals in the country as it is. If the BFI is serious about research it needs to be thinking about creating journals, not destroying them.[64]

The thrust of Nowell-Smith's case is that once *Screen* is taken out of the SEFT portfolio, there is little remaining, even if the *Screen* of the 1980s is apparently but a shadow of the journal in the 1970s.

> On the one side it acts as a ginger group for teachers (mainly in secondary and FE); on the other side it runs a small mail order book service and produces a journal (*Screen*) with some general cultural pretensions and a mainly academic readership.[65]

Whether or not Nowell-Smith's assessment of SEFT's non-*Screen* activities was an accurate one, it clearly represented a general BFI perception that formal contacts between SEFT and BFI had not only failed to change but had served to endorse. Significantly it recognizes two distinct SEFT constituencies and separates the schoolteachers from the *Screen* readers. It also identifies a rapidly expanding and still unaddressed constituency.

> Some grassroots organisation is needed in Higher Education as well. Neither SEFT nor the BFI has done much up to now to help university and polytechnic teachers get together as a profession. The sector needs to be encouraged to organise itself.[66]

The sale of books by SEFT had in fact become a much more substantial operation than Nowell-Smith acknowledged here. The SEFT office based arrangement that had been in place during his Editorship of *Screen* had been replaced by something more substantial and enterprising with stock held in a lock-up in the East End of London. Inserted into copies of *Screen* on a regular basis would be *Publications available from SEFT* – a leaflet revised and re-issued approximately three times a year with the prices of all stock items listed in both sterling and US dollars. In May 1986 an internal stock list reveals some £6,500 worth of books and journals held in the lock-up.[67] The final leaflet was issued in Summer 1988. The range of materials listed demonstrates how far SEFT's original limited intention for stocking publications other than its own had changed.

What had begun as a simple service, whereby SEFT members might be able easily to access copies of 'hard-to-find' texts, had been supplanted by a much larger operation. By 1988 well over one hundred books with academic appeal were held in stock – usually in multiple numbers. BFI publications had a special section. Separately listed were some forty plus Educational Books and Packs including those from the ILEA English Centre. The most heavily stocked items were non-UK journals including *October* and *Camera Obscura*. SEFT was both producing an academic journal and selling academic texts. But it was not recruiting members from those teaching in Higher Education. With the expansion of that sector, an organisation for such teachers would follow in

1989 with the formation of the Association for Media, Film and Television Studies in Higher Education (AMFIT).

Not only had SEFT's routine direct contact with BFI representatives failed to demonstrate that it had other substantial activities but the wider soundings taken by Nowell-Smith within the Institute had reinforced a rather bleak view of SEFT: 'The consensus seems to be that SEFT is useful but not particularly productive'.[68] Where earlier generations of SEFT activists had been able to demonstrate both support and activity at grassroots level, the Society had failed to present the work around *Initiatives* to the BFI as the sustained continuation of the grassroots connection.

> It may be that SEFT has been putting too much of its effort and resources into *Screen* at the expense of its grassroots education work.[69]

Over to Comedia

Just one month after Nowell-Smith's observations had been circulated, Whitehead had written to SEFT's new Chair confirming the offer to the Society of a specific grant of £5,000 'for the cost of a consultancy to review and make recommendations on SEFT's current activities and organisation'.[70] There was one particularly significant stipulation which revealed how far the BFI wanted to extend the enquiry beyond a simple audit of SEFT. To the amended brief as submitted by SEFT the BFI would only release funds on the following 'additional requirement'.

> To examine the potential role of SEFT in a federated organisation encompassing the three main media educational representative organisations in Britain (SEFT, AMES and the MEC).

The two national organisations the Association for Media Education in Scotland (AMES) and Media Education Clwyd (MEC) had had only very loose connections with SEFT and this attempt to examine SEFT in this international context would have been unexpected. SEFT had always had members in both those countries and had never seen itself as simply an English institution. This last minute additional specification was not however queried at the July Executive meeting. Very rapidly after that event, Comedia's consultants began to inspect the SEFT office and to interview staff, volunteers and interested outside parties. The Executive Committee suspended its meetings, pending the report, though both *Screen* and *Initiatives* continued in production.[71]

The Comedia Review appeared in September.[72] It is a contradictory document in that *Screen*, SEFT's most substantial achievement, is barely mentioned other than to be praised briefly, while all other aspects of SEFT are found wanting. The picture is painted of a chaotic office occupied by fiercely territorial staff who operate independently of the weak and ineffectual management, which in turn lacks a proper understanding of the Society with which they are involved. Merck in her letter of response, when members of staff were invited to comment on the draft, made the obvious point that 'the neglect of the concrete achievements of the Society to date is simply staggering'.[73] The Report fails to explain how a successful journal had emerged for so long from such alleged chaos.

It would be surprising if the consultants had not been aware of the outcome the BFI expected and it seems that a possible future for *Screen*, separated from SEFT had already been envisaged for some time. What the report does reveal is the imbalance in SEFT between the staff and the voluntary management and the failure of the latter group to understand the nature of the body with which they were engaged.

> There is an extraordinary level of confusion about where overall responsibility for SEFT's actions is vested. *De facto* control of the organisation seems to be split up between the three major committees: the Executive, the Education Board, the 'Screen' Board. Their respective roles and remits are unclear – both to us and to many of those we spoke to who sit on them.[74]

The consultants also reported that the volunteers occupying the places on the Executive and its two Boards at the time of the review were disengaged from the Society.

> Given the importance of this consultancy for the future of SEFT, we were surprised, to say the least, how few executive and board members came to these meetings or engaged in the process of the study. In total, only six out of a possible 30 plus board members turned up to these crucial meetings.[75]

One interest group which the consultants did interview was 'the BFI'. Unfortunately no further identification of the Institute's spokespersons is provided. Crucially the BFI's concerns were firstly that SEFT's grant took '85 per cent of the budget allocated to media education initiatives' and that the BFI would make better use of the money. Secondly that SEFT 'has not met the Institute's expectations in terms of its function as a national membership organisation for media education'.[76] The 1984 *Screen* figures reveal that there were only 369 individual subscribing members in the UK. Thus at a time when media education was growing rapidly, individual members were a hundred fewer in number in the early 1980s than they had been in the 1960s.[77] Even if SEFT had been minded to mobilize its members to lobby, it had only a tiny base of individuals on which to draw.

One very important interest group that seems not to have been consulted was the *Screen* Editorial Board. There are records of the views only being sought from current SEFT Board members (which one must infer as meaning the SEFT Executive Committee) and of 'current education board members'.[78] This omission is particularly curious when the records in the *Screen* archive show responses protesting to the Report only from members of staff and from *Screen* Board members, but not from members of the Executive or the Education Board whose attitudes to SEFT presumably were in accord with those taken by Comedia. Writing from the perspective of the *Screen* Board, Ginette Vincendeau picks up on the gaps in the report.

> I do not think that the report as it stands gives sufficient information to support the conclusions you are drawing. On the one hand the range of people you have consulted seems rather limited (and I certainly have not been approached to give my opinion); on the other there is a complete absence in the report of *any* information on what SEFT – and *Screen* – actually do and have achieved over the years: eg who SEFT services, what events it has mounted, how many issues *Screen* has produced, what its reputation and standing in the field are, both in Britain and abroad, etc.[79]

She is however concerned now to emphasise that others would certainly have written in similar vein and that the *Screen* archive record must be incomplete.[80]

The Report concludes by listing five options for SEFT only one of which (the fifth) is presented seriously: this is the 'closure/graceful retirement' option.[81] Comedia's conclusion is contained in an extraordinary section of the report which first list as options for the future four alternatives which are then immediately in turn discredited by their authors. Option One (where an attempt would be made to make SEFT operate successfully) is 'a totally unconvincing response'. Option Two (where *Screen* is floated off and SEFT consequently receives a lower subsidy) is 'incomplete and finally unconvincing'. Option Three (where SEFT concentrates only on publishing *Screen*) 'is a wholly unreal proposal'. Option Four (where SEFT might merge with another body) is a route that is not 'seriously available'.[82] To present such discredited alternatives first seems to be a crude mechanism deployed to reinforce the inevitability of Option Five. Since the Report is candid about the BFI's attitude to SEFT at this time, the spurious four options that precede Option Five simply embellish the inevitable. The Report has already commented frankly:

> As one BFI member rather harshly put it "there are those within the BFI who wish SEFT a humane death and those who wish to cut its throat".[83]

It has been one of the themes of the concluding chapters of this investigation that there seem to have been forces at work in SEFT which resisted its maintaining the identity of a teachers' organisation. In the interviews conducted by Comedia with members of the Education Board, this issue is dominant. There is an extraordinary reference to the relation between the teaching profession and SEFT.

> Discussions with this constituency – which would logically form the cornerstone of the Society's work – have led us to the unhappy conclusion that SEFT has quite comprehensively alienated this sector. Media educators of all kinds clearly feel that the Society – whilst claiming to speak on their behalf – is often

dismissive of their concerns. As a result, many of them considered that SEFT was out of touch with class room and lecture hall realities.[84]

It appears that the constituency which was alienated was the Education Board and one might therefore be tempted to infer that SEFT had succeeded in alienating itself.

BFI had insisted that SEFT's positioning in relation to AMES and MEC be included in the consultancy's remit. In the final report these two organisations receive only a passing reference in the final section of the report: 'Beyond SEFT – a sketch of the future'.[85] Here a rather fanciful 'illustrative/indicative' suggestion is for METCO (Media Education and Training Council) to be a body set up solely for England and which would be, predictably as the report chose to emphasise in unsubtle fashion, 'OUTSIDE the BFI and its Education Department'. The 'principle [sic] features' of METCO would include 'a broad view of the media/culture', a broader range of finance support, a quarterly British magazine resulting from collaboration with AMES and MEC. In the self-help spirit of the times Comedia confidently but confusingly states that

> ...this new basis of 'service provision' enhances the organisation's self-esteem, whereby it acts as a professional equals [sic]. (The funder as a client for services and the organisation), rather than as supplicants.[86]

Only as an afterthought is NATE (National Association of Teachers of English) mentioned as possibly providing a potential model for media educators. Comedia's emphasis is for METCO to provide information, training, research and consultancy – at a price. But METCO as envisaged would have been an irrelevance. Rather than AMES and MEC, the consultancy would have been better employed acknowledging Film Education, the English and Media Centre and the BFI's own Education Department, all of which would set out in the 1990s to cater for demand in precisely these areas. What they did not provide was an association for media teachers.

New Providers for Media Teachers

For four decades SEFT and BFI Education had been the 'lead' organisations to which film, television and then media teachers had looked for assistance. Their positions began to be challenged in the later 1980s. When the British film industry decided to celebrate British Film Year in 1985, it established an educational unit under Ian Wall who had headed the Media Department at Holland Park School. During the year Wall collaborated with SEFT in a number of joint ventures in the regions.[87] At the conclusion of British Film Year, its organisers – notably David Puttnam – decided that the educational work should be continued and Film Education was established as an organisation to support teachers, funded by the British film industry.[88] Basing its materials initially around forthcoming film releases, Film Education's remit soon expanded, as did the number of staff it employed. A new and significant player had entered media education.

Film Education represented a beneficial outcome for media education which emerged from the self-help ethos of the 1980s – it was a privately funded operation in contrast to the publicly funded organisations of the BFI and SEFT. Furthermore it met a need for classroom materials which SEFT had on occasions promised to provide but had never actually managed to do. Secondly Film Education saw its target constituency as the schools. The importance of this targeting should be contrasted with the conclusion of the Editorial in the 'Teaching Film and TV' issue of *Screen* where readers were informed that 'teachers at all levels except primary and secondary have contributed'.[89] The Editors clearly considered that the lack of contributions from anyone involved with the pupils in the 12 years of mandatory education did not diminish their claim to have teacher involvement 'at all levels'. By Summer 1988 *Initiatives* acknowledged that Film Education's 'well researched, well produced materials' met a very specific need that classroom teachers had.[90]

Another organisation also offering both the production of materials and the provision of training for teachers was about to move into independence. The Inner London Education Authority was to be abolished in 1990. Its English Centre already had an established presence beyond London through its media education materials, some of which had been made available nationally by SEFT. The Centre's Warden, Michael Simons, and staff took the decision to operate post ILEA as an independent organisation with the significantly amended name of The English and Media Centre which would, like Film Education, provide ready-to-use classroom materials and training courses for practitioners.[91] As the number of teachers involved in media teaching increased during the 1990s, it was the availability of materials and of the advice on how to use them that would make these new providers very attractive to teachers.

The BFI too was having to make adjustments to some of the Education Department's long established commitments. From the 1950s onwards the BFI had maintained control of the content of the Extra-Mural Certificate and Diploma in Film offered by London University. In the 1980s this arrangement ceased when the University's newly appointed Media Studies Officer, Mary Wood, took charge of the programme in 1983.[92] Her job title embodied the change in provision that was envisaged. From just three sessional Media Studies courses in 1982/83 there was a sustained increase during the 1980s so that by 1989/90, 22 sessional courses were offered, a peak of 33 having been reached in 1987/88. Film Study had three groups completing year one of the certificate course in 1982/83; by 1989/90 the number had risen to 14.[93] The Department of Extra-Mural Studies became at this point probably the major UK provider of training in film and media education. This surge in recruitment provides further evidence that the 1980s was the key period of growth for media teaching as it began to become established in education.

Metropolitan film students who wanted a more formal engagement with their enthusiasm had routinely combined attendance at BFI Summer Schools with enrolment for the extra mural classes. The BFI's relinquishing of the evening classes was followed by the discontinuance of its Summer Schools, as BFI course provision became more targeted following the final Summer School in 1991. The summer school had been one of the foundations of film education for many years when there were few other occasions when serious film students might engage with the tiny number of film academics. Many Summer School students recollect the intensity of the experience. The school, which had been reduced in length to one week in the late 1980s, was still, Simpson recalls, very demanding of staff time in its planning and preparation. His view is that the provision of its summer schools in the 1970s had been the process by which BFI Education had at that stage defined itself. He recalls that during this decade they were so influential that he would expect to see summer school material appearing in the syllabuses of higher education some 18 months later.[94] As the provision of film courses expanded, the appeal of the BFI School and its annual selection of a specialist topic had diminished. Simpson was succeeded by Manuel Alvarado who became Head of the Education Department in 1989. Acknowledging the significance of the introduction of the National Curriculum into state schools, the Department took on a strategic role in identifying and promoting where media education might be appropriately accommodated.

When the BFI Education Department had discussed the Comedia Report in November 1988, Lusted's was the only voice raised in support of SEFT existence being maintained. He wrote a lengthy memo to BFI Director Stevenson which raised the same issues as had the few *Screen* people who had responded to Comedia.

> The Report strikes me as being written unsympathetically, even destructively. Did the authors set out with their conclusion in mind or did they reach it during their research?
>
> We have no way of finding this out since we learn so little about SEFT's work, how it's managed and what its outcomes are. This seems to me barely adequate as a report on which to base as dramatic a decision as closure of an organisation like SEFT.[95]

Lusted found no support among his BFI colleagues. The energies of those in SEFT who were involved with *Screen* were busy finding it a new home. But decision-making remained with the SEFT Executive that had shown so little involvement with Comedia during the consultancy and ultimately would require the agreement of the Council of Management.

An Executive meeting was set for August but there is no surviving evidence that it took place. An undated statement was circulated stating that meetings were cancelled at least until November. It would seem that, given the blunt assessment by Comedia, the Officers accepted the inevitable and set about dismantling the Society. The next recorded Executive meeting was in December when diminishing involvement in that body continued to be manifested. Apart from the officers, only three elected members were present.[96] The main agenda item was the future of *Screen* about which as the Treasurer reported pressure was coming from the BFI. While not wishing to take over the journal itself the Institute was demanding the power of veto over the disposal of the journal. A great deal of energy had gone into finding a home for *Screen* and there had been numerous informal discussions about its future with interested parties. Merck reported that

> A wide range of publishers and academic institutions had been approached with regard to the future publication of Screen, including OUP, Routledge, Radius/ Century Hutchinson, Polity Press and PCL, Middlesex Poly, Warwick, Exeter, UEA, Sussex, Stirling and Kent.[97]

The principal dilemma was how to choose between the nature of the very different offers from publishing houses and academic institutions. Present among the committee members was Norman King from the University of Glasgow who was promoting a draft proposal to take over *Screen* from the John Logie Baird Centre, run jointly by the Universities of Glasgow and Strathclyde. Also discussed was what future there might be for a media teachers' association. Marie Gillespie reported that the *ad hoc* working party drawn from Education Board members had met with Stevenson at the BFI. His proposal was for the Institute to fund an extended (six month) consultancy to consider the viability of such an association.[98]

Five Executive members joined the Officers for the January 1989 meeting at which it was reported that the Council of Management 'wanted Screen to go to an academic institution, and resisted the idea of an outright purchase of the title by a publisher'.[99] Again King was present to put the Logie Baird Centre case. Merck was in favour of the offer from the University of Sussex where their taking over *Screen* would coincide with the commencement of an MA in Film and Television Studies. Both academic offers would involve the new Editor in a teaching commitment. At the conclusion 'Logie Baird was recognised as the front runner but Sussex to be given chance to improve bid'.[100] BFI Education was now insistent that – as its Director had said – any media teachers' association would only be considered after the proposed consultancy for which the Department would construct the brief. The future of *Initiatives* was uncertain; Cubitt was approaching various bodies that had indicated some interest in taking it over. The mail order business was the one area where the BFI had shown interest in taking over the operation from SEFT.[101]

For the Executive's final meeting in February, the Officers were joined by four other members of the Committee, plus Christine Geraghty from the Council of Management.[102] *Screen* was to go to Glasgow with the BFI's blessing as in the end Sussex had backed out. To protect the *Screen* legacy, should the move to Glasgow not prove successful, three trustees were put in place to protect the 'title, back issues and copyrights'.[103] The future of *Initiatives* was still uncertain. The only option for the Committee was to pass the responsibility to the informal group that had set itself up and which was based around a few individuals from the Education Board. A deadline of 24 February 1989 was set as the date when the redecorated offices would be vacated after the disposal of SEFT's remaining effects.

Theorising Media Teaching

The educational territory in which all the new providers were now operating had been transformed. Aspects of media education, together with Media Studies as an examination subject, had become established in many schools in Britain by the late 1980s. When Masterman's book *Teaching about Television* first appeared at the beginning of the decade it had had, effectively, no competition. By the mid 1980s there were others ready to publish. The educational terrain had changed: film and television had been subsumed into media. Masterman again headed a new field when, in 1985, he published *Teaching the Media*. This revealed a significant further step describing his shift of position from film, to television, to media as the appropriate and relevant frame of reference within which students might consider popular culture.[104] Masterman was never a SEFT activist. Viewing the Society from his Nottingham base, he detected SEFT's divided loyalties. He described *Initiatives* thus:

> SEFT's termly national newsletter. Invaluable source of information on conferences, meetings and events. Carries articles and book reviews. Recommended.[105]

Screen however did not get a Masterman recommendation.

> Bi-monthly theoretical film and TV journal. Worth looking at but *Screen* has always experienced difficulty in relating its concern with theoretical issues to the realities of educational practices, and remains, at the present time, very remote from the world of most media teachers.[106]

Two years later two further books appeared that did declare a SEFT connection. *Teaching Popular Television* and *Learning the Media*.[107] The author of the former, advisory teacher Mike Clarke, is described on the cover as 'an active member of the Society for Education in Film and Television'. The latter publication had three authors, two of whom had a SEFT connection: Alvarado, former SEFT Education Officer and Editor of *Screen Education* and Tana Wollen, who was the SEFT Chairperson at the time of the book's publication. *Learning the Media* has an initial section on 'Histories' and gives SFT and SEFT a prominent place in that account. But it is clear from the book's twenty packed pages of bibliography that there are now many additional contributors to the development of media education. The 1980s had been a period of great activity. This activity had of course been generated in part by Government decisions, particularly in relation to TVEI (Technical and Vocational Education Initiative) and CPVE (Certificate of Pre-Vocational Education) where opportunities were to be found for media studies developments. Whereas Masterman was hostile to the proposals which he saw as demanding 'regurgitative and reproductive skills, rather than critical abilities',[108] Alvarado *et al* were optimistic.

Moreover, the 'new vocationalism', whatever the intentions of its instigators to return us to a stratified education system, does provide an opportunity to transform liberal education's traditional distinction between an academic 'conceptual' curriculum for some and 'skills' for others – a mode of education which has persisted long after comprehensivisation despite good intentions and many achievements.[109]

For those whose media teaching experience was in further education, CPVE was considered a crucial development. Roy Stafford saw how CPVE allowed the construction of courses specifically in media in an educational environment where previously media had played a subsidiary, servicing role. [110]

There was clearly a role that SEFT might have played in identifying and building on the potential for media teaching within the fast changing educational environment. However BFI pressure had set the Society on a different course that encouraged its National Organiser to intervene across such a wide range of areas of interest that by July 1987, he was owed fifteen weeks of time off in lieu.[111] Higson concedes that the elected officers did not find it easy to manage staff expected to deliver across such a wide remit.[112]

SEFT's staggered obituaries

There is a fourth book that belongs in the sequence of media education texts, although its publication was delayed until 1991 by which time SEFT no longer existed. The Society ceased to trade in early 1989 with the BFI paying its creditors and the costs of staff redundancies.[113] *The Media Studies Book*, edited by Lusted, consisted of articles written in the mid-1980s, though some had been updated.[114] Lusted was presented with a problem since several of the articles included references to SEFT, *Screen* or *Initiatives* that had been current when the articles were first written but his book's eventual publication had followed SEFT's demise. Consequently Lusted had to create a different explanatory reference in his listings for each manifestation of SEFT.

Initiatives, which at the time of Lusted's correction of his proofs, was possibly going to continue with BFI funding, has an ambivalent entry

> *Initiatives*, until 1989, the termly newsletter from SEFT which combines articles with reviews and news. Each of the termly newsletters was edited by one of the many groups in the network of media education initiatives (MEI).[115]

The reference to *Screen*, which was to continue under new ownership, harks back to its time as a SEFT publication when pedagogy was allowed an occasional airing.

> *Screen* incorporating *Screen Education*. Quarterly journal dealing with theoretical issues about film and television. Central but difficult reading. Occasional issues devoted entirely to media education.[116]

The SEFT entry however serves as an obituary.

> Between the 1950s and 1989, SEFT campaigned initially for film education and then television and media criticism and education. It produced *Screen* magazine from 1970, incorporating *Screen Education* journal from the early 1980s, and *Initiatives*, a termly newsletter for media teachers. It organized many events and listed the regional Media Initiative Groups (MEIs), many of which continue since SEFT's demise in 1989.[117]

'Lessons' from SEFT

Some members of the SEFT Education Board, notably David Buckingham and Marie Gillespie, had put the case to Stevenson, Director of the BFI, that a teacher focused successor body to SEFT was essential and had got his agreement to pay for a consultancy to investigate the potential demand.[118] A further outcome of their lobbying was to get financial support from BFI for two further issues of *Initiatives*. In the first of these Buckingham offers an analysis of what had happened to SEFT.[119] He had become, like many who had offered opinions to Comedia, out of sympathy with the organisation in which he had participated. He writes '...for most media teachers in schools and in further education, SEFT was at best an irrelevance, and at worst an obstacle'.[120]

Whereas three years earlier Buckingham had crafted a carefully worded letter to Higson in an attempt to reconnect SEFT's different constituencies, now he was prepared to be forthright. As he saw it, the conflicts he had sought to resolve had in the end destroyed the Society.

> Perhaps the most significant failing here was SEFT's inability to balance and combine the interests of its major constituencies. The long-standing rift between educationalists and academic theorists became more acute in the 1980s, as media education began to gain ground in schools.[121]

His argument is that 'the long-standing rift between educationalists and academic theorists became more acute in the 1980s'.[122] While such separation was undoubtedly the dominant condition in SEFT's final years, Buckingham now considers that it was in earlier attempts to address and involve a third constituency that the imbalance became part of the structure. When he joined SEFT in the early 1980s it had been 'the moment of Channel 4' and SEFT was ready to give representation to those in independent production. Within the tripartite combination of academic writing, independent production and education, the last became the 'poor relation'.[123]

Buckingham's account seeks to describe how SEFT 'appeared deliberately to exclude and intimidate classroom teachers'.[124] He accepts the strategic importance of the different roles played by *Screen* and *Screen Education* in the 1970s and acknowledges the achievement of *Screen* which was influential throughout the Humanities. But he is very critical of how *Screen Education* approached its task of 'identifying a pedagogy for media education in schools'.[125] His concerns are twofold.

> The privileging of theory led to a situation in which writing about classroom practice was not merely hopelessly unglamorous, it was tantamount to bourgeois empiricism.[126]

For Buckingham this meant that very few accounts of classroom practice were published. His second concern was that

> ...much of the rhetoric of *Screen Education* was directed not against the Right, but against the liberal Left, and in particular against the delusions of the 1960s. Child centred education was relentlessly caricatured.[127]

Buckingham's analysis of the position of *Screen Education* in the 1970s reflects a reality. There was considerable distance between the stance taken by its Editors and that being promulgated by the Institute of Education. There was a fundamental difference in how each institution thought working-class children should be educated. But while *Screen Education* existed there was a journal in which media teachers might engage in debate. The absence of anything similar in the mid 1980s was the fundamental problem. *Screen* was staking out its territory as higher level film and media courses spread through the polytechnics. In the schools and further education colleges, the leadership and debates became local.

Notes

1. British Film Institute Special Collections File 141 'SEFT Assessment meeting (4.12.87)' p 1
2. Mandy Merck in interview with the author 14 February 2006.
3. Manuel Alvarado in interview with the author 11 July 2005.
4. 'SEFT Assessment meeting' op cit p 2
5. Ibid
6. Ibid p 4
7. Ibid
8. Ibid p 4
9. Comedia *Society for Education in Film and Television – A Review* London: September 1988 p 8
10. Letter from Irene Whitehead to Sean Cubitt 8 March 1988 p 1
11. Ibid
12. Ibid p 2
13. British Film Institute Special Collections File 141 'Meeting with SEFT Representatives 15 May 1988' p 1
14. Andrew Higson in interview with the author 15 June 2005.

15. Ibid p 2
16. *Screen* Archive University of Glasgow Box 5 1982–86 Letter from David Buckingham to Andrew Higson 30 August 1986
17. *Screen* Vol 27 No 5 September/October 1986
18. Buckingham (1986) op cit pp 1–2
19. Ibid p 2
20. Ibid
21. In the event Buckingham set up his own group of teachers in London who met on Saturday mornings. Their efforts resulted in Buckingham D, Fraser P and Mayman N *Watching Media Learning: Making Sense of Media Education* London: Falmer 1990.
22. David Buckingham in interview with the author 24 November 2005.
23. *Screen* Archive University of Glasgow Box 11 1987 'Minutes of the Joint Meeting of the SEFT Executive and Education Board' 17 October 1987 p 4
24. Higson interview op cit.
25. Buckingham interview op cit
26. Higson interview op cit
27. *Screen* Archive University of Glasgow Box 11 1986 'Amended text of promotional leaflet' 20 August 1986
28. Ibid p 1
29. Ibid p 2
30. *Screen* Archive University of Glasgow Box 11 1986 'SEFT Planning meeting' 23 September 1986
31. Ibid p 1
32. Ibid p 3
33. *Screen* Archive University of Glasgow Box 11 1986 Andrew Higson 'SEFT Policy: Regionalisation, Expansion, Funding'
34. *Screen* Archive University of Glasgow Box 11 1986 'Minutes of the meeting of the SEFT Executive 27 September 1986'
35. *Screen* Archive University of Glasgow Box 11 1987 'Minutes of SEFT Executive Meeting 24 January 1987'
36. *Screen* Archive University of Glasgow Box 11 1987 'Chairperson's Report to the SEFT Executive 14 February 1987'
37. Ibid Item 4 'Post-mortem on 1986 AGM'
38. Ibid
39. SEFT Limited Audited Annual Financial Statements 31 March 1987
40. *Screen* Archive University of Glasgow Box 11 1987 'Minutes of SEFT Executive Meeting' 14 March 1987
41. Ibid p 2
42. *Screen* Archive University of Glasgow Box 11 1987 Jane Arthurs 'SEFT Education Policy: A Discussion Paper' October 1987
43. Ibid p 4

44. *Screen* Archive University of Glasgow Box 11 1987 SEFT Executive Committee/Education Board Briefs for Working Parties to review 'The Job Description of the SEFT National Organiser' and 'The Future of *Initiatives*'

45. *Screen* Archive University of Glasgow Box 11 1987 Andrew Higson 'Re-structuring the elected bodies and management of the Society' 14 February 1988

46. Ibid p 2

47. Efforts definitively to decode this acronym have proved unsuccessful: those involved with media education at the time suggest 'Women In Media Education Network'.

48. *Screen* Archive University of Glasgow Box 11 1988 'Minutes of the SEFT Executive Meeting' 27 February 1988 p 2 This appears to have been the point at which SEFT abandoned the term 'Chairperson' in favour of Chair.

49. *Screen* Archive University of Glasgow Box 11 1988 Minutes of SEFT Executive 21 May 1988 p 2

50. British Film Institute Special Collections Box 141 Caroline Taylor Letter to Executive members 23 June 1988

51. British Film Institute Special Collections File No 141 'Confidential Memo to Wilf Stevenson from Philip Simpson 30th June 1988'

52. British Film Institute Special Collections File No 141 'Brief for consultant for SEFT' attached to letter from Caroline Taylor to SEFT Executive 23 June 1988

53. Ibid

54. Higson interview op cit

55. Merck interview op cit

56. *Screen* Archive University of Glasgow Box 11 1988 Minutes of SEFT Executive 16 July 1988 p 1

57. Ibid p 2

58. Ibid p 1

59. Mandy Merck in interview with the author 16 June 2004

60. Merck interview op cit

61. Buckingham interview op cit

62. British Film Institute Special Collections File 141 Confidential memo to Tony Smith and Wilf Stevenson from Geoffrey Nowell-Smith 9 June 1988 'Thoughts on Funding for Research, Research publications, and Journals' p 1

63. Ibid

64. Ibid

65. Ibid

66. Ibid p 2

67. Stock List 12 May 1986 (Made available to the author by George Foster)

68. Nowell-Smith memo op cit p 1

69. Ibid p 2

70. *Screen* Archive University of Glasgow Box 2. Letter from Irene Whitehead to Caroline Taylor 8 July 1988

71. *Screen* Archive University of Glasgow Box 2. 'Important Notice' Undated but probably August 1988 cancelling Executive Committee meetings until November.
72. *Comedia Review* op cit
73. *Screen* Archive University of Glasgow Box 2. Letter from Mandy Merck to Caroline Taylor and George Foster 18 October 1988
74. *Comedia Review* op cit p 17
75. Ibid p 2 It should however be noted that the main period during which the consultants took evidence coincided with the August vacation, the one month of the year when those engaged in education are most likely to be away.
76. Ibid p 23
77. Sources:Membership Breakdown 17 May 1984 and *Screen Education Yearbook* 1962 London: SEFT 1961. The balance is redressed somewhat in that in that in 1961 there were only 62 overseas members. In 1984 it was 186.
78. Ibid
79. *Screen* Archive University of Glasgow Box 2 Letter from Ginette Vincendeau to Charles Landry at Comedia 21 October 1988
80. Ginette Vincendeau in interview with the author 25 April 2006.
81. *Comedia Review* op cit p 27
82. Ibid pp 26– 27
83. Ibid p 23
84. Ibid p 24
85. Comedia op cit p 30
86. Ibid p 31
87. *Initiatives* 3 February 1986 p 17
88. Ian Wall in interview with the author 12 January 2004.
89. Philip Simpson, Gillian Skirrow, Simon Watney 'Editorial' *Screen* Vol 24 No 3 May/June 1983 p 3
90. Richard Marshall 'Film Education' *Initiatives* 10 Summer 1988 p 25
91. Michael Simons in telephone interview with the author 27 April 2007.
92. Mary Wood in interview with the author 25 July 2005.
93. Data from the Media Studies Archive, Birkbeck College University of London.
94. Simpson interview op cit
95. BFI Education Archive Bretton Hall BH/BFI/MOI 33–4 Memo from David Lusted to Wilf Stevenson 22 November 1988 p 1
96. *Screen* Archive University of Glasgow Box 11 1988 'Meeting of SEFT Executive 10:12:88 Minutes'
97. Ibid p 1
98. Ibid p 2
99. *Screen* Archive University of Glasgow Box 11 1988 'Minutes of the SEFT Executive' 21 January 1989 p 1
100. Ibid p 2
101. Ibid

102. *Screen* Archive University of Glasgow Box 5 1986 'SEFT minutes; Executive; Saturday 11 February '89'
103. Ibid p 1 The trustees were Geoffrey Nowell-Smith, George Foster and Mandy Merck.
104. Len Masterman *Teaching the Media* London: Comedia 1985
105. Ibid p 334
106. Ibid p 332
107. Mike Clarke *Teaching Popular Television* London: Heineman Educational 1987; Manuel Alvarado, Robin Gutch, Tana Wollen *Learning the Media* London: Macmillan Education 1987
108. Masterman op cit p 67
109. Alavarado *et al* op cit p 34
110. Stafford interview op cit
111. *Screen* Archive University of Glasgow Box 11 1987 Sean Cubitt National Organiser's Report 14 July 1987
112. Andrew Higson in interview with the author 15 June 2005.
113. BFI Education Archive Bretton Hall BH/BFI/MOA/33–4 BFI Press Release 'Society for Education in Film and Television (SEFT) and BFI' 22 November 1988
114. David Lusted (Ed) *The Media Studies Book* London: Routledge 1991
115. Ibid p 221
116. Ibid p 222
117. Ibid p 225
118. *Screen* Archive University of Glasgow Box 5 1986 Report of the Working Party on a Media Teachers' Association 5 December 1988
119. David Buckingham 'Lessons from SEFT' *Initiatives* 11 Autumn 1989 pp 3–5
120. Ibid p 3
121. Ibid
122. Ibid
123. Buckingham interview op cit
124. Buckingham 1989 op cit p 3
125. Ibid p 4
126. Ibid
127. Ibid p 5

Epilogue

The current post–SEFT situation is one where the various interests have become very isolated from each other with the inevitable tendency for caricature to replace collaboration.

Simon Blanchard 1991

Some activists from the former SEFT Education Board attempted to promote an organisation to fill the gap that SEFT was about to leave behind. Indeed, as mentioned in Chapter 11, this group chaired by Marie Gillespie did succeed as part of their negotiations in getting money from the BFI for two further issues of *Initiatives*. But they had grander ambitions. Very rapidly at the end of 1988, while the conclusions of the Comedia Report were still being worked through, they had produced a 'Proposal for a National Media Education Association'. Their credentials for promoting the new association were spelled out:

> This document has been prepared by a group of people actively involved in media education at a variety of levels – in secondary, further and adult education, in teacher training and in educational administration.[1]

Absent from these credentials is any mention of higher education. The exclusion is deliberate since they argue it was the imbalance in favour of higher education that had made SEFT 'an obstacle to the continued growth of media teaching within the mainstream educational system.'[2] Their priorities are clear:

> While we would not seek to exclude teachers working in higher education, the major focus of the new association would be on supporting the work of teachers in primary, secondary and further education.[3]

After a meeting with BFI Director Wilf Stevenson in early December Marie Gillespie reported that

> WS responded with encouragement to draft proposal document and agreed on the general principle of continued financial support for media education and for an organisation to service the needs of teachers in the sector.[4]

Having then floated the idea of another consultancy to explore the potential for an association, Stevenson passed the group on to meet with Irene Whitehead and Philip Simpson who refused to engage with the details of the proposal 'whilst awaiting proposals from other groups'.[5] Instead Whitehead and Simpson offered the prospect of a BFI funded consultancy possibly costing £15,000 and taking six months, with a brief to be drawn up by BFI Education.

When the BFI Education Department eventually came to produce this brief, the early lobbying by the former SEFT constituency had clearly had an effect in that 'any new network should be intended to support teachers in primary, secondary and further education'.[6] The object of the investigation was to be the potential for and practicalities of a 'media education network', this term having been deliberately selected in order to be 'a neutral description, not a prescription'.[7] Coinciding with the BFI's involvement with the detail of SEFT's disbandment, the SEFT-shaped absence was dominant in the Department's thinking.

> The consultants should be made aware of the strength of interest of the BFI and other bodies in the question of whether a network should exist, what it should do, and how it should be organised. The question is being put not as a speculative exploration of an open matter so much as an indication of the BFI's concern to respond to pressures, from individuals and groups, for a successor to SEFT to be established quickly.[8]

An additional pressure on Philip Simpson was that he was about to leave the BFI after a decade of rehabilitating the Education Department and possibly he felt the need to set the consultancy process in motion before his successor arrived.

The brief for the consultancy was eventually put out to tender in summer 1989. Boyden Southwood Associates were selected and given the task in February 1990, but the final version of their report did not appear until October 1990, some two years after the Comedia Report.[9] The Boyden Southwood Report was systematic and thorough in consulting with practitioners in the target education sectors and used the services of established figures in those constituencies in order to reflect as comprehensive a view as possible.[10] By the time of its publication in late 1990, the absence of SEFT would have become less marked. Essentially the report focuses on two distinct areas: the possible role to be played by an organisation and the need felt by teachers for a regular publication. The consultants had usefully investigated the membership of well-established subject associations and discovered that even large-scale operations such as NATE followed a national pattern of recruiting only some ten percent of those teachers who were eligible to join. Whereas in the case of NATE 46,000 teachers of English produced 4,600 members, the potential recruitment for a media education association was very much smaller. The Report calculated that the total potential from which the members of a media education association might be recruited was 2270, thus producing a likely membership of 227.[11] Publications were however favoured by teachers, particularly in secondary and further sectors, with a demand both for a regular newsletter and for a more thoughtful, but less frequent, journal.[12]

The Report was discussed at a Media Education Network Seminar held at the NFT in May 1991, an event at which some participants were described as 'argumentative, resistant and on occasion truculent'.[13] The participants were not the teachers who might combine to form the potential membership but representatives of a range of small scale organisations with an involvement in media education. They had been carefully selected:

> We have drawn up the following list of invitees, on the basis that we do not wish to invite everyone we have ever heard of, but strategically important people and institutions in the media education field.[14]

Among the invitees were individuals who were already by then developing media education journals, including Roy Stafford of *in the picture* and Brenda Downes of *Media Education*.[15]

By the time the Boyden Southwood Report had been published, the educational context had changed from that which prevailed during the SEFT decades. The Society had for most of its existence been the only membership organisation in the UK available to those teachers, lecturers, inspectors and advisers in film, television and media who sought to make common cause with others. By 1991, when a possible national successor organisation was being debated, the situation was very different. As already noted, in the mid 1980s nationally based arrangements were developed in Scotland and Wales. The next level of specialisation came later in the decade when distinct professional sub-groups saw their interests as needing separate representation. In autumn 1986, Teacher Educators and Advisers in Media Education (TEAME) was founded, reflecting how local education authorities had addressed the *ad hoc* growth of the various manifestations of media education by making such appointments.

While the 'Gillespie group' wanted a SEFT replacement body for those teaching outside higher education, those in the polytechnics and universities were also seeking assistance from the BFI, having proceeded in late 1989 to form the Association for Media, Film and Television Studies in Higher and Further Education (AMFIT). In London, which had been in effect the SEFT 'heartland', Teaching Media in London (TML) was set up post-SEFT in 1989. Media education, having become widely established in the 1980s, had generated numerous local groups, some dating from SEFT's Media Education Initiative. Where the Comedia Report had been read in 1988 by a small number of disenchanted SEFT Committee members who accepted its negativity, a much more expectant and critical readership had been waiting almost three years for the chance to engage with the Boyden Southwood Report.

The funding necessary to establish an association was examined in detail in the Report and by the time it appeared the realities of the BFI's situation had to be recognised. The SEFT money for 1989/90 had been used up and in the 1990/91 budget that particular line had disappeared from the accounts.[16] Simpson had been replaced by Manuel Alvarado who had long and detailed experience of the intricacies of the SEFT operation. He took an early opportunity of obtaining from BFI accounts a history of the decades of BFI subsidy to SEFT which revealed that over the span of forty years the total grant had amounted to some £750,000.[17] Alvarado's objective was to demonstrate that, for a relatively small annual sum over many years, SEFT had made a very significant contribution to media education.[18] He knew that in order to operate successfully, SEFT had always succeeded year after year in matching whatever sum it received via the BFI grant with income it generated itself. The prospect of a successor body, starting from scratch in the recession years of the early 1990s, being able to achieve a comparable autonomy without BFI funding was very unlikely.

Alvarado had recognised one post-SEFT need that his Department would be able to meet: the provision of an interim replacement for *Initiatives*. Consequently a termly newsletter, *MENU*, appeared – *Media Education News Update*. What did eventually become a possibility in the longer term was the introduction of a new journal. After negotiations, funding additional to the BFI's contribution became available from the Arts Council. The aim of this collaboration was to produce a successor journal to fill the gap that had been created by the demise of *Screen Education* in 1982. Consequently it was planned that the new publication would address 'questions of pedagogy as well as theory' and would command 'a national and international readership amongst teachers of media'.[19] Tenders were finally put out in 1993 for a magazine to cover 'Media and Photography Education'. Whilst it was the case that both *Screen* and *Screen Education* had broken into new territory by printing photographs and introducing articles on photography, teachers of media education and teachers of photography did not at this stage form a common constituency. In practice it was not until the spring of 1995 that *20:20* first appeared and after just five issues it ceased publication with the winter 1996 issue, when the Arts Council funding stopped.[20] The Council's money had been made available from April 1994 for a limited three year franchise, subject to annual review.[21] It would seem that this attempt to meet the requirements of both photography and media teachers had satisfied neither constituency.

A major preoccupation of the BFI Education Department following Alvarado's arrival was the construction jointly with the Open University of a distance learning pack which was 'intended to offer an introduction to media education for teachers in both primary and secondary schools'. It covered 'a basic theoretical background as well as ways of undertaking critical and practical work in the classroom'.[22] This was an important development in that it recognised both the need for training amongst the growing number of teachers directed to teach media and also addressed the reality that schools were increasingly reluctant to release any teachers for training. From an historical perspective it is the 450 page *Reader*, which was edited to accompany the other course materials, that is of greatest interest now.[23] Its publication defines the moment when the initial phase in the development of media education ended, while its content explains how that moment was painstakingly achieved. The term 'media education' was by then already in common currency and covered a recognisable field of knowledge and enquiry. In order to explain how this stage had been reached the *Reader* deploys a comprehensive selection of writing from the previous thirty years, much of it originating in SEFT or BFI Education publications.

Despite this substantial retrospective publication, it might have seemed that media education's best days were already over: no new association had replaced SEFT and the new journal had failed. Success also eluded most of the other member organisations in the field. TEAME's small first Executive of six included four who had been or still were very active in SEFT and there were links between the two organisations.[24] At SEFT's 1987 Annual Conference a range of proposals was agreed concerning the National Curriculum in the expectation that 'they may contribute to discussions at the TEAME event on the National Curriculum'.[25] The TEAME membership was however somewhat restricted. Membership was open to

> ...those officers within a Local Education Authority with responsibility for advising on, developing or supporting media education and to those lecturers in institutions of Higher Education involved in teaching or administering courses in media education within the initial or in-service training of teachers or other educationalists.[26]

With these limitations the individual membership in 1988 had reached only 38. There were a further 17 associate members and 19 corporate members.[27] This was a vulnerable group. As schools achieved greater financial independence, as the powers of intervention by LEAs were diminished and as the constraints of the National Curriculum marginalised the training of media teachers, so the restricted potential for growth and then for survival of TEAME became apparent. In March 1992 TEAME was formally dissolved and its assets transferred to the Association for Media Education (AME).[28] AME had been founded in November 1991 with a very wide brief and a geographical limitation: 'to support and extend media education in England. You do not need to be working in education or the media'.[29]

Coinciding with the disappearance of SEFT, Teaching Media in London was set up in 1989 principally through the efforts of Jenny Grahame who was then working at the English Centre of the Inner London Education Authority (ILEA), though TML had no direct relationship with the Centre. TML was created to address the breaking up of the ILEA into ten borough-based unitary education authorities. While the ILEA had long been supportive of media education, its successor authorities were too small and in most cases too poor to resource innovative curriculum developments. The new group ran successful conferences for the first few years but as the ILEA links between teachers diminished, so TML shrank to become a network with local meetings attracting fewer and fewer people. It was disbanded in 1996 or 1997.[30]

AMFIT however was a very different enterprise which was specifically founded in the aftermath of SEFT's disappearance. It was recruiting in a growth area with membership open to

...people in Universities, Colleges and Institutes of Higher Education, and in the Further and Continuing Education sector.[31]

Within a year of its formation AMFIT had 150 members.[32] It ran a series of well-attended annual conferences with financial support from the BFI and became the front-runner amongst a number of new bodies which were identified in AMFIT's 1993/94 Annual Report:

...the Association for Media Education in England, the Association for Media Education in Scotland, the Association of Cultural Studies, the Media Studies Association, the National Association for Higher Education in Film and Video, the Standing Conference in Culture, Communication and Media Studies and AMFIT itself.

The AMFIT Executive believe that the field (and all its various sectors) could be more effectively represented by a single, vigorous and coherent body that enjoyed the confidence of the appropriate professional communities.[33]

There would be a series of mergers of the organisations recruiting specifically in higher education, but spread over several years. AMFIT joined with the Association of Cultural Studies (ACS) in 1999 to form the Media, Communication and Cultural Studies Association (MeCCSA) which in turn absorbed the Association of Media Practice Educators (AMPE) in 2007.[34] AME which had a much more diverse recruitment strategy was short-lived. Roy Stafford believes that given its wide brief and without a paid employee to co-ordinate its activities, AMEE – as it was subsequently designated to incorporate the English national identifier – simply failed to establish itself.[35] It may also have demonstrated the inevitability of the Boyden Southwood calculation that there were simply not enough eligible teachers who would be prepared to join.

Media education in the late 1980s and 1990s was becoming more widely established in secondary schools, in further education colleges and in higher education. Outside the academy it was media studies at GCSE and A level that dominated while in higher education the range of courses on offer covered a wider terrain. The delivery mechanisms varied between the sectors. In schools, media or film study might be on offer but rarely taught by a specialist. The 'media teacher' would be a specialist in another subject area and only a small proportion of her/his timetable would be given over to the 'media option'. The problem faced by any media teachers' organisation was attracting sufficient members from among those whose priority teaching expertise lay elsewhere. Such teachers, feeling their way in delivering media education, looked to the very specific training provided by the examination boards and specialist centres. These offered a benefit that directly addressed a need and was accordingly perceived as more relevant. By contrast, in higher education whole departments of media specialists serviced the new degree courses. Thus the recruitment potential for an association based in higher education was increasing. Other factors reinforced this tendency: the distinction between polytechnics and universities was abolished in 1993 and with a greater percentage of students expected to study for degrees after 1997, the universities found media based courses to have a particular attraction in their widening participation strategies.

What began as film appreciation for those regarded as on the periphery of organised educational provision, is now manifested in a range of courses that are widely represented in the academy. Many of those who pioneered the work at lower levels are now established as high-ranking academics on these new courses. But those students who achieve their degrees on such media, cultural studies and communication courses are not attracted to teach in schools where the scope for media teaching is constrained by the National Curriculum. Currently the number of students able to train to teach media in schools is tiny: only one institution, the Central School of Speech and Drama, offers training places and these go to fewer than twenty students annually.[36] The teacher training institutions, identified in the 1960s as the locus of innovation in the teaching of film, television and media, no longer play that role.

The argument advanced in the 1960s and 1970s was that only when film and media study were properly represented in the academy would the teaching of those areas in schools achieve status and coherence, qualities that were seen as inevitably lacking in a curriculum that had been created at the margins of mandatory education. Many of those who participated in SEFT during those decades went on successfully to establish media and cultural studies in the academy. The former SEFT journal *Screen*, after forty years in print, has a secure home in the University of Glasgow and remains in regular publication from Oxford University Press. In the schools, the participation of examination boards in expanding their subject offer allowed film and media to achieve popularity and credibility in public examinations. However, teachers trained in media before entering the classroom are missing. The resultant situation is one where much of the training for would-be media teachers is provided by the examination boards, is very specific to the syllabus of each particular board and privileges media studies at the expense of media education.

There is now a new political dimension. A regulatory body, the Office of Communications (Ofcom), has been given responsibility by the Government for developing media literacy in relation to non-print media. However media literacy is a term that still lacks adequate definition. The immediate priority is for the involvement of educational experience and expertise in shaping the debate around this newly recognised form of literacy, which currently remains largely restricted to media professionals. It would seem that a SEFT-shaped gap may be about to re-appear.

Notes

1. *Screen* Archive University of Glasgow Box 5 1986 'Proposal for a National Media Education Association' p 1 – undated but prepared probably in November 1988 by Tim Blanchard, David Buckingham, Andrew Freedman, Marie Gillespie, Simon Greenleaf, Lucy Moy-Thomas, Mary Wood.
2. Ibid
3. Ibid
4. *Screen* Archive University of Glasgow Box 5 1986 Marie Gillespie 'Report of Working Party on Media Teachers Association' 9 November 1988
5. Ibid
6. British Film Institute Education Department Archive Box BFI/MEA/33–4 Philip Simpson Inter-office Memorandum 'Media Education Network' 24 February 1989 p 1
7. Ibid
8. Ibid p 2
9. Inter-office Memorandum from Julian Bowker 21 February 1991
10. Boyden Southwood *British Film Institute Media Education Consultancy* 1990
11. Ibid p 68
12. Section B of the Report 'Interviewee's interests and needs in relation to newsletters and journals' was made available by the BFI as a separate document.
13. Letter to Cary Bazalgette from Paddie Collyer on behalf of the Southampton Media in Education Group (undated)
14. Cary Bazalgette 'Media Education Network Seminar' BFI Inter-office Memorandum to the Education Department 26 April 1991
15. Published list of those attending Media Education Network Seminar 24 May 1991
16. BFI Annual Accounts 1990/1991
17. Inter-office memorandum from Manuel Alvarado to Richard Paterson
18. Manuel Alvarado in interview with the author 8 January 2008
19. 'Media and Photography Education – a new magazine' Tendering document produced jointly by the Arts Council and the British Film Institute for potential publishers, September 1993
20. This journal (*20:20*) should not be confused with the similarly titled *20/20* which appeared in 19 issues between April 1989 and Spring 1991.
21. Tender document op cit
22. Open University *Media Education: an Introduction Workbook* Milton Keynes 1992 p 7
23. Manuel Alvarado and Oliver Boyd-Barrett (Eds) *Media Education: an Introduction* London: British Film Institute 1992
24. Birkbeck College Faculty of Continuing Education Archive TEAME 'First Annual Report' undated but published at some time in the second half of 1988. SEFT personnel on the Executive Committee were Michael Clarke, Phillip Drummond, David Buckingham and Chris Mottershead.
25. *Screen* Archive University of Glasgow Box 11 1987 Paper circulated at TEAME conference 7 December 1987.

26. Birkbeck College Faculty of Continuing Education Archive 'TEAME Constitution' 1986
27. Birkbeck College Faculty of Continuing Education Archive TEAME 'First Annual Report' pp 10–12
28. Birkbeck College Faculty of Continuing Education Archive Letter from TEAME Retiring Chair to the Manager of the Tottenham Court Road Midland Bank
29. Birkbeck College Faculty of Continuing Education Archive AME leaflet
30. Jenny Grahame in interview with the author 13 June 2005
31. Birkbeck College Faculty of Continuing Education Archive Letter from Mary P Wood Secretary AMFIT November 1992
32. Birkbeck College Faculty of Continuing Education Archive AMFIT 'Annual Report 1989–1990' pp 21–24
33. Birkbeck College Faculty of Continuing Education Archive AMFIT 'Annual Report 1993–94' p 3
34. MeCCSA home page http://meccsa.org.uk
35. Roy Stafford in interview with the author 11 May 2005
36. Information in autumn 2007 from Symon Quy Head of Media Teacher Training, Central School of Speech and Drama

Screen education: a timeline 1930–1993

Year	Organisations	Personnel	Events	Publications
1930	The 'unofficial' Commission on Educational and Cultural Films starts work		London County Council (LCC) instructs its school inspectors to investigate children and the cinema	
1931	Empire Marketing Board under John Grierson sets up a film library to distribute to schools and institutes			
1932				Commission Report *The Film in National Life*; Hunter *Scrutiny of Cinema*; LCC *Schoolchildren and the Cinema*; *Sight & Sound* first published by the British Institute of Adult Education
1933	British Film Institute (BFI) is founded	His Grace the Duke of Sutherland is first Chairman of BFI; J W Brown is its first General Manager		Arnheim *Film*
1934	BFI takes over publication of *Sight & Sound*			
1935			First BFI Summer School held in Scarborough	Spottiswoode *A Grammar of the Film*; Lauwerys *The Film and the School*; George *The Cinema in School*

Year	Organisations	Personnel	Events	Publications
1936	BBC starts world's first daily transmission of television programmes	Oliver Bell becomes Director of the BFI in place of General Manager Brown; E Francis Mills experiments with film teaching in the classroom	BFI Conference 'Films for Children' BFI Summer School has first lecture on Film Appreciation	Rotha *Documentary Film*
1937				Denholme *The Cinema and Education* BFI *Films for children*
1938	Northern Counties Children's Cinema Council (NCCCC) set up in Newcastle		Fourth (and last) BFI Summer School to be organised by the Educational Handwork Association	League of Nations *Recreational Cinema and the Young*
1939	BBC ceases television transmission on the outbreak of the Second World War			NCCCC *Film Appreciation in the School*; Ford *Children in the Cinema*
1940	BFI seconds teachers as Teacher Organisers to support war effort			Brian Smith 'The Next Step' (*Sight & Sound*) anticipates 1970s film study
1941	Secondment of Teacher Organisers extended			
1942				Lindgren *Film Appreciation for Discussion Groups and Schools*

Year	Organisations	Personnel	Events	Publications
1943	BFI appoints its first Travelling Educational Representative		BFI Conference 'The Film in National Life' in Exeter	Eisenstein's *The Film Sense* published in English
1944	Education Act successfully steered through Parliament by RA Butler		Interim Report of the Arts Enquiry; BFI Summer School re-established in Bangor	Lindgren *The Cinema*; Manvell *The Cinema and the Public*
1945	BBC television transmission restarts at the end of the war; UNESCO founded	Roger Manvell is BFI's first lecturer in film appreciation		Labour election victory; Pearson *The Film as a Visual Art*
1946	National Committee for Audio Visual Aids in Education (NCAVAE) set up by LEAs with responsibility for film appreciation		BFI/National Council of Women Conference 'Children and the Cinema'; UK school leaving age raised to 15	Jones & Pardoe *A First Course in Film Appreciation*; Penguin *Film Review* appears
1947	British Film Academy established; Wheare Committee on 'Children and the Cinema'		BFI awards £30 to support a film teaching experiment in a secondary modern school	Harman *Good Films and how to Appreciate Them*; Arts Enquiry *The Factual Film*; *Sequence* first appears
1948	Radcliffe Committee redefines the role of the BFI			Lindgren *The Art of the Film*

Year	Organisations	Personnel	Events	Publications
1949	Teachers at BFI Summer School consider forming what will become SFT	Denis Forman becomes Director of the BFI	New Education Fellowship Conference 'The Impact of the Cinema on the Child'	Dilys Powell *Films since 1939*
1950	Society of Film Teachers (SFT) is founded	Stanley Reed becomes BFI's first Film Appreciation Officer; Dr R R Jones becomes first Chairman of SFT	New Education Fellowship Conference 'Film Appreciation' precedes SFT's inaugural meeting	*Report on Children and the Cinema* (Wheare Report); Evernden & Holloway *Our Own Language*
1951	Festival of Britain	E Francis Mills becomes Chairman of SFT	SFT organises exhibition of film teaching work	Buchanan *The Film in Education* BFI monthly wall sheet *Film Guide* first published
1952	BFI begins collaboration with University of London Extra-Mural Department; BFI Experimental Film Fund established; Telekinema from Festival of Britain becomes the first National Film Theatre	Leeds University awards Maurice Woodhouse a PhD for research into film appreciation in the school	Bristol University Drama Department Conference 'The Relation between Universities and Films, Radio and Television'	SFT publishes first issue of *The Film Teacher*; BFI starts *Critics' Choice*; Stanley Reed *Film Appreciation as a Classroom Subject*
1953		Jack Smith becomes Chairman of SFT; Tony Hodgkinson becomes BFI Film Appreciation Officer		Hills *Are They Safe at the Cinema?* BFI/SFT *Twenty Films to Use*

Year	Organisations	Personnel	Events	Publications
1954				Orram & Williams *Preface to Film*; the monthly *Film Guide* poster for schools is developed by the BFI
1955	Independent (commercial) television starts transmission	James Quinn becomes Director of the BFI		SFT replaces *The Film Teacher* (printed) with *Film Teacher* (duplicated)
1956		Tony Higgins becomes Chairman of SFT	Penelope Houston becomes Editor of *Sight & Sound*	SFT organises first public screening of school-made films at the NFT; SFT first publishes *The Film Teacher's Handbook*
1957	BFI opens purpose built National Film Theatre under Waterloo Bridge	Paddy Whannel joins the Film Appreciation Section of the BFI Education Department	Amsterdam Conference 'Film Education and Youth' London Film Festival opens	Hoggart *The Uses of Literacy*
1958			BFI/SFT London Conference 'Film, Television and the Child'	Williams *Culture and Society*; Himmelweit et al *Television and the Child*; ITA *Parents, Children and Television*; Arnheim *Film as Art*
1959	SFT becomes SEFT: Society for Education in Film and Television		BFI/SFT organise 'The Visual Persuaders' week-long event at NFT for Joint Council for Education through Art	SEFT produces first issue of *Screen Education*; *Film Guide* becomes *Screen Guide*

Year	Organisations	Personnel	Events	Publications
1960	*Lady Chatterley's Lover* Trial; First UK university lectureship in Film offered at the Slade School of Art	Victor Perkins leads the attack on the BFI 's film selection priorities in *Oxford Opinion*	NUT Conference 'Popular Culture and Personal Responsibility'	*Screen Education Yearbook* replaces *The Film Teacher's Handbook*; *New Left Review* founded; Kracauer *Theory of Film*
1961			NUT takes over Young Film-Makers Competition from the *News Chronicle*	Groombridge *Study Guide* to NUT Conference; Peters *Teaching about the Film*; BFI produces *Contrast* a quarterly television journal
1962		Don Waters becomes Chairman of SEFT	International Film and Television Teaching Conference, Norway	The first issue of *Movie* is published; Williams *Communications*
1963	BFI lobbies the Ministry of Education for direct funding of its education work			*Half Our Future* (Newsom Report); SEFT completes publication of introductory film-making and screen education pamphlets
1964	Labour wins General Election; Bede College offers first main teacher training course in Film and Television; Council for National Academic Awards (CNAA) is established to award degree level qualifications	Jenny Lee is appointed Minister for the Arts; Stanley Reed becomes Director of the BFI		Hall & Whannel *The Popular Arts*; Whannel & Harcourt *Teaching Film*; Hodgkinson *Screen Education – teaching critical approach to cinema and television*; McLuhan *Understanding Media*; Thompson (ed) *Discrimination and Popular Culture*

Year	Organisations	Personnel	Events	Publications
1965	Funding of BFI passes from Treasury to Department of Education and Science; BFI evening classes become a university certificate course; Certificate of Secondary Education introduced	RC Vannoey becomes Chairman of SEFT		Zwemmer/Tantivy Press introduce paperbacks on film
1966	Whannel offers SEFT the possibility of a joint BFI/SEFT appointment; Bede College and Hornsey College of Art each offer a one term course for established teachers of film and television		SEFT and the London Co-operative Society organise the first biennial 'Let's Make a Film Festival'; BFI offers first 'themed' Summer School on British Cinema	BFI Education publishes *Talking About the Cinema* and *Talking About Television*; BFI abandons *Contrast*; Tucker *Understanding the Mass Media*
1967	Slade School lectureship becomes first UK professorship in film	Alex Richardson appointed BFI Teacher Adviser/Secretary SEFT	BFI Education Department begins programme of regular seminars with invited participants	*Sight & Sound* and BFI Education collaborate on Cinema One books; Movie Paperbacks start; Bazin *What is Cinema?* Vol 1 (in English)
1968		Stuart Hall becomes Acting Director of Birmingham Centre for Contemporary Cultural Studies	BBC transmits *Cinema*, an educational television series for Sixth Form written and presented by Victor Perkins	SEFT publishes the final *Screen Education Yearbook (1969)* and *CSE Examinations in Film*

Year	Organisations	Personnel	Events	Publications
1969	BFI Education Department moves back to Dean Street	Terry Bolas replaces Richardson as full-time Secretary SEFT	Edinburgh Film Festival on 'Samuel Fuller' initiates annual complementary series of paperbacks	SEFT publishes first issue of *Screen*; Wollen *Signs and Meaning in the Cinema*; *Fight for Education: A Black Paper* is the first of a series published from the Right
1970	BFI Members Action Committee formed to confront BFI Governors and Management over BFI policy	Roger Watkins becomes Chairman of SEFT; Sam Rohdie appointed Editor of *Screen*/Secretary SEFT	SEFT/ILEA Film Teaching Experiment	*Afterimage* first published; Wollen (ed) *Working Papers on the Cinema: Sociology and Semiology*
1971	BFI Governors review their Education Department and this triggers six resignations; National Film and Television School opens in Beaconsfield; National Association for Film Education (NAFE) is founded	Jim Cook becomes Chairman of SEFT; Whannel and five others resign from BFI	SEFT calls 'Crisis in Film Education' Conference at the National Film Theatre	Rohdie's redesigned *Screen* appears; Buscombe *Screen* Pamphlet No 1: *Films on TV*; *Brighton Film Review* becomes *Monogram*; First volume of publications from the Birmingham Centre for Contemporary Cultural Studies
1972	SEFT moves out of BFI and goes to 63 Old Compton Street; First candidates sit for O/A Level in Film Studies	Keith Lucas becomes BFI Director; Douglas Lowndes becomes Head of BFI Educational Advisory Service; Christine Gledhill becomes Chairman of SEFT	BFI/ILEA 6th Form Film Study Course begins development	SEFT publishes *Screen Education Notes*; Perkins *Film as Film*; Groombridge *Television and the People*

Year	Organisations	Personnel	Events	Publications
1973	BFI sets up the first pump-primed university lectureship in Film at Warwick University		BFI/SEFT regular seminar programme is introduced; UK school leaving age raised to 16	Murdock & Phelps *Mass Media and the Secondary School*; Johnston *Screen* Pamphlet No 2: *Notes on Women's Cinema*; Barthes *Mythologies* (in English)
1974	BFI university lectureship set up at Keele University	Ben Brewster appointed Editor of *Screen*; Manuel Alvarado appointed Education Officer SEFT/Editor *Screen Education*	SEFT's first Easter School	SEFT publishes the new *Screen Education*; *Framework* first published; Williams *Television, Technology and Cultural Form*
1975	BFI university lectureship set up at Essex University	Chris Mottershead becomes Chairman of SEFT	SEFT programme of Weekend Schools commences; First SEFT Reading Groups are established	*Viewpoint* – a series on mass communications for schools by Douglas Lowndes – is transmitted by Thames Television
1976	BFI university lectureship set up at the University of East Anglia; SEFT moves to 29 Old Compton Street	Four resignations from the *Screen* Editorial Board; Steve Neale becomes Chairperson of SEFT	York Conference 'Film and TV Studies in Secondary Education'; Prime Minister Callaghan's 'Great Debate' speech in Oxford	Buscombe *Making Legend of the Werewolf*, Glasgow University Media Group *Bad News* first volume published
1977	Polytechnic of Central London offers Postgraduate Diploma in Film Study	Geoffrey Nowell-Smith appointed Editor of *Screen*		SEFT *Screen Reader 1 Cinema, Ideology, Politics*; UNESCO *Media Studies in Education*

Year	Organisations	Personnel	Events	Publications
1978	University of East Anglia offers MA in British Cinema; Slade School of Art offers M Phil in Film Studies	Editorial appointments: Mark Nash to *Screen*; James Donald to *Screen Education*; Geoffrey Nowell-Smith appointed Head of EAS at the BFI.		Alvarado & Buscombe *Hazell – the making of a TV series*
1979	Conservative party wins General Election and stays in power until 1997	Anthony Smith becomes Director of the BFI; Phillip Drummond becomes Chairperson of SEFT	BFI and London Institute of Education Conference 'Film and Media Studies in Higher Education'	Mulhern *The Moment of Scrutiny*; SEFT *N and F Studies*
1980	BFI sets up award for new initiatives in media education in memory of Paddy Whannel who died earlier this year	Philip Simpson becomes Head of BFI Education Department; Geoffrey Nowell-Smith moves to Head of BFI Publishing	SEFT Conference 'Culture and Politics'	Masterman *Teaching about Television*; Rogers *Television and the Family*; BFI starts *Film Dossiers*
1981	London Institute of Education offers MA course in Film and Television Studies for Education	George Foster becomes Chairperson of SEFT	BFI/Goldsmiths College 'Media Education' Conference	Birmingham Centre for Contemporary Cultural Studies Education Group *Unpopular Education*
1982	Launch of Channel 4; Introduction of A level Film Studies	Mandy Merck appointed Editor of *Screen incorporating Screen Education*		*Screen Education*'s last issue; SEFT *Screen Reader 2 Cinema and Semiotics*

Year	Organisations	Personnel	Events	Publications
1983	Association for Media Education in Scotland (AMES) is established	Judy Bennett becomes Chairperson of SEFT	BFI and London Institute of Education conference 'Television and Schooling'	DES Report *Popular TV and Schoolchildren; in the picture* first published by Yorkshire Arts
1984	BFI now funds LEA teacher adviser posts annually in place of the university lectureships	Sean Cubitt appointed as SEFT's National Organiser; Tana Wollen becomes Chairperson of SEFT		SEFT produces the first issue of *Initiatives*
1985	'Film Education' is established by the British Film Industry		First SEFT National Conference in Bradford	Masterman *Teaching the Media*
1986	SEFT TV Users Group joins with Campaign for Press and Broadcasting Freedom; Teacher Educators and Advisers in Media Education (TEAME) founded	Andrew Higson becomes Chairperson of SEFT *Screen* 'Pedagogy' issue starts Len Masterman vs David Buckingham debate	SEFT National Conference in Birmingham; BFI/DES National Working Party on primary education	Blanchard *Media Studies and the GCSE*; SEFT *Papers from Bradford*
1987	CSE and GCE O level on offer for the last time before being replaced by the GCSE		BFI/SEFT London conference 'Teaching Alternative Media'; SEFT National Conference in Liverpool	Alvarado, Gutch and Wollen *Learning the Media*

Year	Organisations	Personnel	Events	Publications
1988	Comedia Consultancy recommends discontinuance of SEFT	Wilf Stevenson becomes Director BFI; Caroline Taylor becomes SEFT's final Chair	SEFT's final National Conference in Cambridge	
1989	SEFT ceases after 39 years and Association for Media, Film and Television Studies in Higher Education (AMFIT) is founded	Manuel Alvarado becomes Head of BFI Education Department	First BFI 3-day annual event for teachers of A level Media Studies	*Screen* goes to the Logie Baird Centre in Glasgow; BFI funds two final issues of *Initiatives*
1990	Former ilea English Centre becomes independent as the English and Media Centre	Penelope Houston retires from *Sight & Sound* after 34 years as Editor	BFI Education's International Conference in Toulouse 'New Directions in Media Education'	Boyden Southwood *British Film Institute Media Education Consultancy*; Roy Stafford takes over as Editor and publisher of *in the picture*
1991			Final BFI Summer School	Lusted *The Media Studies Book*
1992	CNAA disappears when higher education institutions given degree-awarding status and polytechnics become universities		Co-op Young People's Film and Video Festival celebrates 25 years; BFI and Birkbeck College recruit eleven students on to their new MA course in Film and TV Studies	Alvarado & Boyd-Barrett (Eds) *Media Education: an Introduction*; Screen *The Sexual Subject A Screen Reader in Sexuality*
1993	Tenders go out for the production of a new Arts Council funded journal for Media and Photography Education			Alvarado, Buscombe, Collins *Screen Education Reader*; BFI publishes first edition of *Media Courses UK*

Expansion of media studies – the statistics

The following tables of statistics illustrate just how extensive has been the expansion of film and media teaching in secondary, further and higher education during the two decades that have followed the period examined in this book. It is however an expansion for which those advocating media education can claim only limited credit: the appeal of the media to the young has worked its own magic.

There has been a curious reversal of priorities in the media teaching situation. From the time of the Wheare Report in 1950 and on through to the 1970s, there was a generally acknowledged concern that the progress of film and then media education must be linked to the availability of suitably trained and qualified teachers in the schools and further education colleges. Now, when there is almost no provision for the training of such teachers, there has been a considerable increase in the availability of public examinations at GCSE, AS and A Levels which has both addressed and stimulated student demand. There are of course graduates with qualifications in a wide range of curriculum areas which fall under the media umbrella and some of these are to be found teaching in schools.

However, the pattern to be found in the secondary and further education sectors is that, while fascination and engagement with the range of media among students has encouraged the introduction of media studies/film at examination levels, media education for younger students is sketchy at best. Consequently relatively few establishments have sufficient numbers to support separate film/media departments; instead much examination teaching is undertaken with varying degrees of willingness by those who regard themselves primarily as teachers of other subjects. Simultaneously the government issues edicts about the importance of media literacy and places responsibility for delivering it on Ofcom, a regulatory rather than educational body.

In higher education the explosion of student interest in media has been addressed more directly at an institutional level. Film and media departments have been established in most universities, recruiting staff with film/media qualifications from similar but longer established departments elsewhere. In some instances departments servicing other disciplines, such as modern languages, have found that offering a film-related option at post-graduate level has generated sufficient student recruitment to help stabilise the department's staffing level.

A consequence of this different but somewhat impromptu growth within each of the two sectors has been the creation of a very indeterminate interface between what is appropriate for study at A Level on the one hand and at first year undergraduate level on the other. How should a university cater in the same introductory course for one student who has achieved an A award in Film Study at A Level and another for whom the degree will provide a first opportunity to study film?

A tiny group of individuals who act independently of each other has, as a consequence, become hugely influential in the dissemination of the practice of teaching film and media studies: those who are employed as Chief Examiners by the Examination Boards. The books they write and the training they design and which the Boards then offer inevitably shape the structure of the subjects at sub-degree level. Undoubtedly the ability of schools and colleges to offer film and media specifically at examination level has guaranteed the acceptability of studying these areas of the curriculum and facilitated their permanent establishment. This has proved to be a definitive move as successive governments have endorsed achievement in examinations as the hallmark of effective education.

In the context of the history of the development of media education, there is an inevitable irony in this outcome. For decades opponents of film and media education at all levels have attacked these subjects as forming the thin end of a popular culture wedge which demonstrated a readiness on the part of other teachers to connive at the dumbing-down of the curriculum. The activists of the 1970s who clustered around *Screen* and *Screen Education* intended their interventions into the study of media and of culture to operate in a precisely opposite direction. They sought to question not just the content of the curriculum but to open up the fissures in the intellectual basis upon which this traditional structure had been established and maintained. *Screen*'s writers of that period drew a deliberate distinction between their approach and that of academics, particularly in the USA, which they rejected. However student preferences for media-related courses have now ensured that such courses are firmly established within the Academy and in schools and colleges. Simultaneously the spread of these media-related qualifications continues to be exploited by conservative academics as evidence of dumbing-down in higher education. For the surviving radicals of the 1970s, the momentum of this institutionalisation of media education represents an altogether more profound dumbing-down.

Percentage of Examination Entries at GCSE & A Level June 2006

	Total Exam Entries	Entries for English	Percentage	Entries for Media	Percentage
GCSE	5752152	721762	*12.5*	57521	*1.0*
A Level	805698	86640	*10.8*	30964	*3.8*

2006 UK Students Sitting for GCE A Level by Gender

Subject Area	Total Students	Female	Male
English	86640	59819	26821
%		*69.04*	*30.96*
Media/Film/TV Studies	30964	16848	14116
%		*54.41*	*45.59*

GCE A Level Results June 2006 Percentages of Grades by Gender

	Year	Students Studying English	% A	% B–C	% D–E	Students Studying Media/Film/TV	% A	% B–C	% D–E
Female	2005	59526	*20.7*	*52.6*	*25.4*	15536	*15.5*	*63.5*	*20.0*
	2006	59819	*22.0*	*53.1*	*23.9*	16848	*16.0*	*64*	*19.2*
Male	2005	26332	*20.7*	*50.1*	*27.6*	12725	*11.3*	*61.1*	*26.1*
	2006	26821	*21.7*	*51.8*	*25.0*	14116	*11.2*	*60.5*	*26.3*

2006 UK Students Sitting for GCSE Level by Gender

Subject Area	Total Students	Female	Male
English	721762	359755	362007
%		*49.84*	*50.16*
Media/Film/Tv Studies	57521	28803	28718
%		*50.07*	*49.93*

GCSE Results June 2006 percentages of Grades by Gender

	Year	Students Studying English	% A*	% A–C	Students Studying Media	% A*	% A–C
Female	2005	354830	4.7	63.2	23732	4.4	63.8
	2006	359755	5.0	63.6	28803	4.7	63.3
Male	2005	353739	2.6	51.3	21951	1.9	51.0
	2006	362007	2.7	52.0	28718	1.9	51.1

Source: Joint Council For Qualifications

Growth of Certain Subject Areas in UK Higher Education – 1996/7 and 2006/7

Subject Area	1996/7	2006/7
English	29455	60310
% of Total HE Students	*1.677*	*2.552*
Media Studies	6888	27225
% of Total HE Students	*0.392*	*1.152*
Cinematics	3204	16055
% of Total HE Students	*0.182*	*0.679*
Total Students in all Subject Areas	**1756179**	**2362815**

2006/7 Recruitment of UK Based Students in Higher Education – By Gender

Subject Area	Total Students	Female	Male
English Studies	51020	36790	14230
%		*72.11*	*27.89*
Media Studies	23710	12250	11460
%		*51.67*	*48.33*
Cinematics	14305	6395	7910
%		*44.70*	*55.30*

UK Higher Education Student Recruitment 1996/7 & 2006/7

Subject Area	Total Students	Full Time Under Grad	Full Time Post Grad	Part Time Under Grad	Part Time Post Grad
English 1996/7	29455	20571	2250	3932	2702
English 2006/7	60310	39000	3660	14195	3460
% Increase	*104.75*	*89.59*	*62.67*	*261.01*	*28.05*
Media Studies 1996/7	6888	4988	607	920	363
Media Studies 2006/7	27225	22420	1995	1740	1070
% Increase	*295.25*	*349.48*	*228.67*	*89.13*	*194.77*
Cinematics 1996/7	3204	2490	276	172	266
Cinematics 2006/7	16055	13405	940	1060	650
% Increase	*401.09*	*438.35*	*240.58*	*516.28*	*144.36*

Source: Higher Education Statistics Agency

Bibliography

Items listed in this bibliography (books and articles in journals) are generally to be found in either the BFI National Library or the British Library. The location of documents to be found in specialist archives is indicated in the appropriate endnote. Those documents are not listed here.

Abrams, Mark *The Teenage Consumer* London: Press Exchange Ltd July 1959

Aldgate, Anthony and Richards, Jeffrey *Best of British – Cinema and Society from 1930 to the present* London: I B Taurus 2002

Alexander, S G P 'Forming the Society of Film Teachers' *Screen Education* No 28 March/April 1968 pp 33–40

Alexander, S G P 'From SFT to SEFT' *Screen Education* No 29 May/June 1965 pp 59–67

Alexander, S G P 'Not so much a philosophy…more a way of life' *Screen Education* No 27 January/February 1965 pp 6–11

Alexander, S G P 'SEFT onwards' *Screen Education* No 30 July/August 1965 pp 66–73

Alexander, S G P 'We've Come a Long Way' *Screen Education* No 31 September/October 1965 pp 53–62

Alexander, S G P *100 Films for Juniors* London: SEFT 1964

Alloway, Lawrence 'Personal Statement' *Ark* 19 Spring 1957

Alloway, Lawrence 'The Iconography of the Movies' *Movie* No 7 February and March 1963 pp 4–6

Alloway, Lawrence Transcript of Extract from the programme 'Comment' transmitted 15 December 1960 on the BBC Third Programme

Alloway, Lawrence *Violent America: The Movies 1946–1954* New York: Museum of Modern Art 1971

Alvarado, Manuel 'Media Education in the United Kingdom' in *Studies in Media Education* Paris: UNESCO 1977

Alvarado, Manuel 'The Development of Film and Television Studies' *Visual Education* April 1977 pp 25–26

Alvarado, Manuel and Boyd-Barrett, Oliver (Eds) *Media Education: An Introduction* London: BFI/Open University 1992

Alvarado, Manuel and Buscombe, Edward *Hazell – the making of a TV series* London: BFI in association with Latimer 1978

Alvarado, Manuel and Collins, Richard 'Editorial' *Screen Education* No 14 Spring 1975 pp 2–3

Alvarado, Manuel and Collins, Richard 'The *Viewpoint* Controversy' *Screen Education* No 19 Summer 1976 pp 74–81

Alvarado, Manuel and Ferguson, Bob 'The Curriculum, Media Studies and Discursivity' *Screen* Vol 24 No 3 p 28

Alvarado, Manuel and Thompson, John O (Eds) *The Media Reader* London: British Film Institute 1990

Alvarado, Manuel; Bazalgette, Cary; Buscombe, Edward 'Editorial' *Screen Education* No 26 p 1

Alvarado, Manuel; Bazalgette, Cary; Grant, Felicity 'Editorial' *Screen Education* No 18 Spring 1976 p 1

Alvarado, Manuel; Bazalgette, Cary; Hillier, Jim 'Editorial' *Screen Education* No 15 Summer 1975 pp 1–2

Alvarado, Manuel; Buscombe, Edward; Collins, Richard (Eds) *A Screen Education Reader: Cinema, Television, Culture* London: Macmillan 1993

Alvarado, Manuel; Buscombe, Edward; Collins, Richard (Eds) *Representation and Photography: A Screen Education Reader* Basingstoke: Palgrave 2001

Alvarado, Manuel; Collins, Richard 'Editorial' *Screen Education* No 19 Summer 1976 p 1

Alvarado, Manuel; Cook, Jim; Goldstein, Geoff; Mottershead, Chris 'Editorial' *Screen Education* No 16 Autumn 1975 pp 1–3

Alvarado, Manuel; Cowie, Elizabeth; Stafford, Roy 'Editorial' *Screen Education* No 27 Summer 1978 p 1

Alvarado, Manuel; Grant, Felicity 'Editorial' *Screen Education* No 24 Autumn 1977 pp 1–3

Alvarado, Manuel; Gutch, Robin; Wollen, Tana *Learning the Media: An Introduction to Media Teaching* London: Macmillan Education 1987

Anderson, Lindsay 'Stand Up! Stand Up!' *Sight and Sound* Vol 26 No 2 Autumn 1956 pp 63–69

Anderson, Lindsay 'The Faculty at the Films' *Sequence* No 2 Winter 1947 p 26

Anderson, Lindsay 'The Manvell Approach' *Sequence* No 2 Winter 1947 p 34

Anderson, Perry 'Components of the National Culture' in A Cockburn and R Blackburn *Student Power* Harmondsworth: Penguin 1969 pp 214–284

Andrew, J Dudley *The Major Film Theories – An Introduction* London: Oxford University Press 1976

Appleyard, Brian *The Pleasures of Peace Art and Imagination in Post-war Britain* London: Faber 1989

Armes, Roy 'A Polemic' *Screen* Vol 10 No 6 pp 75–79

Armes, Roy 'Duplicated Materials' *Screen* Vol 11 No 3 pp 105–106

Armitage, Peter 'The War' *Motion* No 1 Summer 1961 pp 4–6

Arnheim, Rudolf *Film* London: Faber 1933

Arnheim, Rudolf, *Film as Art* London: Faber 1957

Arts Enquiry *Interim Draft of the Factual Film in Great Britain* London: The Arts Enquiry 1944

Arts Enquiry *The Factual Film* Oxford: Oxford University Press 1947

Association of Teachers in Colleges and Departments of Education/ British Film Institute *Film and Television in Education For Teaching* A Report of the Joint Working Party of the Association of Teachers in Colleges and Departments of Education and the British Film Institute London: BFI 1960

Bailblé, Claude 'Programming the Look' *Screen Education* No 32/33Autumn/Winter 1979/80 pp 99–131

Baines, Graham 'The National Association for Film in Education' *Visual Education* April 1977 pp 30–31

Baker, A J 'One Approach to Film Appreciation in the Secondary Modern' *Film Teacher* No 1 April 1955 pp 4–6

Baker, Allan J 'Opening Shots' *The Film Teacher* Spring 1954 pp 6–9

Barker, Francis *et al* (Eds) *The Politics of Theory* Colchester: University of Essex 1983

Barker, Martin *A Haunt of Fears* London: Pluto Press 1984

Barnes, T R 'Art and Ketchup' *The Journal of Education* Vol 90 February 1958 p 61

Barr, Charles 'A Letter from Charles Barr' *Velvet Light Trap* No 21 Summer 1985 pp 5–7

Barr, Charles 'Critics' *Granta* Vol LXIV No 1204 26 November 1960 pp 19–22

Bawden, L-A 'Film and the Historian' *University Vision* No 2 October 1968 pp 32–36

Bawden, L-A 'Film Studies in the University' *University Vision* No 4 November 1969 pp 25–35

Bazalgette, Cary (Ed) *Primary Media Education: A Curriculum Statement* London: BFI January 1989

Bazalgette, Cary 'An Open Letter to Len Masterman' May 1972

Bazalgette, Cary 'Making Sense for Whom?' *Screen* Vol 27 No 5 September /October 1986 pp 30–36

Bazalgette, Cary; Galbraith, Neil; Padmore, Danny 'You saw all the sweat' *Screen Education* No 15 Summer 1975 pp 25–42

Bazalgette, Cary; Cook, Jim; Corbett, Jane; Gledhill, Christine; Hillier, Jim; Mottershead, Chris; Simons, Mike 'Inner London Education Authority Film Study Course for Sixth Form Students' *Screen Education Notes* No 5 Winter 1972 pp 12–18

Bazin, André *What is Cinema?* Vol 1 Berkeley: University of California Press 1967

Bell, Oliver *Memorandum on the promotion of film appreciation in Great Britain* London: BFI 1938

Bennett, Susan 'Mass Media Education – Defining the Subject' *Screen Education* No 18 Spring 1976 pp 15–21

Bennett, Tony 'Popular Culture: A Teaching Object' *Screen Education* No 34 Spring 1980 pp 17–29

Bennett, Tony; Boyd-Bowman, Susan; Mercer, Colin; Woollacott, Janet (Eds) *Popular Television and Film* London: British Film Institute 1981

Bergstrom, Janet (Ed) *Endless Night Cinema and Psychoanalysis, Parallel Histories* Berkeley: University of California Press 1999

Bernard, E G 'Children and the Cinema' *Visual Education* Vol 1 No 6 June 1950

Bethell, Andrew 'Classroom Practice: Observations and Proposals' *Screen Education* No 15 Summer 1975 pp 19–2

BFI 'Editorial' 'BFI Summer School' *Sight and Sound* Vol 3 No 12 Winter 1934/35 p 185

BFI 'Editorial' 'The Film and the Public' *Sight and Sound* Vol 3 No 9 Spring 1934 pp 1–2

BFI 'Editorial' 'Film School for Teachers' *Sight and Sound* Vol 6 No 21 Spring 1937 p 16

BFI 'Editorial' 'Films for Children' *Sight and Sound* Vol 6 No 23 Autumn 1937 p 117

BFI 'Editorial' 'London Film School' *Sight and Sound* Vol 5 No 17 Spring 1936 p 9

BFI 'Editorial' 'Optical Aids in Schools' *Sight and Sound* Vol 6 No 29 Spring 1939 p 39

BFI 'Editorial' 'Projectors for the Schools' *Sight and Sound* Vol 6 No 22 Summer 1937 pp 94–95

BFI 'Editorial' 'The Cinema in Education' *Sight and Sound* Vol 6 No 23 Autumn 1937 pp 152–155

BFI Education Department *Newsom on Film* Education Department London: BFI 1963

BFI *Film Appreciation and Visual Education* London: BFI 1944

BFI Members' Action Committee 'A New Screenplay for the BFI' *Screen* Vol 12 No 3 Autumn 1971 pp 44–50

BFI *Report of an Educational Campaign organised by the British Film Institute* May 1941–April 1942 London: BFI July 1942

BFI *Report of an Educational Film Campaign* London: BFI March/July1940

BFI *Report of the Conference on Films for Children November 20th and 21st 1936* London: British Film Institute 1936

BFI *The Film in National Life* Conference Report London: BFI 1943

BFI/National Council of Women *Children and the Cinema* April 9 1946 Conference Report London: BFI June 1946

BFI/SEFT *Film, Television and the Child* October 1958 Conference Report London BFI/SEFT 1958

Blackham, H J; Britton, James; Young, Dennis (Eds) *A Consideration of Humanity, Technology and Education in Our Time* 22–27 April 1957 Conference Report London: Joint Council for Education through Art 1958

Blanchard, Tim 'The Centralisation of Education' *Papers from the Bradford Media Education Conference* London: SEFT 1986 pp 32–41

Board of Education *Handbook of Suggestions* London: HMSO 1937

Board of Education *Report of the Committee to Consider the Supply, Recruitment and Training of Teachers and Youth Leaders* [McNair Report] London: HMSO 1944

Board of Education *Secondary Education with Special Reference to Grammar Schools and Technical High Schools* London: HMSO 1938

Board of Education *The Youth Service after the War* London: HMSO 1943

Bolas, Terry 'Afraid of the Dark' *Screen Education* No 42 January/February 1968 pp 6–9

Bolas, Terry 'Developments in Film Education' *Screen* Vol 11 No 3 May/June 1970 pp 96–101

Bolas, Terry 'Film and the School' *Screen Education Yearbook* 1967 London: SEFT November 1966

Bolas, Terry 'SEFT/ilea Film Teaching Experiment' *Screen* Vol 12 No 1 Spring 1971 pp 87–92

Bolas, Terry *Projecting Screen* Unpublished MA Dissertation Middlesex University 2003

Booker, Christopher *The Neophiliacs* London: Collins 1969

Bordwell, David and Carroll, Noel (Eds) *Post-Theory: Reconstructing Film Studies* Madison: University of Wisconsin Press 1996

Bower, The Honourable Mrs Robert *Children in the Cinema* Newport: R H Johns Ltd 1950

Bowker, Julian (Ed) *Secondary Media Education: A Curriculum Statement* London: BFI March 1991

Box, Kathleen *The Cinema and the Public* London: The Social Survey DS 34865/1 1946

Brandt, George W '…and at Bristol' *Motion* No 1 Summer 1961 pp 23–25

Brewster, Ben 'Structuralism in Film Criticism' *Screen* Vol 12 No 1 Spring 1971 pp 49–58

British Board of Film Censors Cinema Consultative Committee *The Teaching of Film: A Report and Some Recommendations* London: BFI July 1958

British Film Institute *British Film Institute Library Catalogue* London: British Film Institute September 1948

British Film Institute *British Film Institute: The First Twenty-Five Years* London: BFI 1958

British Film Institute Education Department *Film Study Materials* London: BFI 1962

British Film Institute *British Film Institute Educational Advisory Service Documents* 1973

British Film Institute Educational Advisory Service *Screen Education in Britain* September 1972

British Film Institute *Film Appreciation in Youth Clubs: some suggested approaches* (Second Edition) London: British Film Institute 1955

British Film Institute *Films and Youth Organisations* London: British Film Institute June 1944 and April 1948

British Film Institute *Policy Report* London: British Film Institute 1971

British Film Institute *Proposals from the British Film Institute to the Ministry of Education for the formation of a visual education committee* London: British Film Institute August 1945

British Film Institute Summer School 1944 *Film Appreciation and Visual Education* London: British Film Institute 1944

British Film Institute *The Film In National Life Conference* London: British Film Institute 1943

Britton, Andrew 'The Ideology of *Screen*' *Movie* No 26 Winter 1978/79 pp 2–28

Brock, Eileen *et al* 'Open Letter to the Staff of the British Film Institute' *Screen* Vol 12 No 3 Autumn 1971 pp 2–8

Brown, John 'Film Appreciation in Scotland' *Visual Education* April 1977 p 31

Brumer, Karen; Hagen, Mike; McDonough, Josie; Scurlock, Will and Simpson, Philip 'Report of the NUT/SEFT Easter School "Approaches to the Teaching of Film Studies" York, 1975' *Screen Education* No 15 Summer 1975

Brunsdon, Charlotte and Morley, David *Everyday Television: 'Nationwide'* Television Monograph No 10 London: British Film Institute Educational Advisory Service 1978

Buchanan, Andrew 'Film Appreciation 1 – The Right Approach to the Screen' *Contemporary Cinema* Vol 2 No 3 March 1948 pp 106–110

Buchanan, Andrew *Focus Film Course* London: The Catholic Film Institute 1951

Buchanan, Andrew *Going to the Cinema* London: Phoenix House 1947

Buchanan, Andrew *The Film in Education* London: Phoenix House 1951

Buckingham, David (Ed) *Teaching Popular Culture – Beyond Radical Pedagogy* London: University College Press 1998

Buckingham, David 'Against Demystification – Teaching the Media' *Screen* Vol 27 No 5 September /October 1986 pp 80–95

Buckingham, David 'Lessons from SEFT' *Initiatives* 11 Autumn 1989 pp 3–5

Buckingham, David 'The Technology of Control' *Papers from the Bradford Media Education Conference* London: SEFT 1986 pp 50

Buckingham, David *Media Education* London: Polity Press 2003

Buckingham, David and Sefton-Green, Julian *Cultural Studies goes to School* London: Taylor and Francis 1994

BUFC 'Ernest Lindgren OBE Obituary' *University Vision* No 11 April 1974 pp 6–7

BUFC 'The British Universities Film Council – Past, Present and Future' *University Vision* No 11 April 1974 pp 8–15

Burke, Father John 'Film Morality and Film Taste' *The Film Teacher* Autumn 1953 pp 16–17

Burnett R G and Martell E D *The Devil's Camera – Menace of a film-ridden world* London: The Epworth Press 1932

Buscombe, Ed (Ed) *Football on Television* Television Monograph No 4 London: British Film Institute Educational Advisory Service 1975

Buscombe, Ed *Films on TV* SEFT Pamphlet No 1 London: SEFT 1971

Buscombe, Edward 'The Idea of Genre in American Cinema' *Screen* Vol 11 No 2 March/April 1970 pp 33–45

Buscombe, Edward *Making Legend of the Werewolf* London: BFI/EAS 1976

Buscombe, Edward; Gledhill, Christine; Lovell, Alan and Williams, Christopher 'Statement: Psychoanalysis and Film' *Screen* Vol 16 No 4 Winter 1975/6 pp 119–130

Buscombe, Edward; Gledhill, Christine; Lovell, Alan and Williams, Christopher 'Statement: Why we have resigned from the Board of *Screen* '*Screen* Vol 17 No 2 Summer 1976 pp 106–109

Butler, Ivan *To Encourage the Art of the Film* London: Robert Hale 1971

Cain C and Vannoey R C 'Mutatis Mutandis' *The Film Teacher's Handbook 1959/60* London: SFT 1959 p 3

Cameron A C 'The Case for a National Film Institute' *Sight and Sound* Vol1 No 1 pp 8–9

Cameron, A C 'Films and the School' *Sight and Sound* Vol 3 No 11 Autumn 1934 pp 124–125

Cameron, Ian 'All Together Now' *Film* 25 September/October 1960 p 12

Cameron, Ian 'Films' *Oxford Opinion* No 38 April 30 1960 p 36

Cameron, Ian 'Purely for Kicks' *Screen Education* No 7 March-April 1961 pp 31–33

Cameron, Ian 'What's the Use?' *Film* 28 March/April 1961 pp 10–11

Cameron, Ian; Shivas, Mark and Perkins, V F 'Correspondence – *Oxford Opinion*' *Sight and Sound* Vol 30 No 2 Spring 1961 p 100

Carby, Hazel 'Multi-Culture' *Screen Education* No 34 Spring 1980 pp 62–70

Carr, J F *Teachers' film groups and their contribution to the educational service* London: British Film Institute January 1946

Carroll, Noel *Theorising the Moving Image* Cambridge: Cambridge University Press 1996

Casetti, Francesco *Theories of Cinema 1945–1995* Austin: University of Texas Press 1999

Caughie, John 'Glasgow SEFT Group' *Screen Education* No 22 Spring 1977 p 76

Caughie, John *Television: Ideology and Exchange* Television Monograph No 9 London: British Film Institute Educational Advisory Service 1978

Caute, David *Sixty Eight – The Year of the Barricades* London: Hamish Hamilton 1988

Central Advisory Council for Education (England) *Half Our Future* (The Newsom Report) London: HMSO 1963

Central Advisory Council for Education *Fifteen to Eighteen* (The Crowther Report) London: HMSO 1959

Chambers, Iain 'Rethinking Popular Culture' pp 113–117 *Screen Education* No 36 Autumn 1980

Chambers, Iain; Clarke, John; Connell, Ian; Curti, Lidia; Hall, Stuart; Jefferson, Tony 'Marxism and Culture' *Screen* Vol 18 No 4 Winter 1977/78 pp 109–119

Children's Film Foundation *Saturday Morning Cinema* London: CFF 1969

Chun, Lin *The British New Left* Edinburgh: Edinburgh University Press 1993

Church, Michael 'Film Education: a neglected, misunderstood art' *The Teacher* 20 December 1968 p 10

Clarke, C H *The Elements of Film Criticism* London: BFI 1944

Clarke, Mike *Teaching Popular Television* London: Heineman Educational Books 1987

Clough, D 'American Cinema: a Film Course at Aberystwyth' *University Vision* No 9 November 1972 pp 39–43

Cockburn, A and Blackburn, R *Student Power* Harmondsworth: Penguin 1969

Cockerham, H 'A Film Study Course in a French Department' *University Vision* No 8 January 1972 pp 19–25

Coldstream, Sir William 'Film Lectureship' *Sight and Sound* Vol 29 No 1 Winter 1959–60

Collins, Richard 'A Diploma Course in Film Study at the Polytechnic of Central London' *Screen Education Notes* No 9 Winter 1973/74 p 11

Collins, Richard 'Genre: A Reply to Ed Buscombe' *Screen* Vol 11 No 4/5 July/October pp 66–75

Collins, Richard 'Media studies: alternative or oppositional practice? in Whitty G & Young M (Eds) *Explorations in the Politics of School Knowledge* Driffield: Nafferton Books 1976 pp 166–178

Collins, Richard 'Re-evaluating Leavis' *Screen Education* No 22 Spring 1977 pp 39–47

Collins, Richard *Television News* Television Monograph No 5 London: British Film Institute Educational Advisory Service 1976

Collins, Richard; Grealy, Jim 'Editorial' 'The Education Cuts' *Screen Education* No 16 Autumn 1975 pp 41–46

Comedia *Society for Education in Film and Television – A Review* London: Comedia September 1988

Commission on Educational and Cultural Films *The Film in National Life* London: George Allen & Unwin 1932

Comolli, Jean-Luc and Narboni, Paul 'Cinema/Ideology/Criticism' (translated by Susan Bennett) *Screen* Vol 12 No 1 Spring 1971 pp 27–36

Connell, Myra and O'Shaughnessy, Michael Report *Media Education Conference 1981* London: BFI Education and Goldsmiths College 1982 pp 5–12

Cook, Jim 'Film in English Teaching' 'Review Two' *Screen Education Notes* No 6 Spring 1973 pp 29–35

Cook, Jim 'Teaching the Industry' *Screen Education* No 16 Autumn 1975 pp 4–18

Cook, Jim and Hillier, Jim *The Growth of Film and Television Studies 1960–1975* London: BFI Education 1976, reissued March 1982

Cook, Jim and North, Nicky *BFI Summer Schools 71–79* London: BFI Education Department April 1981

Cook, Pam (Ed) *The Cinema Book* London: British Film Institute 1985

Cook, Pam and Bernink, Mieke (Eds) *The Cinema Book* Second Edition London: British Film Institute 1999

Cousins, R F 'Film and French Studies' *University Vision* No 15 December 1976 pp 14–23

Coward, Rosalind 'Class, "Culture" and the Social Formation' *Screen* Vol 18 No 1 Spring 1977 pp 75–105

Coward, Rosalind and Ellis, John *Language and Materialism: Developments in Semiology and the Theory of the Subject* London: Routledge & Kegan Paul 1977

Crofts, Stephen 'Debate – Psychoanalysis and Film' *Framework* No 4 pp 15–16

Crofts, Stephen 'Film Education in England and Wales' *Screen* Vol 11 No 6 November/December 1970 pp 3–22

Davies, Derek '3D and TV' *The Film Teacher* Autumn 1953 pp 2–3

De Lauretis, Teresa and Heath, Stephen (Eds) *The Cinematic Apparatus* London: Macmillan 1980

Debes, John L and Williams, Clarence M *Visual Literacy, Languaging and Learning* Visual Literacy Center 1978

Denholme, A A *The Cinema in Education* London: British Film Institute 1937

Department of Education and Science *Popular TV and Schoolchildren: The report of a group of teachers* London: Department of Education and Science April 1983

Dickinson, Thorold 'Some Practical Problems of Film Study' *University Vision* No 12 December 1974 pp 5–8

Dickinson, Thorold *Should Britain have a film school?* London: University College March 1963

Donald, James 'Examinations and Strategies' *Screen Education* No 26 Spring 1978 pp 3–11

Donald, James 'Green Paper: Noise of Crisis' *Screen Education* No 30 pp 13–49

Donald, James; Alvarado, Manuel; Collins, Richard; Ferguson, Bob 'Editorial' *Screen Education* No 28 p 1

Drummond, Phillip 'Beginning Film and Television Studies' *Times Educational Supplement* 6 January 1978 pp 27–28

Drummond, Phillip 'Reply to Critics of *Screen Education 20* The Sweeney' *Screen Education* No 23 Summer 1977 pp 65–68

Durgnat, Raymond 'Standing up for Jesus' *Motion* No 6 Autumn 1963 pp 25–28 and 38–42

Durgnat, Raymond 'The Impotence of being Ernest' *Views* No 8 Summer 1965 pp 76–80

Durgnat, Raymond 'The Mass Media – A Highbrow Illiteracy?' *Views* No 4 Spring 1964 pp 49–59

Dyer, Ernest 'Training Film Taste' *Sight and Sound* Vol 3 No 11 Autumn 1934 pp 134–136

Dyer, Peter John 'Counter Attack' *Film 26* November/December 1960 p 8

Dyer, Richard 'Film Studies at the University of Keele' *Screen Education* No 19 Spring 1976 pp 54–57

Dyer, Richard *Light Entertainment* Television Monograph No 2 London: British Film Institute Educational Advisory Service 1973

Dyer, Richard; Geraghty, Christine; Jordan, Marion; Lovell, Terry; Paterson, Richard; Stewart, John *Coronation Street* Television Monograph No 13 London: British Film Institute Publishing 1981

Eagleton, Terry *The Function of Criticism: From The Spectator to Post-Structuralism* London: Verso 1984

Easthope, Anthony 'The Trajectory of *Screen*, 1971–1979' in *The Politics of Theory* Barker, Francis *et al* (Ed) Colchester: University of Essex 1983 pp 121–133

Easthope, Anthony *British Post-Structuralism* London: Routledge 1988 pp 43–59

Easthope, Anthony; Lapsley, Rob 'Manchester SEFT Group' *Screen Education* No 23 Summer 1977 pp 71–72

Easthope, Anthony *Literary into Cultural Studies* London: Routledge 1991

Eaton, Mick and Neale, Steve (Eds) *Screen Reader 2: Cinema and Semiotics* London: SEFT 1981

Edgar Dale 'How to Evaluate the Mass Media' *Film Teacher* 8 March 1957 pp 14–18

Edgar Dale *How to Appreciate Motion Pictures* New York: Macmillan 1933

Education Group at the Centre for Contemporary Cultural Studies *Unpopular Education* London Hutchinson 1981

Eisenstein, Sergei *The Film Sense* London: Faber 1943

Ellis, Jack 'Film at North Western University' *Film Teacher* 15 December 1958 pp 19–25

Ellis, Jack 'Film Societies and Film Education in the USA' *Film Teacher* 13 pp 15–19

Ellis, John (Ed) *Screen Reader 1: Cinema/ideology/Politics* London: SEFT 1977

Ellis, John 'Art, Culture and Quality' *Screen* Vol 19 No 3 Autumn 1978 pp 9–49

Ellis, John 'The Quality Film Adventure: British Critics and the Cinema 1942–48' in Higson, Andrew (Ed) *Dissolving Views* London: Cassell 1996

Else, Eric *The Back of Beyond* London: Longmans Green 1968

English New Education Fellowship *The Impact of the Cinema on the Child* March 1949 Conference Report London: English New Education Fellowship Bulletin No 55 April 1949

Evans, Frederic 'The Silent Film in Schools *Sight and Sound* Vol 7 No 28 Winter 1938–39 pp 175–176

Evans, Frederic 'What Can Be Done' *Sight and Sound* Vol7 No 25 Spring 1938 p 38–39

Evernden, S C and Holloway, R G *English for Citizens* Book IV *Our Own Language* Leeds: E J Arnold & Sons 1950

Exton, Richard; Geraghty, Christine; Gilman, Ian; Lyons, Harry; McKnight, Stephanie; Mottershead, Chris; Williams, Christopher 'Statement: *Screen Education* and *The Sweeney*' in *Screen Education* No 23 Summer 1977 pp 59–64

Ferguson, Bob; Stephens, Robert 'Media Studies and Media Usage in an Institute of Education' *Screen Education* No 21 Winter 1976/77 pp 20–31

Ferguson, Marjorie and Golding, Peter *Cultural Studies in Question* London: Sage 1997

Field, Mary 'The Child Audience' *British Film Academy Journal* Summer 1955 p 3

Field, Mary 'The Children's Film Foundation' in *The Film Teacher* Winter 1952 pp 1–5

Film 27 'The Current Picture' January/February 1961 p 6–7

Film 28 'The Current Picture' March/April 1961 p 4–5

Film Education Working Group *Making Movies Matter* London: British Film Institute 1999

Film Guide was produced by the BFI Film Appreciation Department between January 1954 and September 1959. Renamed *Screen Guide* in October 1959, it was then produced jointly by BFI and SEFT until April 1961

Film Teacher 'Editorial' 'Every Schoolmarm a Critic' *Film Teacher* 5 September 1956 p 2

Film Teacher 'Editorial' 'Film Teachers and Television' *Film Teacher* 13 June 1958 p 2–3

Film Teacher 'Editorial' 'Help Yourself' *Film Teacher* 6 November 1956 p 9–16

Film Teacher 'Editorial' 'Hi Kwai or Die: Some thoughts on the Future of British Cinema' *Film Teacher* 12 March 1958 pp 2–3

Film Teacher 'Editorial' 'Internationally Speaking' *Film Teacher* 8 March 1957 p 2

Fitchett, C E 'Film Teaching – A Training College View' *Film Teacher* 7 January 1957 pp 4–6

Fleming, C M *The Social Psychology of Education* London: Routledge & Kegan Paul 1944

Fletcher, John 'The Film and the Novel' *University Vision* No 5 July 1970 pp 5–10

Ford, Richard *Children in the Cinema* London: George Allen and Unwin 1939

Forman, Denis 'The Work of the British Film Institute' *Quarterly Journal of Film, Radio and Television* Vol IX Winter 1954 pp 147–158

Forman, Denis *Films 1945–1950* London: Longmans Green 1952

Foster, George 'Review of *Making Legend of the Werewolf* *Screen Education* No 24 Autumn 1977 pp 57–60

Foucault, Michel 'What is an Author?' *Screen* Vol 20 No 1 Spring 1979 pp 13–29, translation by Donald F Bouchard Cornell University 1977

Fruchter, Norman 'Two Hours a Week' *Sight and Sound* Vol 31 No 4 Autumn 1962 pp 198–200

Garnham, Nicholas *Structures of Television* Television Monograph No 1 London: British Film Institute Educational Advisory Service 1973; revised edition 1978

George W H *The Cinema in School* London: Sir Isaac Pitman 1935

Gidley, M 'Some American Studies Films at Sussex' *University Vision* No 6 January 1971 pp 4–12

Gillett, B E *Appraising Educational Films* London: British Film Institute December 1946

Gladwell, David 'Editing Anderson's *If* *Screen* Vol 10 No 1 January/February 1969 pp 24–33

Gledhill, Christine (Ed) *Film & Media Studies in Higher Education Conference Papers* London: BFI Education September 1981

Gledhill, Christine and Williams, Linda *Reinventing Film Studies* London: Arnold 2000

Gould, Julius *The Attack on Higher Education: Marxist and Radical Penetration* London: Institute for the Study of Conflict September 1977

Grayson, Dorothy *Films and Youth Organisations* London: BFI 1944

Grealy, Jim 'Notes on Popular Culture' *Screen Education* No 22 Spring 1977 pp 5–11

Greiner, Grace 'Popular Culture and Personal Responsibility' *Education for Teaching* No 54 February 1961 pp 23–26

Greiner, Grace *Teaching Film* London: BFI 1954

Grierson, John 'Art and the Analysts' *Sight and Sound* Vol 4 No 16 Winter 1935–36 pp 157–159

Groombridge, Brian and Whannel, Paddy 'Pop, Posh and Pedagogue' *Times Educational Supplement* 5 January 1950 p 217

Groombridge, Brian *Popular Culture and Personal Responsibility A Study Outline* London: National Union of Teachers May 1961

Groombridge, Brian *Television and the People* Harmondsworth: Penguin 1972

Hall, Stuart 'Impact of Film on the University' *University Vision* No 2 October 1968 pp 28–31

Hall, Stuart 'Recent Developments in Theories of Language and Ideology: A Critical Note' *Culture, Media, Language: Working Papers in Cultural Studies* London: Hutchinson 1980

Hall, Stuart 'The Emergence of Cultural Studies and the Crisis in the Humanities' *October* No 53 Summer 1990 pp 11–23

Hall, Stuart 'The Williams Interviews' *Screen Education* No 34 Spring 1980 pp 94–104

Hall, Stuart and Whannel, Paddy *The Popular Arts* London: Hutchinson Educational 1964

Halloran, James D and Jones, Marsha *Learning about the Media: Communication and Society* Paris: UNESCO 1986 pp 55–60

Halloran, James D *Mass Media and Society* Leicester: Leicester University Press 1974

Harcourt, Peter 'Towards Higher Education' *Screen Education* No 26 September/October 1964 pp 20–30

Harcourt, Peter and Theobald, Peter (Eds) *Film Making in Schools and Colleges* London: BFI Education Department 1966

Harman, Jympson *Good Films and How to Appreciate Them* London: Daily Mail School Aid Department 1947

Hartnoll, Gillian *Reading lists* for *Screen*: Film History Vol 10 No 4/5 pp 187–191; British Cinema Vol 10 No 6 pp 108–109; Theory of Film Vol 11 No 1 pp 101–102; Reference Books Part I Vol 11 No 2 pp 96–98; Reference Books Part II Vol 11 No 4/5 pp 133–136

Hazell, Frank 'Don't be so ashamed of your school reports now' *Film Teacher* 2 June 1955 pp 8–12

Heath, Stephen 'Narrative Space' *Screen* Vol 17 No 3 Autumn 1976

Heath, Stephen; MacCabe, Colin and Prendergast, Christopher *Signs of the Times – Introductory Readings in Textual Semiotics* London: BFI reprint 1978

Heddle, E W M 'Film Appreciation at the University Level – A General Survey' *Film Teacher* 7 January 1957 pp 11–14

Hedling, Erik 'Lindsay Anderson: *Sequence* and the Rise of auteurism in 1950s' Britain' in MacKillop and Sinyard *British Cinema of the 1950s: A Celebration* Manchester: Manchester University Press 2003 pp 23–31

Heller, Caroline *Broadcasting and Accountability* Television Monograph No 7 London: British Film Institute Educational Advisory Service 1978

Hewison, Robert *Culture and Consensus: England, Art and Politics since 1940* London: Methuen 1995 p 105

Hewison, Robert *In Anger: Culture in the Cold War 1945–60* London: Methuen 1988

Heywood, C L 'The Challenge of Television' *The Film Teacher's Handbook 1958/59* London: SFT 1958 pp 23–26

Heywood, L 'Film in the School Curriculum' *Film Teacher* 7 January 1957 pp 17–20

Higgins, A.P. 'Television: Meeting the Challenge' *The Film Teacher's Handbook 1958/59* London: SFT 1958 pp 27–29

Higgins, A P *Talking about Television* London: BFI Education Department 1966

Higgins, Tony; Whannel, Paddy; Williams, Raymond 'Television Supplement' in *New Left Review* 7 January- February 1961 pp 30–48

Higson, Andrew (Ed) *Dissolving Views* London: Cassell 1996

Hill, John and Church Gibson, Pamela (Eds) *The Oxford Guide to Film Studies* Oxford: Oxford University Press 1998

Hillier, Jim and McTaggart, Andrew 'Film in the Humanities Curriculum Project' *Screen* Vol 11 No 2 March/April 1970 pp 46–51

Hills, Janet *Are They Safe at the Cinema? A considered answer to critics of the cinema* London: BFI 1953

Hills, Janet *Films and Children The Positive Approach* London: BFI 1951

Hills, Janet *Fragments: Janet Hills 1919–1956* published posthumously and privately by her family in 1956

Himmelweit, Hilde *Television and the Child* Oxford: Oxford University Press 1958

Hodgkinson, A W 'Films about Films' *Society of Film Teachers Bulletin* Vol 1 No 1 December 1950 p 12

Hodgkin son, A W *Teaching the screen language: a basic method* Worcester: Mass Clark University 1980

Hodgkinson, A W 'Amsterdam and the Virtual World' *Film Teacher* 12 March 1958

Hodgkinson, A W 'Teaching the Art of Film' *Athene* Vol 7 No 4 June 1956

Hodgkinson, A W 'The Continental Scene' *Film Teacher* 6 November 1956 p 12–13

Hodgkinson, A W *Screen Education* Paris: UNESCO 1964

Hodgkinson, A W; Huntley, John; Mills, E Francis; Smith, Jack *School Film Appreciation* London: BFI 1950

Hodgkinson, Tony 'Children's Films and Screen Education' *Film Comment* Vol 2 No 2 1964 pp 14–18

Hodgkinson, Tony 'The British Film Institute' *Film Comment* Vol 2 No 4 Fall 1964 pp 31–34

Hoggart, Richard 'The Quality of Cultural Life in Mass Society' Congress for Cultural Freedom Conference Berlin 1960

Hoggart, Richard *The Uses of Literacy* London: Chatto and Windus 1957

Houston, Penelope 'Critic's Notebook' *Sight and Sound* Vol 30 No 2 Spring 1961 p 62

Houston, Penelope 'Enthusiasm for What?' *Definition* 3 p 8

Houston, Penelope 'The Critical Question' *Sight and Sound* Autumn 1960 Vol 29 No 4 pp 160–165

Hunter, William 'Review of *Film* (Arnheim)' *Scrutiny* Vol II No 2 September 1933 pp 211–212

Hunter, William 'The Art-Form of Democracy' *Scrutiny* Vol 1 No 1 May 1932 p 62

Hunter, William *Scrutiny of Cinema* London: Wishart & Co 1932

Independent Television Authority *Parents, Children and Television* London: HMSO 1958

Instituut Film en Jeugd *Film Education of Youth* 22–24 November 1957 International Conference Report Amsterdam

Isaacs, J 'Review of *Scrutiny of Cinema* (Hunter)' *Scrutiny* Vol I No 4 March 1933 pp 414–416

Johnson, Ian and Durgnat, Raymond 'Puritans Anonymous' *Motion* No 6 Autumn 1963 p 1

Johnson, Ian Editorial *Motion* No 1 Summer 1961 p 1

Johnson, Ian Editorial *Motion* No 2 Winter 1961–2 p 1

Johnson, Richard 'Cultural Studies and Educational Practice' *Screen Education* No 34 Spring 1980 pp 5–16

Johnston, Claire 'Film Journals: Britain and France' *Screen* Vol 12 No 1 Spring 1971 pp 39–46

Johnston, Claire and Willemen, Paul (Eds) *Frank Tashlin* Edinburgh Film Festival in association with *Screen* 1973

Johnston, Claire *Notes on Women's Cinema* Screen Pamphlet Number 2 London: SEFT 1973

Jones, Ceinwen and Pardoe, F E 'Film Study' in *Sight and Sound* Vol 18 No 70 Summer 1949 pp 91–93

Jones, Ceinwen and Pardoe, F E *A First Course in Film Appreciation* London: BFI 1946

Jones, Stephen G *The British Labour Movement and Film 1918–1939* London: Routledge & Kegan Paul 1987

Jones, Stephen G *Workers at Play – A social and economic history of leisure 1918–1939* London: Routledge & Kegan Paul 1986

Journal of Education 'Editorial' 'A Negative Light' *The Journal of Education* Vol 90 February 1958 p 43

Kaplan, E Ann (Ed) 'From Plato's Cave to Freud's Screen' *Psychoanalysis and Cinema* New York: Routledge 1990

Kitses, Jim 'Young filmmakers: some words in their defence' *The Teacher* July 21 1967 p 5

Kitses, Jim *Film and General Studies* London: BFI Education Department 1966

Kitses, Jim *Horizons West* London: Thames & Hudson 1969

Kitses, Jim *Horizons West* Second Edition London: BFI Publishing 2004

Kitses, Jim with Mercer, Ann *Talking about the Cinema* London: BFI Education Department 1966

Knight, Roy (Ed) *Film in English Teaching* London: Hutchinson Educational 1972

Knights, L C 'Will Training Colleges Bear Scrutiny?' *Scrutiny* Vol 1 No 3 December 1932 p 259

Kracauer, Siegfried *Theory of Film: The Redemption of Physical Reality* New York: Oxford University Press 1965

Kubey, Robert W 'Why US media education lags behind the rest of the English-speaking world' *Television and New Media* Vol 4 No 4 November 2003 pp 351–370

Kuhn, Annette and Stacey, Jackie (Eds) *Screen Histories A* Screen *Reader* Oxford: Oxford University Press 1998

Laclau, Ernesto 'Populist Rupture and Discourse' pp 87–93 *Screen Education* No 34 Spring 1980

Laing, Stuart *Representation of Working Class Life 1957–1964* London: Macmillan 1986

Lamb, Stephen 'The place of film in a German Studies course' *University Vision* No 14 March 1976 pp 5–14

Lambert, R S 'How to Get the Films You Want' *Sight and Sound* Vol 3 No 9 Spring 1934 pp 5–9

Langham, Josephine *Teachers and Television: The IBA Educational Fellowship Scheme* London: John Libbey 1990

Lapsley, Robert and Westlake, Michael *Film Theory An Introduction* Manchester: Manchester University Press 1988

Laurence, Margaret *Citizenship through English* Edinburgh: Oliver and Boyd 1946

Lauwerys, J A *The Film and the School* London: Christophers 1935

Laws Frederick (Ed) *Made for Millions* London: Contact Publications 1947

League of Nations Advisory Committee on Social Questions *The Recreational Cinema and the Young* Geneva: League of Nations 1938

Leahy, James 'Post-graduate Diploma at the Slade School of Fine Art' *Visual Education* April 1977 pp 23–25

Learmonth, James 'Organisation and Aftermath' in Lusted, David & Drummond, Phillip (Eds) *TV and Schooling* London: BFI Education Department 1985 pp 19–23

Learmonth, James and Sayer, Mollie *A Review of Good Practice in Media Education* London: British Film Institute 1996

Leavis F R *Education and the University* London: Chatto and Windus 1948

Leavis, F R and Thompson, Denys *Culture and Environment* London: Chatto and Windus 1934

Lewis A Maxwell 'The School Film Society' *Sight and Sound* Vol 3 No 10 Summer 1934 pp 75–78

Lewis, A Maxwell 'Training Young Critics' *Sight and Sound* Vol 4 No 14 Summer 1935 pp 81–83

Lindgren, Ernest 'The selection of films as historical records in the National Film Archive' *University Vision* No 6 January 1971 pp 13–23

Lindgren, Ernest *Film Appreciation for Discussion Groups and Schools* London: BFI 1942

Lindgren, Ernest H 'Nostalgia' *Sight and Sound* Vol 9 No 35 Autumn 1940 pp 49–50

Lindgren, Ernest *The Art of the Film* London: Allen & Unwin 1963

Lindgren, Ernest *The Cinema* London: English Universities Press 1944

Lingstrom, Freda 'BBC Children's Television' *The Film Teacher* Autumn 1953 pp 4–6

Linton, James M 'Values…Theory…Action! Integrating Film Studies' *University Vision* No 12 December 1974 pp 9–26

Lloyd of Hampstead, Lord *A Policy for the Arts* London: HMSO February 1965

London County Council *School Children and the Cinema* London: LCC 1932

Long, Bob 'Photo Practice 1' *Screen Education* No 34 Spring 1980 pp 106–112

Look and Listen 'Editorial' 'A Sensible Attitude to the Cinema – Hertfordshire schools co-operate in evolving a more critical approach' *Look and Listen* April 1950 Vol 4 No 4 pp 76–77

Lovell, Alan (Ed) *British Film Institute Production Board* London: British Film Institute 1976

Lovell, Alan "Editorial" *Screen* Vol 13 No 4 Winter 1972/3 pp 2–3

Lovell, Alan 'Epic Theater and Counter Cinema' *Jump Cut* 1982 Part 1 in No 27 and Part 2 in No 28

Lovell, Alan 'Robin Wood – A Dissenting View' *Screen* March/April 1969 Volume 10 No 2 pp 42–55

Lovell, Alan 'Robin Wood's Criticism' *Screen* Vol 10 No 2 March/April 1969 pp 42–55

Lovell, Alan 'The Aims of Film Education' BFI seminar paper 15 February 1968

Lovell, Alan 'The Best We've Got' *Definition* 2 p 3

Lovell, Alan 'The Common Pursuit of True Judgment' *Screen* Vol 11 No 4/5 pp 76–88

Lovell, Alan 'The Western' *Screen Education* No 41 pp 92–103

Lovell, Alan *Anarchist Cinema* London: Peace News 1962

Lovell, Alan and Hillier, Jim *Studies in Documentary* London: Secker & Warburg 1972

Lowndes, Douglas 'Film Making at Hornsey College of Art' – all day Film Workshop at the National Film Theatre organised by BFI Education Department January 1966

Lowndes, Douglas *Film Making in Schools* London: Batsford 1968

Lusted, David (Ed) *The Media Studies Book* London: Routledge 1991

Lusted, David 'A History of Suspicion: Educational Attitudes to Television' in Lusted, David and Drummond, Phillip *TV and Schooling* London: BFI Education Department and London University Institute of Education 1985 pp 11–18

Lusted, David 'Feeding the Panic and Breaking the Cycle 'Popular TV and Schoolchildren', *Screen* Vol 24 No 6 November/December 1983

Lusted, David 'Introduction – Why Pedagogy?' *Screen* Vol 27 No 5 September /October 1986 pp 2–14

Lusted, David 'Media Education and the Secondary/FE Curriculum' in *Media Education Conference 1981 A Report* London: BFI Education and Goldsmiths College 1982 pp 13–26

Lusted, David and Drummond, Phillip *TV and Schooling* London: BFI Education Department and London University Institute of Education 1985

MacCabe Colin and Petrie, Duncan *New Scholarship from British Film Institute Research* London: British Film Institute 1996

MacCabe, Colin 'Theory and Film: Principles of Realism and Pleasure' *Screen* Vol 17 No 3 Autumn 1976

MacCabe, Colin *Theoretical Essays: Film, Linguistics, Literature* Manchester: Manchester University Press 1985

MacKendrick, Alexander 'As I See It' *The Film Teacher* Spring 1953 pp 8–12

MacKillop, Ian and Sinyard, Neil *British Cinema of the 1950s: A Celebration* Manchester: Manchester University Press 2003

Mainds, Roger 'Editorial' *Screen Education Yearbook 1969* London SEFT 1968 p 5

Mainds, Roger 'The *Teenscreen* Story' *Screen Education* No 18 March/April 1963 pp 53–54

Manvell, Roger *A Seat at the Cinema* London: Evans Brothers 1951

Manvell, Roger *The Cinema and the Public* London: Army Bureau of Current Affairs 1944

Marshall, Richard 'Film Education' *Initiatives* Summer 1988 p 25

Masheder, Mildred; Holme, Anthea and Higgins, Anthony *Family Viewing – a study of early evening television* London: Council for Children's Welfare November 1960

Masterman, Len 'A Reply to David Buckingham' in *Screen* Vol 27 No 5 September/October 1986 pp 96–100

Masterman, Len 'Film and the Raising of the School Leaving Age' *Screen Education Notes* Spring 1973 No 6 p 21

Masterman, Len 'Film in English Teaching' 'Review One' *Screen Education Notes* Spring 1973 No 6 pp 29–35

Masterman, Len *Down Cemetery Road* Wirral: Alpha Media 2002

Masterman, Len *School Knowledge, Media Knowledge: Media Literacy in Teacher Training and Student Learning* Nottingham University May 1983

Masterman, Len *Teaching about Television* London: Macmillan Press 1980

Masterman, Len *Teaching the Media* London: Comedia 1985

Masterman, Len *The Development of Media Education in Europe in the 1980s* Strasbourg: Council of Europe May 1988

Mayer, J P *Sociology of Film Studies* London: Faber 1946

McArthur, Colin 'Two steps forward, one step back – Cultural struggle in the British Film Institute' *Journal of Popular British Cinema* No 4 2001 pp 112–127

McArthur, Colin *Television and History* Television Monograph No 8 London: British Film Institute Educational Advisory Service 1978

McArthur, Colin *The Big Heat* London: British Film Institute 1992

McArthur, Colin *Underworld USA* London: Secker & Warburg 1972

McLuhan, Marshal *Understanding Media* London: Routledge and Kegan Paul 1964

McTaggart, Andrew 'Signs and Meaning in the Cinema' *Screen* Vol 10 No 6 pp 67–75

Mercer, Colin 'After Gramsci' *Screen Education* No 36 Autumn 1980 pp 5–15

Merck, Mandy (Ed) *The Sexual Subject: A Screen Reader on Sexuality* London: Routledge 1992

Meredith, G Patrick *Visual Education and the New Teacher* London: Daily Mail 1946

Mills, E F 'The Classroom Film' *Sight and Sound* Vol 5 No 18 Summer 1936 pp 39–42

Mills, E. Francis 'The Film Lesson' *Sight and Sound* Vol 5 No 17 Spring 1936 p 33

Ministry of Education *Half Our Future* A Report of the Central Advisory Committee (England) London: HMSO 1963

Ministry of Education *The Purpose and Content of the Youth Service* London: HMSO 1945

Moley, Raymond *Are we movie made?* New York: Mary-Massins 1938

Morey, Anne *Hollywood Outsiders – The Adaptation of the Film Industry 1913–1934* Minneapolis: University of Minnesota Press 2003

Morley, David *The* Nationwide *Audience: Structure and Decoding* Television Monograph No 11 London: British Film Institute 1980

Morley, John (Ed) *Art, Science and Education* Whitsun 1958 Conference Report London: Joint Council for Education through Art 1958

Moss, Louis and Box, Kathleen *The Cinema Audience* London: Wartime Social Survey No 37b June/July 1943

Mottershead, Chris 'Teachers' Introduction to Teachers' Guide to Narrative' in *ilea/ bfi 6th form film study course 1983–1984* London: Inner London Education Authority 1983

Mottershead, Chris and Jenkins, Tricia *Children Moving Images* London: British Film Institute 1992 (published to accompany videotapes of the children's work)

Mulhern, Francis 'Notes on Culture and Cultural Struggle' *Screen Education* No 34 Spring 1980 pp 31–35

Mulhern, Francis *The Moment of* Scrutiny London: New Left Books 1979

Mulvey, Laura 'Interview with Peter Wollen' (c 2002) Proof copy *From Cinephilia to Cinema Studies* to be published 2008 by Duke University Press

Mulvey, Laura 'Visual Pleasure and Narrative Cinema' *Screen* Vol 16 No 3 Autumn 1975 pp 6–18

Mulvey, Laura *A short history of the British Film Institute Education Department* London: British Film Institute 1994

Mulvey, Laura *Visual and Other Pleasures* Basingstoke: Palgrave 1989

Murdock, Graham and Phelps, Guy *Mass Media and the Secondary School* London: Macmillan 1973

Murphy, Robert 'Raymond Durgnat and *A Mirror for England*' in MacKillop and Sinyard *British Cinema of the 1950s: A Celebration* Manchester: Manchester University Press 2003 pp 1–22

Nash, Mark *Screen Theory and Film Culture 1977–1987* Unpublished PhD thesis Middlesex University September 2003

National Council of Public Morals *The Cinema: Its present position and future possibilities* London: Williams and Northgate 1917

National Film Theatre *Fifty Famous Films 1915–1945* London: BFI 1960

Noble, Peter (Ed) *British Film Year Book* London: Skelton Robinson 1947

Norris, Terry 'Courses and Creativity at Little Ilford' *Visual Education* April 1977 pp 29–30

Northern Counties Children's Cinema Council *Film Appreciation in the School* London: BFI 1939

Northern Counties Children's Cinema Council *Northern Counties Children's Cinema Council* Newcastle: NCCCC 1938

Nowell-Smith, Geoffrey 'Gramsci and the National Popular' *Screen Education* No 22 Spring 1977 pp 12 -15

Nowell-Smith, Geoffrey 'The Crisis in the British Film Institute 1970–71' Copy of a paper delivered at the 2005 Glasgow *Screen* Conference

NUT 'Will the judges' choice have a bad effect on future productions?' *The Teacher* June 30 1967 p 7

NUT *Popular Culture and Personal Responsibility Conference Programme* October 1960

NUT *Popular Culture and Personal Responsibility Verbatim Report* London: NUT 1961

NUT press release: *Announcing the National Children's Film Awards 1961* London: National Union of Teachers 1961

Oliver, Elizabeth 'The BUFC: Approaches to the Study of Film' *Visual Education* April 1977 p 19

Orrom, Michael and Williams, Raymond *Preface to Film* London: Film Drama Limited 1954

Otley, D Charles *The Cinema in Education* London: George Routledge & Sons 1935

Palmer, J Wood 'Film judgment and appreciation' *The Cinema* pp 19–31

Parnaby, Mary C and Woodhouse, Maurice *Children's Cinema Clubs – A Report* London: British Film Institute March 1947

Pateman, Trevor *Television and the February 1974 General Election* Television Monograph No 3 London: British Film Institute Educational Advisory Service 1974

Paterson, Richard 'Review of EAS publications' *Screen Education* No 19 Summer 1976 pp 45–50

Pearson, George *The Film as a Visual Art* London: BFI 1945

Perkins, V F *Film as Film – Understanding and Judging Movies* Harmondsworth: Penguin 1972

Perkins, Victor 'A Reply to Sam Rohdie' *Screen* Vol 13 No 4 Winter 1972/3 pp 146–151

Perkins, Victor 'Fifty Famous Films 1915–1945' in *Oxford Opinion* No 38 April 30 1960 p 36

Peters, J M L *Teaching about the Film* Paris: UNESCO 1961

Pointon, E M 'Beginners All' in *Film Teacher* No 3 August 1955 pp 6–10

Porter, Vincent 'Video Recording and the Teacher' *Screen Education* No 35 Summer 1980 pp 87–90

Powell, Dilys 'Film in Educational and Social Life' *Documentary Film News* Vol 8 No 71 January 1949 pp 2–4 and 12

Powell, Dilys *Films Since 1939* London: Longman Green 1949

Pronay, Nicholas and Spring D W (Eds) *Propaganda, Politics and Film, 1918–1945* London: Macmillan 1982

Pungente, John J 'Len Masterman: the AML Interview' Media Education Journal 1994

QCA *Media Matters: A Review of Media Studies in Schools and Colleges* London: Qualifications and Curriculum Authority 2005

Quigly, Isabel 'Being a reviewer in the 1950s' in MacKillop and Sinyard *British Cinema of the 1950s: A Celebration* Manchester: Manchester University Press pp 213–220

Quinn, James *The Film and Television as an Aspect of European Culture* Leyden Netherlands: A W Sijthoff 1968

Radcliffe, Sir Cyril J *Report of the Committee on the British Film Institute* Cmd 7361 London: HMSO April 1948

Rand, Helen and Lewis, Richard *Film and School* New York: D Appleton – Century Company 1937

Read, Herbert 'Towards a Film Aesthetic' *Cinema Quarterly* Vol 1 No 1 Autumn 1932 pp 7–11

Read, Herbert *Education through Art* London: Faber 1943

Reed, Bryan H *Eighty Thousand Adolescents* London: Allen & Unwin 1950

Reed, Stanley 'Appreciating the Film' in *The Photographic Journal* August 1950 pp 285–291

Reed, Stanley 'Film and Child' *Visual Education* Vol 1 Nos 9–12 (September/December) 1950

Reed, Stanley 'Film Appreciation in the School' *Society of Film Teachers Bulletin* Vol 1 No 1 December 1950 pp 3–6

Reed, Stanley 'Teaching Film Appreciation in the Classroom' *Sub-Standard Film* December 15 1949 p 122

Reed, Stanley *A Guide to Good Viewing* London: Educational Supply Association 1961

Reed, Stanley *Critics' Choice* British Film Institute (ran from No 1 April 1952 to the final issue in February 1956)

Rees, Sidney and Waters, Don 'Film Making in Schools' *The Film Teacher's Handbook 1956/7* London: SFT 1956 pp 11–19

Rees, Sidney and Waters, Don *Film Making in School* London: SEFT 1960

Rees, Sidney and Waters, Don *Young Film Makers* London: SEFT 1963

Report of the Committee on Broadcasting (Pilkington Report) London: HMSO 1962 Cmd 1753

Report of the Departmental Committee on Children and the Cinema (Wheare Report) London: HMSO 1950 Cmd 1945

Richards, Jeffrey (Ed) *The Unknown 1930s An alternative history of the British Cinema 1929–1939* London: I B Taurus 1998

Richards, Jeffrey 'Thorold Dickinson and the British Cinema' Lanham: The Scarecrow Press 1997

Richards, Jeffrey *The Age of the Dream Palace – Cinema and Society in Britain 1930–1939* London: Routledge 1989

Richardson, Alex 'Postscript to the screen education references in the Newsom Report' *Screen Education* No 22 pp 9–10

Richardson, Alex 'Talking to John Heyer' *Film Society News* 9 Summer 1961 pp 3–6 and *Film Society News* 10 Winter 1961 pp 4–6

Richardson, Alex *Screen Education for Schools* London: Schoolmaster Publishing Company 1967

Richardson, Alex; Vannoey, R C and Waters, Don *A Handbook for Screen Education* London: SEFT 1963

Ridge, Christine 'Reflections on the ILEA 6th Form Film Course' *Screen Education Notes* No 8 Autumn 1973 p 11

Roberts, I E 'Diploma Course Work' *The Film Teacher* Spring 1954 pp 2–4

Roberts, J Morgan 'Cinema Behaviour Problems' *Screen Education* No 9 July/August 1961 pp 42–43

Robins, David (Ed) *The Independent Group: Postwar Britain and the Aesthetics of Plenty* Cambridge: Massachusetts The MIT Press 1990

Robins, Kevin 'Althusserian Marxism and media studies: the case of *Screen*' *Media, Culture and Society* No 1 1979 pp 355–370

Robinson, David '*A Report on the Methods of Higher Education in Professional and Research Subjects related to the Cinema*' London: British Film Institute 1958

Robinson, David 'Building a Cinema' *'Sight and Sound* Vol 26 No 3 Winter 1956–57 pp 137–139

Rodowick, David *The Crisis of Political Modernism* first published by the University of Illinois in 1988 and reprinted by the University of California Press Berkeley 1994

Rogers, Rick (Ed) *Television and the Family* London: University of London Extra Mural Department 1980

Rohdie, Sam 'Editorial' *Screen* Vol 13 No 3 Autumn 1972 pp 2–3

Rohdie, Sam 'Education and Criticism – Notes on work to be done' *Screen* Vol 12 No 1 pp 9–13

Rohdie, Sam 'Foreword' in *Screen* Vol 12 No 4 Winter 1971/2

Rohdie, Sam 'Review: *Movie Reader, Film as Film*' *Screen* Vol 13 No 4 Winter 1972/3 pp 135 -145

Rosen, Philip *The Concept of Ideology and Contemporary Film Criticism: A Study of the Journal Screen in the Context of the Marxist Theoretical Tradition* Unpublished PhD thesis University of Iowa 1978

Rotha, Paul *Documentary Film* Boston: American Photographic Publishing 1936

Rotha, Paul Review 'How to Appreciate Motion Pictures' *Sight and Sound* Vol 3 No 10 Summer 1934 p 81

Rowe, Alan 'As an "O" level Subject' *Visual Education* April 1977 pp 26–29

Ryall, Tom 'Editorial' *Screen Education Notes* Autumn 1972 No 4 p 2

Ryall, Tom 'SEFT Annual Conference' *Screen Education Notes* Winter 1971 p 28–31

Schrire, David 'The Psychology of Film Audiences' *Sight and Sound* Vol 2 No 8 Winter 1934 p 122–123

Sedgwick, John 'Cinema-going preferences in Britain in the 1930s' in Richards, Jeffrey (Ed) *The Unknown 1930s* 1998 pp 1–21

SEFT *Papers from the Bradford Media Education Conference* London: SEFT 1986

SEFT 'Soviet Film 1920s' *Screen* Vol 12 No 4 Winter 1971/72 pp 25–160

SEFT 'The Pilkington Committee A summary of evidence submitted by the Society to the Committee on Broadcasting' *Screen Education* No 8 May-June 1961 pp 4–5

SEFT Nineteenth Annual Report 1969–70 *Screen* Vol 11 No 3 p 102

SEFT working party 'What Every 16 Year Old Should Know about the Mass Media' in *Screen* Vol 24 No 2 March/April 1983 pp 91–95

SFT 'Editorial' *Society of Film Teachers Newsletter* No 2 December 1954 p 2

SFT 'Editorial' *Society of Film Teachers Newsletter* No 3 February 1955 p 2

SFT 'Policy Statement of the Society of Film Teachers' *The Film Teacher's Handbook 1958/59* London: SFT 1958 pp 61–66

SFT Brains Trust Report *Look and Listen* Vol 5 No 8 August 1951 p 170

SFT Festival Exhibition 'The Teacher in School and Out' *The Mini Cinema* Vol 5 No 11 August 1951 p 31

Shivas, Mark 'The Commercial Cinema: a few basic principles' *Oxford Opinion* No 38 April 30 1960 pp 38–40

Simpson, Philip (Ed) *Television and the Family* London: Comedia 1987

Simpson, Philip 'Film and TV Studies in Secondary Education Report of the BFI/SEFT York Conference 1976' *Screen Education* No 19 Summer 1976 p 35

Simpson, Philip 'Appendix I: Film and Media Studies in Higher Education 1977–79' in Gledhill, Christine (Ed) *Film & Media Studies in Higher Education Conference Papers* London: BFI Education September 1981 pp 153–160

Simpson, Philip 'Introduction' *Media Education Conference 1981* London: BFI Education 1982 p 7

Simpson, Philip; Skirrow, Gillian; Watney, Simon 'Editorial' *Screen* Vol 24 No 3 May/June 1983 p 3

Smith, A H; Platnauer, Maurice; Keeley, T C; Coghill, Nevill H *Report of the Oxford Drama Commission* May 1945

Smith, Brian 'The Next Step' *Sight and Sound* Vol 9 No 36 Winter 1940–41 pp 69–70

Smith, G Buckland 'Brentwood School Shows the Way' *Sight and Sound* Vol 6 No 21 Spring 1937 p 38–39

Smith, G Buckland 'Wanted – A Sympathetic Understanding' *Sight and Sound* Vol 8 No 30 Summer 1939 pp 85–86

Smith, Jack 'from the Secretary' *The Film Teacher* Summer 1952 p 27

Smith, Jack 'The Challenge of Television' *Society of Film Teachers Newsletter* No 3 pp 3–5

Smith, Jack 'The teacher and the cinema' *Look and Listen* Vol 7 No 1 January 1953 p 21–22

Smith, Paul 'Historians and Film: A Progress Report' *University Vision* No 4 November 1969 pp 36–39

Sparks, Colin 'The Evolution of Cultural Studies…' *Screen Education* No 22 Spring 1977 pp 16–30

Spencer D A and Waley H D *The Cinema Today* Second Edition London: Oxford University Press 1956

Spottiswoode, Raymond 'Festival Telekinema' *The Film Teacher* Autumn 1953 pp 3–4

Spottiswoode, Raymond *A Grammar of the Film* London: Faber 1935 Second edition 1955

Sproxton, Vernon *Watching Films* London: SCM Press 1948

Stead, Peter 'The People and the Pictures: the British working class and film in the 1930s' in Pronay and Spring (Eds) *Propaganda Politics and Film* London: Macmillan 1982 pp 77–97

Steele, Tom *The Emergence of Cultural Studies 1945–65* London: Lawrence & Wishart 1997

Stevens, Tony 'Reading the Realist Film' *Screen Education* No 26 Spring 1978 pp 13–34

Stone, Margaret '5 years…and then?' *Motion* Summer 1961 pp 21–22 and 25

Strong, L A G *English for Pleasure* London: Methuen & Co Ltd 1941

Swanson, Gillian 'Rethinking Representation' *Screen* Vol 27 No 5 September /October 1986 pp 16 -28

The British Film Institute Act London: HMSO 31 May 1949

The Schoolmaster's Own Correspondents 'Reports on the NUT Conference "Popular Culture and Personal Responsibility"' *The Schoolmaster* November 4 1960 pp 941–948

The Teacher Letters to the Editor 'Young film makers: some words in their defence' *The Teacher* July 21 1967 p 5

TES 'Editorial' *Times Educational Supplement* 8 January 1960 p 25

Thames Television *Viewpoint Teachers' Notes* London: Thames Television 1975

Thompson, Denys (Ed) *Discrimination and Popular Culture* Harmondsworth: Penguin 1964

Thompson, Denys *The Use of English*, originally *English in Schools*, was started in 1939 and continued into the 1960s

Thompson, John O 'Report – SEFT Glasgow Group Weekend School "Television and the Real World"' in *Screen Education* No 23 Summer 1977 pp 69–70

Thompson, Victor 'Story into Screenplay' *Film Teacher* No 2 June 1955 pp 4–7

Tredell, Nicolas (Ed) *Cinemas of the Mind: A Critical History of Film Theory* Cambridge: Icon Books 2002

Trevelyan, John 'The Consultative Committee' *The Film Teacher* Autumn 1953 pp 8–11

Tucker, Nicholas 'Are They Safe in front of the Screen?' *The Teacher* 7 July 1967 p 3

Tucker, Nicholas *Understanding the Mass Media* Cambridge: Cambridge University Press 1966

Turner, Graeme *British Cultural Studies – An Introduction* London: Routledge 1990

Tyrer, Frank 'The development of *Film Guide* in Liverpool' *Look and Listen* Vol 4 No 9 September 1950

UNESCO *The Influence of the Cinema on Children and Adolescents* An annotated international bibliography Paris: UNESCO 1961

V, F H 'Book Review *Film*' *Sight and Sound* Vol 2 No 6 Summer 1933 p 61

Vannoey, R C (Ed) *A Film Society Handbook* London: SEFT 1965

Vannoey, R C 'Ten Years On' *Screen Education Year Book 1960–61* London: SEFT October 1960

Vaughan, Dai 'A Seat for the Tenth Muse' *Film Teacher* 15 December 1958 pp 16–19

Vaughan, Dai 'Films of Innocence' *Film Teacher* 17 May 1959 pp 25–27

Vaughan, Dai 'Letters from the trenches' *Film* 27 January /February 1961 pp 9–10

Vaughan, Dai 'The Critical Question – correspondence' *Sight and Sound* Vol 30 No 1 Winter 1960–61 p 48

Vaughan, Dai 'The Poem as Film' *Film Teacher* 12 March 1956 pp 4–8

Vaughan, Dai 'What is Free Cinema?' *Film Teacher* 14 September 1958 pp 11–17

Vaughan, Dai 'A Brief Reply to Ian Cameron' *Screen Education* 9 July-August 1961 p 50

Vaughan, Dai *Television Documentary Usage* Television Monograph No 6 London: British Film Institute Educational Advisory Service 1976

Vogt, Leiken 'Film Teaching in Norway' *Film Teacher* No 4 July 1956 pp 8–14

Walkerdine, Valerie 'Progressive Pedagogies' *Papers from the Bradford Media Education Conference* London: SEFT 1986 pp 2–8

Wall, W D 'The Adolescent and the Cinema' *Educational Review* Vol 1 1948–1949 pp 34–46 and 119–130

Wall, W D and Simson, W A 'The Effects of Cinema Attendance on the Behaviour of Adolescents as seen by their Contemporaries' *British Journal of Educational Psychology* Vol XIX, Part I February 1949 pp 53–61

Wall, W D and Smith, E M 'Film Choices of Adolescents' *British Journal of Educational Psychology* Vol XIX Part II June 1949 pp 121–136

Ward, J C *Children and the Cinema* London: Central Office of Information – The Social Survey NS131 April 1949

Waters, Don 'Newsom' and 'Newsom on the Screen Media' in *Screen Education 22* January/February 1964 pp 7–9

Waters, W *Visual Education* London: BFI 1946

Watkins, Roger 'Chairman's Foreword' *Screen* Vol 12 No 1 Spring 1971 pp 7–8

Watkins, Roger *CSE Examinations in Film* London: BFI/SEFT 1969

Watney, Simon 'Canvassing *Screen*' *Screen* Vol 27 No 5 September /October 1986 pp 50–53

Whannel, Paddy 'Film Education and Film Culture' *Screen* Vol 10 No 3 May/June 1969 p 49

Whannel, Paddy 'Know a Good Film' *Times Educational Supplement* 29 June 1962 p 1329

Whannel, Paddy 'Receiving the Message' *Definition* 3 p 14

Whannel, Paddy 'Servicing the Film Teacher' *Screen* Vol 11 No 4/5 1970 p 48

Whannel, Paddy 'The Problem of Film Availability' *Screen* Vol 10 No 1 January/February 1969 pp 67–73

Whannel, Paddy 'Towards a Positive Criticism of the Mass Media' *Film Teacher* 17 May 1959 pp 28–30

Whannel, Paddy 'Where Do We Go From Here?' *Screen Education* 7 March-April 1961 p 7

Whannel, Paddy and Harcourt, Peter (Eds) *Film Teaching* London: BFI Education Department 1964 (Revised edition 1968)

Whannel, Paddy and Jacobs, Alex (Eds) *Artist, Critic and Teacher* London: Joint Council for Education through Art 1958

Whannel, Paddy *The Work of the Education Department* London: BFI 1963

Whitty, Geoff and Young, Michael (Eds) *Explorations in the Politics of School Knowledge* Driffield: Nafferton Books 1976

Wickham, Glynne (Ed) *The Relation between Universities and Films, Radio and Television* London: Butterworth 1956

Willemen, Paul 'Introduction' in Willemen, Paul and Pines, Jim *The Essential* Framework London: Epigraph Publications Limited 1988 pp 1–11

Willemen, Paul 'Remarks on *Screen* A Spiralling Trajectory' *Southern Review* Vol 16 No 2 July 1983. The references in the text are to a typescript version of the article distributed by Willemen to students on the BFI MA course in the early 1990s

Williams, Christopher 'Theory, Misadventure and Critical Choices' *Screen* Vol 42 No 2 Summer 2001 pp 230–238

Williams, Linda 'Hiroshima and Marienbad – Metaphor and Metonymy' *Screen* Vol 17 No 1 Spring 1976

Williams, Raymond *Culture and Society* Harmondsworth: Penguin 1961

Williams, Raymond *Britain in the Sixties: Communications* Harmondsworth: Penguin Books 1962

Williams, Raymond *Television: Technology and Cultural Form* London: Fontana 1974

Wills, H R (Ed) *Young Film Makers Symposium* London: SEFT 1964

Wills, H R 'Concern for Children' *Screen Education* No 7 March/April 1961 pp 4–5

Wills, H R 'Cuttings' *Film Teacher* 12 March 1958 pp 21–23

Wollen, Peter 'Towards a New Criticism?' *Screen Education* No 41 September/October 1967 pp 90–91

Wollen, Peter *Signs and Meaning in the Cinema* London: Secker & Warburg 1969

Wollen, Peter (Ed) *Working papers on the cinema: sociology and semiology* London: British Film Institute Education Department 1971

Wollen, Peter 'Film Studies at the University of Essex' *Screen Education* No 19 Spring 1976 pp 57–60

Wollen, Peter *Signs and Meaning in the Cinema* Expanded Edition London: BFI 1998

Wollenberg, H H *Anatomy of the Film – an illustrated guide to film appreciation* London: Marsland Publications 1947

Wood, Robin 'New Criticism?' *Definition* 3 p 11

Wood, Robin 'Ghostly Paradigm and HCF: An Answer to Alan Lovell' *Screen* Vol 10 No 3 May/June 1969 pp 35–48

Wood, Robin 'Film Studies at Warwick' *University Vision* No 12 December 1974 pp 27–36

Wood, Robin 'Film Studies at the University of Warwick' *Screen Education* No 19 Summer 1976 pp 51–54

Wood, Robin *Personal Views: Explorations in Film* London: Gordon Fraser 1976

Wood, Robin 'Courses at Warwick University' *Visual Education* April 1977 pp 19–23

Woodhouse, M T 'Children's Film Judgments' *Researches and Studies* No 1 December 1949 pp 33–45

Woodhouse, Maurice T *Film Appreciation in the School* Unpublished PhD thesis Department of Education University of Leeds January 1952

Wright, Ian 'National Film School' *Sight and Sound* Vol 36 No 4 Autumn 1967 pp 197–198

Young Screen 1969 Entry form and information London: NUT 1969

Young, Colin 'National Film School' *Sight and Sound* Vol 41 No 1 Winter 1971/72 pp 5–8

Index

Individuals mentioned in this account of the evolution of film and media education

References to the following regular publications of SFT and SEFT would be too numerous to be useful. They are detailed when relevant in the endnotes to each chapter.

Society of Film Teachers:
The Film Teacher
Film Teacher
The Film Teacher's Handbook

Society for Education in Film and Television:
Screen Education (1959–1968)
Screen Education Yearbook
Teen Screen
Film Society News
Screen
Screen Education Notes
Screen Education (1974–1982)
Initiatives

Abbreviations denoting organisations mentioned in the text

Readers

Readers unfamiliar with the output of *Screen* and *Screen Education* during the period covered by this account may wish to explore the selection of articles published in the following *Screen* and *Screen Education Readers*.

Screen

John Ellis (ed) *Screen Reader 1: Cinema/ Ideology/Politics* SEFT 1977

Mick Eaton and Steve Neale (eds) *Screen Reader 2: Cinema and Semiotics* SEFT 1981

Barbara Creed and Mandy Merck (eds) *The Sexual Subject: A Screen Reader in Sexuality* Routledge 1992

Screen Education

Manuel Alvarado, Edward Buscombe and Richard Collins (eds) *The Screen Education Reader: Cinema, Television, Culture* Macmillan 1993

Manuel Alvarado, Edward Buscombe and Richard Collins (eds) *Representation and Photography: A Screen Education Reader* Palgrave 2001